Soviet Agricultural Policy

Stephen Osofsky

The Praeger Special Studies program—
utilizing the most modern and efficient book
production techniques and a selective
worldwide distribution network—makes
available to the academic, government, and
business communities significant, timely
research in U.S. and international economic, social, and political development.

Soviet Agricultural Policy
Toward the Abolition
of Collective Farms

PRAEGER SPECIAL STUDIES IN INTERNATIONAL ECONOMICS AND DEVELOPMENT

Praeger Publishers New York Washington London

Library of Congress Cataloging in Publication Data

Osofsky, Stephen.
    Soviet agricultural policy.

    (Praeger special studies in international economics
and development)
    Bibliography: p.
    1. Agriculture and state—Russia.   2. Collective
farms—Russia.   I. Title.
HD1993 1974.083   338.1'847   74-1747
ISBN 0-275-08870-7

PRAEGER PUBLISHERS
111 Fourth Avenue, New York, N.Y. 10003, U.S.A.
5, Cromwell Place, London SW7 2JL, England

Published in the United States of America in 1974
by Praeger Publishers, Inc.

Printed in the United States of America

This is dedicated to
my mother and my father,
to whom I will always be grateful

I want to acknowledge
the inestimable contribution of

Professor John Hazard

to whatever is worthwhile in this book,
and to my professional career

S. O.

CONTENTS

LIST OF ABBREVIATIONS

Akad.	Akademia
CDSP	Current Digest of the Soviet Press
Gos.	Gosudarstvo, Gosudarstvenni
Izdat.	Izdatel'stvo
Iurid.	Iuridicheskii
IASP	International Arts and Sciences Press
Kom.	Komsomol, Komsomol'skaia (adjective)
Lenin.	Leningrad (adjective)
Mosk.	Moscow (adjective)
MTS	Machine Tractor Station
NEP	New Economic Policy
RSFSR	Russian Republic
SGIP	Sovetskoe Gosudarstvo i Pravo
Sov. Iust.	Sovetskaia Iustitsia
Sots. Zak.	Sotsialnaia Zakonnost'
Stat.	Statistika
Ts. Kom.	Tsentral'nyi Komitet
Univ.	Universitet
Uprav.	Upravlenie

PART

I

CONTINUITY AND CHANGE IN THE POST-KHRUSHCHEV ERA

THE KHRUSHCHEVIAN
LEGACY

With the recent adoption of the ninth five-year plan by the Twenty-Fourth CPSU Congress and the analyses by both Soviet and non-Soviet experts of the results of the eight five-year plan, the post-Khrushchev leadership faces the prospects of its new plan set against the rather disappointing results of the last five-year plan, their first attempt to disentangle Soviet agriculture from the stagnancy of the period from 1958 to 1963. The leadership has been active on the agricultural front since deposing Khrushchev, whose campaigning approach and subjectivism in respect of technical agricultural questions, and whose penchant for frequent and profound agricultural administrative reforms that alienated the bureaucrats of both party and state they have frequently denounced. According to the late Naum Jasny, Khrushchev made many serious and inexcusable mistakes in the realm of cropping patterns. First, the supplanting of rotational hay and oats as feeds by maize, which is poorly suited climatically to the Soviet Union. Second, reducing the share of winter wheat in the wheat area and abolishing much bare fallow in semi-arid regions growing winter wheat, and then using the liberated land for maize and sugar beets, whose yields in such areas are well below that of winter wheat. Third, Khrushchev defied world practice by growing labor intensive and costly sugar beet as a feed crop. Not only is it expensive but it is a poor feed because of its low protein content. Jasny concluded that the major Soviet grain imports in 1963 would not have been needed but for the wasteful growing of maize and the common practice of utilizing it before it fully matured on land perfectly suited to winter wheat.[1] In many cases Khrushchev's innovations and prescriptions have been reversed. But in many others Khrushchev's reforms have been extended. So there is both continuity and change in the two periods in terms of policy. The change in styles, however, is unmistakable. The current leadership eschews the barnstorming, personalized, peasant-wisdom-spouting style of Khrushchev. It prefers the controlled clinical language of the Central Committee resolution to the aphorisms of the pseudo-peasant. And the major policy initiatives that have come from this leadership do not bear the personal stamp of any one of the leaders.

The purpose of this study is to probe for the major problem areas in the kolkhoz sector rather than in Soviet agriculture as a whole, although in many cases the problems overlap and are inextricably bound together. In posing the problems, the differences between Soviet and Western formulations will become evident. Moreover, in some cases the Soviet politicians or experts will not acknowledge the existence of a problem that the Western critic poses. Or, where both agree on the existence of a given problem, the prescriptions for ameliorating or solving it are often quite irreconcilable. This, in many instances, is understandable because of differing ideological convictions. And the extent to which ideology colors both problem identification and problem solution will be quite evident in studying kolkhoz problems. The kolkhoz problems, although certainly in good measure economic in nature, are also in part sociological and ideological. Ultimately the problems are political, and it is the political aspects that will be weighed most heavily.

By way of general background a rather quick listing of the more significant post-Stalin and Khrushchevian agricultural innovations, with particular reference to the kolkhozy, is in order.[2] The most dramatic agricultural policies were the Virgin Lands project, the kolkhoz mergers, the conversion of kolkhozy into sovkhozy, the procurement price increases, the disbanding of the MTS and the sale of its machinery to the kolkhozy, the assault on the Ministry of Agriculture and an oscillating policy on decentralized party-state control of agriculture, and significant changes in both the formulae and methods of procuring agricultural produce from kolkhozy. The Khrushchev era saw the inculcation of internal cost accounting within kolkhozy, to better measure kolkhoz performance in general, as well as its use for internal kolkhoz production subdivisions—links, brigades, and farms—so as to judge their performances individually. Along with the inculcation of cost accounting in the kolkhozy went the monetization of kolkhoz labor payments, that is a diminution in the percentage of in-kind pay in the earnings of kolkhozniks, a feature that was not only to boost incentives of kolkhozniks but also to help simplify the cost account problem. In addition the monetization of kolkhoz labor payments was accompanied by the increased use of money and in-kind monthly or periodic earnings and advances in an attempt to create incentive by making rewards available to kolkhozniks as they worked instead of making them wait for the traditional accounting with the

4

kolkhoz at the end of the economic year, their wages then being only
a residual left after certain prior claims of kolkhoz income and
produce—such as state delivery quotas and mandated by law reserve
funds, insurance taxes, credits payments, and natural insurance funds—
were met. Hence, there was no guaranteed wage at all for kolkhozniks.
In theory they were all co-owners entitled only to a share of whatever
residual of income and produce remained after meeting all state
obligations. Moreover, under the prevailing system of determining
individual shares through labor days earned—with the labor day representing no fixed amount but rather a share unit based on the grade
of one's job in relation to other jobs, with one day's acceptable performance earning a certain fraction or number of labor days—one
could not know what a labor day was worth until the total earned by
all was divided into the residual profit left at the end of the economic
year. The theory of the kolkhoz as a cooperative not only excused
the seeming anomaly in a socialist society of a not even minimum
wage for a large segment of the work force, but also allowed for these
nonstate employees, the kolkhozniks, to remain uncovered by the state
old-age pension and social security system in the main, although both
guaranteed pay—the right to be paid in accordance with the quality
and quantity of one's work—a cardinal principle of Soviet socialism,
and the right to security in old age and in case of incapacity are
vouchsafed as constitutional rights to all citizens in the Soviet constitution.

In the last year of Khrushchev's rule a state social security
and pension fund for kolkhozniks was mandated, financed only in small
part by the states, the rest by the kolkhozy themselves, in contrast
to the wholly state-financed state workers and employees pensions.
In the post-Khrushchev era the fund for kolkhozniks would be augmented
and brought closer to the more liberal eligibility and benefit provisions of the state system, thus bringing the kolkhozniks closer to the
benefit level of the state employees. In 1966 the post-Khrushchev
leadership implemented the guaranted pay system for kolkhozniks,
with the pay level recommended to be at the sovkhoz worker levels.
It should be noted that no actual fixed minimum pay was mandated
and that the state had not directly assumed the duty of paying kolkhoznik
wages. Rather the kolkhoz was to create out of its own means a wage
fund that would be a first charge on its gross income. The amount was
obviously dependent in part on the economic performance of the
kolkhoz. Only to the extent that the kolkhoz could not meet its wage
fund was the state to extend credits necessary to meet the wage fund
level. This should be seen in perspective as a logical extension of the
Khrushchev innovations—the money advances already referred to and
certain experiments abolishing the labor day and substituting man-
day pay units not hitherto mentioned. In a few wealthy kolkhozy there
actually were guaranteed labor days or man days with a fixed value.

Moreover, certain other innovations of the Khrushchev era have been further developed. The encouragement and official promotion of kolkhozy creating subsidiary enterprises—a policy started by Khrushchev in recognition of the need to make better use of local natural resources, surplus agricultural produce, and surplus agricultural labor, and also in recognition of the inability of the state's light industry to supply localities with what they wanted, as well as the strain increased rural consumer demands would make on the fragile transportation and state retail network—has been very emphatic and enthusiastic, coupled, however, with the warning that it must remain subsidiary. Production ties between kolkhozy and sovkhozy, or between kolkhozy and other state enterprises, by way of their pooling resources to build, for example, power stations, mills, processing facilities, irrigation works, and artificial insemination plants, thereby allowing for a self-help, localist approach to the need for new facilities, services, and power without draining off scarce state investment capital, had been well advanced under Khrushchev and was known as the interkolkhoz or state-kolkhoz movement. The resultant enterprises or facilities, or in some cases, funds—for instance, insurance seed funds—were joint property of all participants and jointly managed. Under Khrushchev the fervor for organically combining industry and agriculture in giant enterprises and combines or complexes under the vague title of agraro-industrial enterprises was seen not only as economically rational, but perhaps more importantly as portending in this first, crude form the ultimate Marxian ideal of the industrialization of agriculture and the extinction of peasant-worker class differences. It should be noted that these first agraro-industrial units were basically agricultural raw material processing plants that had entered into direct ties with kolkhozy or sovkhozy, that is, they had concluded bilateral long-term supply contracts with kolkhozy without assimilating or merging with these suppliers. Under Khrushchev's successors the agraro-industrial units were enthusiastically advertised and their numbers grew. Khrushchev's policy toward the subsidiary-acre-and-a-cow economy of the kolkhoznik was, on the whole, oscillating. He alternately liberalized state taxes and procurement policies toward them only to shift later to repression. In his last years, he had reverted to a repressive policy, which the new leadership almost immediately reversed.

As a fitting monument to their agricultural policy, the current leadership made good—apparently not without some internal dissent—on the long-overdue, long-promised new kolkhoz Model Charter to replace the obsolete 1935 charter. Khrushchev had promised a new charter and had been allowing economists and jurists to engage in academic polemics over its shape and contents. Finally, in January 1966, Brezhnev was announced as heading a commission to draft a new charter. Their draft charter appeared only in April 1969, and the final version was ratified by the Third All-Union Congress of Kolkhozniks in November 1969. Its appearance and contents seemed to preclude any radical restructuring or transformation of the kolkhoz system. It is a document embodying relatively minor structural and theoretical changes, except insofar as it reflects the changes that had already been accumulated. Thus it did not enact any major changes, but rather updated the 1935 charter to take account of the post-Stalin changes. Still, it did initiate certain changes that could prove very significant in conjunction with future policy initiatives. These changes will be discussed later.

To sum up the Khrushchevian legacy on the agricultural front in general and on the kolkhoz question in particular: first, there was a major redistribution of national income in favor of agriculture in general and the kolkhozy in particular. This redistribution of income was necessitated by the overall poor condition of Soviet agriculture, especially the poor performance of the kolkhozy, and took varied forms. For the kolkhozy the major form was the state raising its procurement prices. The state also canceled many debts owed by the kolkhozy. Prices of agricultural machinery were lowered. Moreover, indirectly, the benefit of greater state capital investments in agricultural facilities and irrigation, drainage, better roads, and so on, was significant, as was accelerated state agricultural research in developing new chemical fertilizers, pesticides, and pedigreed livestock, items all of this made available to kolkhozy.

Second, there was less dictation from above to the kolkhoz in terms of how to run its internal production affairs—fewer planned-from-above targets—and a concomitant encouraging of the kolkhozy to devise new methods of reward and forms of labor organization so as to inspire more output and increase labor productivity. Firm output quotas had to be met, but the dictation of the detail of how to go about meeting them was renounced. Moreover, the production targets were based on more realistic criteria and reflected greater sensitivity to local production conditions. The idea was to relieve kolkhozy of as much petty tutelage from party and state central and local organs as possible, thus allowing full play for local initiative and judgment, based on presumed better familiarity of local personnel with local conditions, without, however, removing party and state monitoring of kolkhoz implementation of state policies and targets or the party's educative-exhortatory role on the farms.

Third, there was a recognition on the part of the regime that the quality of life of the kolkhoznik had to be drastically upgraded, especially as to income and social security, if labor productivity and output were to grow on the kolkhozy.

Fourth, there was a recognition that rational allocation of capital and other state resources required a more scientifically based analysis of kolkhoz production cost. This would provide in part a sound basis for judging individual kolkhoz economic performance and constructing rational regional procurement prices that would take into account the legitimate costs of production and insure the kolkhoz enough profit for proper accumulation and a sufficiently high wage fund to provide work incentives. This also involved the problem of equalizing the differential income of kolkhozy where such differences in income were not attributable to the skill or energy of the individual higher income farm but rather to its good location near a market, or to the fact that it enjoyed a better climate or soils or was endowed with more and better machinery, experts, power resources, facilities, or critical materials.

Fifth, as a corollary of the above point, it became part of the conventional wisdom that systematic, scientifically based specialization both within and among kolkhozy and sovkhozy, as well as concentration of functions within a farm, would lead to economies of cost and positive quantitative and qualitative changes in output. This functional specialization, as well as territorial specialization, based on analyzing production costs for particular crops and livestock in different climatic and soil zones, again required a more sophisticated approach to cost analysis, as well as some land cadastre or comprehensive land-rating system in terms of suitability of fields for different crops in different areas and suitability of soils for different animals.

Sixth, Khrushchev recognized the need for both intensive as well as extensive cultivation as the key to increasing total agricultural output. The Virgin Lands program was an example of the latter, as were his irrigation and drainage projects and his jettisoning of the Vil'yams grassland fallow system. An example of the former was his chemical fertilizer campaign. On the whole the extensivity tack took precedence because it promised quicker, more dramatic results and less capital investment. Now intensity was to be stressed.

Seventh, Khrushchev tried, as far as possible, to solve certain seemingly intractable problems with the poorer performing kolkhozy by administrative measures pure and simple. He tended to merge poorer kolkhozy with the better performing ones at an incredibly fast rate and on a grand scale. Some kolkhozy were converted into sovkhozy. Bad harvest years were attributed at times to maladministration, and reallocations of jurisdiction over kolkhozy and sovkhozy among central republican and local ministries and administrations as well as between the state and party committees and councils were frequent. The pattern of centralization-decentralization-recentralization was recurrent. Moreover, Khrushchev felt that, at least to some extent, the source of much of the ills of agriculture was to be found in poor administrative guidance and poor leadership on the farms and in the party-state control units, and that more and better propaganda and better use of moral incentives could take the place of more investment funds. This led to the typical Khrushchevian forays into the hinterlands to drum up grass-roots enthusiasm for the latest notion or nostrum.

Eighth, Khrushchev had what one might term a Marxian bias in favor of large production units. He combined kolkhozy not just for the sake of eliminating the economic weak sisters but in good measure because he truly believed that the bigger a farm, the better it would perform economically. Although he at times admitted that "gigantomania" was to be curbed, none the less he was reluctant to explore the problem of the law of diminishing returns and the concept of the optimal size of kolkhozy.

Last, Khrushchev, despite occasional concessions to the private subsidiary economy of kolkhozniks, on balance had a pronounced negative attitude toward them based on his belief, perhaps again attributable to Marxian rigidity, that small-scale production was economically retrograde and ideologically tainted because it perpetuated the private property mentality among the kolkhoz peasantry and undermined their commitment to the public economy of the kolkhoz. He believed that time spent on the private plot came largely at the expense of participation in the public sector.

NOTES

1. Naum Jasny, Khrushchev's Crop Policy (Glasgow: Outram and Co., Ltd., 1966), pp. 11-17.
2. For an in-depth study of Khrushchev's agricultural policy, see Sidney Ploss, Conflict and Decision-Making in Soviet Russia (Princeton: Princeton University Press, 1965).

2

THE BREZHNEV-KOSYGIN
RECORD

The first year of the post-Khrushchev leadership was a most eventful one on the agriculture and the kolkhoz front. In the official explanation tendered by party historians for Khrushchev's resignation as First Secretary and Chairman of the Council of Ministers, his "subjectivism" and the mistaken policies it bred loomed large. The poor state of Soviet agriculture was emphasized in official accounts. Subjectivism is described as the attempt to solve practical problems of communist construction without taking into account the objective laws of development of socialist society. No attempt to resolve these problems by voluntarist methods and hasty administrative measures in disregard of scientific methods can be successful. Veteran party leaders may get the false impression that the party can achieve anything it sets its mind on.[1] Khrushchev, by implication, had been a subjectivist par excellence. Price policy is all important under socialism and the prices of commodities fixed by the party-state must not be arbitrary. Khrushchev had sinned by establishing in the early 1960s the so-called sliding purchase price system for farm products. Prices were fixed annually depending on the results of the annual harvest. Good harvests meant lower prices and bad harvests higher prices, with consequent uncertainty before the harvest results were predictable as to prices. This was alleged to have adversely affected kolkhozniks' incentives, since they were aware that whether or not the harvest was good or bad, they would, through the sliding price mechanism, come out about the same. So why work for higher yields? An "instant" official history of this period states that the 1961 and 1963 crop failures coincided with the introduction of this system and that the consequence was that grain production and the livestock population decreased.[2] There is a clear implication that the Khrushchev system caused or aggravated these crop failures and livestock losses.

On October 27, 1964, a Central Committee decree entitled "About the Removal of Unfounded Limitations of the Personal Subsidiary Economy of the Kolkhozniks, Workers, and Employees" was published, which reversed a major Khrushchev policy of restricting the private sector by tightening the restrictions on both the size of private plots and the numbers of private livestock. Khrushchev had hoped to raise labor participation in the public sector of the kolkhoz by making the private sector less attractive through restrictions on the kolkhoz selling essential fodder for private livestock as well as on loans of equipment and transportation for working the plot and marketing its produce. Also, he encouraged the establishment by kolkhozy of minimum yearly labor participation quotas in the public sector in man days for kolkhozniks, with sanctions for failure to work the minimum time, including further loss of privileges as to getting kolkhoz feed and help as well as possibly losing the private plot entirely. Now the new leadership reversed this by calling for restoration of norms of cattle and plot sizes in effect before the Khrushchev limitations. The same decree also commissioned the USSR Ministry of Finance and Gosbank to introduce within a month a new proposal for giving credits to kolkhozniks and others with subsidiary plots so as to allow them to buy cows and calves.[3] The new leadership seemed to have concluded that the private plots' prosperity was either a necessary evil tolerable because they did not threaten to undermine participation in the public sector by kolkhozniks or because they supplied kolkhozniks with the supplementary income and food products that the state was either unwilling or unable to supply. Moreover, the kolkhoz markets somewhat relieved the food shortage pressure emanating from the urban population's growing food demands—which demands the state retail stores were apparently unable to meet.

The Soviet economist N. S. Nazarov, writing in 1965, tried to refute the formerly widely held official view that private plots lure away manpower from the public sector and that both they and kolkhoz markets increase the trend toward private property and encourage the black market, especially when certain foodstuffs are in short supply.[4] The Soviet economist G. Shmelev pointed out in 1965 that in the main the subsidiary economy consists of those kinds of crops the production of which in the public economy is insufficiently mechanized, for example, potatoes and vegetables, both of which are insignificant in the public economy's total production.[5] Implicit in this observation is the reassurance that the new liberality toward the private sector is a safe policy because there is no direct competition between the two sectors in that they do not concern themselves with the same crops. Moreover, the labor-intensive crops raised by the private sector are better left to it, since the state does not have to subsidize this inefficient use of labor time. M. Makeenko, another economist,

11

is even more reassuring. Writing in 1966, he calls the idea that the private sector detracts from kolkhozniks' participation in the public sector a big myth. He notes that female labor predominates in the private sector. The private sector is not only an essential source of a critical portion of kolkhozniks' food requirements, but helps to prevent the agricultural population from leaving the farms in larger numbers than already is the case.[6]

By a decree of the USSR Council of Ministers and CPSU Central Committee of March 1, 1965, "On Increasing the Role of the Ministry of Agriculture USSR in Management of Kolkhoz and Sovkhoz Production,"[7] two of Khrushchev's administrative rearrangements were undone. The Union-Republic USSR Ministry of Agriculture resumed its traditional powers over most aspects of kolkhoz and sovkhoz production, powers Khrushchev had disaggregated, beginning in 1961,[8] and redistributed among various central, republican, and local state organs and administrations, including Gosplan and the Khrushchev-created kolkhoz-sovkhoz administrations, whose jurisdiction straddled raion (district) lines, thus upstaging both raion party and state organs, which traditionally had collaborated as the ultimate raion agricultural overseers. According to the decree, the Ministry of Agriculture's responsibilities now included yearly and prospective planning of kolkhoz-sovkhoz production, measures to implement the plans and state agricultural procurements, working out and implementation of measures for specialization and intensification of kolkhoz and sovkhoz production, research on and implementation of new technology and techniques, supervision of capital investments and construction in agriculture, implementation and supervision of financial control, cost accounting, agro-chemical services, and control over proper land use and the observance of party and state policies as well as conformity of kolkhoz practices with their charters and the norms of kolkhoz democracy. Gosplan's function of analyzing the economic activities and financial condition of kolkhozy and sovkhozy was to be absorbed by the Ministry of Agriculture. And the kolkhoz-sovkhoz administrations were transformed into raion production agriculture administrations, which were local organs of the ministry.[9]

Brezhnev's March 1965 report at the Central Committee Plenum, entitled "On the Urgent Measures for Further Development of the USSR's Agriculture," was a comprehensive survey of the ills of agriculture, a stinging indictment of Khrushchev, and a battle plan for dispelling the stagnant conditions he found. This speech is, functionally, like the famous Khrushchev report of September 7, 1953, "About Measures for Further Development of the Agriculture of the USSR,"[10] delivered at the Central Committee Plenum. Just as Khrushchev criticized the then state of agriculture and, by implication, his predecessor, Stalin, while announcing a "new deal," so did Brezhnev promise a "new deal" for agriculture, and with much less euphemizing. The key fact was that the seven-year plan (1959-65) was to have increased gross agricultural production by 70 percent, but in fact increased it by only 10 percent. Whereas gross yearly agricultural production over the period from 1955 to 1959 had average increases of 7.6 percent, for the period from 1960 to 1965 it had dipped to 1.9 percent. Why? First, because the law of planned proportional development had been violated, as had the principle of combining public and personal interests. There had been too much subjectivism, especially in planning, price policy, finances, and credit. Purchase price in many cases, he noted, did not even cover production expenses.

Second, state investment in agriculture was too low. For the period from 1954 to 1958 it was only 11.3 percent of all investments in the economy, and according to the control figures for the seven-year plan (1959-65), it was set at 7.5 percent. This has resulted, among other things, in kolkhozy and sovkhozy being underequipped.

Third, crop-rotation principles had been violated and elementary rules of agrotechnology had not been observed (allusions to Khrushchev's voluntarism, his personal crusade for indiscriminate widening of the corn cropping areas, his long-term devotion to Lysenko's unsound schemes and Vil'yams grassland system).[11] Also, there had been too much dictation from the center in disregard of local conditions.

Fourth, and last, the work of party, soviet, and land organs had been inadequate in various ways.[12]

Next came prescriptions for correcting these conditions. The purchase system had to be changed from one of sliding yearly prices to one of a firm plan of purchase at set prices for a number of years ahead—the grain purchase plans of the last ten years were fulfilled only three times![13] More realism was needed in setting the plan targets. The price paid for grain crops by the state would be raised.[14] Fifty percent higher prices would be established for above-plan purchases of wheat and rye.[15] Since livestock production was generally unprofitable given the traditional level of state purchase prices, obviously this provided a disincentive to increasing meat production, which is sorely needed. Brezhnev admonished kolkhoz presidents and sovkhoz directors as well as party and state organs to correct this situation. He announced that above-plan purchase prices for meat would be raised without raising existing levels of retail prices for bread, meat, and meat products.[16] Thus the state rather than the consuming public is to subsidize livestock production.

Brezhnev hoped that the lifting of limitations on the personal subsidiary economies or private sector would stimulate production of livestock production. He also promised stable six-year purchase plans for agricultural produce at this point.[17]

Brezhnev devoted a great deal of the remainder of his report to the problems of the kolkhozy. Significantly, he prefaced his particular proposals for remedying some of their ills with a reassurance that the regime values them and will not administratively transform them into sovkhozy, the ideologically superior state farms, as Khrushchev at one time did on a limited but nonetheless substantial basis. Brezhnev stated:

It is necessary to assume that these two types of social economies . . . will exist and develop for a long time yet. At the contemporary stage our duty consists not in speeding the transformation of one form into the other but rather in rendering all-around aid to develop and make powerful both types of social economy.[18]

Brezhnev next reviewed the call for a new kolkhoz Model Charter, a call made by Khrushchev in the 1950s. He indicated that an All-Union Congress of Kolkhozniks would tackle the job in the coming year, a pledge that was finally redeemed in late 1969. He emphasized that it was now essential to commission the Ministry of Agriculture, the Ministry of Finance, and Gosbank to work out propositions for improving the financial system and credit policies toward kolkhozy and to report back to the Central Committee. Debts owed to the state by weaker kolkhozy would be canceled and the income tax on kolkhozy would be reformed so as to fall on net income, rather than gross income as was the case.[19] This then in broad terms was Brezhnev's "new deal." What follows is a description of its partial implementation, supplementation, modification, and even reversal. A decree entitled "About the Purchase Plan for Agricultural Products for 1966-70"[20] set the amount of grain per year at 55,700 thousand tons per year, the wheat component stable at approximately 37,600 tons. The purchase (procurement) organs were admonished to be guided by the principle of differentiated approach to each farm, taking account of the perspective development of its economy, in compiling their purchase plans. Moreover, the state and party republican and local committees were ordered to work out state purchase plans for individual kolkhozy and sovkhozy so as to accelerate national production specialization and to compensate for branches dropped by some farms by promoting these for other farms. The planning-control organs were also to widen direct ties of kolkhozy and sovkhozy with industrial enterprises and trade organizations so as to cut costs of supply.

The decree "About Raising the Material Interest of Kolkhozy and Sovkhozy in Increasing Production and Sale of Meat to the State,"[21] introduced as of May 1, 1965, raised for kolkhozy, sovkhozy, and other state economies, average supplemental payment increases on top of actual prices for sales to the state of cattle, sheep, goats, and pigs. For cattle the additional amounts ranged from 20 to 55 percent, and for pigs, between 30 and 70 percent of the regular price, depending on the union republic. As to sheep and goats, there was not only a union republic differentiation but also separate schedules for kolkhozy, on the one hand, and sovkhozy and other state economies on the other. Generally, the kolkhoz schedule was 10 percent higher than the state schedule. Moreover, supplementary payments for sheep and goats in the mountainous areas of the USSR were well above the established supplements, being set at 100 percent of the regular quota price. Also, the Union Republic Councils of Ministers were told to zonally differentiate price supplements for cattle, sheep, goats, and pigs within the limits of the average size of the supplemental payments established by the schedules.

By a ukaz (edict) of the USSR Supreme Soviet Presidium of April 10, 1965, entitled "On the Income Tax on Kolkhozy,"[22] the income tax on kolkhozy, hitherto levied against gross income, now was to fall on net income only and only after 15 percent of this was deducted. Kolkhoz social security payments were included in costs, along with labor and costs of produce, production, and services. There was a separate tax on that part of the labor payment fund of the kolkhoz that exceeded the average monthly earnings per kolkhoznik as established by the USSR Council of Ministers. This tax was independent of the profitability of the kolkhoz. The tax rate was a flat 12 percent on both net income and the excessive labor fund. The USSR Council of Ministers was given the right to free some kolkhozy from tax payments or to offer some of them tax privileges in order to stimulate the development of separate branches of agriculture. Also, Union Republic Councils of Ministers could allow individual kolkhozy an extension of the tax payment deadline and even write off part of the tax due. Kolkhozy suffering material disasters could, by decision of local state organs, be given stays of tax payment.

The USSR Council of Ministers decree of July 28, 1965, entitled "About Improving the Work of the All-Union Association Soiuzsel'khoz-teknika for Material-Technical Securing of Agriculture,"[23] admonished this organization for insufficiently supplying agriculture with machines and spare parts and materials, largely because of insufficient studying of kolkhoz and sovkhoz demands, although refusals by kolkhozy and sovkhozy to accept order deliveries, as well as the practice of local soviet and agricultural organs of raising orders for machinery given to them by kolkhozy and sovkhozy without any real need for the additions, were also cited as factors contributing to the organization's poor work. The organization was cited as being derelict in propagandizing and advertising new machinery, which led to overstocking of unsold machinery. Also at fault was its poor organizational work in respect of its trade network, which resulted in excessive internal crossing of materials and unjustified scattering of spare parts for tractors, autos, and other machinery among too many warehouses and bases. The practice of writing off obsolete machines and equipment that had never been used was cited. The decree lays down the principle that henceforth all of the organization's dealings with its customers must be on the basis of customer orders alone. A draft statute on the material liability of the organization to its customers for violating its delivery obligations or other duties was to be worked out within two months.

In a decree of November 5, 1965,[24] "About Wholesale Prices for Automobiles, Agricultural Tractors, Agricultural Machines and Spare Parts for Automobiles, Tractors, and Agricultural Machines," kolkhozy and sovkhozy were made the beneficiaries of lower prices for these items, prices traditionally denied to them. Moreover, permanent wholesale prices for new types of agricultural tractors machines and their spare parts, to be based on prices for analogous machinery, meant further economic benefits to the farms. By decree of the Council of Ministers of December 17, 1965, the rates for electric energy supplied by the state to kolkhozy, sovkhozy, and other agricultural enterprises were lowered.[25] That same day the Council of Ministers issued a decree entitled "About Improving Crediting of Kolkhozy,"[26] which called for putting kolkhozy on direct bank credit basis so as to allow them to use bank credits to cover seasonal shortages in money, including money to pay kolkhozniks, per their production plan. This program was to be begun by Gosbank in 1966. Long-term credits would be given to kolkhozy on the basis of economically grounded plans for capital investments. Gosbank could give out supplementary five-year credits for purchase of pedigreed cattle and for construction of homes, and fifteen-year credits for construction of children's institutions, baths, and other cultural-domestic construction, with repayment beginning with the second year for the five-year credits and in the fifth year for the fifteen-year credits. In 1966, 3,200 kolkhozy were put on a direct credit basis.[27]

Up to 1958 the kolkhozy were primarily receiving credits indirectly through the MTS (Motor Tractor Station). After the demise of the MTS, credits came primarily via the advances of the procurement agencies and only secondarily via direct bank credits, which play an insignificant role.[28] For the period from 1958 to 1963, the role of long-term credits in the formation of kolkhoz capital investments and indivisible funds actually decreased relative to 1957. At the beginning of 1964, 87 percent of the whole value of basic production funds of kolkhozy was self-generated.[29] The insufficiency of long-term credits available to kolkhozy, coupled with the expenses they incurred after 1958 associated with their buying up MTS machinery, led to many kolkhozy sacrificing pay funds for the sake of capital investments. And short-term credit policy also was conservative, so that while in 1957 it constituted 37.4 percent of the value of goods produced in kolkhozy, by 1962 the figure was only 27.2 percent.[30] And short-term credits are especially crucial to kolkhozy in the first half of their production year, when their receipts are small and their expenses are heavy. The average kolkhoz receives no more than one-fourth of its money credits in the first half.[31] With the 1965 decree, direct bank credits replaced the indirect system, until by 1972 approximately 95 percent of all kolkhozy received it and it constitutes about 30 percent of all kolkhoz capital investments.[32] The American economist James R. Millar concludes from his study of Soviet financial policy toward the agricultural sector that financial channels, despite recent improvements in policy, are not likely to become major sources of funds for farms in the foreseeable future and that the consequence of this is to burden the price and procurement policies of the regime.[33]

A joint Central Committee and Council of Ministers decree of January 15, 1966, "About Further Improvement of the System of Raising the Qualifications of Guiding Cadres of Kolkhozy and Sovkhozy and Agricultural Specialists,"[34] was an attempt to speed the flow of more qualified agricultural experts to the farms. It called for a reorganization of the one-year schools for preparing management cadres for kolkhozy and sovkhozy, of courses for raising the qualifications of management cadres of the farms, and of courses for raising the qualifications of specialists. Six-month courses were to be set up for preparing farm management cadre, and three-month courses for raising the qualifications of management cadres and courses of up to three months for agricultural specialists were to be started. The schools for raising qualifications of agricultural cadres would be financed at the expense of union republics. Its pupils would continue to get their average monthly pay while studying.

At the end of March 1966, the Twenty-Third Party Congress took place. Brezhnev delivered the report of the Central Committee on March 29th. He reviewed the reforms of 1964-66 and claimed that they were in good measure responsible for the significant increase in 1965 in livestock.[35] He emphasized intensive agriculture and the application of chemical fertilizers to obtain the best possible yield per hectare.[36] He suggested that the formation of elective kolkhoz organs at the raion, oblast, krai, republic, and all-union levels be on the agenda of the coming Congress of Kolkhozniks.[37] Brezhnev admitted that rural housing construction had been neglected for years and promised a significant program to remedy this.[38] But the major proposal as far as the kolkhozy were concerned came with his announcement that a guaranteed monthly wage for kolkhozniks comparable to the sovkhoz pay level was to be introduced during the new five-year plan.[39] The directives on the economy adopted by the Congress in its new five-year plan called for an increase of the average yearly production of agricultural produce by 25 percent as compared to the level of the previous five-year plan. The yearly output of grains was to increase by thirty percent as compared to the previous plan.[40] Productivity of labor on the farms was to grow by 40-45 percent over the period.[41] Also noteworthy was the call to develop on the farms as well as in interkolkhoz organizations subsidiary enterprises and handicrafts for processing agricultural produce.[42] The money and natural income of kolkhozniks from the public economy was to increase on the average by 35-40 percent and thus come much closer to the level of workers and employees.[43] The minimum size of old-age pension for workers and kolkhozniks was to be raised and the eligibility age for receiving old-age pensions as well as the method of calculating its size was to be equalized to give kolkhozniks the same rewards as workers and employees.[44]

By way of implementing the directive on developing subsidiary enterprises on the farms, the Central Committee and Council of Ministers issued a decree entitled "On the Development of Subsidiary Enterprises and Handicrafts in Agriculture," dated April 14, 1966.[45] This decree expressly and officially superseded decrees of 1938 on illegal organization in kolkhozy of industrial enterprises not connected with agricultural production and another decree of 1939 on the order of transferring such enterprises from kolkhozy to the state. The drive for subsidiary enterprise to be encouraged on the farms had begun under Khrushchev, but it remained for the law to catch up with practice and policy.

Brezhnev had announced in his report to the Congress that guaranteed pay for kolkhozniks was to be implemented. A combined Central Committee and Council of Ministers decree of May 16, 1966, "About Raising the Material Interest of Kolkhozniks in the Development of Social Production,"[46] translated this into law. The decree prefaced its reform of the kolkhozniks traditional pay system by stating that the present system in many kolkhozy failed to provide the necessary material interest for kolkhozniks in work in the public sector. It recommended as of July 1, 1966, that kolkhozy introduce guaranteed pay in money and in kind, based on pay rates for corresponding jobs in the sovkhozy. Norms of output were to be established taking account of the concrete conditions and the norms prevailing for analogous jobs in sovkhozy. Together with the guaranteed pay, payment per final results—quantitatively and qualitatively—was to be implemented. The kolkhoz production-financial plan was to earmark funds and natural produce as a payment of labor fund. Guaranteed pay was to be paid out at least once a month and the natural payments when produce became available. The payment of labor fund had priority in the distribution of kolkhoz income. Allocations to the indivisible and other social funds came only after allocations to the guaranteed pay fund, to the state for obligatory payment, and payments into the central social security fund of kolkhozniks.

In order to satisfy the needs of kolkhozniks for agricultural produce, it was recommended that they create a quaranteed natural fund of distribution for payment of labor. To this fund there should be allocated a definite share of the gross harvest of grain and other produce in order that kolkhozniks who want produce as fodder for their private livestock can choose natural payment in part instead of taking the whole of their pay in money.

The decree stated that guaranteed pay was in the future to rest upon increased production, increased labor productivity, removal of deficiencies in the norms of output for jobs and the pay scale, liquidation of superfluous numbers of administrative and service personnel, a sharp decrease in nonproduction expenses, and a strict observance of the regime of economies. Thus the guaranteed pay was to be "earned" from the new income guaranteed by these measures. Yet the decree provided what was intended as a temporary means of implementing guaranteed pay to the weaker kolkhozy who could not go over to the new system immediately on the basis of their current economic situation. For those weaker sisters, Gosbank was to extend credits during the period from 1966 to 1970 for up to five years, in the amount of the difference between the guaranteed pay fund and the means of the individual kolkhoz, that is, the loan was to cover only the amount the kolkhoz could not itself supply to make good the guaranteed pay. Repayment by the kolkhoz was to begin with the third year after receipt of the loan, and be a preferred charge on kolkhoz income after payments into the state budget and before payments into kolkhoz indivisible and social funds.

It should be noted that no definite minimum wage is guaranteed, nor is the state paying the kolkhoz wage bill. All that is guaranteed is regular monthly payments for work done, at rates ultimately approximating those in sovkhozy for similar jobs. Moreover, there are ambiguities in the scheme. For example, how do the kolkhozy calculate the money value of natural payments—by state purchase prices, retail prices, and so on? Also, what happens if the natural pay fund is needed to meet state procurement quotas or if it is inadequate to meet the demands of kolkhozniks? May a kolkhoznik resell natural pay produce on the kolkhoz market? Roger Clarke, a British specialist on Soviet agriculture, wonders whether the right to guaranteed pay extends to winter months, when there is no work available for a kolkhoznik.[47]

A decree of the Central Committee of July 11, 1966,[48] highlights a recurring problem—the potential for distortion built into the high above-plan purchase prices. Apparently the low quotas set for grain had become a problem because many kolkhozy and sovkhozy were choosing to underfulfill some grain quotas and concentrate on over-fulfilling others—apparently the rewards based on higher above-plan prices for wheat and rye more than compensated for losses on the underfulfilled crops, oats, corn, and buckwheat. Also many farms were not selling their above-plan quantities but rather chose to keep them. This was condemned and local party organs were ordered to vigorously combat these unconscientious attitudes. So in order to avoid a bread shortage, pressures were to be applied to the farms to sell much more of their surplus grain. In theory such sales were purely voluntary on the part of the kolkhozy.

A decree "On the Further Development of Subsidiary Enterprises and Handicrafts in Agriculture,"[49] of September 16, 1967, was intended to stimulate subsidiary enterprises on the farms and in interkolkhoz organizations, as the Party Congress had urged, but not at the expense of agricultural production. By doing this it was hoped to fully utilize seasonal surplus labor on the farms as well as surplus of unused raw material. It envisioned processing of fruits, berries, the production of local construction materials and consumer goods. Production ties with industrial enterprises were to be developed. Contracts with consumer cooperatives, state trade organs, and industrial enterprises to sell produce were to be established. But such goods could be sold on city and village markets. Gosbank was to extend six-year credits to farms and interkolkhoz organizations for construction of subsidiary enterprises. State enterprises were allowed to sell surplus equipment, raw materials, byproducts, fuel, transportation means, and apparatus they did not need. Union Republic Councils of Ministers were to introduce recommendations on pay for kolkhozniks working in subsidiary enterprises. The ultimate question as to the development of subsidiary enterprises on the farms in whether, despite the qualification in the decree that they would not adversely affect agricultural production, farms will not invest more time and capital in those enterprises that turn out to be very profitable and ultimately curtail their strictly farming pursuits.

Brezhnev's promise that kolkhozniks would be given equality with workers and employees in respect of pension benefits and eligibility requirements was made good in an edict of the USSR Supreme Soviet's Presidium of September 26, 1967.[50] The age at which a kolkhoznik has a right to an old-age pension was lowered from sixty-five to sixty for men and from sixty to fifty-five for women. For women with five or more children and having raised them to age eight, the age limit was lowered from fifty-five to fifty. These eligibility ages for old-age pensions were now the same as for workers and state employees. The minimal size of pensions for invalids in consequence of labor accident or occupational disease was raised. A further advance for kolkhozniks came with a Supreme Soviet decree of June 5, 1971, which brought them into the same system for pension deductions enjoyed by state employees. This decree also raised the size of the pension for old age for kolkhozniks to a minimum of 20 and a maximum of 120 rubles a month.

On October 31, 1968, the Central Committee Plenum issued a decree entitled "About the Course of Fulfillment of the Decisions of the Twenty-Third Congress and CPSU Central Committee Plenums on Agricultural Questions."[51] Reporting on results for 1965-67 as compared with 1962-64, the average yearly harvest for grain was up 10.5 percent, cotton 20.4 percent, sugar beet 34.5 percent, rice almost 100 percent, meat 15 percent, milk 21.3 percent, eggs 11.2 percent. The state purchase plans for 1965-67 in both crops and livestock were successfully fulfilled. In 1968 the state purchase plans for meat, milk, eggs, and wool were fulfilled before the end of the year. Still in general the production levels of some products and the growth in the productivity of labor still were below the Twenty-Third Congress' five-year plan target levels. Ineffective use of technology, machines, agronomical science, and fertilizers was blamed. Livestock's high costs of production had not been cut down appreciably. Many kolkhozy still had excessive expenditures on the administrative-directional apparatus. The state organs, general and specialized, dealing with the farm were blamed for laxity in flushing out hidden capacities and checking up on implementation of policies. Despite these problems, the principle of firm plans for purchase, initiated in 1965, were to be used again for 1971-75, and the grain target for 1971-75 was to be the same as in the last five-year plan. In order to increase production and encourage farms to sell produce, higher above-plan prices used for grain were now to be used for certain other produce as well.

On December 13, 1968, a new USSR Fundamentals of Land Legislation was adopted.[52] Article 8 reaffirmed the principle of free land use, that is, no conventional rent charge for land use. Article 9 reaffirmed that land occupied by kolkhozy was secured to them in use for an unlimited period. Article 16 states that the taking of kolkhoz land must be agreed to by the general meeting or meeting of representatives of the kolkhoz. Article 19 establishes the principle that taking of agricultural land for nonagricultural purposes must compensate the users for loss of agricultural production connected with this taking. Article 25 is devoted to the right of the kolkhoz dvor (kolkhoz household) to a garden plot. This right is preserved when the only able-bodied dvor member is in military service, is away for studies or elective duty, or is temporarily transferred to other work with the consent of the kolkhoz through state order, and also preserved when the dvor only has underage members. If all dvor members are incapacitated, through old age or any incapacity, the right to the plot is preserved. In accordance with the kolkhoz's charter, the dvor is alloted pasturage for its cattle. Kolkhozy, as well as other state agricultural enterprises, per Article 28, can transfer lands of theirs temporarily not being used to the use of other kolkhozy, sovkhozy, and so on, if the raion executive committee approves. The user, whose use is limited to a definite period only, compensates the expenses related to that land incurred by its permanent possessor for the period of the loan. Article 46 calls for the introduction of a state land cadastre for securing the rational use of land. Article 50 reaffirms that the buying, selling, pledging, transmission by will, gift, renting, voluntary exchange of plots, and other deals in direct or hidden form all violate the right of state ownership of the land and are invalid.

Thus the Fundamentals in essence reaffirm the traditional Soviet land tenure system. They update the last comprehensive legislation on the subject, the 1922 Land Code. The new elements as far as the kolkhoz is concerned are more safeguards for the land user against the land taker, more protection for the kolkhoz dvor against the kolkhoz as to its garden plot rights, and the allowance of a very limited right to temporarily loan out unused land to third parties, but without levying a rent charge, the only compensation being that of costs accumulating on the loaned land during the period, which are payable by the temporary user.

NOTES

1. A Short History of The Communist Party of the Soviet Union (Moscow: Progress Publishers, 1970), pp. 350-351. (Hereafter cited as Short History.)

2. Ibid., p. 352.

3. For excerpts of the decree, see Resheniia Partii i Pravitel'-stva po Khoziastvennym Voprosam, Tom 5 (Moscow: Izdat. Polit. Lit., 1968), p. 517. (This multivolumed work hereafter cited as Resheniia.)

4. Simon Kabysh, "New Policy on the Private Plots," Studies on the Soviet Union VI, no. 1 (1966): 26-27, in which he cites R. S. Nazarov in Kommunist, no. 16 (1965).

5. G. Shmelev, "Ekonomicheskaia Rol' Lichnogo Podsobnogo Khoziaistva," Voprosy Ekonomiki, no. 4 (1965): 35.

6. M. Makeenko, "Ekonomicheskaia Rol' Lichnogo Podsobnogo Khoziaistva," Voprosy Ekonomiki, no. 10 (1966): 61-65.

7. Resheniia, Tom V, pp. 581-583.

8. "O Reorganizatsii Ministerstva Sel'skogo Khoziaistva," Postanovlenie Tsentral'nogo Komiteta KPSS, Soveta Ministerov SSSR, February 20, 1961, No. 152. Text in Sbornik Reshenii po Sel'skomu Khoziaistvu, (Moscow: Izdat. Sel'skokhoziaistvennoi Lit., 1963), pp. 448-458.

9. R. Conquest, ed., Agricultural Workers in the USSR (New York: Praeger Publishers, 1969), p. 76.

10. See Sbornik Reshenii po Sel'skomu Khoziaistvu, op. cit., pp. 78-114.

11. For two in-depth studies of Lysenko's career and its effects on Soviet agriculture, see Z. Medvedev, The Rise and Fall of T. D. Lysenko (New York: Columbia University Press, 1969) and D. Joravsky, The Lysenko Affair (Cambridge: Harvard University Press, 1970). The Vil'yams system of rotation involved alternating crops with grasses in order to replenish soil fertility.

12. L. I. Brezhnev, O Neotlozhnykh Merakh po Dal'neishemu Razvitiiu Sel'skokhoziaistva SSSR, Deklad na Plenume Ts. R. KPSS, March 24, 1965 (Moscow: Pelitizdat, 1965), pp. 5-7.

13. The period adopted for fixed procurement quotas was five years. In 1972 one prominent Soviet legal specialist called for fifteen- to twenty-year state purchase plans as a better way to stimulate specialization. See M. I. Kozyr', "Pravo i Sel'skoe Khoziaistvo," SGIP, No. 6 (1972), p. 18.

14. L. I. Brezhnev, O Neotlozhnykh Merakh po Dal'neishemu Razvitiiu Sel'skokhoziaistva SSSR, op. cit., pp. 9-10.

15. Ibid., p. 12.

16. Ibid., pp. 15-17.

17. Ibid., pp. 18-19.

18. Ibid., p. 30.

19. Ibid., pp. 31-33.

20. Resheniia, Tom 5, pp. 613-617.

21. Ibid., pp. 618-619.

22. Ibid., pp. 622-626.

23. Ibid., pp. 633-637.

24. Ibid., pp. 735-736.

25. Ibid., p. 738.

26. Ibid., pp. 739-740.

27. Ekonomika i Organizatsiia Sel'skokhoziaistvennogo Proizvodstva (Moscow: Izdat. "Myal '," 1970), p. 495.

28. G. Belovsenko, Oborotyne Sredstva Kolkhozov i Kredit (Moscow: Izdat. Finansy, 1968), p. 86.

29. V. A. Peshekhonov, Rol'Tovarno-Denezhnykh Otnoshenii v Planovom Rukovodstve Kolkhoznym Proizvodstvom (Leningrad: Izdat. Lenin. Univ., 1967), p. 99.

30. Ibid., p. 101.

31. L. I. Dolychev, Kredit i Effektivnost' Kolkhoznogo Proiz- vodstva (Moscow: Izdat. Finansy, 1972), p. 61.

32. Ibid., p. 128.

33. James R. Millar, "Financial Innovation in Contemporary Soviet Agricultural Policy," Slavic Review 32, no. 1 (March 1973): 114.

34. Resheniia, Tom 6, pp. 7-12.

35. L. I. Brezhnev, Leninskim Kursom, Tom 1 (Moscow: Izdat. Polit. Lit., 1970), p. 320.

36. Ibid., p. 321.

37. Ibid., p. 323.

38. Ibid., p. 329.

39. Ibid., p. 332.

40. Resheniia, Tom 6, p. 67.

41. Ibid., p. 72.

42. Ibid., p. 72.

43. Ibid., p. 77.

44. Ibid., p. 79.

45. Ibid., pp. 103-104.

46. Ibid., pp. 111-113.

47. Roger Clarke, "Soviet Agricultural Reforms Since Khru- shchev," Soviet Studies XX, no. 2 (October 1968): 162.

48. Resheniia, Tom 6, pp. 166-168.

49. Ibid., pp. 596-600.

50. Ibid., pp. 610-618.

51. Resheniia, Tom 7, pp. 176-183.

52. Ibid., pp. 198-220.

3

THE NEW KOLKHOZ
MODEL CHARTER

On April 24, 1969, Soviet newspapers printed both the draft
kolkhoz charter arrived at by the Commission for Working Out a
Draft Model Charter for the Agricultural Artel and the news that the
Central Committee had accepted the Commission's call for the
covening of a Third All-Union Congress of Kolkhozniks in November
1969 in Moscow. The forthcoming Congress would finally replace
the 1935 Kolkhoz Model Charter, which it was agreed had long been
rendered obsolete by numerous laws and practices, especially by
events of the Khrushchev and post-Khrushchev years. There were
three major questions about the long-overdue event. First, why had
it been so long in coming—Khrushchev had encouraged a full-scale
debate over the shape of a new charter in the middle 1950s. Second,
how far beyond merely reflecting and codifying the post-Stalin welter
of laws and de facto practices that had made the 1935 charter obsolete
would the new charter go? Were there to be any fundamental changes
in the structure or powers of the kolkhoz that might indicate an attempt
to solve certain perennial problems besetting the kolkhoz sector's
economic performance? Third, why did the regime want a new charter
at all?

First, the draft charter.[1] Brezhnev had renewed Khrushchev's
promise for a new draft charter in his March 26, 1965, speech, a
charter to be submitted to a third All-Union Congress of Soviets in
1966. Pravda of January 26, 1966, published the names of the members
of the Draft Commission, which was headed by Brezhnev and presumably to be dominated by him and the other Politburo members
among its 149 members, who included M. Suslov, N. Podgorny, P.
Shelest, A. Pel'she, A. Kosygin, and A. Shelepin.[2] After some two
years of obscure toil, it was announced in the March 26, 1969, edition
of the newspaper Sel'skaia Zhizn' that the draft would soon be forthcoming. Very probably one reason for the delay in working out the

new charter was the inability of the leadership to decide on the ideologically sensitive "link" issue, discussed below. The issue of kolkhoz unions, as well as the issue of a fee for land use, were also probably factors in this delay. Karl Eugen Wadekin feels that the issue of the size of garden plots was a cause for the delay.[3]

Both the draft and the final version issued by the Congress reincorporated the rent-free perpetual use principle by which the state deeds land to individual kolkhozy. The 1968 USSR Fundamentals of Land Legislation had already done this, so all talk of a rent charge or of a flexible and variable land allocation system for kolkhozy had come to nothing. And any drastic approach to the subsidiary plot— either to extend it or drastically curtail it—also found no echo. In general the new charter reflects more concern for the rights of kolkhozniks in relations to the kolkhoz management and sanctions a certain devolution of administrative authority from the central kolkhoz organs to the production subdivisions. The application of the principle of the electivity of kolkhoz officials is significantly broadened and the secret ballot is allowed for. Yet there are several reservations in this seeming democratization. First of all, the absolute right of kolkhozniks to leave the kolkhoz, a right that is implicit in the fundamental principle of the kolkhoz as a voluntary association, is not explicitly insured. Moreover, the Soviet internal passport system, which precludes residence in many urban and suburban areas for kolkhozniks who cannot obtain the requisite passport, a matter of administrative discretion, is left in effect.

The Congress of Kolkhozniks, heeding Brezhnev's suggestion of 1965, passed a resolution creating a system of elective kolkhoz councils at all levels—raion, oblast, krai, and All-Union. What was made clear is that they have only the power to make recommendations, and although the intricacies of their interrelations remained to be seen,[4] it seemed clear enough that they were not meant to be a kolkhoz parliament or a corporate spokesman for kolkhoz interests, considering their highly decentralized, probably confederative structure. Moreover, from the rather considerable proportion of central party and state agricultural bureaucrats elected to the All-Union Council it looks like the All-Union Council is clearly meant not to reflect grass-roots rumblings but rather to smother, disguise, or channelize these into harmless "further studies."[5]

Now, as to the details of the new charter. In article 4 certain rights are expressly provided for the kolkhoznik as against the kolkhoz that were not in the 1935 charter. He had the right now to receive assistance from the kolkhoz to improve his skills, which might be a basis for demanding the right to get paid leave for studies, although this is far from clear. He has the right to use kolkhoz pastures and draught cattle as well as transportation facilities for personal needs in the manner established by the kolkhoz. Previously, although the practice of rendering such help was common, it was not by right. It perhaps remains for a "case law" or set of formal rules and regulations governing this right to evolve before the abstract right is translated into meaningful specifics. Moreover, it is unclear what recourse a kolkhoznik denied such rights has. Without norms as to what the quantum, frequency, and form of such rights are, the "right" lacks the specificity necessary to make particular claims on the basis of it in, let us say, a court. The court would have no criteria by which to judge the claim of a kolkhoznik that he was so unreasonably limited in his right to, let us say, transportation facilities in a particular case. The same is true as to his new right to help in repairing his dwelling.

Perhaps the local soviet will provide the "case law" over time, backed up by the raion soviets. The lawyer A. Pervushin sees the local soviets as playing a special role in examining complaints of kolkhozniks and in enforcing the charter.[6]

Another new right is that of article 6, the maintenance of status as a member when on active military duty, when elected to government or cooperative office, when engaged in full-time study, or when engaging in work in the national economy for a period fixed by the kolkhoz board. Article 7 states that the application by a kolkhoznik to leave must be considered by the board and the general meeting within three months after the application is filed. First of all, it is not clear from this whether it is the board or the general meeting that has the final say. More importantly, although there was no reference at all to the application to leave in the 1935 charter, this article 7 application procedure does not amount to the bestowal of even a conditional right to leave the kolkhoz. And apparently there is no appeal from the decision nor any formal criteria by which to judge the cogency of an application to leave.[7] The jurist Vl. Petrov does not consider this a limitation of personal freedom.[8] The jurist G. Kharatishvili discusses cases of those refused permission with resultant hardship for them in having to change residence due to changed family circunstances. Yet he does not raise the underlying issue.[9]

Article 10 states that a reduction in the amount of kolkhoz land or a change in its boundaries, on the basis that the state or public needs will be served, requires the consent of the kolkhoz general meeting and the respective state bodies. It also states that, as a rule, it is not permissible to turn over irrigated and drained lands, ploughland, and land taken up by perennial fruit trees and berry shrubs and vineyards for nonagricultural use. The kolkhoz has a right to compensation for losses connected with permanent takings of its land or its temporary use. Compensation is set by legislation. It certainly is an improvement in protecting the rights of the kolkhoz to have the right expressly stated in principle, which was not done in the 1935 charter. Still, there are some problems. First, who or what decides as to whether or not state or public needs require certain lands? Can the kolkhoz general meeting prevent an administrative decision in favor of a taking? Exactly what losses are connected with the taking—lost profits if the land had been cultivated? On what basis is the land taken evaluated? Perhaps the reference to "legislation in effect" is a partial solution, yet it seems that more detailed elaboration of both the determination of state needs, even a list, as well as the principles to be employed in order to award compensation, would have far better suited the demands of protecting the kolkhozy. Even if it is allowed that the charter, being a document of principles, is not in theory the proper place for elaborations or detailed description of processes to implement declared rights, still to declare that the kolkhoz general meeting's consent is required for any taking and then to confuse this by coupling it with the consent of respective state bodies is merely to render the text unfathomable without further explanation. That these are problems is evident from the legal literature. The "legislation in effect" fails to define exactly which types of loss are compensable and or to give criteria for determining the amount.[10] And the losses involved in agricultural land being appropriated for nonagricultural use have an economic aspect as well.

Article 13 states that kolkhozniks who negligently cause the destruction, spoilage, or loss of kolkhoz property, or who without authorization use tractors, automobiles, farm machinery, or draught livestock, or who inflict material damage on the kolkhoz must make compensation to the kolkhoz. The kolkhoz board is to determine the size of actual damages. If damage results from a kolkhoznik's negligence, recovery is made to the fullest extent possible of the damages but not above an amount constituting one-third of the kolkhoznik's monthly earnings. But if the damage is done intentionally, all the damages must be compensated. The board carries out the action and collects the damages, but if litigation occurs, then it goes into a court. The 1935 charter did not discuss the liability of the kolkhoznik to the kolkhoz for civil damages. What this provision amounts to is the codification of kolkhoz practice in these cases, with the difference that the one-third limitation on recovery is taken by analogy to the liability of workers to their enterprises, provided for in the labor code, and represents the triumph of those jurists and economists who for years had urged limiting kolkhoznik's liability to that of workers, since the court practices that had evolved did not so limit their liability to one-third of monthly earnings.

Yet there are circumstances where full liability or even extraordinary or "raised" liability, as opposed to the limited liability spoken of in article 13, is imposed. Unlike the labor legislation from which the article 13 one-third-of-monthly-earnings-limit was borrowed, the model charter does not list the cases and bases in which full and extraordinary liability can be applied.[11] Full liability is generally applied if acts are intentional or criminal, or if it is specifically provided for by legislation.[12] Also, full liability applies if damage done by the kolkhoznik occurred outside the scope of his membership duties.[13] Demands are being made now by lawyers for an exhaustive list of the cases in which extraordinary liability can be applied, so as to better protect the kolkhoznik in undefined cases. The problems of defining exactly which production "expenses" can be recovered and the meaning of "unreceived income" that is not recoverable are seen as important.[14] They highlight the ambiguitity of article 13. Yet another problem is the jurisdiction of the kolkhoz Comrade's Court as opposed to the People's Court in article 13 litigation.[15] Article 26 goes beyond article 14 of the 1935 charter, which spoke only of the brigade as the one production subdivision on the farm, although links and farms were in fact used both before and after this time. Article 26 lists departments, brigades, links, and other production units. Land, plots, tractors, machinery and implements, livestock and buildings are to be secured to those production units. Thus article 26 is flexible enough to sanction all kinds of experiments in creating more incentive-producing work units like the mechanized link. Here again the charter is not so much innovative as reflective of the practices prevailing. Article 26 also states that the activities of the production units are conducted on the basis of internal cost accounting (khozraschet). Thus the new types of subbrigade production units are legitimized as actual independent economic-financial entities the better to test their economic potential and maximize incentives by insuring that, to the greatest extent, workers are paid on the basis of the results of their own work. Of course, smaller work units, being more successful than larger ones, would undermine the dogma that the larger the production unit the more economical and productive it is. Also, there is a distinct fear that the smaller links, which often resemble the old family-farm-sized operation—and they often do involve members of one or two families—would rekindle the private property mentality of the peasants and perhaps become, in disguised form, private family farming. In any case practice and ongoing experiments have yielded very positive economic results from different types of links with different sizes, both specialized and unspecialized, mechanized and nonmechanized. The new charter allows for the experiments to continue. It is noted by one Western expert on the kolkhoz that the final draft of article 26 dropped the qualification "for several years" affixed to the description of the production subdivisions being endowed with lands, machinery, livestock, and so on, that was in the draft charter's article 26.[16] This could either be because the more flexible approach was taken or because conservatives feared that the "for several years" provision could be the germ for kolkhozniks recreating stable mini-farms on their relatively secure tenure in certain land, livestock, and personnel.

Article 28, inter alia, states that kolkhozniks who without valid reason fail to make the established minimum labor contribution to the public sector or who avoid work may, by decision of the kolkhoz board, be deprived in whole or in part of their bonuses or premia and other forms of material reward. Thus insufficient labor participation becomes a basis for forfeiture of earned benefits or denial of privileges. In the 1935 charter there was no such offense mentioned and no notion of any minimum yearly labor participation. Yet the practice grew up out of necessity within kolkhozy of enforcing some minimum number of labor days or work appearance days to be earned or accumulated or else suffer penalties and even expulsion from the kolkhoz, the latter carrying with it loss of the right to the all-important garden plot. This practice was formalized in a joint party-state decree of March 6, 1956, entitled "About the Charter of the Agricultural Artel and the Further Development of the Initiative of Kolkhozniks in the Organization of Kolkhoz Production and Administration of Kolkhoz Affairs." A landmark decree, it recognized that in many ways the 1935 charter was obsolete. Ostensibly for the purposes of democratizing the internal working of kolkhozy and freeing them from the shackles of the sterotyped and inflexible approach of the 1935 charter, which did not allow for local initiative and adaptation by individual kolkhozy to their own peculiar local circumstances, it granted kolkhozy the freedom to modify and mold their own charters in enumerated areas to their own circumstances free of the straight jacket of the 1935 charter. In particular, it was strongly recommended in it that the size and allocation of both garden plots as well as the privilege of use of kolkhoz pastures for private cattle and feed allotments from the kolkhoz be made to depend upon the degree of the kolkhoznik's labor participation in the public sector. To this end it was recommended that the sizes of the garden plots indicated in the 1935 charter be jettisoned in favor of letting each kolkhoz define size, taking into account both local conditions and labor participation. The 1935 charter norms on private cattle could also be reconsidered by each kolkhoz. It was recommended that an obligatory minimum of labor days, based on each kolkhoz's labor expenditure plan, be instituted.[17] This decree laid a legal basis for many abuses being perpetrated by kolkhoz officials on kolkhozniks and in periodic campaigns against the private sector with consequent negative results on the level of private livestock and on the supply of vegetables, potatoes, and meat products locally and in cities from the private sector. By January 1, 1966, an overall 8 percent reduction in gross output of private plots had resulted despite Khrushchev's successors' rollback of most abuses.[18]

It is notable that the new charter's provision does not specify any minimum labor participation. Nor did article 28 in the draft charter. Dmitri Poliansky, in his report "Concerning the New Model Rules of the Kolkhoz," delivered at the Congress of Kolkhozniks, in discussing the debate over the draft charter, rejected on behalf of the charter commission the suggestion of some that the charter stipulate the number of working hours and the minimum amount of work to be done in the public sector. This would, he said, complicate the charter. There was no need for unnecessary detail.[19] Nor was there any mention of the size of the supplementary or bonus pay fund. While the jurist N. A. Ivanovich does not urge an amendment to this effect, he does call attention to what he considers the malpractice of some kolkhozy that allow supplementary pay to actually exceed basic pay. In some republics there is legislation limiting the percentage of supplementary to basic pay to 12 or 20 percent of the latter, which is in line with what Ivanovich feels is the proper priority of accumulation over consumption.[20] There are those who feel that the model charter is defective in not placing a maximum on the wage fund as well as on the administrative expense fund. But the jurist A. M. Kalandadze disagrees.[21]

The rights of pregnant women and adolescents are increased as compared to the 1935 charter. Instead of just one month before and after giving birth as leave at one-half of average monthly pay, as per article 14 of the 1935 charter, the new article 33, in addition to announcing a right to maternity leave, speaks of mothers being afforded the necessary conditions for timely feeding of their infants and provides that they may be given additional leave. Article 33 stipulates that the kolkhoz establish a shorter work day for adolescents and benefits for them. There was no reference to this in the 1935 charter.

Article 35 stipulates that penalties can be imposed on the kolkhoz president and the president of the auditing commission and its members by the general meeting. Senior specialists, the head bookkeeper, and heads of production units can be penalized by either the general meeting or the board. In the 1935 charter there was no reference to penalties for these officials. Perhaps it was inherent in the general meeting's theoretically supreme position that it could penalize any and all. Still, this clause would seem to be a strengthening of the rank and file at the expense of the officials and thus at least a formal increase in kolkhoz democracy.

The new charter's arrangements in respect of gross income and produce are notable in many respects. First, unlike the 1935 charter, they do set aside a guaranteed pay fund, but neither article 28 nor 36, which speak of this, respect Brezhnev's recommendation that the level of guaranteed pay be set at approximately the sovkhoz level for analogous jobs. Is this an innocent, benign omission or perhaps in execution of an international policy of retreat or hedging on the previous policy of quickly raising kolkhoz pay levels to those of the sovkhoz? The question is not easily resolved. Alan Abouchar, a Western student of Soviet agriculture, feels this omission may be due to the regime's feeling that kolkhoz wages had already grown too fast.[22]

Second, article 36 stipulates that allotments for increasing the fixed and circulating assets are obligatory but the annual amount is to be fixed by reference to the need for insuring continuous expansion of production. Article 11(e) of the 1935 charter mandated a 10 to 20 percent deduction from total annual money income to be put into the indivisible fund (fixed and circulating assets fund). That there was a major dispute over the necessity of specifying a certain fixed percentage to the indivisible fund is admitted by Poliansky in his Congress report. Poliansky cites that as proof of the new economic independence bestowed on the kolkhozy.[23] Actually, the crucial element in this respect is the mandatory nature of the yearly allocation to replenish and extend the indivisible fund. This is done in order to make sure kolkhozy do not use their profits wholly for consumption, that is, mainly to increase members' pay. In theory this is purely an internal kolkhoz matter, since kolkhozy are supposedly cooperatives outside the state's control. Of course, the Congress of Kolkhozniks is not legally a state agency, so that its dictates in the form of a new charter—which in theory all kolkhozy participated in the writing of through their representatives' work in the Kolkhoz Charter Commission and the Congress—are not a state-ordered interference in internal kolkhoz affairs.

Third, the 1935 charter's article 10 division of the kolkhoz entrant's socialized property into that which goes to the indivisible fund, and is hence nonreturnable, and that which is considered his "share," which he is entitled to have returned on leaving, is not mentioned in the new charter. No longer is the socialization of the property of new members a factor in adding to kolkhoz assets. This represents merely a recognition of the realities. Yet in dispensing with this, the theory of the kolkhoz as a cooperative is undermined. The kolkhoz has developed into a cooperative that no longer depends on the assets of new members other than their continuing work contribution.

Article 39 incorporates the old-age and disability pensions and pensions for loss of breadwinners already enacted by legislation. But article 40 breaks new ground by stipulating that kolkhozniks are to receive temporary disability benefits and accomodations at rest homes and sanatoria out of the kolkhozniks' centralized social insurance fund, rather than such provision being at the mercy of each

32

kolkhoz's own funds, as per the 1935 charter. (Under the old system such funds were uncertain as to amount or even as to whether there would be any surplus funds available after all other prior claims on kolkhoz income were met.)

Article 42 provides for kolkhozniks to be sent to schools for upgrading themselves, but they are obliged to return to the farm that sends them and work on it. So, although upward mobility at kolkhoz expense is spelled out, the price is a legal obligation to return.

The new charter provides that the subsidiary plots can be up to one-half hectare—only one-fifth of a hectare on irrigated lands— including land under buildings. Within this maximum each kolkhoz general meeting defines the actual sizes, taking account of the family and its labor participation in the public sector. Under the 1935 charter's article 2, the size was to vary from one-fourth to one-half hectare (2.471 acres), and in some areas, up to one hectare. In a sense, since there is no minimum of one-fourth hectare, the rights of the dvor are distinctly inferior to those provided in the 1935 charter. Moreover, the maximum includes space occupied by buildings, where- whereas the 1935 allotment was exclusive of buildings. Thus, the new charter is less liberal in this area than its predecessor. The actual size in the 1960s of garden plots was slightly less than one- third, .31, of a hectare.[24]

There is another potentially limiting aspect to article 42. It is stated that in case of compact residential construction in rural areas, the kolkhoz may allot the kolkhozniks farmyard plots of a smaller size near their new dwellings or apartments, giving them the rest of their total plot beyond the bounds of the residential zone of the area. This almost echoes the old Khrushchev agrogorod (agricul- tural town) scheme of some two decades ago whereby Khrushchev proposed a radical plan to rebuild kolkhoz villages as high-rise apart- ment house complexes with the garden plots located well away from these living areas, in effect rendering the plots more difficult and inconvenient to use and thus discouraging kolkhozniks from investing time that might otherwise be spent in the public sector. In this charter scheme only part of the plot would be cut off from the residen- tial area, yet perhaps it portends eventual total severance.

There is one provision in article 42 affording more protection to plot users. It preserves the right of plot use to dvors in cases when all its members are unable to work because of old age or dis- ability, when the only able-bodied member has been called to military service or elective office or has temporarily left for work with the consent of the kolkhoz, and when only minors remain in the dvor.

Article 43 provides that a dvor may have one cow with offspring up to one year and one head of young stock up to two years of age, one sow with offspring up to three months old or two pigs for fattening, up to ten sheep and goats (combined), beehives, poultry, and rabbits. The one cow, one pig formula is approximately the same as in the 1935 charter, except that the offspring of the one cow were limited to two calves. Also, per article 5 of the 1935 charter, there could be two sows with sucklings. The ten sheep and goats together were also in the 1935 charter. In the 1935 charter the provision for fowl and rabbits was unlimited as to number and the limit on beehives was set at twenty. In the new charter's article 43, it simply allows for beehives, poultry, and rabbits without any qualification. This could allow for each kolkhoz charter to supply its own maxima. On the whole then, the livestock provisions of the new charter are somewhat more restrictive, and potentially even more so.

Some of the most interesting changes occur in the charter's provisions for the kolkhoz administrative structure. The new tone is one of increased sensitivity to democratic procedures and controls from below. The general meeting decides whether or not to allow the kolkhoz to participate in interkolkhoz and state-kolkhoz organizations and associations, rather than the kolkhoz management or some external state organ. Unlike the 1935 charter, which set no fixed or minimal number of yearly general meetings, article 47 states that the board must convene a general meeting at least four times a year and also whenever one-third of the membership of the kolkhoz or the auditing commission request one. Moreover, unlike the 1935 charter, which had no provision for prior notice to the membership of a general meeting, article 47 provides that at least seven days before a general meeting the board must give notice. Still, the preparation of the agenda, so crucial a power, is not discussed in the new charter, just as it was ignored in the old one. As to the quorum, it is now two-thirds for all questions, whereas under the old charter it was a simple majority, except for expulsions of members, election of the board and president, and questions of the size of funds.

Article 48 provides for a meeting of representatives or delegates on larger farms where it is difficult to convene general membership meetings. The meeting of representatives or delegates can decide matters hitherto solely within the competence of the general meeting. Representatives are to be elected at meetings of farmers in brigades and other production units. The representational ratios and election procedures are set by the board. Questions to be decided by the meeting of representatives are first discussed at meetings held by brigades or other production units. Representatives report decisions taken at production subdivision meetings. The quorum for the meeting of representatives is three-fourths. The meeting of representatives had been legally recognized by the joint party-state decree of March 6, 1956, cited above, so that this represents no innovation by the new charter, although no such institution was provided

for in the 1935 charter. The significance of this development is unclear. Perhaps it is a genuine attempt to recreate the general meeting
on a practical scale, or it may be an attempt to undermine the principle of direct democracy on the pretext of its impracticality.

The kolkhoz board's term is extended to three years by the new
charter (article 49), whereas previously it had been two years, and
instead of its membership being limited to from five to nine, the
number is left for the general meeting to decide, as is also the case
with the size of the auditing commission. The sessions of the kolkhoz
board are to be held at least once a month—formerly once every two
weeks—and a three-fourths quorum is required, whereas before a
quorum was not mentioned. The board's decisions are by simple
majority. This was not mentioned before. The general meeting elects
a president for three years who is simultaneously the board's chairmen. Previously no specific term was mentioned in connection with
the election of a president. Brigadiers and livestock farm managers
were previously appointed by the board for two-year terms, whereas
now their terms are not specified. There is an interesting provision
in article 52 that states that instructions of chief (senior) specialists
on questions within their competence are binding on members as well
as officials of the kolkhoz. This is an innovation of the new charter
and it represents not only an attempt to bolster the authority of specialists in relation both to their superiors and subordinates but also
to lay a basis for holding them personally responsible for the consequences of their work. It would provide a basis for civil damage
actions against them in cases where the kolkhoz suffers material
losses because of their operational decisions. On the other hand, the
positive side of it could be a greater respect and status for specialists
that might go far in cutting down their tendency to switch farms or
leave the countryside all too frequently.

Article 53 describes brigade and brigade subdivision meetings,
which elect brigadiers with the choice subject to board approval.
The brigadier acts as the brigade executive. The brigade may also
elect a brigade council, analagous to the kolkhoz board. These organs
are subordinated to the kolkhoz board, which determines their powers.
Here is a set of new institutions that represents a real possibility
for decentralized responsibility and localized decision-making for
local production matters. There is also the possibility that these
bridage meetings could ultimately be the nuclei for new small farms
if the regime should ever decide to drastically cut down in size the
monstrous, administratively unwieldy farms it has created. This can
be done in a disguised, gradual form, and without ideologically embarrassing the regime, by gradually increasing the economic independence and legal rights of the brigades in relation to the central organs
of the kolkhoz.

Article 54 structures the auditing commission, and a new element as compared to the 1935 charter is its three-year term, whereas before it had no specified term. Also, now it must conduct two annual audits of kolkhoz financial-economic activity instead of the previous four. There was nothing in the 1935 charter about the time within which the auditing commission's reports had to come before board sessions, whereas now these were to be introduced within ten days (article 55). Moreover, the auditing commission now was expressly empowered to demand necessary documents from officials and members.

Article 56 provides that the board, auditing commission, and kolkhoz chairman are to be elected by secret or open ballot, at the discretion of the general meeting. There was nothing specific in the 1935 charter about the method to be used for these elections, but there was a reference to general meeting resolutions being adopted by a show of hands (article 20). Poliansky, in his address to the Congress of Kolkhozniks, stated that some favored the secret ballot and others the open ballot, the latter being the actual practice among kolkhozy. Considering this difference in opinion, the commission decided to let each general meeting decide for itself, said Poliansky.[25] It would seem that this failure to mandate the secret ballot may leave the rank-and-file kolkhozniks on farms dominated by their officials to the latter's tender mercies. On balance this failure might be a very significant one.

There is an unprecedented right of recall of the chairman and board members before the expiration of their terms. It is peculiar that the auditing commission members were not made recallable as well. In article 58 it is stated that an economic council, a cultural and service commission, and mutual assistance funds may be created if desired. What is new in this is the economic council, although what role it may play or who should be on it is not gone into.

Now to weigh the significance of the new charter as a declaration. It seems to be a compromise—it contains some important procedural safeguards for the individual kolkhoznik and affords some relief for the kolkhoz management from petty tutelage at the hands of local state and party organs as well as from the center. Mainly it codified previous legislation and defacto practices. On the truly crucial issues— such as the right of the kolkhoz to have total freedom to produce what it wants and sell to whom it wants, the right of kolkhozniks to freely leave the farm, the issue of a rent charge for land or some arrangement to allow farms to lease unused lands, and the freedom of the kolkhoz to choose any method of payment and organization of its labor force—it failed to act. Even the draft model charter was more liberal than the final version in that it allowed allocations of equipment and inventory to links and other production subdivisions for a number of years,[26] whereas article 26 of the final version omitted this and simply states that land plots, tractors, machinery and implements, and so forth, are secured to the production units. As Dmitri Pospielovsky observed, this leaves it up to local kolkhoz officials whether to give links and other production subdivisions a sense of permanency.[27] And this sense of stability is perhaps the crucial ingredient in their success. Yet the Soviet leadership seemed to fear this stability being institutionalized even in the face of the evidence of the economic success of the links. Again it seems to be a case of an aversion to officially enshrining a potentially ideologically abhorrent institution, a work unit that approximates in size and operation the pre-collectivization peasant family work unit.

NOTES

1. For its texts, see Sovetskaia Rossiia, April 24, 1969, pp. 1-3. For the final version see Pravda, November 30, 1969, pp. 1-2.

2. For the full list of members, see Tretii Vsesoiuznyi Sezd Kolkhoznikov, Stenograficheskii Otchet (Moscow: Izdat. "Kolos," 1970), pp. 470-478.

3. Karl-Eugen Wadekin, "Private Production in Soviet Agriculture, "Problems of Communism XVII, no. 1 (January-February 1968): 30.

4. The model statutes structuring these councils as the All-Union, Union Republic, Autonomous Republic, krai, oblast, and raion levels were published in Ekonomicheskaia Gazeta, no. 32, August 1971, and will be discussed in Appendix B.

5. The All-Union Council elected had 125 members, including the Minister of Agriculture, all the Union Republic Ministers of Agriculture, important party and state agricultural experts, the USSR Minister of State Purchases, the President of the All-Union inter-kolkhoz construction organizations, the Head of the Agricultural Workers Trade Union division, the USSR Minister of Land Reclamation and Water Economy, the President of the All-Union "Soiuzsel'khoz-tekhnika,"and the President of the All-Union Academy of Agriculture Sciences. Others included numerous kolkhoz presidents, specialists, and workers. For the full list of members, see Tretii Vsesoiuznyi S'ezd Kolkhoznikov, op. cit., pp. 310-321.

6. A Pervushin, "Zashchita Sub'ektivnyk Prav Chlenov Kolkhoza," Sov. Iust., no. 19 (1971): p. 11.

7. G. Shvets, "Nekotorye Voprosy Sviazannye Primeneniem Primernogo Ustava Kolkhoza,"Sov. Iust., no. 24 (1971): 14.

8. Vl. Petrov, Primernyi Ustav i Problemy Sotsialisticheskoi Zakonnosti v Kolkhozakh (Kazan: Izdat. Kazanskogo Univ., 1971), p. 167.

9. G. G. Kharatishvili, "Chlenskie Pravootnosheniia po Primer-nomu Ustavu Kolkhoza," SGIP, no. 2 (1972): 51.

10. Iu. Zharikov, "Okhrana Prav Zemlepol'zovaniia," SGIP, no. 12 (1971): 52; V. Egorev, "Sudebnaia Praktika po Delam O Vozmeshchenii Vreda Prichinennogo Nepravomernym Ispol'zovaniem Zemel'," Sov. Iust., no. 3 (1972): 14.

11. V. Romanov, "Spornye Voprosy Primeneniia Kolkhoznogo Zakonodatel'stva," Sov. Iust., no. 3 (1972): 14.

12. G. Dobrovol'skii, "Material'naia Otvetstvennost' Kolkhoznikov za Ushcherb, Prichinennyi Kolkhozam," Sov. Iust., no. 18 (1971): 20.

13. S. Dontsov, "Material'naia Otvetstvennost Dolzhnostnykh Lits Kolkhoza i Inykh Lits za Vred, Prichinennyi Kolkhozy," Sov. Iust., no. 5 (1972): 13-14.

14. N. V. Storozhev, "Material'naia Otvetstvennost' Kolkhozni-kov," SGIP, no. 11 (1971): 38-39.

15. For a good discussion of this, see G. F. Dobrovol'skii, "Spory o Material'noi Otvetstvennosti Chlenov Kolkhoza," SGIP, no. 3 (1972): 52-53.

16. Keith Bush, "The Third All-Union Congress of Kolkhozniks," Bulletin, Institute for the Study of the USSR XVII, no. 1 (January 1970): 22.

17. For the text of the decree, see Sbornik Reshenii po Sel'-skomu Khoziaistvu, op. cit., pp. 251-258.

18. John W. DePauw, "The Private Sector in Soviet Agriculture," Slavic Review 28, no. 1 (March 1969): 64-65.

19. Tretii Vsesoiuznyi S'ezd Kolkhoznikov, Stenograficheskii Otchet., op. cit., pp. 55-56.

20. N. A. Ivanovich, "Nekotorye Voprosy Oplaty Truda v Kolkhozakh," Vestnik Mosk. Univ., Pravo 2 (1972): 69.

21. A. M. Kalandadze, "Printsip Dispozitivnosti v Deiatel'nosti Kolkhoza," Pravovedenie, no. 1 (1971): 76.

22. Alan Abouchar, "The Private Plot and the Prototype Collec-tive Farm Charter," Slavic Review 30, no. 2 (June 1971): 358.

23. Tretii Vsesoiuznyi S'ezd Kolkhoznikov, op. cit., p. 49.

24. Keith Bush, "The New Draft Kolkhoz Model Charter," Bulletin, Institute for the Study of the USSR, XVI, no. 7 (July 1969): 39.

25. Tretii Vsesoiuznyi S'ezd Kolkhoznikov, op. cit., p. 55.

26. See article 26, paragraph three, of the draft charter in Sovetskaia Rossia, April 24, 1969, p. 2.

27. Dimitry Pospielovsky, "The Link System in Soviet Agricul-ture," Soviet Studies XXI, no. 4 (April 1970): 434.

On January 13, 1970, a decree of the USSR Council of Ministers was issued entitled "On Evening Out Expenses of Kolkhozy, Sovkhozy, and Other Agricultural Enterprises and Organizations Connected with the Transporting of Material-Technical Means."[1]

The essence of this was to place the physical burden of delivery on the state supply agency, Soiuzsel'khoztekhnika, rather than on the farms, although the latter would have to reimburse the agency for the expenses by paying a surcharge added to the wholesale price. But such expenses would be uniform within a union republic zone. And where the farms supplied the transportation, they would be compensated. These delivery fees too would be per set rates. There had appeared a complaint by a kolkhoz chairman about the burden of deliveries, pleading that responsibilities for them be switched to collection centers.[2] Here then is another attempt to introduce equal economic conditions for farms in approximately equal stituations and also to perhaps minimize the farms unproductive use of their own transportation facilities.

On February 10, 1970, the USSR Council of Ministers decreed that Gosbank USSR should make long-term credits available to certain types of interkolkhoz enterprises and organizations engaged in fattening cattle and fowl.[3] These loans were to be for construction of new complexes for fattening and were to be for up to ten years, with repayment to begin from the fourth year after receipt of the loan. There were other types of loans also, one to cover expenses for the introduction of new machinery and mechanization of production, with repayment after six years. To qualify, an interkolkhoz enterprise or organization had to be on khozraschet (cost accounting), have its own independent bank account and circulating means, and be profitable. This new policy would obviously encourage the expansion of interkolkhoz activity in that it would no longer be limited to dependency on internally generated capital investment funds.

Two articles in Komsomol'skaia Pravda in April 1970 boosted the link as a production unit. A report from Cheliabinsk Oblast talks of their popularity in crop production, while the same is true in the Kuban.[4] Mechanized links, without assigned work duties (beznariadnaia sistema), were hailed as highly successful at a conference. The assembled experts seemed to feel that a heightened sense of being masters of the land and of personal involvement were the chief virtues of the links. Unlike the piecework system, which tends to be individualistic, the link system unites its members in a collective spirit and this results in stimulating performance.[5] These periodically favorable references to and publicity for the links might yet eventuate in an institutionalization of them via an amendment to the new model charter, or perhaps through a special statute structuring them or an individual decree authorizing or even mandating their extensive or even universal use and also guaranteeing the rights and duties of their members.

Brezhnev's report at the Central Committee Plenum of July 2, 1970, and the Central Committee resolutions based on it point the way toward the party's position on agriculture adopted at the Twenty-Fourth Congress. There are no significant innovations revealed in the report and resolutions, just a bit more of the old standard remedies. Yet the report is evidence of the continuing problems experienced since 1965 in agriculture. Brezhnev notes that in May 1970 the Politburo approved the policy of increasing the volume of capital investments and strengthening the material-technical supply of agriculture.[6]

On the whole, Brezhnev was well satisfied with gross crop productions totals for 1966-70. The average gross yearly harvest of grain for 1966-70 was 37.2 million tons more than the average for the previous five-year plan.[7] The fact that all the major crop average yearly harvests were up over the last two five-year plans, and that this was due mainly to greater yields rather than to more acreage being sown, is notable. Especially noteworthy, Brezhnev felt, was the breakthrough on the eight-ten centners per hectare barrier on grain yields in the last four years to achieve levels of 13.2 centners per hectare. The eight-ten centner barrier had stood for over a decade.

All major livestock products made significant progress for 1966-69 by comparison with the last two five-year plans. The yield of milk per cow was up by 266 kilograms over 1965. All qualitative indicators were up as well, and Brezhnev attributed all this progress directly to his course of chemicalization, reclamation, and complex mechanization worked out at the Twenty-Third Congress. The benefits to the farms were cited. The average gross income of kolkhozy for the last four years was 5.8 billion rubles above that of 1962-65. In 1969 the average monthly earnings of kolkhozniks was 33 percent above 1965.[8] Yet there were failures. For a complex of reasons, agriculture had not fully received the amount of capital investments foreseen by the plan, nor the defined quantity of machinery. The energy and mineral fertilizer supply plans were unfulfilled. There were notable violations of the rules for use of machines, premature writing off of machines, and underutilization of many machines.[9]

Brezhnev announced that intensive cultivation as opposed to extensive was not only the policy but a necessity since the USSR no longer had any free agricultural land. The key to intensive cultivation was the continued strengthening of the material-technical base of agriculture. Brezhnev, equating intensification with industrialization, is typical of the Soviet approach to agriculture. Intensification of cultivation does not necessarily require industrial managerial techniques nor even mechanized labor. The best example of this in the Soviet context is the highly intensive work, largely hand labor, in the private sector.[10] In fact industrial management techniques can be counter-productive in agriculture. As he had already indicated, there were organizational failures responsible for agricultural backwardness. State and party control organs would have to heighten the fight against indiscipline, irresponsibility, and uneconomic practices. Not a small part of the insufficiencies found among kolkhozy and sovkhozy were the direct results of weak guidance, especially by some party and state organs in respect to financial-economic activities of kolkhozy and sovkhozy. One noteworthy abuse was that of quite a few kolkhozy decreasing their allocations into the indivisible fund. The central and local agricultural organs were very weak in making sure kolkhozy and sovkhozy more fully utilized their reserves for increasing the production of produce, for raising the productivity of labor and lowering its cost.[11]

Brezhnev announced that in the forthcoming five-year plan the average yearly production of grain was to reach 195 million tons. And this figure was based only on minimal needs. To raise this amount a four centner increase per hectare of grain nationally on the average was necessary. And this required delivery of the requisite mineral fertilizers, machinery, and some land reclamation. The state grain purchase plan is to be unchanging for the whole five-year plan, thus reaffirming Brezhnev's 1965 innovation. The total purchase target is 60 million tons. But Brezhnev makes it clear that each kolkhoz and sovkhoz should sell over the coming five-year plan, as a minimum, 35 percent of the grain produced above the plan at the 50 percent higher-than-basic purchase price (above-plan) prices.[12] In effect this is mandated, although in theory and form those are voluntary sales.

In order to stimulate livestock production, the Politburo adopted in March 1970 a policy of raising purchase prices for milk and cream

41

on the average by 20 percent, introducing new purchase prices for livestock, including the previously established markups. Prices are raised for sheep, goats, and rabbits, and in some provinces and republics, on cattle as well. Purchase prices on all types of animal husbandry produce are established at the same rates for kolkhozy, sovkhozy, and the private sector, per the zone system. To stimulate the intensive fattening of young cattle and their delivery in better condition, markups are established amounting to 35 to 50 percent of the purchase price on young animals weighing 300 to 420 kilograms sold to the state by kolkhozy and sovkhozy, differentiated per zones. Purchase prices on some types of wool are raised by an average of 20 to 30 percent, and kolkhozy and sovkhozy were to be paid markups amounting to 50 percent of the purchase price for livestock, poultry, milk, wool, and eggs sold to the state above the annual plan. These markups would be paid for cattle and poultry if there was an increase in the heads of livestock on a given farm at the beginning of the year. These new purchase prices on animal husbandry products have been established without raising the retail prices on meat, milk, and other products. Yet Brezhnev insists that the additional income this new price policy brings to the farms must be channeled primarily into the expansion of production, the development and strengthening of the feed base, the construction of livestock sections, and the technical outfitting of animal husbandry. And on this basis, he warns, there must be a substantial increase in the very near future in the production and sale to the state of meat, milk, eggs, and wool. The kolkhozy and sovkhozy were expected to sell annually 8 to 10 percent of their animal husbandry products above the plan at higher prices, and this required not just a rise in productivity but also an increase in the number of livestock and poultry. At this point Brezhnev makes it clear that an increase in private livestock and not just in that of the public sector is what he has in mind. Realism dictates a policy of liberally making available to the private sector young animals to replenish personal holdings and also ample feed. Thus it should be recommended that kolkhozy issue grain and coarse and succulent fodder to kolkhozniks against their guaranteed pay.[13] Brezhnev thus reinforced the immediate post-Khrushchevian policy of a liberal line on the private sector in spite of the emphasis in the theoretical literature on the kolkhoz progressively metamorphosing into all-people's property and, as a concomitant of this, the progressive, voluntary curtailing of the private subsidiary economy (as, with the growth of the public sector, the private sector becomes unnecessary as a source of food and income) by those engaging in it without administrative pressure being applied to this end. Yet this "liberal" line should not be taken to amount to an official encouragement of the private sector. One of the post-Khrushchev leadership's first reversals of their deposed leader's policies was in removing Khrushchev's more recent administrative restrictions on private plots in order to improve the food and livestock situation. In the kolkhoz Model Charter the provisions that touch and concern the private sector, although they reflect a concern for securing the rights of the farmers not always observed by Khrushchev, do not, in the main, represent an expansion of these rights.

Brezhnev noted that the Politburo has decided to allocate to agriculture capital investments for the new five-year plan at a level 70 percent greater than such investments in the current five-year plan. But in addition to this the kolkhozy, thanks to their economic growth, will be able to invest more money than before in capital construction and in the purchase of machinery. According to his preliminary calculations, the capital investments of kolkhozy in the new five-year plan will increase by roughly 50 percent.[14] Hence, the kolkhozy implicitly will self-finance much of their capital investments and will not be allowed to use their net income frivolously on more pay, cultural-domestic facilities, and fringe benefits.

Brezhnev cited some other priority areas. The development of interkolkhoz construction organizations should be promoted in every way. Not only are larger quantities of mineral fertilizers needed, but also higher quality. And the delivery of mineral fertilizers to consumers is starting to become a major problem. Transportation, storage and utilizations of fertilizers, and liming of acidic soils are not going well.[15]

Brezhnev announced that for the first time in Soviet history, during the new five-year plan large grain-producing areas will be created on irrigated lands. Also, in light of the vast sums spent on land reclamation, he warns that the regime can no longer tolerate it when certain executives look calmly on while irrigated land is used at only half capacity.[16]

Another perennial refrain on the agricultural front, mechanization, is taken up. Brezhnev blames regional autumn plowing mainly on shortages of equipment. Together with increased deliveries of equipment, the rate of electrification of agriculture must progress.[17]

Both the training of farmers in the proper use of machinery and the need for more machine operators on the farms are seen as major problems by Brezhnev. He suggests that local units of Soiuz-sel'khoztekhnika, the machinery supply agency, be charged with the maintenance and repair of machinery and be made liable, along with firm executives, for the uninterrupted operation of equipment. This would no doubt relieve the apparently already overburdened farms of the formidable task of maintaining full-fledged repair shops. Addressing himself to the problem of the seeming perennially short supply of on-farm mechanizers, he admitted that a final solution has eluded the regime. Although large numbers of these cadres are trained, yet owing to extensive turnover within their ranks, farms are short of tractor drivers, combine operators, and other specialists. Why? In good measure the shortage is due to the insufficient attention given to the farm's working and living conditions. Brezhnev suggests what he labels some immediate "radical" measures: putting the pay system in order, with appropriate incentives for length of service and qualifications, and improvements in working and living conditions.[18] Here then is official recognition of the problem of the outflow of skilled workers from the farms. Yet the "radical" measures proposed are simply old bromides seemingly reflexively proffered as solutions, a rather pious and perfunctory treatment of a major problem.

Brezhnev's report ended on a note of exhortation to the farms to increase their sale of agricultural products to the state. He bemoans the seeming disappearance of the traditional "first commandment," that is, the primary duty of the farms to deliver and sell grain and other products to the state.[19] And the raion agricultural organizations, a key to agricultural control, have recently been strengthened so as to better insure discipline on the farms. The raion agricultural production administrations were recently reorganized as the agricultural administrations of the district executive committees. Now the directors of these administrations are at the same time vice-chairmen of the district soviet executive committees. Brezhnev sees this reorganization as heightening the role of the district soviets in the development of agricultural production. Actually, outside of the obvious reconcentrating of control at this level, this move seems to be yet another in a seemingly endless succession of administrative tinkerings with the agricultural bureaucracy, further evidence of an endless faith in administrative pill-taking, as if faulty chains of command, fuzzy jurisdictional areas, or new organizations can solve underlying economic problems or at least substantially ameliorate them. More of the same old medicine being administered is to be seen in another recent administrative innovation Brezhnev cites, the establishment of state inspectorates for the purchase and quality verification of agricultural products in districts, territories, and provinces. Brezhnev voiced the hopes that their work will facilitate an increase in state discipline and in responsibility for fulfilling the established plans for the production and purchase of grain, cotton, meat, milk, and other products. The inspectorates are to strengthen business relations between the producers of output and the procurement, marketing, and processing organization.[20] No doubt this will not be the last restructuring of the state procurement system. While it is true that Khrushchev's penchant for administrative restructuring was more obvious than that of his successors and, moreover, was more profound in both scope and depth, still, those who rebuked him for "administrativitis" seem to be afflicted with a milder version of the same disease.

Thus the most meaningful policies to emerge from Brezhnev's report seem to be the new price increases and an explicit commitment to help out the private livestock sector. Beyond this one finds a reiteration of stale old cliches and exhortations and a conspicuous lack of analysis of the underlying problems. The production upturn in comparison to the last two five-year plans has allowed Brezhnev to focus on the positive side of the ledger, ephemeral as this upturn may be, and positive only in a relative sense, that is, in reference to the last years of the Khrushchev regime, a time of distinct stagnancy in agriculture.

The advantages of interkolkhoz organizations were extolled in Izvestia of August 15, 1970, by Doctor of Economics I. Lukinov, director of the Ukranian Agricultural Research Institute. According to Lukinov, the deepening of specialization and the concentration of production are inevitably accompanied by a strengthening of cooperative ties and the combining of branches into the most rational economic structure. Yet the objective preconditions for large-scale interfarm associations appear only when production and technology have reached a sufficiently high stage of development. Then, in certain branches of agriculture, the "closed circle" within the framework of a single enterprise or association of farms becomes economically the most justifiable pattern for the organization of the production process, up to and including the production of finished output. The virtue of this, says Lukinov, is the elimination in such an organization of superfluous intermediate links, with reduction in losses and spoilage of raw produce, and optimum routes selected for the movement of output. Fixed productive assets and labor resources are utilized more fully and seasonal fluctuations are leveled. Still, the construction of a large-scale, modern plant is not only beyond the powers of the individual kolkhoz generally, but unless the plant has enough raw materials resources to keep it operating for more than just a few days, it is pointless.

Lukinov is a cautious advocate. The major obstacles to interfarm associations include the tremendous diversity of the majority of farms and the necessity of surmounting barriers along departmental boundaries. Typically each farm now delivers many kinds of produce — and often in small amounts—to state enterprises for processing. The area served by these enterprises embraces raw materials regions that vary greatly in size. So, concludes Lukinov, a mechanical approach to the economic unification of raw materials and processing complexes is unthinkable in such conditions. Such unification requires the creation of suitable economic and organizational preconditions, such as proper concentration and specialization of agricultural production and precisely regulated forms of raw material marketing and processing. Yet there has been notable progress of late in construction and processing of agricultural output. Especially outstanding economies

have been achieved by the large-scale production associations formed
by poultry farms. Here the process of deepening intrabranch specialization has been linked with the necessity of the unification of and
rational collaboration between several technologically interconnected
enterprises engaged in the incubation of eggs, the raising of young
fowl, the keeping of commercial flocks, and the maintenance of pedigree
stock farms, poultry-dressing plants, refrigerators, and feed-con-
centrate plants. Taken as a whole, says Lukinov, these enterprises
represent a unified economic complex. Its assets are obvious. Because
its incubators and slaughterhouses and all its other productive assets
are more fully utilized, the poultry-raising economic complex operates
more efficiently than the poultry farm within the framework of a closed
production cycle. And in such a complex, Lukinov claims, the overall capital investment per unit of output is less. Thus, Lukinov sees
great progress in industrialization of animal husbandry.[21]

That Lukinov's views are not at all to be considered ahead of
the times is obvious from reading the Soviet agricultural and economic
media. Interkolkhoz enterprises are given constant publicity. The
theme is their demonstrated economic success and their widening
scope. It is reported from Krasnodarsk Krai that interkolkhoz organizations, already important in construction, are beginning to be organized for feeding livestock, to run rest homes and fruit processing
plants.[22] There is a report on the Tirasopol interkolkhoz gardening
enterprise created in 1970. Its orchards go on for twenty-six kilometers and occupy 5.5 thousand hectares. It will soon set up a canning
plant and refrigerator facilities, and refrigerated transport also is
being acquired.[23] It is reported that in Moldavia in recent years
there has been significant growth in interkolkhoz pig-fattening enterprises. Some can handle twenty-five to thirty thousand pigs a year.
In 1966 in Moldavia the first interkolkhoz fodder combine plants were
established.[24] Another report comes from Lithuania on a highly
successful pig-fattening interkolkhoz union formed by twenty kolkhozy.
Its statute allowed for sovkhozy of the raion to gain membership in
it. Each member pays in five thousand rubles as a share fee as well
as contributing construction work by its labor worth twenty thousand
rubles. Per its statute, 15 to 30 percent of its net income goes into
its indivisible fund. Its highest organ is a meeting of representatives
elected by individual kolkhoz general meetings. This organ chooses
a seven-man council to act in the organization's board.[25] This is an
example of one particular interkolkhoz organization's statute. M.
Kovalenko, a party official, feels that with interkolkhoz ties more
and more transcending raion and even oblast lines, perhaps unions
of interkolkhoz organs at raion, oblast, and republican levels should
be formed.[26] It seems that the centralization issue will loom large
as the interkolkhoz organizational form grows.

46

In the Penza Region an interkolkhoz pig-fattening organization gives the state almost two-thirds of all pig meat sold in the oblast. And the production costs per centner of meat is ten times lower than that of the average per kolkhoz of the oblast.[27] An article entitled "The Collective Farmers Personal Farming" by a Soviet executive committee chairman, A. Malikov, in Izvestia of August 27, 1970, played on the theme that the kolkhoznik's personal farming continues to play a definite, although naturally diminishing role in the total output of agriculture. And it does not require capital expenditures from the state. Moreover, it soaks up supplementary labor resources not always utilizable in the public sector. And, administrative repression of it led to milk and meat shortages recently.[28] The lesson for local kolkhoz and state and party officials is that in aiding the personal economy you are increasing the market output of the communal annual husbandry sector because the individual engaged in personal animal husbandry will make fewer demands on the kolkhoz's marketable livestock supply. Moreover, the state procurements of meat from personal holdings, as well as of eggs and fruits, are significant.[29]

Brezhnev's demands put forward in the July 1970 report at the Central Committee Plenum that kolkhozy and sovkhozy owed it to the state to sell significant proportions of their above-plan grain surpluses to the state were apparently finding a mixed reception, according to an article in Pravda of September 1, 1970, by I. Lukin entitled "Put Grain into the State's Granaries." Lukin reports cases where farm directors have displayed "careless attitudes concerning the fulfillment of their assignments to sell grain. They see this matter from their own vantage points, so to speak, and forget that the state's interests have priority."[30] Voluntary response to Brezhnev's plea was apparently no better by the spring of 1971, and the economist P. Bakal proposed the setting of centralized norms of above-plan sales of grain for republics, krais (territories), and oblasts.[31]

In an article in Pravda of October 23, 1970, Doctor of Economics S. Semin, on the subject of ways of overcoming differences between city and countryside, discusses future plans to consolidate the highly dispersed rural settlements so as to facilitate servicing them. He states that there are some seven hundred thousand communities in the country now, of which about 70 percent have fewer than one hundred inhabitants each. There are about eight villages per kolkhoz. This fragmentation, he feels, is in large part the reason for the small scale of production, including that of livestock sections. And this hampers their mechanization and creates complications in the specialization and concentration of production and in providing cultural and everyday services to the rural population. Semin reveals that in the past ten years, the design organizations of the USSR State Construction Committee have worked out schemes for the planning of more than 80 percent of the rural districts. Yet the farms themselves operate on an ad hoc basis, largely based on the principle that the fewer the settlements the better, since this will insure larger and presumably more economical villages. But this is done without considering the actual size of kolkhozy and sovkhozy and their subdivisions or specializations, and the possibility of having personal plots. Still, work on the concentration of the rural population has begun, and in Orel Province, with 4,500 communities on 412 kolkhozy and sovkhozy, it has been decided to reconstruct eight hundred villages, with the result that each kolkhoz and sovkhoz would have approximately two settlements with all the amenities instead of the nine or ten it has now.

Of course there are some problems with rural concentration. First, if done on a national scale it would drain all other sectors of capital investments funds. As of today, 60 percent of the total volume of village housing construction is individually financed by the citizens themselves.[32] Second, it would make easier the curtailment of the private sector by divorcing the living area physically from the garden plot area, although this need not be. The idea of dividing the land plots of rural inhabitants into physically separate living and garden zones seems to be gaining adherents.[33] Third, it would facilitate greater control over the rural population, whose greatest insulation from the authorities so far has been its dispersal and the physical distances and hence the time involved in overseeing its activities. For instance, in Belgorod oblast on the average in each kolkhoz party organization there are only sixty-four kolkhozniks.[34] In Moldavia the average kolkhoz has 4.5 thousand hectares and fifteen hundred kolkhozniks.[35] Today's kolkhozy often encompass ten population points and two to three thousand people.[36] In fact one motive in consolidating kolkhozy was to thereby concentrate more party members on each farm. Preconsolidation kolkhozy were so strapped for party members to form party organizations that they commonly allowed nonfarm party members living on the farms to join them.[37]

It will, of course, be crucial to know just what type of settlements will become the official models for restructuring the rural areas. Some of the alternatives are described and evaluated by G. Golovko in an article entitled "Appearance of Our Village: An Architec Is Indispensable."[38] He recognizes the dispersals of villages as primarily an economic problem. Dispersed villages both obstruct the rational utilization of land and deprive their residents of the benefits of sewers, cultural facilities, and other amenities. Taking the village of Vysokoe in Zaporozhye Province of the Ukraine as an example of the economic advantages of village consolidation, Golovko notes that it will occupy a territory one-fourth the total area of the seven hamlets that presently comprise it. Buildings will be of one to three stories. Each family will be alloted not more than one hectare of land near its home for a vegetable garden. The principal household plot will be beyond the village outskirts. Compactness of the housing area is crucial to cutting down on paving and water main costs. Height of the buildings is not. Golovko rejects the extreme plan for building multistory buildings of a purely urban type. These, he notes, make it difficult for rural residents to tend their personal plots. Thus one might say that the types of village plan the regime ultimately standardizes will depend upon their attitude toward the private plots.

Another factor involved is the influence of the dispersal of population points on the farm on the forms of internal organization of labor. The more scattered the population on a farm the more likely it is to have a multitude of small brigades, and the smaller the brigades the less able they are to attract specialists.[39] This results in lower productivity for the small brigades.

The control factor from the party standpoint is illustrated by an article written by an obkom (oblast committee) party secretary in Kazakhstan. In his region there are seventeen hundred small villages, with more than five thousand shepherd brigades. One party group armed with a car has fifty to sixty livestock brigades and work points to cover, spread over sixteen to seventeen villages. The average auto radius of their route is two hundred to three hundred kilometers. They are able to visit each place once or twice a quarter.[40] Perhaps this is an extreme case but there is no reason to assume so.

On the theme of advantages and problems of the association, two Ukrainian republic agricultural officials, A. Sennikov and M. Mezentsev, writing in Izvestia of December 11, 1970, dwell upon the great success of large specialized poultry farms in the Ukraine, with egg production increasing more than fivefold and dressed poultry production almost quadrupling on these farms over the last five years. They claim that both labor productivity and unit costs of output also were lowered. The search for ways to speed the growth of output led to the amalgamation of poultry farms into associations. The authors discuss the first association of this type, the Starin Association. The Starin Poultry Farm, the parent enterprise, took charge of general production process operations (the keeping of the breeding flock of turkeys, the production of eggs for incubation, the hatching and rearing of turkey chicks up to the age of fifteen days, and slaughtering). The subsidiary farms specialized solely in the raising of turkey chicks for meat. The authors suggest that when an association is being set up, each ministry and department has to work out for itself just what the relationships are to be among member farms, as well as the rights and duties of parent and subsidiary farms, bonus-pay systems, and so on. Apparently the authors believe in strict financial controls over the associations. They also advocate convening an all-union conference on associations in order, ultimately, to prepare and ratify a statute on such associations.[41]

The jurist I. V. Pavlov discussed the legal nature of the agraro-industrial complex, which he calls a production organization uniting the production of agriculture produce with its processing on an industrial basis. He notes that it is not only of economic significance but also of social significance, since within it, ultimately, will occur the merging of kolkhozy cooperative property with all-people's property and, on this basis, the formation of a single form of public property.[42] Pavlov explores the different types of these complexes, trying to arrive at some general principles by which to govern their internal structure, the relations of the member units to each other and to the complex itself, the nature of the internal government of the complex, and its external relations. He concludes that it is primarily an agricultural rather than industrial unit.[43] He addresses himself to a consideration of just what controls the state would have over the formation and operation of these complexes.[44] In the end Pavlov raises the question of the legal capacity of the complexes and the need for some legislation on them.

What emerges from these articles is a growing awareness of the potential economic benefits of these agraro-industrial production units and of the need to lay a firmer legal foundation for them to develop on in the form of some model statute structuring them. Yet what is the real barrier to accelerating their development? Certainly not the absence of enabling legislation or a model associational charter. Actually there are no opponents of agricultural associations in principle They are lauded as the precursors of the ultimate agraro-industrial complex, which will organically combine industry and agriculture, thus ending the class division between the peasantry and the workers. The real question is that of priorities. The agricultural sector and its satellite, the food industry, despite recent increases in the amount of capital investments allocated to them, are still not receiving the investments required to industrialize them.

This problem is linked to the low level of technology and mechanization in Soviet agriculture, which results in the agricultural labor force's lagging rate of growth in labor productivity. The economist K. Ia. Lemeshev notes that in most economically developed countries of Europe and America the growth rate of labor productivity in agriculture is now one and a half to two times higher than in industry. The result has been a sharp reduction in the size of the agricultural population, with the consequence that the share of agricultural workers does not exceed 5.8 percent of the total able-bodied population in such countries, whereas in the USSR this index is approximately 30 percent. This high percentage, notes Lemeshev, indicates that manual labor still plays a large part in agriculture, and this in turn restricts the

possibility of releasing manpower to work in other branches of the
economy. Lemeshev puts the problem of the rural exodus in broad
perspective:

> At the present time, the level of production equipment
> and power per worker in agriculture is lower; the pay-
> ment for labor and the incomes of the rural population
> in general are lower; the level of general and special-
> ized education in the village is lower; and housing,
> cultural and living conditions are relatively worse.
> All these factors are the source of the relatively low
> prestige of agricultural labor, of the spontaneous
> migration of the agricultural population to the cities
> and to industrial centers, of the increasing problem of
> keeping skilled personnel and especially young people
> in the village. Unless this problem is solved, there
> can be no harmonious development of industry and agri-
> culture, nor can the unity of the economic interests of
> the city and village be effectively realized.[45]

A major theme in all the agricultural discussions, and especially
applicable to the kolkhozy, is that of the exodus of the rural population.
An important article by the economist V. Perevedentsev focused, inter
alia, on the facts of the rural outflow. Writing in the journal Voprosy
Ekonomiki of September 1970, he cites the statistics that in 1967 3.1
million people moved from rural areas to cities and only 1.5 million
from cities to rural areas. Also, several million people moved from
one rural area to another. What is particularly significant about this
is that these movements concerned primarily young, able-bodied
people. Perevedentsev concludes that the main results of migration
were the growth of the urban population at the expense of the rural
population. Perevedentsev indicates that in an eleven-year period
(1959-69) the number of urban residents increased by 36 million (by
36 percent), while the rural population decreased by 3.1 million (by
2.8 percent). And he concludes that the main source for the growth
of urban residents was the rural population—two-thirds of it. And
this urban growth at the expense of the rural population is not merely
regional but general, being true for all the country's Union Republics
and economic regions. Perevedentsev notes that this outflow is not
a wholly negative phenomenon by any means. He believes it was an
absolutely necessary condition for the expansion of the "urban" branches
of the national economy to their present dimensions.

Yet the rural exodus has its negative side. The question emerges
as to why there was an apparent rural manpower surplus. Citing 1959
statistics, Perevedentsev indicates that the level of manpower supply

51

to kolkhozy during the period of greatest intensity in agricultural work was as follows: 70 percent in western Siberia, 71 percent in Kazakhstan 76 percent in the northwest, 8 percent in Estonia, and 83 percent in eastern Siberia. But at the same time, the labor supply level was 122 percent on the kolkhozy of Kirgizia, 128 percent in the Ukraine and Moldavia, 142 percent in Belorussia, and as high as 199 percent in Georgia. Whereas each able-bodied kolkhoznik worked an average of 255 working days in the communal sector of the kolkhozy in the northwest and 249 days in eastern Siberia, the figure was 198 days in the Ukraine, 183 in Lithuania, 163 in Moldavia, and 148 in Georgia. Thus, concludes Pervedentsev, the rural localities in many areas possessed extensive surpluses of labor resources, and movements out of such areas would only benefit the national economy. But the rural exodus was larger from labor-short rural areas, not labor-surplus areas. And this only aggravated the situation in labor-deficit areas. In 1965 an able-bodied kolkhoznik worked 261 work days in the communal sector in the northwest (six days more than in 1959), 188 days in the Ukraine (ten days less than in 1959), 153 days in Moldavia (ten days less), and 135 days in Georgia (thirteen days less).

In general, Pervedentsev feels that the rural outflow has not been excessive, and, reassuringly, the size of the rural population has shown almost no decrease for ten years. And, he notes, since the share of labor resources employed in agriculture is substantially higher than in other economically highly developed countries, he has no doubt the outflow will continue. Yet he is aware of the problem of outflow from the labor-deficit short areas, especially the economically important ones, in particular all of Siberia and the northwest. Perevedentsev sees the rural outflow problem as one of the irrational distribution of the outflow rather than as merely involving the quantity of the total outflow.

His solution is more use of economic measures in regulating the territorial redistribution of labor resources rather than a resort to organizational and administrative measures, which he refers to but fails to discuss. He advises establishment of a definite correlation between urban and rural living standards, both between and within regions and between and among various occupational and skill groups. He proposes the establishment of a higher living standard for workers of the same occupation and skills in places with a shortage of labor resources in comparison with places of labor surplus and smaller differences between the living standards of the urban and rural population in areas with manpower shortages in agriculture in comparison with areas of surplus rural population.

In one report a kolkhoz rewarded young workers who stayed on the job a 20 percent monthly increase in their pay during their first two years.[46] But even here there is a threshold problem. There is

apparently a lack of data. Perevedentsev confesses that very little
is known about the actual correlation of living standards and even
about the real wages of the population in various places. Still, he feels
it would not be difficult to establish that the living standard of the population of a given area is higher or lower than the living standard for
the USSR. This, of course, is quite a commentary on the sensitivity
of the regime to such contrasts and the secrecy surrounding the gathering of the basic information itself. But although Perevedentsev acknowl-
edges that no methodology for calculating synthetic living standard
indices has yet been worked out—in spite of the discussion of this in
the scientific literature for some time—still it is easy enough to locate
the lower standard of living areas by the net population outflow from
certain areas.

Of course, Perevedentsev is only scratching the surface of the
problem. It has always been known that kolkhozniks and sovkhoz workers
earned much less than state workers and employees, enjoyed few of
the amenties associated with urban life, and that kolkhozniks had, until
recently, no state social security and insurance benefits. Moreover,
to the extent the regime wanted to discourage rural outflow, it merely
enforced or expanded the internal passport system to make increasingly
larger numbers of rural people ineligible to live in urban areas. Actually it is apparently a commonplace for factories that need labor to
accept kolkhozniks for work who have not been officially released by
their kolkhoz, although there in fact is no law prohibiting kolkhozniks
from taking work outside their kolkhoz without its permission. There
is a 1957 USSR Council of Ministers order that may amount to a prohibition. Two jurists conclude that such unauthorized hirings by factories are in fact illegal.[47] But it is one thing to keep them down on
the farms and quite another to get them to be productive there. And
this requires inputs of investment capital on a vast scale to improve
living conditions in the traditionally capital-deprived rural areas,[48]
plus a basic redistribution of national income in the form of wages,
fringe benefits, social security, and bonuses for farmers. To a significant extent such investment and redistribution has occurred since
1953. But much remains to be done, and Perevedentsev's proposal,
even if put forward in a rather abstract way, of a locally determined
wage level or standard of living correlated to the local labor resource
situation is a significant contribution to the continuing problem of
attracting and retaining farm labor.

A reminder of the importance, economically, of the peasant
household for the national economy, given in an Izvestia editorial of
January 16, 1971, was meant to reinforce the liberal policy of the
new kolkhoz charter toward the households as well as to remind party
and state officials that the households' production could play a significant role in fulfilling the above-plan procurement purchase plans of

the new five-year plan, emphasized by Brezhnev in his July report
to the Central Committee. The personal cattle, fowl, and vegetable
patch, says the editorial, have lost none of their significance in the
peasant's everyday life. It notes that surplus produce from the household is sold to the state and that a few hundred households are equivalent
to a subsidiary meat-and-dairy complex. Local soviets are admonished
to bring together state, kolkhoz, and household interests.[49]

A particularly important aspect of the rural population outflow
ignored by Perevedentsev is the large component of the more able-
bodied, younger element in the outflow. An article in Pravda of
January 27, 1971, by Iu. Grebennikov on the theme of keeping young
people on the farms stresses the acuteness of the manpower shortage
in Vitebsk Province. The supply of manpower varies drastically from
district to district. In one district, Shumilino, there are 9.7 able-
bodied workers for every one hundred hectares of arable land, while
in Glubkoe District the figure is 19.2. Often in the kolkhoz annual
reports the number of able-bodied workers is considerably overstated.
Retired persons are counted as active. In one particular kolkhoz, instead of the 240 able-bodied workers listed in the report, the farm had
only 206. Grebennikov, a kolkhoz president, admits that he has undertaken a great deal in recent years to retain his young cadres—helped
the young to acquire specialties, found agreeable jobs, built cultural
and sports facilities—but the results have been disappointing. He
concludes that young people are attracted above all to industrial labor.
Thus the retention rate hinges on industrialization of agricultural
labor, which is no immediate possibility.

Noting that in his krai after 1959 the agricultural population
dropped by 358,000 and that among those leaving, youths between fifteen
and twenty constituted 44 percent, the first party secretary of the Altai
Kraikom cites as causes lack of educational opportunities and the low
level of domestic amenities.[50] Another major reason for outflow of
youths in one study he cites is their heavy use in unskilled jobs.[51]
The first secretary of the Novosibirsk party relates a similar experience. Every year in his oblast approximately twenty thousand migrate
from rural to urban areas, and this worsens the age structure of the
agricultural population. Many leave to get more education, and the
young who go generally do not return.[52] The theme of holding onto
young specialists is especially strong now.[53] Apparently many of the
young specialists leave.[54]

Another problem is the still significant role of the personal
subsidiary economics. According to Grebennikov, during the past
decade there was a substantial reduction in the amount of grain and
potatoes issued to the kolkhoznik from the kolkhoz storerooms. This
was because the kolkhozy wanted to increase the percentage of produce
from the communal sector that is marketed. This resulted in a greater

dependency of the kolkhoznik on his subsidiary plot. And the introduction of guaranteed pay on kolkhozy has not reduced the role of
personal holdings in supplying peasant families with produce. Kolkhozy
should help the peasant by lightening his work load on the subsidiary
plot through generous help; for example, by giving him haying areas
near his plot. Yet many do just the contrary, and this too exacts its
toll in those who leave the farm.[55]

An item in Pravda of March 12, 1971, entitled "Kolkhoz Council
at Work," by A. Panchenko, announced a meeting of the Union Kolkhoz
Council in Moscow the day before. Representing the 17 million Soviet
kolkhozniks, the Council discussed the tasks posed for the kolkhozy
by the Twenty-Fourth Congress Draft Directives for the 1971-75 five-
year plan. The participants approved draft statutes on the kolkhoz
councils, elected an eleven-member presidium to carry on the council's
daily work, and formed nine sections, covering every branch of kolkhoz
production.[56] The council also heard proposals for a project model
statute on interkolkhoz enterprises.[57] This item is one of the few
evidences of the functioning of the Union Kolkhoz Council formed by
the All-Union Congress of Kolkhozniks in November 1969.

Yet another cautionary note on the issue of the acceleration of
the development of interkolkhoz production associations and industrial
complexes and the denigration of the private sector was sounded by
Gosplan Chairman N. R. Gusev in an interview with writer Yu.
Chernichenko entitled "About Bread and Other Things by Which Man
Lives" in the Literary Gazette of February 17, 1971. Referring to
zealots of accelerated livestock production complex construction as
some "hotheads" who need a shower, Gusev emphasizes that you cannot establish industrial-method livestock-raising on a handicraft construction base. And one cannot counterpose the complexes to existing
types of livestock farms or even to the personal auxiliary farming
sector. Even after the new five-year plan, he cautions, the complexes
will account for less than 16 percent of the total output of pork and
only one-fifth of total beef output. Even for eggs, the area of their
greatest success, the poultry factories alone will not meet normal
supply requirements. Personal plots now provide 30 percent of all
meat, and the decision of the Central Committee and state to remove
unjustified restrictions on the maintenance of livestock by kolkhozniks
and sovkhoz workers has had a positive effect. Still locally kolkhozniks
are not getting enough help with pasturing and haying, and not many
calves or other young stock are sold to them for raising. Chernichenko
interjects that new sociological factors are in good part responsible
for the decline in cows kept in personal farming. With the rise in
cash incomes, he holds, more villagers go to the food store to buy
foodstuffs rather than give up their leisure time to raising livestock.
Young couples do not want to burden themselves with personal farming,

according to Chernichenko. But Gusev emphasizes that the process of the diminishment of subsidiary farming should proceed naturally, without artificial acceleration.[58] In other words, there should be no return to Khrushchev's administrative suppression of the private sector from 1959 on.

NOTES

1. For text, see Spravochnik Partiinogo Rabotnika, Vypusk Desiatyi (Moscow: Izdat. Polit. Lit., 1970), pp. 199-201.

2. Ekonomika Sel'skogo Khoziaistva, no. 2 (1970): 34-39.

3. For the text or the decree, see Spravochnik Partiinogo Rabotnika, op. cit., pp. 204-205.

4. Kom. Pravda, April 14, 1970, p. 1.

5. Kom. Pravda, April 24, 1970, p. 2.

6. L. Brezhnev, Ocherednye Zadachi Partii v Oblasti Sel'skogo Khoziaistva, Doklad na Plenume Ts. K. KPSS, July 3, 1970 (Moscow: Politizdat, 1970), p. 3.

7. Ibid., pp. 4-5.

8. Ibid., pp. 6-7.

9. Ibid., pp. 8-9.

10. Karl-Eugen Wadekin, "Kolkhoz, Sovkhoz and Private Production in Soviet Agriculture" in W. A. D. Jackson, editor, Agrarian Policies and Problems in Communist and Non-Communist Countries (Seattle and London: University of Washington Press), 1971.

11. Brezhnev, Ocherednye Zadachi, op. cit., pp. 9-10.

12. Ibid., pp. 11-13.

13. Ibid., pp. 17-20.

14. Ibid., p. 26.

15. Ibid., pp. 27-30.

16. Ibid., pp. 31-33.

17. Ibid., pp. 34-35.

18. Ibid., pp. 35-36.

19. Ibid., pp. 44.

20. Ibid., p. 45.

21. Izvestia, August 15, 1970, p. 2.

22. G. Zolotukhin, "Pod'em Sel'skogo Khoziaistva Trebevanie Vremeni," Kommunist, no. 3 (1971): 36.

23. Sel'skaia Zhizn', April 22, 1971, p. 4.

24. Ibid., March 5, 1971, p. 2.

25. See the item by Ia. Glazer and A. Duberov in Ekonomicheskaia Gazeta, no. 27 (July 1971): p. 18.

26. M. Kovalenko, "Nov' Kolkhoznogo Sela," Kommunist, no. 4 (1971): 34.

27. L. Ermin, "Nash Kurs-Spetsializatsiia," Pravda, July 19, 1971, p. 2.

28. P. Kozyr', "Sochetanie Obshchestvennykh i Lichnykh Interesov v Kolkhozakh," Kommunist, no. 16 (1969): 51-52.

29. Izvestia, August 27, 1970, p. 3.

30. Pravda, September 1, 1970, p. 1.

31. P. Bakai, "Above-Plan Sale of Grain," Ekonomicheskaia Gazeta, no. 12 (March 1971): 14.

32. V. P. Balezin, "K Voprosu o Normirovanii Razmerov Pridomovykh Zemel'nykh v Sel'skykh Naselennykh Puntakh," Vestnik Mosk. Univ., no. 1 (1972): 11.

33. B. Erofeev, "Pravovoi Rezhim Zemel' Perspektivnykh Sel'skikh Naselennykh Punktov," Sov. Iust., no. 9 (1970): 27.

34. N. Vasil'ev, "Vedoshchaia Sila Kollektiva," in Sel'skaia Partiinaia Organizatsiia (Moscow: Izdat. Polit. Lit., 1970), p. 6.

35. P. Paskar, "Demokraticheskie Formy Upravleniia," in Kolkhoz—Shkola Kommunizma dlia Krest'ianstva (Moscow: Izdat. Pravda, 1969), p. 361.

36. I. Bendarenko, "Kolkhoznyi Brigadir," in Ibid., p. 366.

37. N. Barsukov, "Partiinaia Organizatsiia Brigady i Fermy," in Sel'skaia Partiinaia Organizatsiia, op. cit., p. 115.

38. Pravda, May 22, 1971, p. 3.

39. V. Komissarov, "Kadry Srednego Zvena v Kolkhozakh i Sovkhozakh," Partiinaia Zhizn', no. 16 (August 1971): 24.

40. B. Zhumagaliev, "Politicheskaia Rabota Sredi Zhivotnovodov," Partiinaia Zhizn', no. 3 (1971): 29.

41. Izvestia, December 11, 1970, p. 6.

42. I. V. Pavlov, "Pravovoe Polozhenie Agrarno-Promishlennykh Kompleksov," SGIP, no. 9 (1971): 29-30.

43. Ibid., p. 32.

44. Ibid., p. 36.

45. M. Ia. Lemeshev, "On the Elaboration of a Program for the Development of the Agraro-Industrial Complex in the USSR," Izvestiia Sibirskogo Otdeleniia, Akademii Nauk SSSR, no. 11, Issue 3, translated in Problems of Economics, IASP XIV, no. 4 (August 1971): 32.

46. M. Savilev, "From the Experience of Local Soviets: The New Generation of Peasants," Izvestia, August 11, 1971, p. 3.

47. A. Bezina and M. Mavliatshin, "Uvol'nenie iz Predpriatii i Uchrezhdenii Nepravil'no Priniatykh Chlenov Kolkhozov," Sov. Iust., no. 23 (1970): 9.

48. A. Emel'ianov, "Technical Progress and Structural Changes in Agriculture," Voprosy Ekonomiki, no. 4 (1971), translated in Problems of Economics, IASP, XIV, no. 4 (August 1971): p. 5.

49. Izvestia, January 16, 1971, p. 1.
50. A. Georgiev, "Sel'skii Trud i Molodezh'," Kommunist, no. 9 (1971): 26-27.
51. Ibid., p. 28.
52. F. Goriachev, "Ukrepliat' Soiuz Nauka i Sel'skokhoziastvennogo Proizvodstva," Kommunist, no. 1 (1971): 85.
53. "Novyi Otriad Sel'skikh Spetsialistov," Sel'skaia Zhizn', July 30, 1971, p. 1.
54. V. Taratuta, in Sel'skaia Zhizn', July 27, 1971, p. 2.
55. Pravda, January 28, 1971, p. 2.
56. Ibid., March 12, p. 2.
57. Sel'skaia Zhizn', March 12, 1971, p. 2.
58. Literaturnaia Gazeta, February 17, 1971, p. 3.

THE TWENTY-FOURTH CONGRESS
AND BEYOND:
THEMES AND ECHOES

On March 30, 1971, the Twenty-Fourth Congress began. Brezhnev's report of the Central Committee gave prominence to the regime's accomplishment in agriculture. Gross agricultural production for 1970 was increased over that of 1965 by 21 percent, whereas 1965 gross production in comparison to 1960 was up by only 12 percent. The annual average gross output of grain was up by 30 percent, and the production of meat, milk, eggs, and other produce had markedly increased.[1] As for the next five-year plan, Brezhnev reaffirmed the principle of stable procurement plans for a number of years ahead, and the introduction of such incentive prizes for products delivered in excess of the plan as would stimulate the growth of production. Both of these principles had been endorsed in 1968 and in July 1970. Agricultural investments for the new plan would amount to as much as those for the two preceding five-year plans combined. The traditional emphasis on grain production was retained but with a new emphasis on forage grain and not just food grain, in view of the necessity, according to Brezhnev, of rapidly developing animal husbandry.[2] Brezhnev once again emphasized that since at present the personal auxiliary husbandry still plays an appreciable role in the production of meat and milk, necessary help should be given kolkhozniks and sovkhoz employees in acquiring livestock and poultry and the essential supplies of feed.[3] It seems that Brezhnev finds it necessary to admonish apparently balky kolkhoz and sovkhoz officials into selling livestock to their rank and file. Brezhnev also praises the acceleration of the development of interkolkhoz and state-kolkhoz production associations and the establishment of agraro-industrial complexes as signs of the industrialization of agriculture.[4]

He cited as proof of the socio-economic development of the Soviet peasantry the fact that as of the end of 1970, more than half the rural population had finished a secondary school or an institution of higher learning, whereas in 1941 the figure was 6 percent and, according to Brezhnev, the growing supply of agricultural machinery to the farms is making agricultural labor much more attractive, especially for the younger people, who are now more willing, after finishing their education, to stay in the country. Brezhnev also praised the election of the newly created kolkhoz councils at the union, republican, territorial, regional, and district levels. The councils, he stated, represent the interests of the peasants. And this is a spur to the development of kolkhoz democracy.[5]

Premier Alexei Kosygin's report on the Congress' directives for the 1971-75 five-year plan, delivered on April 6, contained a more detailed picture of the contours of the new plan for agriculture. According to Kosygin's data, the average monthly income of kolkhozniks in cash and kind from the public sector increased by 42 percent over the 1965 level, which meant that the Twenty-Third Congress, directive on this point was exceeded by at least 2 percent. And in respect of only two crops—potatoes and vegetables—were the planned targets for 1970 underfulfilled.[6] Even for these two crops, the percentage increase in production for 1966-70 in comparison to 1961-65 was appreciable—31 percent for potatoes and 40 percent for vegetables.[7] As for the new targets for 1975, grain yields must be increased by at least four centners per hectare, which Kosygin regarded as not easy but feasible. Agricultural power resources are to be increased over the next five years by 50 percent and the tractor fleet by 27 percent. Consumption of electricity in agriculture will practically double. In 1975 agriculture will get 75 million tons of mineral fertilizers and feed phosphates as against 46 million tons in 1970.[8]

Kosygin announced that the minimum monthly wage is to be raised in 1971 to seventy rubles, but this does not include kolkhozniks. Also, the rates for farm machine operators were to go up in 1971. The Western economist Andrei Babich finds that the Directives' figure of a 42 percent kolkhoznik pay increase over 1965 is only superficially impressive since it is not translated into rubles per month. And on the basis of published indirect data (the cost of man days on collective farms and the number of man days put in by each kolkhoznik on average per year) Babich concludes that the kolkhoznik's average monthly earnings are little over half those of a factory or office worker, some 60 rubles a month. The kolkhoznik must resort to the private plot for added income.[9] As of July 1, 1971, the minimum pension for kolkhozniks was to be raised and the regulations for determining pensions for workers and employees were to be applied to kolkhozniks as well.[10] Not only was this done, but other benefits were added.[11] The average monthly cash wage of workers and employees is to rise by 20 to 22 percent in the next five years, and kolkhozniks' pay for work in the communal sector for this period is to go up by 30 to 35 percent.[12]

Despite the claim in the Directives of a 42 percent increase in kolkhozniks' earnings, there was an obvious gap between the living standards of the urban and rural population, and a directive on this states that on the basis of higher labor productivity on the kolkhozy, kolkhoznik earnings are to be brought considerably closer to the wages of comparable categories of sovkhoz workers.[13] This is a very conditional and limited pledge to raise earnings of kolkhozniks. First of all, the raise must be based on rises in the productivity of labor, and to some extent productivity depends on technical equipment that may not be available. Second, "considerably closer" is still not equal to sovkhoz workers pay, and that pay level is not equal to that of workers and employees. "Considerably closer" is imprecise and is obviously less than a commitment to parity or a specific level by 1975.

Of course, on the obligation side of the ledger the Directives are characteristically precise. The average annual output of farm products is to increase by 22 percent as compared with the preceding five-year period.[14] Kolkhozy and sovkhozy are directed to provide the rural population with the necessary assistance in their subsidiary husbandry and in increasing the livestock and poultry population in the subsidiary economies. Echoing Brezhnev's July 1970 report to the Central Committee Plenum, the Directives declared that for every kolkhoz and sovkhoz engaged in the production of marketable grain and for every region, territory, and republic, the target shall be not only the fulfillment of the fixed plan but the selling to the state, on the basis of increased agricultural production, of a minimum of 35 percent of grain over and above the plan during the five-year period. And, it shall be insured that every kolkhoz and sovkhoz shall annually sell to the state not less than 8 to 10 percent of its livestock output over and above the plan.[15] This officially mandates a veritable above-plan compulsory sale system, sweetened, of course, by the higher prices paid to above-plan sales, which are, in theory, still voluntary.

Direct links between industrial enterprises and trading organizations and kolkhozy and sovkhozy shall be developed and strengthened to the utmost.[16] During the five-year period labor productivity on kolkhozy and sovkhozy shall be increased by 37 to 40 percent, and production costs shall be substantially lowered.[17] The further development of subsidiary industries, chiefly for processing and storing farm produce and producing building materials and consumer goods from local raw materials, is to be insured on the farms in order to secure fuller and more rational utilization of the labor resources in rural localities throughout the year. Production links shall be promoted between agricultural and industrial enterprises. The building and improvement of interkolkhoz and state-kolkhoz enterprises and organization, and the creation of agraro-industrial complexes and amalgamations shall be facilitated.[18]

In sum, the Twenty-Fourth Congress had little to say about the problems of Soviet agriculture other than to repeat the now well-known bromides about "direct links between industry and agriculture," the "industrialization of agriculture"—mechanization, specialization, chemicalization, concentration, the development of interkolkhoz and kolkhoz-state joint enterprises and agraro-industrial complexes, increased pay for kolkhozniks based on rises in their labor productivity,

increased development of subsidiary enterprises on farms, and the
rendering of aid by farms to the personal subsidiary economies.
Leonard Schapiro characterizes the Twenty-Fourth Congress as
dominated by compromise, producing no surprises, its proceedings
bland, colorless, and smooth-running. There were, he notes, no out-
ward indications of the serious policy disputes that are believed to
have been going on within the top leadership for the last few years.[19]
These policy disputes may explain why the Congress was delayed by
a year[20] and why the speech of Brezhnev at the December 15, 1969,
session of the Central Committee Plenum was never published.[21]
This is reminiscent of the great delay in convening the All-Union Congress of Kolkhozniks.[22] In any case, the only significant policy changes
emerging from the Congress seem to be the backing of the promise
to significantly improve living conditions by significant increases in
the resources allocated to production of consumer goods and the ideologically ticklish departure from the orthodox principle of the pre-
ponderance of heavy industry over light industry in regard to their
respective growth rates. Also notable is the modesty of the figures
for economic growth.[23] Certainly for agriculture the Congress was
a disappointment.

MECHANIZATION, SPECIALIZATION, AND LABOR PROBLEMS

In the April 26, 1971, issue of Pravda there appeared a joint
decree of the Council of Ministers and Central Committee entitled
"On Measures for Further Increasing the Production of Eggs and
Poultry Meat on an Industrial Basis." Taking note of the livestock
production specialization and concentration on sovkhozy and kolkhozy
in recent years and the creation of large animal-husbandry complexes
for the production of pork, beef, and milk on an industrial basis, and
the construction of poultry factories—all of which have made it possible
to increase output, to reduce feed outlays, substantially to curtail
manpower requirements for work with livestock and poultry, and to
make more effective use of production buildings and equipment—the
aim in the new five-year plan will be to more broadly develop the
construction of large animal-husbandry complexes and poultry factories.
Construction plans for 1,170 large state complexes for the production
of meat and milk on an industrial basis and the construction and expansion of 585 poultry factories are approved. The network of state
and interkolkhoz incubator and poultry-breeding stations will receive
further significant expansion, and it is hoped they will fully insure
the requirements of kolkhozy, sovkhozy, and the population for young
breeding stock.[24]
Agraro-industrial unions and complexes are increasingly being
touted, not only in livestock production. Specialized sovkhozy are

being linked to factories, using their outputs under a unified management—a move it is assumed has significantly lowered costs in wine production. These sovkhoz factory unions supposedly simplify production relations among the constituent parts or the union, effecting large reductions in administrative staffs.[25] The literature talks of growing horizontal and vertical integration, the latter involving merger or production, supply, transportation processing, preservation, and trade. Ultimately the process will lead to an organic merger of agriculture and industry. But at first agraro-industrial complexes arise based on territorial branch enterprises. This takes the form of localized merger of farms raising a product and local processing enterprises. In agraro-industrial unions the economic independence of the member enterprises and farms is preserved. The agraro-industrial complex involves a looser set of interrelationships on a permanent basis.[26] While Soviet economists arc differing on the distinctions between agraro-industrial complexes, unions, and enterprises and the consequent form of property arising from these,[27] there is no disagreement over the idea that they signify the concentration, specialization, and mechanization of agriculture. But the economist M. Vasilenko sounds a warning note in urging experiments to determine the optimal size of agraro-industrial complexes so as to avoid "gigantomania."[28]

Despite these ambitious plans and visions for an industrialized livestock production, there were still recurrent problems in this area. An article by A. Chudnaia in the May 9, 1971, issue of Pravda, entitled "Time to Proceed from Words to Deeds," reveals that livestock production is lagging in many kolkhozy and sovkhozy in Uzbekistan, mainly because of some farm and district officials continuing to regard it as a secondary branch. Chudnaia cities as evidence of negligence the wintering of sheep on the steppe without shelter and keeping cows outside too much and thus reducing their productivity. While hailing the accelerating pace of construction of huge livestock-raising complexes for the production of pork, beef, and milk, Chudnaia notes that all this takes time, and so it would be impermissible for farm officials to use this as an excuse for further reducing their meat production. Another problem singled out by Chudnaia is the shortage of milkmaids in her republic. This is because owing to the lack of mechanization in milking, the work must be done almost entirely by hand. Also, no two-shift system has been organized, so that milkmaids have to stay on the job from dawn to dusk.[29]

The plight of the milkmaid condemned to heavy work and long hours, with consequent poor morale and low productivity, has been focused on in the campaign to increase livestock productivity. One widely sponsored reform, along with mechanization of milking, is the two-shift system referred to by Chudnaia. E. Vavilin, head of an agricultural investigatory station, writing in the agricultural paper Sel'skaia Zhizn' of July 20, 1971, remarks that two-shift work depends on mechanization and electrification. He reports that in Leningrad Oblast over seven thousand livestock workers are on two-shift work. Experience shows that the effectiveness of the two-shift system depends on administrative and technical measures. Its application cuts labor expenses and reduces administrative personnel. In Leningrad Oblast milking is 98.3 percent mechanized. But gathering manure and distributing fodder are still overwhelmingly manual. Another problem in two-shift work is making sure that the pairs selected are really volunteers. Otherwise morale is undermined.[30]

V. Tsarov, a kolkhoz official from Tambov Oblast, notes a conspicuous absence of youth among livestock personnel on his kolkhoz, although in contrast there are many workers under twenty years of age to be found in the jobs of tractorists and drivers. Tsarov, acknowledging the formidability of the physical labor aspect of livestock work, stresses psychological and morale problems as the main reason youth reject such work. A job must be attractive, something one can take pride in doing. Tsarov pleads for the creation of new professions.[31]

The ultimate solution to the milking problem is described by S. Botvinnik in a new model milking complex near Moscow that utilizes a carousel milker servicing two hundred cows in an hour. Six men per shift can milk 1,570 cows. The whole farm with two thousand cows occupied only seven hectares, whereas the typical milk farm takes up 17.5 hectares per head.[32] Yet short of this "nirvana," M. Glinka, in a comparison of dairying operations on a sovkhoz and kolkhoz in his district, comes up with some practical suggestions for improving productivity. The kolkhoz outperforms the sovkhoz in terms of man days per centner of milk and rubles expenditure per centner. The reason is that on the kolkhoz each milker is free of caring for the cows and feeding them. On the sovkhoz the milker cleans and feeds them. This results in significant time losses.[33]

D. Buslov, a district party raikom secretary, cites as a major impediment to effective kolkhoz management the inefficient placement and use of specialists, that is the inactivity of specialists in actual production management. The Kantemirovka District Party Committee decided to urge a switch to the branch system of management, under which the leaders of the various branches—plant, livestock, construction, and so on—become the specialists, each leader answering personally for fulfillment of directives in his branch. The leaders of the specialized brigades are subordinated to the branch leader. The local party organization is even thinking fo restructuring their farm organization to parallel the branch principle.[34]

THE PROBLEM OF A RATIONAL
PURCHASE PRICE MECHANISM

Whereas the mechanisation of jobs involving heavy manual labor and the cutting down of the hours worked at such jobs as well as the better use of farm specialists will no doubt spur productivity and are not measures that in any sense could be deemed controversial, the state's policy on differentiation of purchase prices is a highly controversial policy area and involves the state in a direct way whereas, to some extent, the aforementioned problems are strictly the internal affairs of particular farms and in theory are resolvable by unilateral action of their management. But when we come to prices for agricultural produce and the state procurement system in general, we have entered the realm of high policy. On the issue of what system of differentiated purchase prices is best there is an article by a Pravda economic observer, V. Boldin, of May 16, 1971, entitled "The Conditions Must Be Equalized."[35] In the Penza area 80 of 167 kolkhozy have grown so strong economically that they almost never need bank credits. Yet a certain group of kolkhozy have been lagging economically despite increased material and financial assistance of late and the writing off of debts. The profitability level of most of the kolkhozy rose from 34 percent to 41 percent on the average during the past five years. But among the lagging group of farms it declined from 13 percent to 7.8 percent, and this is not merely a local phenomenon. The net income per hectare of agricultural land on the strong farms in Estonia increased by 140 percent from 1965 to 1970 while that of the weak farms grew by only 30 percent. This is happening all over. As a result, there are many profitable farms and many unprofitable. V. P. Gorbachev, a Penza Gosbank official, accounts for this phenomenon in his area as the result of unequal natural-economic conditions among the farms. The poorer farms are located in the province's interior, on poor soil, and limited by poor roads. But how to equalize the conditions of economic management? In the past redistribution of differential income from the best land was by means of differing rates of income tax, insurance payment, and norms of obligatory deliveries of output. In time the function of redistributing differential income came to be played increasingly by the purchase prices for output, which were established according to the natural-economic differences in the conditions of economic management. Very significant reforms in this regard came after the March 1965 Central Committee Plenum. Presently, wheat prices in the Russian Republic have been differentiated for eighteen zones. Still, the zones are too large and encompass differing soil and climatic conditions. Some propose further perfecting the differentiation of prices. Boldin reports that in Lithuania the differentiation of prices has facilitated rapid development. In 1970 Lithuanian officials conducted an experiment. Prices were no longer differentiated for administrative groups of districts but for four groups of farms with similar natural-economic conditions. This system takes the specific conditions of economic management more fully into account, and it has proven effective. The levels of the economies of the various kolkhozy groups are drawing together, but without incentive-killing "leveling." The farms where the intensification of production is high continue to make substantially greater profits. The upswing in the weaker farms is not harmful to the stronger ones.

Boldin notes that the differentiation-of-prices approach to the equalization of economic performance criteria issue has the virtue of yielding definite gains without requiring additional investments, certainly a virtue anywhere but expecially so in the Soviet Union in relation to agriculture. Yet, puzzles Boldin, why has not the Lithuanian experiment been tried elsewhere? Certain state agricultural administrators Boldin has interviewed pass the buck by saying the responsibility lies outside their jurisdiction. But Boldin feels that coolness toward the experiment is not just attributable to bureaucratic paralysis. He thinks that some scientists and economic managers simply do not accept the concept of the differentiation of prices down to the level of groups of districts or groups of farms. Charitably, he allows that they may have valid reasons and that the Lithuanian experience probably should not be copied everywhere, at least not yet. The final judgment on it can be made only when the experiment has been thoroughly analyzed and generalized. To reject it without having studied it, and not to study it because it deviates from established ideas, laments Boldin, would be a mistake. But what if the "established ideas" are Marxian theory? Boldin also fails to go into the possible valid objections of the opponents of the experiment. Boldin's article has touched on a major problem—that of devising an economically objective set of criteria whereby to judge relative economic performances of farms operating with differing soil, climatic, technical, machine, organizational, personnel, and locational factors, and thus with differing objective costs of production factors and productivity levels. This problem has loomed large in Soviet agricultural journals over the last two decades but has found little echo of late in high party policy statements.

MEASURING AND REWARDING QUALITY

A series of interviews in Izvestia of May 13, 1971, entitled "Argument over the Tuber," conducted by correspondent Matukovsky, touches upon yet another major problem, not just for Soviet agriculture but for the whole economy. The problem is how to reward quality production when the administratively easier method of gauging successful performance is the quantity of output. The problem of the distortive effect of quantitative success indicators on product mix, quality, and usefulness of products has been discussed at length and in depth for the industrial sector.[36] Much less attention has been turned on quantity-at-the-cost-of-quality in Soviet agriculture, in part because the major problem in agriculture always seemed to be assuring sufficient quantity. In any case, Matukovsky's piece in Izvestia is most revealing of a problem that plagues more than just potatoes. The quality of a potato depends on its starch content. Yet Matukovsky shows that the starch content of Byelorussian potatoes received in processing plants over the years has gone down—from 18.9 percent starch in 1940 to 17.3 percent in 1948, to 16.3 percent in 1956, 15.1 percent in 1966, 13.6 percent in 1969, and 13.4 percent in 1970. The Byelorussian Deputy Minister of the Food Industry notes that loss of starch content causes a decrease in alcohol yield per ton of potatoes. With the decline in starch content, the state purchase agencies must purchase more potatoes now than previously in order to get the amount of starch and alcohol called for by the plan. This lengthens the processing season significantly and leads to longer periods of storage, which in turn results in greater quality loss in the potatoes. Also the labor-intensiveness of many processes increases. Why has starch content gone down? It seems that since the payoff in the plans is on gross output of potatoes and since an increase in yield is not always in the short run compatible with increases in quality, quality is sacrificed for the sake of quantity so as to fulfill and overfulfill plans. Two hundred centners per hectare with 22 percent starch content is not considered as good as three hundred centners with a 12 percent index from the standpoint of the farm, although the processing plant may have other ideas. The result of the neglect of the qualitative factor in judging farm performance is that farms have no economic interest in producing good potatoes. Moreover, state procurement personnel today are not even in a position to judge the quality of potatoes other than by size. They do not have laboratories for determining starch content. And, to maximize production of particular types of potatoes—eating versus processing—you would have to scientifically ascertain the identity of various types and then devise a price system to reward quality. This would require more stores and storehouses to sort out the different types. Construction funds for such facilities are already in short supply. So, as Matukovsky concludes, a strange picture emerges: "It is not very advantageous for the farms to produce good potatoes; it is not very convenient for procurement personnel to procure them for sale or for trade personnel to sell them. It is inconvenient and disadvantageous for everyone except the consumer."

The economist Paige Bryan reports that the Soviet agricultural paper Sel'skaia Zhizn' on March 23, 1972, revealed that too many hogs for lard are being raised as opposed to hogs for meat. Since the purchase prices for bacon and lard are identical in many republics, and since bacon is more difficult to produce, farmers produce practically only lard, although feeding hogs for lard is more expensive in terms of feed costs.[37]

A similar picture emerges from the wheat front. In an article entitled "An Ear of Russian Wheat,"[38] a team of Izvestia correspondents analyzes the problem of Saratov Province, a traditional producer of the most valuable varieties of wheat, hard and durum, the varieties containing larger amounts of albumen and gluten, the elements determinative of baking quality. Yet there has been a decline in or at least no increase in procurements of these varieties of late. Hard wheat requires a high level of agricultural technology. Otherwise its harvests will substantially decline. The soft varieties are less capricious and yield a relatively good "gross" with an average level of technology. So, since the payoff in plans is on the gross production, and since ordinary wheat is often raised with less trouble and is more reliable than the valuable high-albumen varieties, more and more of it is grown, even though less is paid per unit for it than for hard wheat. Apparently higher and more stable yields of the inferior wheat more than make up for the difference. Farms must take more of their valuable time up during harvest to segregate out the hard wheat, time that would be used to get in more wheat. Moreover, there is a general shortage of the mineral fertilizers needed for hard wheat. On top of all this, the grain procurement stations do not have up-to-date methods for rapid and reliable determination of the percentages of albumen and gluten in grain. There are few experienced laboratory workers at the grain elevators and there are no instruments to aid in carrying out high-speed analyses. And, conclude the authors, the obviously outmoded system of receiving wheat and evaluating its quality takes away many economic managers' desire to constantly improve grain quality. Thus the problem of quantity versus quality calls out for reforms. And it is certainly not just confined to potatoes and wheat. Another Pravda article notes the problem of lean, low-grade livestock.[39]

The problems of coordinating and perfecting farm links with procurement agencies and even processing factories can be seen to be an especially actual and acute one with respect to vegetable production. I. Titov, in an article entitled "Why There Is a Shortage of Vegetables in Stores in Voronezh,"[40] cites the lack of large-capacity refrigerators and storehouses for vegetables both on the farms and in the state procurement centers and then alludes to the Twenty-Fourth Congress directive on shifting to the reception of output directly on the farms and its delivery to the procurement organization. Ye. Kirichenko, in an article in Izvestia entitled "Will the Vegetables Be Left in the Field?"[41] talks of the need to create a "ripening ladder," that is a perfecting of a sequential ripening period for different crops so that they do not all have to be harvested at once, thus throwing a tremendous burden on both limited farm personnel and transport facilities. In vegetable growing this is especially acute because of its notorious labor-intensivity, almost everything having to be done by hand. Direct ties between Moscow trade organizations and stores, on the one hand, and local potato and vegetable producers on the other have significantly increased over the period from 1965 to 1970.[42] V. Konev, in an article entitled "Receiving Station in the Field . . ."[43] describes how a canning factory organized vegetable procurement so as to avoid losses. It sent specially trained personnel out to receive vegetables right in the kolkhoz fields, and the provincial soviet executive committee has recommended to all processing enterprises and consumers' cooperative procurement offices that they organize receipt of vegetables directly on the farms. Of course, the key to solving this problem is investment in both new equipment to mechanize vegetable production as well as for more investment in freezers, refrigerated storage areas, and refrigerated trucks to move out produce. Yet the press plays up the theme of "direct ties" between farm and factory as if it were the crucial organizational missing link. A classic example of this touting of "direct links" as an administrative and "cheap" solution to the problem can be seen in an article in Sel'skaia Zhizn'. The author, V. Pshenichnyi, reports on the progress in Tambov in carrying out the Twenty-Fourth Party Congress directive on developing and strengthening direct ties between trade and industrial enterprises, on the one hand, and farms on the other. He relates that in 1971 purchase (procurement) agencies were commissioned to accept directly potatoes, fruit, and vegetables and melons in some farms in Krasnodarsk Krai, Astrakhan, Voronezh, Gorkovskii, and Briansk oblasts. On-the-site acceptance points with weighing and sorting of produce fresh from the field and with the purchaser's staff and equipment, as well as warehouse facilities permanently stationed there are all part of the Tambov Oblast scene. On the basis of the limited experience of one canning combine, the Tambov Oblast executive committee recommended direct ties for other processing enterprises and purchase organizations of consumer cooperatives of the oblast.[44]

Just as rewarding high quality produce is neglected in favor of quantitative indicators of output, so there is a somewhat similar problem involved in rewarding farm workers not just for the quantity of their output but also for its quality. The issue is presented in an Izvestia item, "The Chairman's Question," by S. Iarmoliuk.[45] The gist of it is that a conscientious kolkhoz chairman introduced payment based on quality of work in the form of an additional percentage added to the piece-rate earnings for excellent work. Yet the system does not seem to work because the disappointed kolkhozniks who fail to get the increment and are told to do the job over again feel they have not been fully paid, regarding the quality increment as basic pay. All this causes the kolkhoz chairman to think about the whole problem of disaffection among rural workers. Nothing that the Labor Research Institute is sponsoring numerous sociological investigations into rural labor problems, he wonders what they have learned. Such questions as how to most effectively combine moral and material incentives and how to enhance the social prestige of farm work remain unanswered. That the regime is commissioning in-depth sociological studies on such questions is itself an indication of the acuteness of the problems.

The search for better methods of rewarding kolkhozniks, methods that truly create incentives to increase quality and not just quantity, seems to be more readily attainable when final results depend on individual rather than team effort, that is, when the method individualizes the work and thus most clearly links individual effort and final results. Such is the gist of a new piece-work contract method reportedly used in Bolgrad Raion in the Ukraine.[46] Under this particular scheme, a cattle worker concludes a special piece-work order contract with his kolkhoz board. The contract sets forth mutual obligations of both sides. The worker is given a certain number of heifers to bring up to a certain weight and condition within a certain period and is guaranteed the necessary quantity of feed to do so. There are supplementary rewards for qualities above those stipulated by the contract. The reports of the results are very favorable. Another incentive-creating proposal comes from the jurist I. F. Kuz'min. He proposed that in cases where the ideas of a kolkhoz will result in direct monetary economies for the kolkhoz, the author of the idea should receive a certain percentage of the savings effected. He notes that the proposal is already used in industry.[47]

OF UNEDIFYING EXHORTATION
AND SIMPLISTIC SOLUTIONS

The causes for some kolkhozy lagging behind others in better soil or cimate zones are fairly obvious. But what about the cases where neighboring kolkhozy are at oppostie ends of the performance spectrum? There is an almost continual citing of the sins of kolkhoz managers and local state control officials in allowing farms to deteriorate by slackening in their financial and general economic surveillance. These "man-made" disasters, so the line goes, need not have happened, and to rectify them what is needed is not some basic reform but rather more vigilance. Obviously vigilance is a very cheap input. Typical of the treatment of this problem is a story entitled "Reflection on a Fact: The Good Thing About a Debt Is Its Repayment."[48] This particular Soviet morality tale concerns kolkhozy operating at a loss in the black earth region of Kursk Province, a rather unlikely area for this to occur. In fact, the particular kolkhoz singled out for treatment in this article ostensibly did operate profitably, but only in a formal sense, since in reality its expenditures exceeded its income and its indebtedness to the state continued to grow. Physically it is in good shape, with splendidly appointed village houses complete with all kinds of amenities that would seem to belie its poor economic condition. The problem is that it is getting by on seemingly inexhaustible credits from the local bank, which it is unable to repay. The penalties for nonpayment are paid. The main vice involved is apparently low productivity of labor, combined with the squandering of large amounts on nonproductive assets. One remedy prescribed is obvious: make the bank become more discriminating in issuing credits. Another is not so obvious: more control from below over the kolkhoz management's financial policies. This latter proposal is very odd since, although "kolkhoz democracy" is invoked to show the self-participatory and thereby truly cooperative nature of the kolkhozy and thus their own responsibility for their economic performances,[49] yet it has never been hailed by economists as a method for maximizing the effectiveness of management.

In another Pravda story, entitled "Put Under the Control of the Masses: A Proprietor's Concern for Every Ruble,"[50] staff correspondent A. Platoshkin relates that cases of violations of financial-estimate discipline by kolkhozy have been multiplying lately in the Republic. First of all, administrative staffs are expanding at unjustifiable rates. Managers are awarding themselves large cash bonuses and overpaying hired construction workers. In another case history from Kursk Oblast two neighboring kolkhozy are quite a contrast, growing similar crops and raising similar animals. The unprofitable one has higher labor costs per unit of output, lower yields per hectare, and this despite equivalent manpower resources per unit of area. Two causes are cited. First, the far greater size of the indivisible fund of the profitable farm. Second, losses suffered by the weaker kolkhoz from absorbing transportation costs that are not fully compensated by the supply organs. Actually this is really no explanation, since the vastly lower worth of the fixed assets of the weak kolkhoz requires an explanation. It is hardly enough to cite this fact as an explanation for why it is a weak farm. The reasons behind this fact are the crux of the matter. But the conclusion of the article is simply that the problem of lagging kolkhozy is a complex one!

The theme of developing to the utmost subsidiary enterprises within individual kolkhozy has been given more emphasis of late in connection with two other themes—the industrialization of agricultural labor and the rural outflow. The use of subsidiary enterprises as a school for industrializing agricultural labor is obvious. As to the second connection—the use of subsidiary enterprises as a sponge to soak up underutilized labor during the slack season, a euphemism for seasonal unemployment, and also as a means of holding the young down on the farms by providing a more attractive outlet for their ambitions and skills right there—there is much to be said. Yet an undue emphasis on subsidiary enterprises on farms could further exacerbate the very problem it is in part intended to allay. It could draw off from the traditional unskilled labor-intensive jobs most of the young, who then would stampede into the jobs created in a highly developed subsidiary enterprise. Moreover, a kolkhoz itself could gradually become more a canning enterprise and less a producer of that which goes into the cans, especially if its canning operation produced more profits than the field work.

While the regime makes much of the ultimate organic fusion of industry and agriculture in agraro-industrial combines, still they must make sure the fields are prepared, cultivated, and harvested. In other words, the farming function remains to be done, regardless of how industrialized the farm becomes. The farm must remain to some extent a farm. As much as the party likes to think of every farm as ultimately becoming a factory, this is eminently impractical today despite the rhetoric. The point of departure for encouraging subsidiary enterprises on kolkhozy is the winter slack-labor period.

According to one economist, there is almost one-third less work in the public sector in winter than in the summer.[51] A kolkhoz agronomist reports that from November to April many kolkhozniks are not fully occupied in his raion.[52] The main direction of the development of subsidiary enterprises has been and still is the processing of agricultural materials and produce and the production of local construction materials. Thus they are not, in the main, in handicrafts production. It has been suggested that in light of their economic significance or potential, they should be put under the control of planning and agricultural organs of the state. In fact, many oblast agricultural administrations have formed departments for subsidiary enterprises.[53] The subsidiary enterprise often springs up less as an attempt to find a new source of profit than as a way to prevent waste or losses. In one suburban kolkhoz that specialized in meat and milk production, a secondary interest in vegetables grew up, only to encounter marketing problems because the state would not buy up its nonstandard, fast-spoiling vegetables. Then the idea of a canning factory emerged. And this did, in fact, greatly increase the kolkhoz's income.[54] Implicit in this success story is the problem of the success of a subsidiary enterprise undermining the farm's primary mission.

The economic and agricultural journals and papers are rather superficial for the most part in portraying the causes of lagging farm performances. Lurid comparisons of neighboring kolkhozy are a stock device for edifying officialdom and the rank and file in the countryside as to what not to do. The search for cheap and quick methods for bolstering farm efficiency and increasing production results in a propensity to devise and implement administrative reshufflings and new methods of organizing and using labor units on the farms, especially the kolkhozy, accompanied by great fanfare and professions of extravagant expectations of success from them. These "morality tales" of the two neighboring farms become especially abundant during the launching of a new five-year plan so as to fire up the agricultural sector with the requisite enthusiasm. Enthusiasm is certainly a virtue, but it is no substitute for a sound prognosis and deeper theoretical approach to recurrent and seemingly intractable problems. Typical of this approach is the contrasting of the neighboring Kursk Oblast kolkhozy "Leninskii Put" and "Gigant," both having equal quality land and both being grain, sugar beet, meat, and milk producers. Manpower per unit of area for both is approximately the same. But "Leninskii Put" is a prosperous farm, whereas "Gigant" is unprofitable. In 1970 "Gigant" lost 17,000 rubles and made no contributions to its indivisible fund, circulating fund, social security, material aid, or cultural funds. Its debts are overdue. In the same year "Leninskii Put" paid out 4 rubles and 5 kopeks per man hour and "Gigant" paid out 2 rubles and 85 kopeks. Hence, it is not because of inordinate labor payments that "Gigant" is in bad shape, as is sometimes the case with lagging farms. The gross income in "Leninskii Put" per one hundred hectares of

arable land was 12,573 rubles, whereas it was 7,314 rubles in "Gigant."
"Leninskii Put" harvests its sugar beets in a month, whereas "Gigant"
takes two months. In "Leninskii Put" the value of basic funds per able-
bodied worker is 2,415 rubles, whereas in "Gigant" it is 1,262. In
"Gigant" one milkmaid services twelve or thirteen cows, while on
neighboring farms it is sixteen.[55] And so on. But why is this—mis-
management, poor morale, poorer labor force? No real analysis of
the reasons behind this poor performance is given. It is perhaps considered therapeutic to turn the spotlight on this deplorable state of
affairs. Yet merely to show that one farm has far greater assets per
worker is not to explain why.

Another typical anecdote involves the kolkhoz "Shliakhom Lenina"
of Vinnitsa Oblast in the Ukraine. It went from being a backward farm
to a veritable model of progress, with extremely impressive yields
per hectare.[56] Exactly what the secret of its success is is not made
clear. In another case the answer is apparently more productivity
per worker. But again no explanation why. This involved a comparison
of the sovkhoz "Danchenskii" and the kolkhoz "Novaia Zhizn'." The
sovkhoz has 600 cows and 87 men, while the kolkhoz has 770 cows and
47 workers. The sovkhoz require 1.23 man days to produce one centner of milk and almost 18 rubles of other means. In the kolkhoz the
corresponding figures are 0.4 man days and 14.5 rubles of means per
centner.[57]

Three other success stories leave one with less than a clear
understanding of why some succeed where others fail. In the kolkhoz
"Karl Marx," in the last year of the eighth five-year plan, a yield of
22.9 centners of grain per hectare was achieved. And this was to
increase by three centners more in the next year. How? By raising
the fertility of the soil, using the latest technological devices, using
mineral fertilizers and land reclamation, applying the better quality
seeds, and mastering the best crop rotation systems.[58] The question
is, are these supposed to be unique procedures? If so, it simply might
exculpate managers of lagging farms if they did not have the technical
aids and labor force necessary to utilize such techniques. But the
comparisons imply managerial responsibility for lagging farm performance. Another dramatic success story is also explained as the
result of purely technical innovations. The kolkhoz "Avangard" in
Gorkovskii Oblast, RSFSR, has experienced an incredible rise in its
per hectare potato yield—233 centners per hectare now. The profitability rate for potatoes in the last five-year plan was 137 percent.
The success is attributed to use of the correct crop rotation and the
aid of the local agricultural chemical laboratory, which systematically,
for over four years, conducted soil investigations that culminated in
a cartogram of the kolkhoz's fields. On the basis of the cartogram,
the exactly appropriate fertilizers and crops were used.[59] On the
kolkhoz "Radishchev" in Smolensk Oblast, there are very impressive
milk yields per cow. Its president attributes this to better breeding
of the cows and better care.[60] Again, this is hardly a revelation.

THE KHOZRASCHET PRINCIPLE
AND THE "LINKS"

In agriculture the problem of pinpointing individual responsibility for poor performance is especially difficult in view of the physically dispersed labor conditions involved and the delayed time sequence of the biological process. Sowing results only become apparent months later. That is why economists like Michael Bradley see the use of small group work units (links) as easier on a centrally managed system like the kolkhoz. They better pinpoint responsibility.[61]

Successes attributable to the use of new types of production subdivisions and of internal cost accounting (Khozraschet) within them is a recurrent theme. According to K. Tarchokov, the link, traditionally the subdivision of the brigade, is most successful. Links and detachments of highly qualified mechanizers with full responsibility for a given plot for a whole crop rotation period, all voluntarily working together, and working on a full khozraschet basis, are ideal. Tarchokov claims that mechnaized links are superior, with better labor discipline, self-imposed, characteristic of them. Tarchokov claims that in specialized links there is a definite resolve, a personal input, and a feeling of personal responsibility involved for each member for his labor, for the land, and for the machinery he uses.[62] Ideally, he feels, with the progressive mechanization, the "labor cell" (iacheika), endowed with land and machinery, will embody the principle of clearly defining the responsibility of each member and connecting it with that of the others so as to make actual "the one for all and all for one" spirit.[63]

V. Koshelev feels that the key to full inculcation of khozraschet in kolkhozy is the planning of the production activities of production subdivisions, which will be derived from the kolkhoz's production-financial plan.[64] What is new here is that Koshelev is suggesting the institutionalization of "mini-plans" for brigades, links, farms, and plots, and this has implications of self-sufficiency and even economic independence, which some ideologically rigid officials might see as the degeneration of the kolkhoz into a series of smaller, vaguely interlocking production units that might in effect amount to decollectivization on an installment basis.

The khozraschet, production subdivision, and new methods of payment of labor questions are interrelated. The common trend is the search for more productivity through better work incentives and a clearer pinpointing of individual responsibility. I. Mikulovich's discussion of the disincentive built into the traditional system for paying tractor drivers is illustrative. They have been paid not by the quantity and quality of the end product of their work but rather by the number of hectares plowed, a purely quantitative approach that has the virtue of being easily measured. Under this system there was no incentive for a tractorist to hope his plowing would help to obtain better yields. Mikulovich describes the use of the mechanized link in his oblast since 1963. It includes five or six mechanizers, who remain together usually for a crop rotation. Their work is evaluated at the end of the crop and the yield. Mikulovich also describes the creation of production plots. These are mechanized links with land and machines, auxiliary links, and livestock farms distributed on the plot. They are significantly larger than certain brigades. On his kolkhoz the board gives them and the mechanized links a production plan and a detailed technological map that includes norms of expenditures on certain jobs of both labor and materials and in money.[65] Although link heads are in fact designated by the kolkhoz board, Mikulovich feels it would be better if they were elected by the mechanizers themselves.[66] Mikulovich feels that the creation of specialized links is a big step toward liquidating impersonality in the use of land and machines.[67] For him the advantages of links are that they embody democratic bases of administration, develop independence and initiative of the workers, and raise their responsibility for entrusted work. Mikulovich proposed new departments of field production—including livestock, planning, supply, and dispatch services. These can contract with each other for services and products per planned norms of costs. The contract will provide discipline. And he is confident that all these new forms will cut down on administrative personnel.[68]

That the pace of converting production subdivisions of kolkhozy to a khrozraschet basis is proceeding rapidly is testified to by A. Esin's claim that more than 70 percent of kolkhoz subdivisions have implemented "elements" of khozraschet. He adds that the lagging sectors are auxiliary and service units.[69]

A successful Uzbek cotton kolkhoz president boasts that all his subdivisions are now on khozraschet. All their tasks are set out on technical charts in both in-kind and cost terms, including labor payment limits. Comparison of the work of individual subdivisions gives better control over production.[70] The chief economist of a Krasnodar Krai kolkhoz relates that four years ago the autopark and repair shop of his kolkhoz was put on khozraschet, and over the four-year period expenses for transportation of loads were lowered by almost 110,000 rubles.[71] V. Zhulin describes a system in his kolkhoz of monthly reporting by production subdivisions to the kolkhoz planning department, with the indicators for the subdivision including a minimum monthly number of work days.[72] In another kolkhoz with all brigades and farms on khozraschet, each subdivision that economized on norms of expense by the end of the year was awarded supplementary pay distributed proportional to earnings of individuals.[73]

Another variant of the mechanized link on behalf of which great claims are made is the "orderless" links. They are not given specific detailed tasks. They are given land for a long period of time—in this particular case, five years—and told to raise the fertility of the soil as well as the crop yields.[74] This seems to be successful in that it transcends the mere qualitative approach by making rewards hinge on fulfillment of both quantitative and qualitative indicators. Mechanized links of the kolkhoz "Kama" have their earnings based on final results of yields, plus premia for above-plan production and for economizing on expenses. It is found that under this system link leaders commonly stay after their shifts to help their comrades, says I. Masaulov. Extra ordinary yields per hectare are claimed under this system, even from unfertile lands. And all this is attributed to the link form.[75] A more sophisticated price-work system in which a "norm-shift" is used is highly praised by A. Novikov. Essentially, a norm-shift is a criterion for defining the labor effort involved in fulfillment of piece work. For tractor work, sowing may have the coefficient of 1.2 and loading or unloading a coefficient of 0.6.[76] In other words, this system further sophisticates the judgment of work like tractor operations, hitherto undifferentiated, and values different types of tractor functions by one driver differently.

In sum, V. N. Dem'ianenko claims that the introduction of khozraschet is connected with a higher stage in the organization and payment of labor, a rational decentralization of administration, and a transfer of a maximal number of functions from above (from the kolkhoz board) to below (to the production subdivisions). He asserts that the system of material interests—the dependence of the factual size of pay not only on the general kolkhoz indicators, but in great measure on the results achieved by the production subdivision—encourages each to relate economically to raising the effectiveness of social production. This is especially true of the orderless system of links and brigades.[77]

THE PARTY AND KOLKHOZ DEMOCRACY

A traditional theme played upon by the media is the positive role of kolkhoz party organizations in spurring the kolkhoz's economic performance and in making sure that kolkhoz democracy is operative. The party organization is supposed to monitor economic and administrative performance but not to interfere with actual administrative and economic functions. Rather its role is to admonish the management and warn state and party organs outside the farm of alleged malfunctions and misdeeds. Although the kolkhoz party organization's role in insuring the integrity of kolkhoz democracy looms large, the literature is also directed at autocratic kolkhoz officials and presidents who ignore the rank-and-file kolkhozniks in policy-making, violate the charter, and do not feel accountable to the rank and file. Other culprits are the state procurement agencies, construction trusts, and individual factories that violate the right of the kolkhoz. The notion seems to be that if kolkhoz democracy became operative, if the kolkhozniks were secured their rights under the kolkhoz charter, and if the state agencies did not transgress on the kolkhoz's rights, then the morale of the kolkhoz would be raised and so would work incentives. The idea is not so much to affirm the integrity of kolkhoz democracy for the sake of principle, but rather because in so doing economic benefits will accrue thereby, or certain economic problems will be solved. There is a rich rhetoric extolling the pro-liferation of new grass-roots, mainly voluntary, advisory kolkhoz organs—economic councils, councils of pensioners, technical councils—as betokening a new flowering of kolkhoz democracy. The newly created kolkhoz councils at the All-Union, republican, krai, oblast, and raion levels are hailed as corporate representatives of the kolkhozniks and as further proof of the vitality of kolkhoz democracy and evidence of its further development.

The kolkhozy, encompassing almost half of the whole sown area of the country and containing approximately two-thirds of all the heads of cattle, have supposedly been duly recognized within the soviet re-presentative organs through the election of the kolkhozniks to the soviets to the extent of their constituting 30 percent of all soviet de-puties.[78] Yet kolkhozniks constituted only 15.1 percent of the party membership in 1971,[79] whereas in 1966 they composed almost 24 per-cent of the total population.[80] Yet the kolkhoz peasantry is hailed as the "reliable ally" of the working class, and the new five-year plan calls for a 30 to 35 percent growth in the income of kolkhozniks from the public economy.[81] And kolkhoz democracy, as a form of socialist democracy, involves all of the masses of workers in administration, so that each feels responsible not only for his own job but for the whole collective's work.[82] The best indication of the social effective-ness of kolkhoz democracy is the achievement of a new stage in the development of the productive forces and social relations in the coun-try, according to the jurist V. N. Dem'ianenko.[83] So, according to Dem'ianenko, kolkhoz democracy is primarily a method of increasing production. And the projected pay increase for kolkhozniks is sup-posed to be based on increased labor productivity.[84]

According to Dem'ianenko, the role of the ordinary kolkhoznik does not reduce to that of an unthinking executant of orders from above.[85] Yet A. Kozhevnikov, a raikom first secretary in Tambov Oblast, reiterates the all-too-familiar story of a kolkhoz in which the general meeting was not convened from election to election and brigade meetings ceased. Then a new president was "recommended" by the raikom and department party organizations were created. Thereafter all important questions were systematically discussed at brigade and general meetings,[86] as in theory they are supposed to be. Now, in contrast to earlier general meetings where typically only twelve to fifteen spoke out, there are discussions prior to a general meeting at the brigade meeting level and typically seventy to eighty discussants take part.[87] Thus one would gather that the kolkhoz party organization is a key element in preserving kolkhoz democracy.

Organizationally, the party presence within the kolkhoz has been undergoing changes. Department, brigade, and party groups are proliferating.[88] Traditionally, because of the shortage of party members among the peasantry, a kolkhoz was fortunate to have enough members to form a farm primary party organization. The average number of party members per kolkhoz is now thirty-one.[89] What is seen as crucial is the choice of a primary party organization secretary and the decisive role in this selection is played by the party obkom and raikom rather than the party membership of the kolkhoz.[90] An example of successful party work in converting a lagging kolkhoz sector into a progressive one is cited by M. Nikonov, a party first secretary in Tambov Oblast. The grain yield of the third brigade of the kolkhoz "Dawn of Communism" was only thirteen centners per hectare, while neighboring brigades got eighteen or nineteen centners. In 1965 a party group was formed, and it soon became a brigade party organization with over twenty members and candidates. The big problem, it felt, was lack of stable leadership. The brigade party organization requested a certain well-thought-of link leader be sent to a one-year course and then return as brigadier. This course of action proved successful.[91] An example of a strong, all-pervasive party network in his kolkhoz is given by the secretary of a kolkhoz Party Committee. It has 109 members in thirteen department party organizations. In the garage, repair shop, and construction brigades there are permanent party groups and seven temporary party groups created for periods of seasonal work, for example, for harvest time.[92]

Yet the party's role, even in those kolkhozy where it is quite strong, is not to replace either the kolkhoz officials or the spontaneity of the rank and file. In the words of the Belgorod obkom first secretary, M. Trunov:

> Not party guardianship of kolkhoz cadres, but educating
> them to a feeling of independence determines the success
> of the matter. . . . The party organization strives all-
> around to support the creative initiative of workers, to
> see ahead, to concentrate the attention of the collective
> on basic questions of production. And therefore it is
> very important to arm cadres with economic knowl-
> edge.[93]

Within the ranks of kolkhoz party members, those with higher and intermediate education now constitute 95.5 percent, whereas in 1965 the figure was 74 percent. Every third member is an agricultural specialist.[94] Still, though both quantitatively and qualitatively the party's presence in the kolkhozy is increasing, there are new problems in the wake of this prosperity. With the proliferation of production subdivisions, how closely should party organization follow the production pattern? According to V. Mikulich, a Belorussian obkom first secretary, many department party organizations within a kolkhoz are created unthinkingly, allowing artificial combinations of members of various brigades, farms, and plots without taking account of the specifics of their work. The big question for Mikulich is whether to have department party organizations or party groups in all production brigades, plots, departments, and livestock farms within a kolkhoz.[95] In addition, although Mikulich does not raise it, there is the question of kolkhoz Komsomol organizations, especially important since many of the mechanizers are young and are the key personnel on a farm[96] and since they tend to be party members to a much greater extent than the rank-and-file kolkhozniks.[97]

SOCIALIST LEGALITY AND THE RIGHTS
OF FARMS AND FARMERS

As to the violation of rights of kolkhozniks by the kolkhoz, the literature points toward two major areas of abuse today. First, despite Brezhnev's repeated pledges to help the kolkhozniks in their personal subsidiary economies and the formalization of these pledges in the new Model Charter of the kolkhoz, apparently many kolkhoz officials have not taken them seriously. Not only do kolkhoz chairmen introduce provisions in their kolkhoz charters contrary to the Model Charter, but they illegally decrease private plots, ignore quorums, or even fail to call the meetings as specified in the charter. Second, despite the exhaustive and explicit lists of penalties for violations of labor discipline in article 35 of the new kolkhoz Model Charter, some kolkhoz officials continue to resort to disciplinary measures not sanctioned by the charter, such as fines.[98] Moreover, there is apparently still a generally less than scrupulous attitude of kolkhoz officials toward observance of the norms of kolkhoz democracy.

In article 25 of the USSR Fundamentals of Land Legislation it is provided that each kolkhoz dvor has the right to a garden plot obtained in the order and within the limits of norms foreseen by the kolkhoz charter. The new kolkhoz Model Charter, unlike its predecessor, has an independent section in which it regulates in detail the basic questions of subsidiary economic activity of the kolkhoz dvor. This is to be explained, according to the jurist N. Sirodoev, not by the growing role of the subsidiary economy, but rather by the necessity of more fully securing the constitutional right of citizens (the constitution grants a right to all citizens to have a subsidiary plot) to conduct a subsidiary economy.[99] The new Model Charter, in setting the size limits of the garden plot at between one-fifth to one half a hectare, inclusive of land under buildings, allows each kolkhoz to determine the particular size of an individual plot within these limits, specifying, however, that in so doing the kolkhoz should take into account the labor participation of members of the particular dvor in the public sector of the kolkhoz as well as the number of dvor members. The plot is assigned without charge and for an unlimited period. The reason for this, according to Sirodoev, is to insure the incentive of investing in it over the years without fear of it being transferred to another user.[100] Only legally sanctioned bases for taking it away can be invoked. And the right to preserve the use of plots for dvors consisting only of invalids, the under-aged, and the elderly has been affirmed in the new Model Charter so as to better protect these groups from the kolkhoz officials and even the rank and file at general meetings. However, the kolkhoz board must supervise observation of the limits of plot size and take back land appropriated by a dvor in excess of the maximum without giving any compensation for the crops raised on the illegally appropriated excess.[101]

The kolkhozy are not the only culprits in infringing upon the rights of the garden plot user. There have been cases where state enterprises have seized garden plot lands as well as communal kolkhoz lands, the latter being the more common abuse.[102] The same reporter notes that many kolkhoz presidents and their deputies have personally decided questions that are within the jurisdiction of kolkhoz boards alone to decide and that they continue to dispose of kolkhoz monies and property unchecked by internal kolkhoz control organs. Many illegal decisions are being made and the kolkhoz auditing commissions are often feeble.[103] Apparently the auditing commissions are not performing their roles as fiscal watchdogs over the kolkhoz officials any better than they were before the new Model Charter was passed. Reports from Astrakhan, Saratov, and Volgograd oblasts indicate the alarming proportions of embezzlements, appropriations, and other abuses of official positions by kolkhoz officials and the fact that auditing commissions facilitate this by not taking inventory for years.[104] The problem is especially acute during sowing and harvesting campaigns.[105] There are other reports of violations of the Model Charter and other laws reported by procurators' offices.

In the charters of some small kolkhozy in Latvia there have been provisions that amount to a replacing of the general meeting by the meeting of representatives, an eventuality only justified where a kolkhoz is very large, thus making the general meeting unwieldy and impractical. One kolkhoz directly contradicted the Model Charter by putting in its charter a provision for a fine of from three to five norm days. Another kolkhoz's charter sharply decreased the size of the garden plots of incapacitated kolkhozniks. And in some charters the norms for livestock in the personal possession of the dvor were raised beyond the legal maxima. The jurist M. Kozyr' urges Union Republic Ministries of Agriculture to carefully check out charters adopted by individual kolkhozy.[106]

As noted above, some kolkhozy have attempted either by introducing a provision in their charters or rules of internal order or simply by adopting it as a policy, to levy fines as a form of penalty. Others resort to levying "lost profits" from kolkhozniks guilty of acts resulting in loss of income for the kolkhoz. The problem is that article 35 of the Model Charter does not allow fining of kolkhozniks guilty of violating work discipline. The jurist T. Sviatetskaia believes that fines are only to be imposed by the kolkhoz on kolkhozniks if a piece of legislation authorizes this.[107] And so does the jurist M. S. Sakhipov.[108]

The new Model Charter embodies a new approach to the traditionally troublesome problem of the material liability of kolkhozniks for harm done to the kolkhoz. Apparently there were two abuses common in respect to the problem of damages inflicted on the kolkhoz by its members. In some cases the kolkhoz could not actually recover by way of compensation the full amount of the damages because of the fuzziness of the legal doctrines applicable and the lack of a uniform, authoritative approach by the courts as to the measure of liability. Quite apart from this problem was, and is, the one of the kolkhoz that unjustifiably writes off losses caused by kolkhozniks without seeking compensation at all. The 1935 Model Charter simply did not speak to the matter of a kolkhoznik's material liability. But the new Model Charter's article 13 states that kolkhozniks who, owing to negligence or carelessness, have caused the destruction, spoilage, or loss of kolkhoz property or are guilty of unauthorized use of tractors, automobiles, farm machinery, or livestock, and who have inflicted material harm on the kolkhoz, must compensate it to the kolkhoz. The size of the actual damage is determined by the kolkhoz board. If damage results from a kolkhozniks' inefficiency, recovery is made to the fullest extent possible of the damage but not over one-third of the kolkhoznik's basic monthly earnings. If damage is inflicted deliberately, as well as in cases foreseen by legislation, the guilty party compensates the damages in full and perhaps a penalty is imposed on top of this. Recovery is effected by the kolkhoz board or, if litigation occurs, by a court.

The lawyer G. Dobrovol'skii sees article 13 as not only promoting a feeling of responsibility on the part of kolkhozniks toward kolkhoz property, but as also creating a legal guarantee protecting their earning from illegal and unfounded withholdings by the kolkhoz.[109] Sakhipov asserts that levies of a kolkhoz on a kolkhoznik's salary cannot occur except through a court action if the kolkhoznik disputes the right of the kolkhoz to levy on his salary.[110] Article 13 applies only to kolkhozniks, not nonmembers working on the farm on the basis of a labor contract. They are subject only to norms of labor legislation. If the nonmember causing harm to the kolkhoz is not working for the kolkhoz at all, then his liability is determined by civil law norms.[111]

As for the kolkhoz itself, its property and income have been given greater protection of late through better legal protections of its lands as well as more comprehensive insurance coverage of its property[112] and a more equitable income tax policy. And there has been some sympathetic attention paid of late to the poor and in many cases nonexistent legal staffing of kolkhozy. All of these new policies or concerns highlight long-standing problems that have no duobt been contributors to the poor performance of many kolkhozy.

The Soviet doctrine of securing lands to kolkhozy in deeds of perpetual use is officially justified as the only way of convincing them that they have a real vested interest in the lands assigned to them and thus an incentive in making long-term investments in land amelioration, which presumably a short-term use regime would not encourage. Yet there are more and more complaints heard that some of the better agricultural lands are being irrationally and even illegally appropriated by construction and other industrial interests and, moreover, with inadequate compensation being made to the victimized kolkhoz.[113] Up to the introduction of the new Fundamentals of Land Legislation in 1968, compensation of losses due to appropriation of kolkhoz lands was limited, as a rule, to the cost of sowing (if crops had ripened), of plants, and certain other expenses incurred by the kolkhoz on the land's preparation for that season. Expenses associated with anti-pollution measures for water or antisoil erosion were not taken into account. The jurist Iu. Zharikov feels that unreceived income (lost profits) should be compensated. He sees these as the value, per state purchase prices, of produce that would have been received from the land if it had not been either taken or damaged, as the case may be.[114] Another jurist, F. Adikhanov, feels that those suffering illegal deprivation of land should recover lost profits for lost use. He also feels that a fine should be imposed, the amount of which would depend on the quantity of land seized, its value, and the length of the taking. All of the fine should go to the agricultural organs, not the farm since the farm would get the lost profit. Another jurist regrets that the RSFSR Criminal Code does not define the intentional taking of agricultural land as an independent crime, although article 199 does foresee liability for all types of land violations.[115] According to article 50 of the Fundamentals of Land Legislation, persons guilty of intentional taking of land are brought to criminal or administrative liability according to legislation.

NEW INSURANCE AND TAX POLICIES

As to the change in insurance policy, up to 1968 the greater part of agricultural crops remained uninsured from drought, insufficeint heat, excessive moisture, agricultural pests, and diseases, and fruit and berries could not be insured against destruction. By state decree of August 28, 1967, "On State Obligatory Insurance of Property of Kolkhozy," there was introduced a rate of payments for insurance of agricultural crops at their full value, based on actual state purchase prices. Now the circle of disasters against which crops are insurable has been widened. Included now are drought, insufficient heat, excessive moisture, disease, and harmful growths and also other meteorological and natural phenomena unusual for the given locality. Practically all unfavorable natural factors are covered as to crops. Certain premiums were lowered, whereas some were increased. The system was rationalized in that payments in different republics were differentiated in relation to probable risks. Payments by kolkhozy with above-average crop yields were increased. Previously insurance of agricultural crops was at equal premium rates for all kolkhozy in a raion, based on 40 percent of the average value of the crop. The terms and conditions for insuring livestock have been liberalized, as they have for insuring buildings, structures, and other kolkhoz property. For instance, livestock destruction by lightning is now covered under "natural disasters."[116]

As to the new tax policy, a ukaz of the Presidium of the USSR Supreme Soviet of February 2, 1970, introduced a differentiated income tax based on the level of profitability. It is not based on a single percentage rate for all kolkhozy as before (12 percent), but rather on a differentiated rate running from 3 percent for each percent of profit over 15 percent profitability rate, but no more than 25 percent of taxable net income. Previously the income tax fell on gross income. The labor payment fund of the kolkhoz is taxes separately and a certain part of it is tax free.[117]

STRENGTHENING FARM LEGAL STAFFS

It has been noted by one student of kolkhoz problems that there is great need for trained economists and accountants on kolkhoz staffs.[118] The need for professional legal staff is also notable. That the kolkhozy have been victimized in part because they lack adequate legal staff is the contention of the jurist A. Denisov. According to Denisov, large material losses occur often because of insufficient legal service being available. In many cases huge debts owed to kolkhozy pile up and the statute of limitations runs out on the kolkhozy without them asserting their claims. Up to 1967 there actually was no legal service for farms. As of September 1967, in all of agriculture there were only 137 jurisconsults (special full-time staff legal advisers).[119] The USSR Ministry of Agriculture on November 6, 1967, issued a special order on the organization of juridic service for the village, and it foresaw the creation in all links of the agricultural apparatus and in the larger kolkhozy and sovkhozy of a staff juridical service.[120] Today in agriculture there are more than fifteen hundred jurisconsults. Still, most kolkhozy and sovkhozy have none and use advokats (lawyers), although Denisov feels that this is ineffective.[121] I. F. Pankratov agrees with Denisov and feels that kolkhozy should have their own staff jurisconsults.[122]

A staff juridical (legal) service has been created in oblast and raion agricultural administration links and these, especially in the raions, will help the kolkhozy. The USSR Ministry of Agricilture published an order of January 18, 1971, No. 18, which confirmed a plan of basic measures to improve legal services for the farms.

For 1972-75 it is planned to create a legal service in agricultural administrations' raion soviet executive committees, that is, there will be introduced the post of legal work within the staff. In all krai and oblast agricultural administrations and within the Ministries of Agriculture of Autonomous Republics and sovkhoz trusts, the post of legal worker was introduced in 1971-72. And the Russian Republic's Council of Ministers, in a decree of January 29, 1971, No. 69, "About Improving Legal Work in the Economy," obliged its Ministry of Agriculture, the Councils of Ministers of Autonomous Republics, and executive committees of krais and oblasts to work out during 1971, per agreements with the USSR Ministry of Agriculture, concrete measures to improve legal servicing of farms and other agricultural enterprises and organizations.[123]

That the kolkhozy in dealing with state procurement organs could benefit from the presence of permanent legal staff is evident from L. N. Bakhovkina's description of the commonplace sloppiness of kolkhozy in not weighing goods or defining and verifying quality and not using proper forms. All of this, she related, leads to kolkhozy being taken advantage of by unscrupulous employees of the procurement agencies. There are many cases of outright fraud in weighing produce perpetrated by state organs, and also of their delay in pouring milk, for instance, leading to quality deterioration at the expense of the kolkhoz, which is actually blameless.[124] There are, then, not only voices to be heard in favor of advancing legal services to each farm on a par with what the typical state enterprise now has, but the first few decrees on this. Although the decrees have not yet changed much in practice, they have underlined the rather "defenseless" position of the farms, especially the kolkhoz, up till now.

The new concern for protecting the kolkhozy in their dealing with the state procurement service, as well as the need for clarifying the mutual rights involved, is indicated by the jurist A. Pervushin. He cautions local state organs against dictating the terms of the contract of the kolkhoz, stressing the voluntary bilateral nature of the contract between the two. He notes the legislative gap in regulating significant incidents of kolkhoz-procurement agency legal relations, such as the period within which acceptance or nonacceptance of produce must be made. Pervushin favors placing more of the risk of spoilage during transit and storage on the procurement agency, and in general is very sympathetic to the kolkhoz's interests.[125] The jurist S. Dontsov notes that suits by kolkhozy against state and inter-kolkhoz organizations to recover compensation for jobs either not done or poorly done constitute, from year to year, a fifth of the total yearly court cases. Commonly the kolkhoz-plaintiff is unaware of the nature of limitations on such suits or the legal requirement to put certain contracts in writing. And often losses suffered by kolkhozy through the negligence of their officials are not recovered through a suit against such officials when such a remedy is available.[126]

S. Lur'e, a consultant to Gosarbitrazh, the state arbitration service, urges letting Gosarbitrazh have jurisdiction over disputes of kolkhozy with state procurement and supply agencies in the interests of expediting economic flows.[127]

Kolkhozy are also sloppy about recovering loans made to their members, and some indulge in the illegal practices of paying the agricultural tax and other personal obligations of their members. Frequently kolkhozy are victimized by mistaken decisions of courts holding them liable to repay sums paid out mistakenly as pension benefits to their members without any establishing of guilt on their part.[128] All this seems to indicate the need for more legal aid for them.

Of course, adequate legal staffs alone will not result in any major improvement in the economic positions of the weaker kolkhozy. Yet the seeming commitment to a "new deal" on this minor problem is symptomatic of the regime's willingness to address itself to the allegations of discriminations and abuses suffered by the kolkhozy at the hands of state organs. And this is in itself evidence of a more objective attitude toward the kolkhozy and their performance.

NOTES

1. Twenty-Fourth Congress of the CPSU, Documents (Moscow: Novesti Press Agency Publishing House, 1971), p. 43. (Hereafter cited as "24th Congress.")
2. Ibid., pp. 58-59.
3. Ibid., p. 60.
4. Ibid., p. 62.
5. Ibid., pp. 89-90.
6. Ibid., pp. 133-134.
7. Ibid., p. 140.
8. Ibid., pp. 164-165.
9. Andrei Babich, The Party Issues Draft Directives for the Ninth Five-Year Prosperity Plan, Analysis of Current Developments in the Soviet Union, Institute for the Study of the USSR, no. 644 (March 30, 1971): 2.
10. 24th Congress, pp. 190-191.
11. S. Luk'ianenko, "Pensionnoe Obespechenie Chlenov Kolkhozov," Sot. Zak., no. 12 (1971): 39-40; M. Kozyr',"Zakon Kolkhoznoi Zhizhi," Chelovek i Zakon, no. 8 (1971): 15.
12. 24th Congress, p. 193.
13. Ibid., p. 248.
14. Ibid., p. 272.
15. Ibid., pp. 275-276.
16. Ibid., p. 276.
17. Ibid., p. 277.

18. Ibid., p. 279.
19. Leonard Schapiro, "Keynote—Compromise," Problems of Communism (July-August 1971): 2.
20. Ibid., p. 3.
21. Sidney Ploss, "Politics in the Kremlin," Problems of Communism (May-June 1970): 10-11.
22. See "Confirming of the Meeting of the Third All-Union Congress of Kolkhozniks for 1966," Izvestia, January 26, 1966, pp. 34-40.
23. C. Olgin, "The Ninth Five-Year Plan: Economics and Party Politics," Bulletin, Institute for the Study of the USSR XVIII no. 4 (April 1971): 34.
24. Pravda, April 26, 1971, p. 1.
25. A. V. Rimachenko and G. Vasilenko, "Agrarno-Promishlennye Ob'edineniia—Progressivnaia Forma Organizatsii Proizvodstva," Ekonomika Sel'skogo Khoziaistva, no. 12 (1971): 70-71.
26. G. Loza, "Razvitie Agrarno-Promyshlennykh Kompleksov i Ob'edinenii," Ekonomika Sel'skogo Khoziaistva, no. 11 (1971): 101-102.
27. A. Kalambet, "Ispol'zovanie Osnovnykh Fundov V Agrarno-Promyshlennykh Obedineniiakh," Ekonomika Sel'skogo Khoziaistva, no. 1 (1972): 81-82.
28. M. Vasilenko, "Effektivnost' Sochetaniia Sel'skokhoziaistvennogo i Podsobnogo Promyshlennogo Proizvodstva," Ekonomika Sel'skogo Khoziaistva, no. 2 (1972): 84.
29. Ibid., May 9, 1971, p. 2.
30. E. Vavilin, "Rabochii Den'doiarki," Sel'skaia Zhizn', July 20, 1971, p. 2.
31. V. Tsarov, in Sel'skaia Zhizn', July 7, 1971, p. 2.
32. S. Botvinnik, "Shchapovskii Kompleks—2,000 Korov pod Odnoi Kryshei," Sel'skaia Zhizn', July 7, 1971, p. 2.
33. M. Glinka, "Dva Podkhoda k Odnoi Probleme," Sel'skaia Zhizn', July 8, 1971, p. 2.
34. See D. Buslov, "Partiinaia Zhizn'," Pravda, May 11, 1971, p. 2.
35. Pravda, May 16, 1971, p. 2.
36. For instance, see Alec Nove, The Soviet Economy (New York: Praeger Publishers, 1961).
37. Paige Bryan, "Bacon Prices Causing Production Problems," Radio Liberty Dispatch, April 4, 1972.
38. Izvestia, May 15, 1971, p. 3.
39. See the article, "Rising to the Level of Advanced Farms," in Pravda, May 29, 1971, p. 3.
40. Pravda, June 16, 1971, p. 2.
41. Izvestia, June 23, 1971, p. 3.
42. V. Karavaev, "Priamye Sviazi i Puti Ikh Dal'neishego Razvitiia," Ekonomika Sel'skogo Khoziaistva, no. 12 (1971): 75.
43. Ibid., June 4, 1971, p. 3.

44. V. Pshenichnyi, "Vygoda Priamykh Sviazei," Sel'skaia Zhizn', July 13, 1971, p. 2.
45. Izvestia, May 26, 1971, p. 2.
46. I. Chikanchi, "Po Akkordnomu Nariadu—Dogovoru!" Ekonomicheskaia Gazeta, no. 29 (July 1971): 19.
47. I. F. Kuz'min, "Pravovye Sredstva Povysheniia Effektivnosti Proizvodstvennoi Deiatel'nosti Kolkhozov," SGIP, no. 8 (1971): 69.
48. Pravda, May 19, 1971, p. 2.
49. M. Seslavin and A. Trubnikov, "Liuboe Delo Distsiplinoi Krepitsia," Sel'skaia Zhizn', August 17, 1971, p. 2.
50. Pravda, June 5, 1971, p. 3.
51. E. Rusanov, "To Develop Agraro-Industrial Complexes," Ekonomicheskaia Gazeta, no. 12 (March 1971): 14.
52. A. Shershukov, "V Interesakh Razvitiia Obshchestvennogo Khoziaistva" Ekonomicheskaia Gazeta, no. 32 (August 1971): 18.
53. Ibid., p. 19.
54. See A. Batov, "The Development of Subsidiary Production in a Kolkhoz in Rovensk Oblast," Ekonomicheskaia Gazeta, no. 18 (April 1971): 18.
55. A. Shershukov, "Na Mezhe Kontrastov," Ekonomicheskaia Gazeta, no. 28 (July 1971): 19.
56. I. Sirovatko and A. Khamlak, "Novye Rubezhi Kolkhoznogo Sela," Partiinaia Zhizn', no. 9 (1971): 37-38.
57. M. Glinka, "Dva Podkhoda k Odnoi Probleme," Sel'skaia Zhizn', July 8, 1971, p. 2.
58. A. Dimin, "Slovo Truzhenikov Sela," Partiinaia Zhizn', no. 6 (1971): 71.
59. I. Razumovskii and V. Siviakov, "Za 280 Tsentnerov Klubnei s Gektara," Sel'skaia Zhizn', July, 1971, p. 2.
60. I. Denisenkov, in Sel'skaia Zhizn', June 23, 1971, p. 2.
61. Michael Bradley, "Prospects for Soviet Agriculture," Current History (October 1970): 231.
62. K. Tarchokov, "Dukhovnyi Rost Kolkhoznogo Kresti'ianstva," Kommunist, no. 16 (1969): 83-84.
63. Ibid., p. 84.
64. V. Koshelev, "Polnyi Vnutrikhoziaistvennyi Raschet—Vazhnyi Proizvodstvennyi Rezerv," Kommunist, no. 9 (1971): 52.
65. I. Mikulovich, "Sovershenstvuem Organizatsiiu Truda i Upravleniia v Sel'skom Khoziaistva," Partiinaia Zhizn' no. 5 (1971): 27-28.
66. Ibid., p. 28.
67. Ibid., p. 29.
68. Ibid., p. 31.
69. A. Esin, "Internal Accounting in Kolkhozy," Ekonomicheskaia Gazeta, no. 27 (July 1971): 18.
70. Ekonomicheskaia Gazeta, No. 1 (January 1971): 7.
71. Ibid., no. 22 (May 1971): 10.

72. Ibid.
73. Ibid., no. 4 (January 1971): 18.
74. Dimin, op. cit., p. 72.
75. I. Masaulov, "Primer Mekhanizatorov," Sel'skaia Zhizn', June 30, 1971, p. 2.
76. A. Novikov, "Akkordnaia Oplata," Ekonomicheskaia Gazeta, no. 25 (June 1971): 11.
77. V. N. Dem'ianenko, "Sovershenstvovat' Kolkhoznoe Proizvodstvo," SGIP, no. 6 (1971): 14.
78. "Kolkhoznoe Krest'ianstvo," Pravda, July 22, 1971, p. 1.
79. Darrell Hammer, "The Dilemma of Party Growth," Problems of Communism XX (July-August 1970): 19, Table 2.
80. Society and Economic Relations (Moscow: Progress Publishers, 1969), p. 203.
81. Pravda, July 22, 1971, p. 1.
82. M. Seslavin and A. Trubnikov, "Liuboe Delo Distsiplinoi Krespitsia," Sel'skaia Zhizn', August 17, 1971, p. 2.
83. Dem'ianenko, op. cit., p. 12.
84. I. Denisenkov, in Sel'skaia Zhizn', June 23, 1971, p. 2.
85. Dem'ianenko, op. cit., p. 17.
86. A Kozhevnikov, "Nikto Ne Stoit v Stornoe," Sel'skaia Zhizn', August 5, 1971, p. 2.
87. Ibid., p. 2.
88. V. Mikulich, "Obkom i Sel'skie Partiinye Organizatsii," Partiinaia Zhizn', no. 2 (1971): 39.
89. I. Mikulovich, "Sovershenstvuem Organizatsiyu Truda i Upravleniia v Sel'skom Khoziaistve," Partiinaia Zhizn', no. 5 (1971): 32.
90. Mikulich, op. cit., pp. 43-44.
91. M. Nikonov, "Kommunisty v Brigade," Pravda, July 20, 1971, p. 2.
92. A Nikollenko, "Strogii Spros i Pomoschch," Sel'skaia Zhizn', August 21, 1971, p. 2.
93. M. Trunov, "Za Uglublenie Spetsializatsii v Sel'skokhoziaistvennom Proizvodstve," Partiinaia Zhizn', no. 13 (1971): 18.
94. Mikulich, op. cit., p. 44.
95. Ibid., p. 45.
96. A. Georgiev, "Sel'skii Trud i Molodezh'," Kommunist, no. 9 (1971): 25-26.
97. V. Stepanov, "Kliuchevaia Problema Razvitiia Sel'skogo Khoziaistva," Partiinaia Zhizn', no. 8 (1971): 32.
98. M. Kozyr', "Zakon Kolkhoznoi Zhizni," Chelovek i Zakon, no. 8 (August 1971): 16-17.
99. N. Sirodoev, "Pravo Zemlepol'zovaniia Kolkhoznogo Dvora," Sov. Iust., no. 13 (1970): 6.
100. Ibid., p. 7.
101. Ibid.

102. I. Balurov in "Nazor za Ispolneniem Zakonov v Selskom Khoziaistve," Sots. Zak., no. 8 (1970): 21.

103. Ibid.

104. V. Kornoukhov, "Rabota Narodnykh Sudov po Preduprezhdeniiu Khishchenii Kolkhoznogo Imushchestva," Sov. Iust., no. 5 (1970): 26.

105. Ibid., pp. 26-27.

106. M. Kozyr', "Primernyi Ustav Kolkhoza i Problemy Zakonodatel'stva," Sots. Zak., no. 2 (1971): 6.

107. T. Sviatetskaia, "Pravovoe Regulirovanie Distsiplinarnoi Otvetstvennosti Chenov Kolkhoza," Sov. Iust., no. 17, (1970): 9.

108. M. S. Sakhipov, "Otvetstvennost' po Kolkhoznomu Pravu," SGIP, no. 4 (1971): 31

109. G. Dobrovol'skii, "Material'naia Otvetstvennost' Kolkhoznikov po Novomu Primernomu Ustavu Kolkhoza," Sov. Iust., no. 14 (1970): 5.

110. Sakhipov, op. cit., p. 35.

111. V. Paniugin, "Materialnaia Otvetstvennost' Chlenov Kolkhoza," Sots. Zak., no. 4 (1971).

112. V. Iakovlev, "Strakhovanie Imushchestva Kolkhoza," Sov. Iust., 1971 no. 22, pp. 3-4.

113. S. Foteev, "Sotsialisticheskie Zemel'nye Otnosheniia i Ratsional'noe Ispol'zovanie Zemli," Kommunist, no. 16 (1969): 73.

114. Iu Zharikov, "Okhrana Imushchestvennykh Prav Zemlepol'zovatelei," Sov. Iust., no. 7 (1971): 12.

115. F. Adikhanov, "Otvetstvennost' za Samovol'noe Zaniatie Zemel' Sel'skokhoziastvennykh Predpriiatii," Sov. Iust., no. 5 (1971): p. 30.

116. Iu. Iuldashev, "Ekonomicheskie Rezul'taty Perestroiki Gosudarstvennogo Strakhovaniia Imushchestva Kolkhozov," Finansy SSSR, no. 10 (1969): 77-78.

117. A. Matveev, "Income Tax on Kolkhozy," Ekonomicheskaia Gazeta, no. 25 (1971): 18.

118. Robert C. Stuart, The Collective Farm in Soviet Agriculture (Lexington: D. C. Heath, 1972), p. 184.

119. See Permanent Consultants on Legal Questions on the Staffs of Most Institutions and Enterprises, Kratkii Iuridicheskii Slovar'-Spravochnik dlia Naseleniia, Gosiurizdat, 1960).

120. A. Denisov, "Iuridicheskoe Obsluzhivanie Kolkhozov i Sovkhozov," Sov. Iust. no. 12 (1971): p. 3.

121. Ibid., p. 4.

122. I. F. Pankratov, Gosudarvstvennoe Rukovodstvo Sel'skim Khoziaistvom SSSR (Moscow: Izdat. Iurid. Lit., 1969), p. 167.

123. Denisov, op. cit., p. 4.

124. L. N. Bakhovkina, "Zakupki Kolkhoznoi Sel'skokhoziaistvennoi Produktsii," SGIP, no. 3 (1971): 62.

125. A. Pervushin, "Ispolnenie Dogovora Kontraktatsii Selskokhoziaistvennoi Produktsii," Sov. Iust., no. 14 (July 1971): 6-7.

126. S. Lur'e, "Pravovoe Regulirovanie Kontraktatsii Sel'skokh-oziaistvennoi Produktsii," Sov. Iust., no. 23 (1971): p. 21.

127. S. Dontsov, "Sudebnaia Praktika Razresheniia Sporov, Odnoi iz Storon v Kotorykh Iavliaetsia Kolkhoz," Sov. Iust., no. 16 (August 1971): 15.

128. Ibid., p. 16.

SOVIET AGRICULTURE TODAY:
PROBLEMS AND PROSPECTS
FOR REFORM

6

SOVIET AGRICULTURE TODAY:
AN OVERVIEW

A citation from Erich Strauss provides an appropriate starting point for a discussion of current dilemmas facing the Soviets in agriculture: "After having been for a whole generation primarily a political issue with economic consequences, Soviet agriculture has now turned into a mainly economic problem with political overtones."[1]

As Strauss sees it, the main question of current and future Soviet agricultural policy is the balance of human and material resources in agriculture compared with other sectors of the economy and the terms of exchange between them.[2] The regime has apparently established its hegemony over the peasants and is confident of its control over agriculture. With the successful industrialization and the housebreaking of the peasantry via the kolkhozy, the task now is no longer perpetual exploitation of the peasantry for the sake of heavy industry, but how best to pull agriculture out of the doldrums it was seemingly indefinitely condemned to by both the logic of maximal industrialization in the minimal time and the Marxist bias against the reactionary peasantry and the idiocy of rural life.

Strauss believes that ideological rigidity and prejudices are giving way to economic pragmatism. The lagging behind the rest of the Soviet economy of agriculture has now become a drag on the whole economy. The symbols of Soviet agricultural failure are a low volume of agricultural production per head of population, generally accompanied by high costs of production, periodic food difficulties—in either quantity or quality or both—and limited supplies of raw materials for the food, textiles, and leather goods industries.[3] Moreover, given the Soviet Union's political need to remain wholly independent economically of the nonsocialist world, this excludes any possibility of reliance on food imports as a normal economic occurrence.[4] This need for increased agricultural output at home is complicated by the exodus from farm to factory. This means that fewer farm hands must produce even more output, which requires them to increase their labor productivity to a point even beyond that of merely compensating for the loss of manpower.[5]

Strauss feels that the uneasy relations between Soviet power and the peasants have been the most formidable constraint on the regime's internal freedom of action on a number of occasions. He believes that unless and until the agricultural basis of the system is secure, the system as a whole remains under pressure.[6] Lord Walton more than agrees: "The problem of the land and of the men and women who work on it has been the greatest problem that the Soviet Union has had to face within its own borders, and it is a problem which even after forty years it has not succeeded in finally solving."[7] Strauss sees Khrushchev's rise and fall as tied to the agricultural question. His rise to supremacy was linked in time and substance with the partial success of his policy of raising the level of agricultural output through a gigantic crash program designed to get quick results at the cost of taking considerable risks. The revival of the threat of agricultural stagnation after 1958 may well have been one of the causes of the increasingly erratic policy of the Soviet government under his leadership in many fields. The feverish and almost desperate attempts to improve the position of agriculture through repeated administrative reshuffles and the severe setback of the crop failure of 1963 must have undermined his position in the party hierarchy and contributed to his downfall.[8]

In his chapter on bureaucratic dictatorship and agricultural policy, Strauss makes some telling points about how bureaucratic dictatorship tends to distort the upward flow of communications and turn local economic problems into bureaucratic politics, thus creating false issues as well as exacerbating the real underlying problems by neglect. Strauss begins by stating that the prohibition of any independent center of social, political, or economic interests outside the recognized official bodies limits the expression of such interests to their influence on sections of the party and government officially in charge of their respective spheres. In other words, the monitoring and service agricultural organs of party and state inevitably become wedded to the interests they manipulate and supervise. Strauss feels that clashes of interest between social groups thus tend under a system in which direct expression of particular interests is illicit to assume the form of difficulties in the operation of the bureaucratic machines, and particularly of friction between different bureaucratic organs. This fools the top leadership into crediting the bureaucratic difficulties as the real source of problems instead of searching below this level. As Strauss puts it, the function of the bureaucracy as intermediary between different interests tends to disguise these interests to such

an extent that not even the top leadership may be aware of the true
causes of the so-called administrative problems.[9]

THE HEAVY HAND OF BUREAUCRACY

Another key proposition in Strauss' theory is that excessive
centralization distorts the system of upward communication of information and impedes advance notice about important developments,
particularly if they are not in line with current policy, until they cause
administrative difficulties, and, of course, the administrative difficulties are only the symptoms of the underlying problem. So the treatment—administrative reform—touches only the symptoms, not the
disease. And in a hierarchical system where there are vested interests below in misleading those above, frequently it will be the case
that local agents of the bureaucracy are genuinely ignorant or are
misled about the true situation, and obviously their reports then are
either incomplete or outright misleading. And since the upward flow
of incomplete or distorted information is distorted in the direction
of confirming official policies and dogmas so as not to risk a confron-
tation, the distorted information, since it is reinforcing of upper-level
policies, is not as critically sifted as it would be if it challenged such
beliefs and policies. Moreover, as Strauss neglects to say, it is always more comforting to attribute mistakes and disasters to individual
actions improperly taken rather than to policies.
    The result of this distortion is that since policy is determined
at the top on the basis of defective and often out-of-date information,
adjustment to important external changes will also be late and incomplete. Strauss observes that, as a rule, the machine continues to
operate on this basis of existing policies until it comes up against
obstacles that do not yield to local pressure. This may cause more
or less prolonged deadlock, until a new policy is agreed to at the top
and communicated to the lower echelons.[10] Apparently some problems
can be covered up by administrative reshufflings or salved by half-
measures and palliatives. And in fact administrative reorganizations,
attended by prolonged propaganda about how they will cure the problem,
deflect attention from the still unsolved problem. Usually the propaganda accompanying the restructuring makes it clear that the salutary
effects of the reform require time to become manifest, and meanwhile
more "devils" are uncovered and these are invoked to explain continued
difficulties.
    The "devils" have to be continually exposed as the real causes
of the continuing problems. Of course, all this gains more time for
the new administrative reforms to prove themselves. And meanwhile
this is normally accompanied by an intense campaign to arouse the

farms to redouble their own personal efforts and to correct their own deficiencies, which have contributed to the problems besetting them. Again the effect of this is to deflect the critical spotlight away from mistaken efforts, and thereby to deflect the sense of guilt for the continuing malfunctionings on to the farmers themselves. Apparently it is only when the regime can no longer fail to treat the real problem except at the expense of tremendous economic losses that put a strain on the whole economy that it proceeds to a deeper analysis, even at the cost of shedding certain traditional beliefs and dogmas where these directly confound any progress toward a solution. But it must be stressed that the economic costs of maintaining the unrealistic policy must be very great indeed and the side effects of the medicine administered as a cure must not be too unpredictable or threatening to the party's core beliefs and control system. Otherwise, the hard costs of the continuing malfunctions will be endured for the sake of system maintenance. But since the benefits derivable may be immediate and palpable, there seems to be a tendency within more and more of the leadership to assume the risks. Moreover, since the short-run political fortunes of individual leaders depend in some measure on their ability to associate their names with prestigious achievements, earning them "prestige-capital" with which to bargain with their fellow leaders for a bigger share of the power, there would seem to be more and more receptivity at the top to economic reforms.

Since the top leaders have the power to redefine or modify that which is orthodox in theory, they can to some extent bend theory to accommodate the needs of economic necessity. Hence they can minimize the shock to the belief system of reforms that involve seeming reversals of Marxist tenets by redefining and qualifying the traditional doctrine and by covering up the heretical aspects of the concession to economic necessity. The particular problems to be focused on below in great depth are approached from this broad perspective.

To what extent is this regime at this time willing to recognize the problems as more economic than political, to view them in more practical than ideological terms, and just what are the costs, as they as well as others see it, of continuing to cope only with the symptoms. The costs can be seen as both short and long-term. The fundamental question is to what extent does the regime recognize that certain problems exist. And can they further delay addressing themselves to these problems? In other words, how acute are the problems? Is the regime aware of the possible costs of solutions if they do recognize the problem rather than just the symptoms? And, given that they are willing to recognize the existence of the problem, how realistic is their appraisal of its dimensions and how uninhibited are the discussions of possible remedies? What factors impair their ability to cope with the problem and realistically evaluate possible solutions or remedial policies, given their belief system and the logic of system preservation?

An extremely important factor in this is the role of the experts—ideologists, economists, agronomists, jurists, and other specialists. To what extent do their "interests" propel them into the arena to plead for new initiatives and new policies, and to what extent do they affect the top-level policy? Is intense conflict among the experts over remedies and solutions to these problems predictable in terms of personal, occupational, and professional rivalries, or is it more often the genuine, normal conflict of experts over tough technical questions in regard to which there are no hard and fast answers? Moreover, to what extent does the divergence among the various specialists and experts, once a question has apparently been allowed as one open to discussion, in the scholarly press affect the speed with which the regime takes action on this question? All these are appropriate questions.

THE IMPACT OF IDEOLOGY

From the Soviets' standpoint there remain two institutionalized ideological concessions to practicality or economic expedience in agriculture that their Marxist theory tells them must ultimately disappear. First, there are the kolkhozy, which are cooperatives and hence theoretically group and not state property, and thus ideologically inferior to the state-owned sovkhozy. Another ideologically retrograde aspect of the kolkhozy is that they are economically independent of each other, and the level of coordination and mutual aid among them is low despite the advent of kolkhoz-state and interkolkhoz organizations. Their independence of each other thwarts rational specialization and concentration of economic activities.

The second institutionalized concession is the private sector of "acre and a cow" garden plots and livestock, constitutionally guaranteed not just to kolkhoz and sovkhoz workers but to all citizens, although only the two aforementioned groups are major factors in the private sector's marketings. This is a remnant of private farming and keeps alive the spirit of the private property mentality. Its survival is officially viewed as a necessary concession because of the inability of the public sector in agriculture to supply sufficient quantities of the food needs of both the farmers and the nonfarm population, given the level of financial support the regime is willing to extend to agriculture. But it is made quite clear that it will die a "natural death" through the growth of the public sector to a point where it can supply more, better, and cheaper foods for all, so that those engaged in the private sector will give it up voluntarily in recognition that they can buy food from the state that is cheaper and better than that which they raise.

Lord Walton captures the dilemma of the Soviet regime in harboring these deviations:

No one can say for certain that the success, under any other system of government, would have been greater or less. But of two things one can be sure. First, the Soviet Government has so far failed to evolve a system which, in the case of livestock, gives it the increase in production which it requires, but which does not at the same time involve a relatively high degree of private ownership, individual skill and responsibility, and personal reward. Secondly, so long as it is found necessary to retain this private sector of production, the flame of private possession which burns in every peasant's heart will never be extinguished.[11]

In a sense not only the private sector but the kolkhozy themselves are a continuing sign of the imperviousness of the human clay to the divine Marxian design, an irritating reminder of the limits of human engineering and the weakness of the flesh. In a more practical vein they underline the continuing failure of the regime to complete the internal revolution so successfully applied to industry. Agriculture is surely that most perverse of sectors. As Strauss, Walton, and the late Naum Jasny put it, it is the regime's Achilles' heel. So, before charging into the woods to examine the particular problems, let us dwell for a time on the overarching problems involved in the Soviet approach to agriculture.

Roy Laird, the veteran American student of Soviet agriculture, has often ventured that the Soviet approach to agriculture is based on fundamentally unsound assumptions about the nature of agricultural production, and therefore the current problems besetting it cannot be solved, as many Soviet and non-Soviet experts agree, through economic correctives, especially more capital investment. According to Laird, new investments alone will not satisfactorily alleviate Soviet rural ills. Laird believes, contrary to many students of Soviet agriculture, that Khrushchev's emphasis on management problems was basically sound, whereas the first acts of his successors point to an emphasis on economic shortcomings.[12] Laird's contention that the Soviet approach to agriculture is fundamentally in error proceeds from his belief in the significance of the outdoor and hence inherently uncontrollable environment in which agriculture is conducted—the outdoor factory is essentially different than the indoor one. Moreover, the Soviets not only mistakenly view the production process in agriculture as fundamentally unchanged, but make the false assumption that the bureaucratic administrative system that is essential for efficient industrial production is also the best scheme for organizing and managing agriculture. They fail to realize the absolute necessity and virtue of decentralization of decision-making on the farms if individual farm efficiency is to be maximized. As far as Laird is concerned, fundamental revisions in the system are needed:

> Given the oftimes crucial factors of special local conditions, and the constant and often unpredictable alterations in the environment imposed by nature, the successful farm manager needs the fullest freedom in production decision-making to respond to the ever-changing demands of the plants and animals that he is nurturing. Yet to a degree greater than in any other system in the world, the Soviet "on the farm" farm administrators are continually required to respond to outside, "above-the-farm" directives.[13]

Roy and Betty Laird developed their ideas about the fundamental fallacies of Soviet agricultural thinking and practices at great length in a recent book, Soviet Communism and Agrarian Revolution. In their book they set out to explode the "false myths" at the basis of Soviet agricultural policy. To the Lairds, too many communist policies have been disastrously counterproductive because they have been rooted in misconceptions of the needs of agriculture, which in turn are derived from "false myths," the value-impregnated beliefs and notions that men hold. The Lairds are concerned with doctrines that have guided Soviet society in making agricultural policy, the "false myths" that go counter to scientific discovery yet have become so deeply ingrained in men's minds that even after new evidence has pointed in a different direction, old habit and views persist.[14]

Unlike in industry, the Lairds note, there has been no agricultural revolution. The shift to machine farming still leaves relatively undisturbed the sequential pattern of operations that has prevailed. This is the source of a number of urban misconceptions about agriculture. There is a widespread failure to see the great discrepancy between industrial and agricultural growth rates. And, the low agricultural rates are little affected ever by great industrial growth rate in the same country.[15] Another important misconception is that chemical fertilizers and modern machines for applying them invariably produce the maximum yield per acre. In fact, although they almost always result in significant labor savings and do greatly increase yields, they do not always produce the best yield possible.[16] In many instances chemical fertilizer is not as effective as natural fertilizer, or a combination of the two, and mechanization, they believe, often leads to farm specialization, which means many modern farms keep no livestock and save on labor, but much of the land is left without any natural fertilizers.

Another rebuttable assumption is that machine cultivation and harvesting of crops increase yield because they reduce weeds more rapidly and speed up harvest. But, opine the Lairds, given ample and eager labor, human hands will pull weeds next to a plant that machines could not touch. Similarly, gleaners can pick up fallen grain the machine would miss, and Asian farmers often reseed small gaps in their fields that a machine could not detect. A particularly pernicious myth, in their eyes, is the one to the effect that centralized industrial management practice has greatly enhanced farm production. On-the-farm management is directly involved in production, and is not in some remote centralized office. Success is very much dependent on an intimate knowledge of the constantly changing physical environment on each acre.[17]

THE FAILURE OF BIGNESS

Moreover, there are important limits on farm size, varying with the type of farm, if peak efficiency in management and production is to be maintained. One cannot blithely assume, as do the Soviets, that the bigger the farm the better. The notion of optimal size is a corrective to the naive worship of "gigantomania."[18] The Lairds dispute the commonly held urban dwellers' assumption that modern equipment allows a farmer to impose industrial production controls over his production. Yet natural changes still confound such controls, and it is most unlikely that the rigidly controlled production environment that is essential for industrial success can ever be imposed on the "roofless production plant of the farmer."[19]

The American economists Michael Bradley and M. Gardner Clark, like the Lairds, feel that the sequential nature of farm work, as well as its dispersal over large areas, represents tremendous control and management problems. American corporate farms minimize supervision problems by creating a structure that allows for a minimal work force. The Soviets multiply the inherent supervision problems by insisting on huge farms and huge numbers of farmers, since the latter are not given freedom to leave the farms.[20] In direct contrast to the inefficiency of the public sector is the relative efficiency of the private sector, based on unsupervised self-initiative. The Soviets could greatly increase efficiency by revising structural forms to allow for minimal supervision.[21]

The Lairds conclude that evidence from Soviet and Polish practice indicates that the price of collectivization is not only dissatisfaction among farmers, but also an enormous waste of labor and a loss of food output that may be more than 15 percent of the possible maximum:[22] "Causes for this waste are not economic, but stem from distorted beliefs that ignore problems of farm organization and management as related to size, and from central interference in farm decision-making."[23]

But they believe that the emotional investment in the Soviet agricultural system is so deep that to repudiate it would be unthinkable, because the Soviets' claim that it is universally applicable would then be undermined.[24] To drop collectivization would be to repudiate Marx's belief in the application of the industrial principle to agriculture.[25] Stalin's contribution was forced collectivization, a step Lenin repudiated. Stalinist literature expressed the belief, say the Lairds, that the sovkhozy were a higher form of production than the kolkhozy, and that a marriage of the Marxist-Leninist "science" and natural science would ultimately allow the transformation of nature to a point where agriculture would enjoy the same controlled conditions of production that had been achieved in much of industry.[26]

The Lairds conclude:

Stalin's successors may well wonder at times whether Lenin's voluntary path would not have been better than the Stalinist road of force. Nevertheless, the collective and state farms that exist are part of the heritage that must be believed in, and there is no evidence that the post-1953 leadership has rejected the myth of the superiority of large-scale collectivized agriculture—after all, they combine the communist and industrial organizational forms.[27]

The Lairds stress, correctly, I believe, that although the post-Stalin press has emphasized repeatedly the virtual equality between sovkhozy and kolkhozy as to degree of socialist development, yet belief in the slight superiority of the sovkhozy persists as official doctrine.[28] Khrushchev's kolkhoz amalgamation drive, from the 1950s through the early 1960s, led to the average size of kolkhozy becoming much larger, making the kolkhozy in this respect more like the traditionally larger sovkhozy. But Brezhnev recognized that this process had gone too far. Still, the Lairds note, Soviet studies today on the optimal size of the farms reiterate faith in the present large units, even though the key to increased production in today's official language is intensivity rather than extensivity.[29]

The myths of the voluntariness of collectivization and of the reality of kolkhoz democracy are still the official views. The Lairds feel the regime is wedded to collectivization for at least three reasons: first, it serves to control peasant society. Second, and most importantly, the kolkhozy and sovkhozy are seen as the correct media for industrializing agriculture, however mistaken and costly this aim may

be. Third, the farms satisfy a penchant for bigness. The Lairds see
this penchant manifesting itself at the level of the internal kolkhoz
production subdivision farms:

> The size of the farms and of the work brigades can be ex-
> plained up to a point by the need for maximum controls, but
> particularly in the face of evidence that the small zveno
> work units are much more efficient, there is hardly any
> compelling economic argument that the present system of
> huge brigades is the most desirable form of organizing the
> work; it seems to spring from a faith in size for its own
> sake.[30]

The Lairds venture that perhaps the most important of the myths
that make collectivization attractive is that fashioned from a wedding
of Marxist-Leninist "science" with scientism, the faith in the perfect-
ibility of human institutions, with collectivization seen as the best
way to organize the transformation of nature in search of heaven on
earth.[31]

The Lairds feel that nothing short of fundamental changes in the
system that would seriously challenge these beliefs is needed if Soviet
agriculture is to solve its very grave problems.[32] There are signs,
however, of a more flexible approach toward agricultural science,
a begrudging willingness to defer on more technical questions to
experts, a depoliticizing of certain technical agricultural questions.[33]
Yet as to the more crucial questions, farm size and organization,
deference to the agricultural experts clashes with preservation of the
cherished myths.[34] Here is the rub.

The heart of the dilemma is that the hugeness and industrialization in agriculture to which ideological and political considerations
have committed the regime cost enormous losses in food output. These
two criteria are incompatible with the needs and demands of the farming
operation, which for maximal efficiency must be of such a size and
structure that the management can be aware of all farm activity at
all times and make the on-the-spot decisions required by constantly
changing conditions.[35] And the application of industrial techniques
to the agricultural labor force is inappropriate.

The Lairds feel that agricultural production, in contrast to
industrial, requires much more concealed worker time and much more
worker judgment and individual attention. If a farmer is not properly
skilled or sufficiently interested to treat his plants and animals with
care, they stress, these highly perishable products can be seriously
damaged or destroyed.[36] And the paralyzing effect of overcentraliza-
tion characteristic of industrial management on the farm's operation
is illustrated by the following: suppose that a kolkhoz chairman has

insisted on all changes in work orders coming from him alone, and thus while he is away, great losses occur before the appropriate orders are forthcoming to meet changing circumstances.[37]

Human caprice can have much more impact on the strictly production side of agriculture than it has on the carefully planned operation of an assembly line.[38] Timeliness in making decisions is crucial to agricultural success, but because of the system, the kolkhoz chairman has to make decisions that should be made by peasants dealing directly with the plants and animals. Not only is this bad because of the manager's remoteness, but it also robs the workers of the satisfaction of exercising their own initiative, thus dulling incentives. Moreover, the collective farmer realizes that most of his income is not directly dependent upon the quality of his work. And, in many important instances, only the agricultural production worker himself can have the grasp of the situation that is necessary if farm production is to succeed.[39]

The Lairds conclude that if it is true that decision-making is vital in agricultural production, then the optimal size for a given type of farm will be related to the limits within which managers can remain fully informed about changing environmental conditions.[40] The Lairds obviously feel Soviet kolkhozy, not to speak of the even larger sovkhozy, are too large for this.

The American economist David Conklin suggests that the archly centralized Stalinist planned economy has continually encountered 3 problems: an information problem, a coordination problem, and a flexibility problem. All three increase in both difficulty and importance as the economy develops. With increasing development comes more interrelatedness in the production process due to increasing specialization. Coordination problems increase and flexibility is more difficult because unforseen developments in any one enterprise affect others in chain reaction. The modern economy's emphasis on quality and appropriateness adds to the planner's difficulties, since many aspects of quality cannot be quantified easily,[41] and, in general, the costs of poor coordination and poor quality are especially great in agriculture, because of the perishability of produce and the inherently nonuniform nature of the final products. Conklin's analysis seems to suggest that the Soviet economy would benefit from a decentralization of decision-making with guidelines such as centrally determined prices for each industry and region.[42] Linkages between producer and consumer should and would be shortened. Local personnel could adapt more rapidly to changing local conditions, and the information overload on central planners would be drastically reduced. They would be relieved of the burden of determining how much growth farm "X" should produce. All they would need to plan is the yearly amount of grain needed by the economy. Control over production would be indirectly exercised through tax, credit, and price policies.[43] The champion of such ideas in relation to agriculture today in the Soviet Union is the economist Lisichkin, whose ideas are discussed in Part III.

Exiled to a western Siberian kolkhoz as a social parasite, the Russian dissident Andrei Amalrik concludes, from first-hand observation, that each kolkhoz should be given the freedom to make its own plan, with the state exercising indirect control by setting wholesale prices. Amalrik emphasizes the need for real kolkhoz democracy to instill self-respect and a sense of personal responsibility for results. He calls for abolishing administrative restraints on the freedom of farmers to leave the farms, stressing that agriculture should be improved by raising the skill level and not the number of workers. Intensivity not extensivity is the key.[44]

THE QUESTION OF OWNERSHIP

Yet if the Soviets oversubscribe to "false myths" about agriculture, what of the one so popular among critics of Soviet agriculture that farmers, to be successful, must love their land, a myth which leads to another one to the effect that private ownership of land is essential to efficient farming. Certainly, based on the experience of the United States, this is not so, say the Lairds. They hold that neither love of the land nor ownership as such can be demonstrated as essential to agricultural efficiency. What is required is pride in one's work and the feeling of personal accomplishment, which they feel is probably best represented by tangible economic reward from sustained and intelligent care of soil and animals.[45] This explains to a great extent the apparent success of the Soviet farmer in farming his private plot.[46] The Lairds liken the rank-and-file kolkhozniks in their labor in the public sector to "hired hands" rather than co-owners, as the theory of kolkhoz holds.[47] They dismiss the official Soviet propaganda stressing the vitality of kolkhoz democracy as impractical. Huge farms do require strict discipline, which kills individual initiative. Such discipline flows not only out of the mechanical transference of industrial experience to agriculture, but also from other ideological and political demands imposed by the authoritarian system.[48] The Lairds in the end urge the Soviets to disband the vast majority of kolkhozy and sovkhozy, arguing that they are no longer needed as control agencies.[49] Genuine cooperatives might be encouraged.[50] This is the ultimate "solution."

Short of this, the Lairds are by implication urging smaller farms, smaller production work units, and much more decentralization of decision-making and room for personal initiative to flourish. There

104

should be work units and reward systems that promote a clear relationship between individual efforts, final results, and pay. That such ideas
are being explored in depth by Soviet agricultural experts, economists,
and jurists is evident from the materials above and will become the
center of attention in subsequent chapters. How viable would genuine
producer cooperatives be if all the obstacles facing them today in the
Soviet Union—such as output quotas, administrative interference,
shortage of strategic inputs, depressed prices of outputs, and poor
coordination from above—were removed, if the kolkhozy found themselves in an economic environment where everything could be bought
and sold at market price, and if the peasants were free to run their
farms provided the essential structure of the kolkhoz was retained?
This is the question a trio of American economists addressed themselves to. In other words, under market conditions and working
according to pure cooperative theory, how could kolkhozy perform?
The question is relevant to the problem of alternatives to the present
Soviet system and poses the possibility of a less drastic alternative
than total decollectivization. In his model of the kolkhoz under these
conditions, Evsey Domar assumes the kolkhoz pays a fixed rent for
its land, strives to maximize its total profit, and can hire or admit
members and deploy its labor force in response to prices. Domar
concludes that freedom in hiring is quite important to the kolkhoz,
a freedom it today lacks. Nonetheless, inability to fire members in
response to deteriorating market conditions is an inherent disadvan-
tage of the kolkhoz. Domar's "pure model" performs below that of
his comparable competitor capitalist corporate farm, which is based
on hired labor.[51] In light of present realities, Domar recommends
that the Soviets adopt four reforms for the sake of making the present
kolkhozy operate more efficiently: (1) allow material inputs and outputs to be determined by supply and demand; (2) abolish the income
tax on kolkhozy; (3) impose a rent on each farm based on its location,
soil fertility, and other natural conditions; (4) let the kolkhoz hire
or fire labor freely.[52]

A model of the kolkhoz created by Walter Oi and Elizabeth Clayton modifies Domar's to reflect the response of the kolkhoz to market
conditions, by reallocating its work force between the private and
public sectors, and also to reflect response to state quota restraints.
Oi and Clayton also allow for the kolkhoz to fire its members as well
as its hired help. They conclude that a kolkhoz can always achieve
an optimum labor input so long as membership is variable.[53]

The overarching issue with regard to the kolkhoz is whether
its transfiguration into an agaro-industrial complex, or something
intermediate to that penultimate form, is to occur sooner or later and,
although this issue seems to have been blunted of late, whether
kolkhozy would be transformed into sovkhozy. In other words, of what

value are the kolkhozy, as presently constituted, to the regime? What vested interest, if any, does the post-Khrushchev leadership have in them? In the light of recent agricultural policy changes, especially since 1964, it is quite possible that certain advantages that traditionally accrued from the kolkhoz form are no longer accruing. If this is so, the question becomes one of evaluating just why the regime continues to tolerate and even bolster this ideologically inferior form of farm instead of converting them all into sovkhozy.

The ideologically superior form exists as a beacon. As Robert Conquest sees it, the regime has derived four distinct advantages from the kolkhoz system. First, it (collectivization) finally destroyed the power of the peasants to hold the regime up to ransom, that is, to withhold its produce for either the right price or the right goods at the right time. No longer could independent peasants decide how much to sow, what to sow, and at what price to sell. Second, it made possible the extension into the countryside of detailed political control and of methods of labor organization and discipline similar to industry, and, as the Lairds make abundantly clear, this is seen by the Soviets as a good in itself, promoting the industrialization of agriculture and agricultural labor on the basis of the presumption that this is the only way to maximize efficiency and also realize the goal of ending the classic gulf between rural and urban life. Third, it made possible control of the level of peasants' home consumption and thus insured procurements of agricultural produce at terms and quantities dictated by the regime. Finally, it facilitated the mobilization of rural labor resources for large-scale transfers to industry and for colonization of underpopulated areas in Siberia and the Far East.[54]

EXPLOITING THE PEASANTRY

Certainly the peasantry has been housebroken and has in effect become the tributary sector, with a standard of living and status well below that of the industrial workers and, until recently, of the sovkhoz workers. Agriculture was bled for the sake of rapid industrialization, a view even shared by certain non-Soviet marxists.[55] But now that a full-pledged industrial complex has been established, this advantage has lost its meaning. The second advantage, one of the Lairds' "myths presumably still holds sway but is being eroded by the new "economic rationality" and deference to technical experts, except to the extent that political controls must not be sacrificed even for the sake of economic efficiency. The third advantage still applies but it too has been eroded by the dictates of economic rationality. The "carrot" has proved more important than the stick in stimulating more productivity. Higher wages, more and better fringe benefits, state-guaranteed wage system paid at regular intervals, usually monthly, all have contributed to a rising standard of living and a major redistribution of income in favor of the kolkhozniks, so that they are not far below the sovkhoz workers in terms of income derived from the public sector. Yet whereas the kolkhoz form justified the low level of income of kolkhozniks in the past because it was, in theory, due to their own poor efforts, they were, of course, every bit as much under state orders and state plans as the sovkhozy, whose inefficiency was subsidized because they were state enterprises. Yet the kolkhozy were in theory cooperatives and hence not entitled to state subsidies, and their members could not be guaranteed any state-mandated minimum wage or retirement or disability pay. So the kolkhozy had the worst of both worlds—they were totally under state orders yet without any state subsidies. Moreover, as ideologically inferior, they were discriminated against by the state in respect to taxes, credits, procurement prices and investments, and machinery and materials supply. So the macro-economic environment was hostile to them.

Now that many of these unfavorable policies have been withdrawn and the kolkhozy are treated almost on an equal basis with the sovkhozy by the state, what do the differences that remain between sovkhozy and kolkhozy add up to, and why should the regime perpetuate these? In theory the kolkhozy are still self-administered by the collective of workers, so-called kolkhoz democracy. Moreover, the kolkhozy still has more freedom in determining its production tasks, allocating its resultant income and produce free of all but the state-mandated planned target figures, funds, and legislatively defined contributions to the state budget. In other words, the kolkhoz management—although not the kolkhoz rank and file, as the theory of kolkhoz democracy holds—plays a significant role in marketing a proportion of the output and in allocating gross income between investment and consumption. By contrast, in sovkhozy production tasks and investments are mainly state-mandated,[56] and salaries do not in the main depend upon profitability, though sovkhozy are now supposed to be financially self-supporting and are all being put on a khozraschet basis. The sovkhoz director, unlike the kolkhoz president, is appointed rather than elected and is subordinated to his superiors in the trust to which his sovkhoz belongs and, ultimately, to the USSR Ministry of Agriculture.[57]

FAVORING THE SOVKHOZY

Just as the proletariat play the leading role in Soviet society, thus leading the peasantry, so do the sovkhozy officially play the leading role in Soviet agriculture. G. Aksenenok feels that despite the existence of some kolkhozy that operate more efficiently than many sovkhozy, the latter still are the models for the conduct of large-scale socialist agriculture. They are based on a higher form of property, state property.[58] Sovkhozy are asserted to be attuned to the interests of society, not their collective of workers, like the kolkhozy. They are better equipped, and their labor force is supposedly better and is utilized more productively. They have bigger land masses, which presumably makes their operation better economically.[59] Thus they are more multibranched and in better position to utilize complex machinery. They are more profitable, it is claimed by Aksenenok.[60] They have more staff agronomists and zootechnicians. Their labor productivity is allegedly considerably higher than that of kolkhozy, supposedly due to superior technical help and more machinery.[61] Yet all these alleged advantages are far from proving any inherent superiority of sovkhoz over kolkhoz. Seemingly all such statements show is that if you have more and better equipment and more skilled cadres you will do better.

The true test is whether under equal conditions and with equal quality material and manpower, the one type of farm outperforms the other. Nothing decisive has been shown to prove this. In effect, then, the much vaunted superiority of the sovkhoz is simply a product of propaganda and ideological prejudice plus a policy of state preference given to them in respect of supplies, equipment, and fiscal advantages. Erich Strauss concludes that, in numerical terms, there is no evidence whatever of economies of scale in the employment of managerial and technical sovkhoz staff.[62] Whatever advantages through size the generally larger sovkhozy have may very well be matched by kolkhozy of the same size, perhaps indicating that it is not the sovkhoz form that is superior at all. Moreover, the use of new types of links and the introduction of khozraschet within the sovkhozy, which is continually reported in the Soviet press,[63] actually put them operationally closer to the kolkhozy. The April 15, 1967, Pravda carried a decree announcing the initiation of the transfer of sovkhozy to full economic self-reliance. The first group of sovkhozy experimentally placed on this basis were expected to cover all their production costs, productive capital investment, increases in working capital, the formation of incentive funds, and due repayment of bank credit out of their own revenue, but not their housing, cultural, and social amenities bill. In order to enable them to do this, they were to receive for the produce sold to the state the same prices as were established in 1965 for kolkhozy.[64] Although previously indifferent to whether they made a profit or a loss, now sovkhoz management has to generate a profit or lose its only source of investment funds.[65] More and more economic autonomy would be given to them in the future so that in this key area of distinction between kolkhozy and sovkhozy, internal economic independence, the gap was and is narrowing. As Clarke puts it:

the guaranteed pay for kolkhozniks following the introduction of pensions . . . and, on the other hand, the 1967 sovkhoz reform . . . have diminished sharply the difference between the two types of farms. . . . Both . . . will now receive and pay the same prices, including for labor, have more or less the same degree of autonomy . . . and for both the ultimate financial responsibility will rest with the state.[66]

It would seem then that the two types of farm are in fact becoming more like each other. The outstanding difference between the two is reduced to the different managerial systems. All it would take to erode this would be for the chief sovkhozy officers to become officials elected by the sovkhoz workers. There are at times oblique suggestions that this may be done.[67]

In any case, if the trend toward greater use of the market—that is, price policy—as a replacement for detailed central planning, together with more thorough inculcation of khozraschet—that is, close attention to minimizing costs so as to maximize profits—continues and is accompanied by more autonomy for farm managers, and if the gap in pay and fringe benefits between sovkhoz workers and kolkhozniks also continues to close, then it would seem that the distinction between kolkhozy and sovkhozy would be reduced solely to the fact that the kolkhoz was still theoretically operating on the basis of kolkhoz democracy. At this point the American economist Howard Sherman feels all kolkhozy will become sovkhozy, since all income distribution will depend only on wages and on bonuses for high rates of profit ability.[68] What Sherman says is in essence true, but there need be no abolition of the kolkhoz form, since the propaganda value of kolkhoz democracy may, from the regime's standpoint, be worth saving.

NOTES

1. Erich Strauss, Soviet Agriculture in Perspective (New York: Praeger Publishers, 1969), p. 8.
2. Ibid., p. 9.
3. Ibid., p. 21.
4. Ibid., p. 28.
5. Ibid., pp. 28-29.
6. Ibid., p. 29.
7. Lord Walston, Agriculture Under Communism (New York: Capricorn Books, 1968), p. 45.
8. Strauss, op. cit., p. 22.
9. Ibid., p. 33.

10. Ibid., p. 34.

11. Lord Walston, op. cit., p. 44.

12. Roy Laird, "Political and Economic Trends in Soviet Agriculture," in Denis Dirscherl, editor, The New Russia (Dayton, Ohio: Pflaum Press, 1968), pp. 43-44.

13. Ibid., p. 45.

14. Roy and Betty Laird, Soviet Communism and Agrarian Revolution (Baltimore: Penguin Books, 1970), p. 10.

15. Ibid., p. 15.

16. Ibid., pp. 16-17.

17. Ibid., p. 17.

18. Ibid., pp. 17-18.

19. Ibid., p. 18.

20. Michael E. Bradley and M. Gardner Clark, "Supervision and Efficiency in Socialized Agriculture," Soviet Studies XXII, no. 3 (January 1972): 469-470.

21. Ibid., p. 471.

22. Roy and Betty Laird, op. cit., p. 26.

23. Ibid., pp. 26-27

24. Ibid., p. 47.

25. Ibid., p. 50.

26. Ibid., p. 53.

27. Ibid., p. 54.

28. Ibid., p. 57.

29. Ibid., p. 58.

30. Ibid., p. 59.

31. Ibid., p. 60.

32. Ibid., p. 61.

33. Ibid., p. 66.

34. Ibid., p. 74.

35. Ibid., p. 84.

36. Ibid., p. 86.

37. Ibid., p. 88.

38. Ibid., pp. 88-89.

39. Ibid., pp. 90-91.

40. Ibid., p. 93.

41. David W. Conklin, An Evaluation of the Soviet Profit Reforms (New York: Praeger Publishers, 1970), pp. 103-104.

42. Ibid., pp. 106-107.

43. Ibid., pp. 111-112.

44. Andrei Amalrik, Involuntary Journey to Siberia (New York: Harcourt Brace Jovanovich, Inc., 1970), pp. 251-253.

45. Roy and Betty Laird, op. cit., pp. 119-120.

46. Ibid., p. 120.

47. Ibid., p. 121.

48. Ibid., p. 122.
49. Ibid., p. 123.
50. Ibid., p. 125.
51. Evsey Domar, "The Soviet Collective Farm as a Producer Cooperative," The American Economic Review LVI, no. 4 (September 1966): 741 and 749.
52. Ibid., p. 749.
53. Walter Y. Oi and Elizabeth M. Clayton, "A Peasant's View of a Soviet Collective Farm," The American Economic Review LVIII, no. 11 (March 1968): 53.
54. Robert Conquest, Agricultural Workers in the USSR (New York: Praeger Publishers, 1969), pp. 29-30.
55. See Ernest Mandel, Marxist Economic Theory, Vol. II (New York: Monthly Review Press, 1970), p. 575.
56. G. A. Akenenok, Pravovoe Polozhenie Sovkhozov v SSSR (Moscow: Izdat. Akad. Nauk SSSR, 1960), p. 27.
57. Ibid., p. 15.
58. Ibid., p. 13.
59. Ibid., p. 15.
60. Ibid.
61. Iu. Kumachenko, Prevrashchenie Sotsialisticheskoi Sobstvennosti v Kommunisticheskuiu Sobstvennost' (Moscow: Izdat. Mosk.. Univ., 1970), pp. 56-57.
62. Strauss, op. cit., p. 277.
63. See "Knizhka Zven'evogo," in Eknomicheskaia Gazeta, September 1971, p. 11.
64. Roger Clarke, "Soviet Agricultural Reforms Since Khrushchev," Soviet Studies XX no. 2 (October 1968): 163.
65. Ibid., p. 165.
66. Ibid., pp. 176-177.
67. Ekonomika Sotsialisticheskogo Sel'skogo Khoziaistva v Sovremennykh Usloviiakh (Moscow: Izdat. "Ekonomika," 1971), p. 301.
68. Howard J. Sherman, The Soviet Economy (Boston: Little, Brown and Company, 1969), p. 173.

7

THE RURAL
POPULATION OUTFLOW

Questions about the quantity and quality of the agricultural work force are being posed today in the Soviet academic press in connection with the problem of increasing efficiency on the farms and especially increasing the productivity of labor on the kolkhozy. Whereas there is a tendency to reduce this very complex socioeconomic problem to one of simply coming up with the right mix of administrative control, ideological exhortations, and material incentives, more serious students of the problem have proceeded to a more total critique of the poor material conditions found on the average kolkhoz and in the countryside in general. There is increasing use of field investigations seeking the opinions of country dwellers and kolkhozniks.

THE URBAN-RURAL BALANCE

To start with, the birth rate in the countryside has traditionally been and still is higher than in cities of the USSR. However, there has taken place during the period 1959-67 a lowering of the birth rate in the rural areas. This is explained by the economist V. N. Iakimov as a result of the sharp worsening in the age structure of the agricultural population and the consequent effect on marriages. Also, the educational and skill level among the agricultural population is much lower than that among the urban population.[1] Farm workers' children start work in the public sector significantly earlier than do city children.[2] In 1966, 69.5 percent of all kolkhozniks had less than a seven-year education.[3] Iakimov feels that an increase in skills, cultural level, and mechanization of labor among the rural population will accelerate the tendency to have fewer children.[4] Hence, quantitatively the forecast is for continued contraction in the rural population.

112

In 1926 the city population constituted some 26.3 million and the rural population 120 million.[5] As of 1967, the respective figures were 130.9 million and 105.8 million.[6]

As to long-term migration trends, for the thirty-two years between the censuses of 1926 and 1959, the city population increased by more than 70 million; 63 percent of this growth occurred directly as a result of the migration of agricultural population into the city and 27 percent as an indirect result of this.[7] From 1959 to 1964, 8.4 million village inhabitants left for towns.[8] Looked at from another perspective, from 1939 to 1965 the population of the USSR increased by 20 percent, but the village population decreased by 17 percent. For the period from 1951 to 1964 the number of kolkhozniks decreased by 8.4 million.[9] One study concluded that the most important motives for both intrarural and rural-city migration are, first, to change jobs, second, to continue one's general or special education and, third, to improve the material and cultural domestic conditions of one's life.[10] These outflows should continue in the near future, since it is practically inconceivable that the regime can create educational facilities and enough incentives in the form of higher pay for farm jobs and much greater village amenities to offset the causes for migration.

In general, the city or urban population constituted in 1969 56 percent and the rural population 44 percent of the total population.[11] As of 1970, kolkhozniks constituted approximately 20 percent of the population.[12]

RURAL OVERPOPULATION AND AGRICULTURAL LABOR PRODUCTIVITY

Unlike industry, whose growth is accompanied by an increase in its work force, the growth of agricultural production is accompanied by a decrease in the size of its work force. From 1960 to 1968 the agricultural work force was reduced from 26.1 million to 23.8 million.[13] In 1968 the gross produce of agriculture of the USSR grew by comparison with 1913 by 2.9 times and the number of agricultural workers decreased by 2.5 times. And, unlike the workers, the kolkhozniks share in the total labor force is gradually lessening: in 1940, 44.2 percent; 1950, 44 percent; 1955, 37.1 percent; 1960, 30 percent; 1965, 20.5 percent; 1968, 17.3 percent. According to the economist V. F. Melnikov, the essence of the problem of labor resources in agriculture is no longer how to speed up the outflow reserves but rather how, in the first place, to secure better able-bodied young cadres, especially machine operators, and secondly, to more fully and rationally use the presently available labor resources.[14] Actually there has never been a manpower shortage in Soviet agriculture. In fact, the problem has been quality rather than quantity. There are too many unskilled and not enough with technical training. One typical soviet sociological study classifies the kolkhozniks into three groups according to their jobs and skills. The first is the engineer-technician and administrative-directing personnel, those with higher and intermediate education. These are said to constitute 6 to 9 percent of all kolkhozniks. Second are the mechanizers, the machine operators and truck drivers, constituting approximately 10 to 13 percent of all kolkhozniks. The rest are all those without specialized education, predominantly manual laborers.[15] And, due to the very poor living conditions in rural areas, those who can, want to leave, especially the young. So the work force in the country tends to get older, with a disproportionately high number of those leaving being in the younger age brackets. This is a world-wide phenomenon, and so in the Soviet situation it is a matter of the degree. Since the young are the better-educated element in the rural areas, this further undermines the quality of the rural work force.[16] Because of the priority given to industry, capital investments for agriculture were extremely low, and this capital starvation lasted well into the early 1960s. As a result, the level of mechanization, as well as its quality, was and is woefully low. Moreover, the rural infrastructure—production buildings sheds, animal shelters, storage buildings, and roads—is poorly developed. Erich Strauss notes that the mechanization of animal husbandry is in its infancy and cites a 1965 figure indicating that in that year only 27 percent of the cows on all the farms were machine milked and feeding and manure disposal were almost always carried out by hand. By 1970 mechanized milking was up to 56 percent.[17] This lavish use of manual labor, Strauss concludes, is one of the main causes of the high cost of meat, dairy produce, and eggs.[18] He also feels that there is an almost unlimited need for capital investments in such things as buildings, electrification, equipment machinery, and higher quality feeds in order to create favorable conditions for a cut in the labor component of meat, milk, and eggs.

The Belgian Marxist economic theorist Ernest Mandel believes that in the absence of adequate mechanization and of extensive investment in fertilizers and infrastructural works (for example, roads, silos, and storage facilities), complete collectivization of agricultural holdings produced harmful economic and social effects. Output has been depressed and it was necessary to create a bulky apparatus of kolkhoz officialdom, the cost of which reduced the margin of accumulation of the farms above and beyond the exploitative terms of exchange unilaterally imposed on the farms by the state.[19] Certainly one can agree with Mandel that this was one of the causes, but certainly not the main one.

Erich Strauss cites data indicating that the milk yield per cow for the whole of Soviet agriculture in the record year 1966 was less than half the average yield of the best dairying countries, and the live weight of cattle at slaughter is considerably lower compared with the United States and England. The number of piglets per sow is very low compared to advanced agricultural countries, as is the average number of eggs per laying hen.[20] Strauss credits expensive feeds as contributing to the high costs of Soviet livestock produce[21] and suggests that more livestock products could be produced from smaller herds and flocks with a substantial improvement in the utilization of feed.[22]

Soviet agriculture claimed only a 5.6 percent growth rate for the period from 1950 to 1958 and only 1.1 percent growth rate for 1958 to 1963. A 1971 Soviet economics book reports that approximately 29 percent of all the able-bodied population works in agriculture, and that this group creates a corresponding share of the national income. Another more recent Soviet source states that the agricultural sector creates approximately one-third of the national income.[23] The official statistical handbook for 1970 shows 27 percent of the labor force engaged in agriculture. Agriculture also absorbs about 20 percent of all basic production funds (capital stock).[24] It emerges that the USSR uses far more land and labor than the United States in agricultural production. Almost all Soviet crops yields per acre for the same crops are much lower than United States yields, as are the Soviet yields per worker. And the farm share of total employment in the United States is only 7 percent, whereas it is 38 percent in the USSR. Howard Sherman observes from the figures on United States and USSR material inputs into agriculture that the reason for the greater use and lower productivity of labor in Soviet agriculture is that the Soviets use far fewer tractors, trucks, and combines and less electricity and fertilizers. A recent Soviet source states that as of 1964 for every thousand hectares of ploughland in the United States, there were approximately thirty-four tractors, as opposed to eight in the USSR, and the figures for hauling trucks were twenty-two and four respectively. For each thousand hectares of sown grain in the United States, there were three times more combines.[25] Yet Sherman believes that this is not the whole answer to why Soviet farm labor productivity is so low. Organizational and incentive problems also play a role.[26] And low labor productivity is also in part due to the poor quality of labor, that is, a lack of skilled mechanics, machine operators, and the advanced age of the rural work force and the large number of women in this force. In 1959 women constituted 57 percent of all kolkhozniks employed in nonspecialized or unskilled work.[27] It is to the problem of poor quality of the rural work force that we now turn.

RURAL OUTFLOW AND THE SPECIALIST PROBLEM

Today 40 percent of all workers participating in the sphere of material production are in agriculture. Almost one-third of the whole national income and up to 30 percent of net income are created by Soviet agriculture.[28] The rural infrastructure is freely acknowledged as poor by the Soviet literature. Too many jobs are still manual, and yearly 5 to 8 million men are occupied in loading and unloading operations in agriculture, which accounts for 20 to 30 percent of the cost of agricultural produce.[29] Approximately 75 percent of all kolkhozniks as of 1963 were involved in manual labor.[30] The poor condition of roads in rural areas makes normal exchanges very difficult and leads to quick wearing out of auto and other transportation equipment plus supplementary expenses for repair, all of which increases the cost of produce. Hard-surfaced road building to alleviate this problem over the next ten to fifteen years is estimated to need expansion to four or five times the present capacity.[31] But the growth of the skill level of the rural labor force is emphasized. For the period from 1959 to 1968 the skill level of agricultural cadres is proclaimed to have risen significantly. The segment of kolkhozniks with higher and intermediate education is said to have grown by almost seventeen times. The number of specialists with diplomas working in agricultural enterprises increased from 65,000 in 1940 to 821,000 in 1968. By 1980 the number of specialists with higher and intermediate education in all specialties should reach over 1.3 million. There have already been significant changes in the quality of managing cadres of kolkhozy. Statistically now 78.1 percent of kolkhoz presidents and 94.7 percent of sovkhoz directors have completed higher and intermediate specialized education. But there is acknowledged to be an acute shortage of engineering-technical middle link personnel.[32] Yet it is admitted that in 1963 farm labor productivity went down as to grain and sugar beet, and that for the periods from 1961 to 1963 and from 1967 to 1969, the productivity of labor in RSFSR sovkhozy with regard to grain went down.[33] So the specialist shortage is acknowledged. Let us look at this problem in more depth.

The specialist shortage is tied to the problem of the outflow of the young from rural areas to the cities in quest of greater opportunities and to escape the scarcity of domestic services and the cultural poverty of the typical rural area.[34] One Soviet economist holds that the generally poorer pension provisions for kolkhozniks has been a major cause of both the specialist and youth outflow.[35] The Soviet economist Iakimov pinpoints the most intensive outflow as occurring in the sixteen- to twenty-seven- or twenty-eight-year-old age group.[36] A non-Soviet economist claims that the agricultural outflow applies almost exclusively to the working section of the population, especially its younger part, with almost two-thirds of the net balance of migrants to the towns being in the fifteen to twenty-nine age group.[37] Another Soviet study of western Siberia finds that of those leaving for the cities, more than 72 percent were between sixteen and thirty years of age.[38] Yet another west Siberian study finds that two-thirds of the outflow falls in the under thirty age category.[39] If the rate of youth leaving the farms is approximately the same for both kolkhozy and sovkhozy, then the kolkhozy would be worse off because they have less skilled staff on the average per thousand employed than the sovkhozy. For each 1,000 workers in kolkhozy production in 1960, there were 79 mechanizers (machine-operators) and in 1968, 106. The same figures for the same years for the sovkhozy were 135 and 160.[40] Since the living conditions, employment benefits, and work regimes are inferior on the kolkhozy in comparison to the sovkhozy as a whole, one would expect that a disproportionately large amount of the rural outflow comes from the kolkhozy.

When one looks at the number of those with higher or intermediate education per 1,000 population of kolkhozniks and industrial workers, one finds that, as of 1959, the figure for the workers was 451 and for the kolkhozniks, 226. In 1967 the corresponding figures were 594 and 330.[41] As of today, for every 1,000 in industry, there are 116 engineering-technical workers, whereas in agriculture, in general, there are 3.4. This is obviously a tremendous gap. Moreover, as if the shortage of skilled workers in agriculture is not enough, there is acknowledged to be a great problem in that there is too much fluidity among farm guiding personnel. Bulavin states that the length of service of kolkhoz and sovkhoz heads in the majority of cases does not exceed three years, whereas in the average industrial enterprise the manager's tenure is six to seven years.[42] Another source indicates that out of each hundred specialists working in kolkhozy and sovkhozy of west Siberia, who are obliged to begin work there at the end of their studies, yearly fifteen to sixteen leave and thirteen to fourteen of these go to the city. The average work length of the specialist in agriculture in the region of west Siberia in recent years has been seven years. This outflow is supposed to have decreased after the March 1965 Central Committee Plenum.[43]

Obviously the lack of stability of leadership on the farms can undermine performance to some extent. Moreover, it is indicative of underlying problems. It is interesting that Bulavin does not attempt to explain why this situation exists but rather simply considers it a negative phenomenon. Of course it would be easy to attribute it to the generally unattractive conditions on the farms and the rather arduous challenge of making backward kolkhozy into progressive ones without sufficient machinery, investments, and so on. And it would be helpful if we knew where those who leave farm headships go —to other farms in the same capacity or, perhaps, into the state agricultural bureaucracy. In other words, how many of these shifts can be considered punishment for failure or promotions or neither reward or punishment? No Soviet materials I have seen speculate on or discuss this.

The situation is improving in respect to the skill level of managerial personnel. Bulavin states that the number of persons with higher and intermediate education among brigadiers and livestock farm managers in kolkhozy increased from 5.3 percent in 1959 to 15.5 percent in 1960. The figure in 1969 for analogous sovkhoz personnel was 22 percent.[44] Still, despite such selective and moderate upgrading, the main problem has not been attacked. Bulavin admits that in agriculture in general, and especially among kolkhozy, with each year there are fewer and fewer able-bodied workers in the eighteen to forty age group.[45] He concludes that the quantity and especially the quality of all agricultural cadres still does not answer contemporary demands and continues to lag well behind in terms of average skill levels of all other sectors. Moreover, the outflow mainly involves the more qualified, that is, the most essential element.[46] According to an American economist, the late Jerry Karcz, the flight of the young from the farms has driven the average age of the farmers presently up to fifty years, and the share of the able-bodied in the general declining rural population of the Russian Republic dropped from 54 percent in 1959 to 47 percent in 1967. Karcz cites Soviet data that state that only 17 percent of the rural youngsters who continue their education choose agricultural curricula.[47] Karcz ventures the thought that serious local shortages of manpower may have been one of the reasons why the new kolkhoz Model Charter did not grant kolkhozniks outright freedom to leave the farm.[48] A Soviet source states that the average age of the agricultural population in European districts of the USSR for the period from 1955 to 1965 rose from thirty-six to thirty-eight to forty-six.[49]

THE SEASONALITY OF LABOR PROBLEM

Erich Strauss focuses on the acutely seasonal character of agricultural labor as a major cause of its low productivity in the USSR. He cites 1959 data on the number of kolkhozniks and their families working in public agriculture as varying from 18 million in January to 30.7 million in July. Ironically, during work peaks outside labor is needed temporarily, say for harvest,[50] whereas during the long slack periods during the long winter and autumn, there is a great deal of rural employment. Strauss sees growing

118

mechanization of labor plus the increased emphasis on livestock production as helping to correct this. So will the development of subsidiary enterprises on the farms and the bringing of new industry into the rural areas to provide off-season employment, thus obviating the need to migrate seasonally in search of work and also making for more productive use of the underemployed or unemployed potentially migratory rural labor force.[51] One Soviet text on kolkhoz economics lays down the role that the greater the weight of livestock production on a farm the less the seasonality of labor problem. Hence farms should try to increase livestock components. The text also recommends improving the structure of field crops so that sowing and harvesting periods do not coincide and limited machinery will not be spread thin.[52] Bulavin refers to the problem of "industrializing" agricultural labor, that is, essentially converting the largely manual into machine labor.[53] Bulavin analyzes the problem and makes some suggestions for improving the situation. At the root of the problem is the dependence of the economic process of reproduction on the biological process of reproduction in agriculture. For the maturation of the winter wheat nature mandates 270-350 days, whereas the actual work period associated with it does not exceed twenty-five or twenty-six days. For sunflowers the natural process takes eighty to ninety days and the work time only three to five days. Of course climatic conditions are the major variable here as to the length of the biological process, but they also affect the work period. The seasonality of work leads to a significant part of the means of production. especially cultivators, harvest machinery, and so on, remaining unused for long periods in the course of a year, which results in certain maintenance problems.[54] But the seasonality problem's main impact is on the use of the work force. Bulavin states that for July 1968 the kolkhozy of the USSR used on the average 61 to 82 percent of their members. Huge masses of agricultural labor, especially on the kolkhozy, are not utilized, a euphemism for their being unemployed. According to Bulavin. in the winter of 1952 in USSR kolkhozy, 13.2 million did not work. In the winter of 1959 the figure was 12.7 million and in the winter of 1967-68 over ten million.[55] In another study of kolkhozy, one-fourth of the adult able-bodied kolkhoznik in winter were almost entirely unoccupied in the public sector.[56] It seems obvious from these figures that agricultural underemployment or unemployment has not been substantially reduced over the last decade and a half despite the much heralded campaigns to industrialize labor, consolidate the kolkhozy, convert some kolkhozy into sovkhozy, and develop subsidiary enterprises on the farms. The creation of more agraro-industrial complexes—which would exchange temporarily unneeded workers from farm to nearby factory and vice versa, especially to factories dependent on agricultural raw materials that flow in only seasonally—has also been suggested.[57]

Bulavin bemoans the inability to harness agricultural labor to that strict subordination to the production process characteristic of industry. In order to make agricultural labor more productive and less arduous he suggests going over to two-shift work wherever feasible.[58] Another unique problem of agriculture with no analogue in industrial production and one that negatively affects the productivity of agricultural labor is the dispersal of the production units over large areas, thus necessitating tremendous expenditures of nonproductive work time and resources on trips to and from work sites.[59] Although he cites with relish the statistic that by mechanization of milking one milkmaid could service thirty to fifty cows instead of the present ten to twelve through hand-milking, still he does not address himself to the problem of what to do with the manpower released by mechanization. Can it be productively absorbed on the farm, or should the rural outflow be encouraged but on a more selective basis? Bulavin does not discuss the optimal size of farm work forces. He simply reiterates the more conventional Soviet line that combines of agricultural processing with agricultural production (factory farms) will save society transportation costs, reduce spoilage, and better utilize by-products[60] and that industrial enterprises on the farms will better utilize farm labor all year round[61] and import to kolkhozniks industrial skills, thus accelerating the fusion of the farmers with the workers.[62]

The Soviet economist V. N. Iakimov, in grappling with the problem of kolkhoz labor resources and their effectiveness, emphasizes the variability in the number of man days worked per year according to jobs on the kolkhoz. According to his figures, the average able-bodied kolkhoznik worked 195 man days in 1967. This is a bit misleading, he feels, because there are more women—53 percent—among this group and they, significantly more than men, expend time on the subsidiary economy and domestic work, and thus in 1967 each able-bodied kolkhoznik worked 173 days in the public economy but the able-bodied male worked 221.[63] Administrative personnel on kolkhozy work 298 man days; brigadiers in crop growing, 309; tractorists, 218; livestock workers, 305; hand workers in crop production, 181.[64] Out of all kolkhoz workers in 1967 approximately 25 percent were specialists and skilled workers, 18 to 19 percent semiskilled, and 56 to 57 percent unskilled. In 1965 in kolkhoz production, mechanized labor constituted only 15 percent of all labor performed. The figure for sovkhozy was 24 percent and for industry, 40 percent.[65] It would seem, then, on the basis of this data, that although there are relatively few skilled and semiskilled workers on kolkhozy, there is a waste of their talents because there is not enough mechanized work for them to perform. This would, in part, seem to account for the inclination of specialists to leave the farms. And Iakimov concludes that part of the outflow of youth problem is due to the impossibility today for kolkhozy to utilize the skills of the better educated youngsters.[66] Yet all he can offer as advice is an exhortation to kolkhozy to better utilize their underemployed work force.[67] Iakimov thus documents the overwhelming dominance of unskilled hand labor in agriculture and the inability, given the present low level of mechanization, to utilize the more skilled on the farms. He does not face up to the implications of this—the youth exodus must continue, especially of those with some skill. Moreover, the fluidity of specialists problem will remain. And the age structure will worsen with the average age of the agricultural worker getting higher, and the number of women in the total increasing, all this negatively affecting the productivity of labor.

The question emerges, should the Soviets encourage the un-skilled farmers to leave the farms at this point, in order to implement a policy of quality instead of quantity? The problem with the rural outflow is that it is in good measure an outflow of the skilled and more able-bodied. Could the underemployed on the farms be more profitably made use of in other sectors of the economy? Or is not the rural underemployment a necessary part of the policy of under-investing in agricultural equipment and the necessary rural infrastructure? Perhaps the constant lament over the outflow of the youth and the specialists has a hollow ring in that there is an awareness that, given the costs involved in overcoming this, the regime is not prepared to pay it. Yet it piously drones on about how agricultural labor must be industrialized when it is not willing to make the expenditures that this policy requires. What it is really concerned about in the short run is the falling productivity of agricultural labor because of the losses of the young and semiskilled through the outflow and also the bad effect of such a phenomenon on the morale of the remaining farmers and the poor image it gives to the Soviet agricultural system. Basically the regime is still wedded to the "quantitative" approach in farm labor, at least as long as labor costs in the form of salaries and fringe benefits can be kept down so that under-utilized farm labor, especially on the kolkhozy, is not paid "full-time" wages by the state. The underutilized still, in effect, subsidize themselves by indulging in private subsidiary economy in the slack periods. Even with the new guaranteed wages for kolkhozniks, the state does not really bear the brunt of the kolkhoz labor bill, and thus it can still afford to let three do the job of one, since it refuses to pay for the machine that would render the two extra pairs of hands superfluous. Of course, if a more sophisticated macro-economic calculation were made here, the regime might become aware that it is paying a high price for agriculture's backwardness and its decision to rely on sheer manpower, however inefficient in terms of productivity per man. For bad morale on the farms and the consequent loss in maximal productivity affect other sectors of the economy, especially light industry and foodstuffs, causing periodic food shortages that ultimately may cause politically adverse effects.

The Soviets are still adhering to a "minimalist" approach to agricultural production for a complex of reasons. By this I mean that they are satisfied by a combination of positive and negative incentives, although clearly the stick predominates over the carrot, to force agriculture to come up with as much as is considered minimally adequate to feed the population, supply industry with raw materials, and provide necessary reserves. In some years targets have been overly ambitious in terms of past targets and present capabilities, and given the overall system of controls from above, irrational price policy, lack of infrastructure and capital investment, bad wage policy, and the consequent distortions at the micro level by managers and farmers so as to beat or befuddle the system. There is little evidence of any enthusiasm for a rethinking of the problems the system as presently constituted spawns. Maximalization of productivity and production seems to be thought of only in terms of ferreting out hidden capacities and slack sectors within the present system. The West German Karl-Eugen Wadekin opines that a drastic shrinkage of the agricultural labor force is to be expected if Soviet economic development is successful.[68] In other words, agricultural labor productivity must increase. But this does not mean, according to Wadekin, that the outflow of the young need not be checked, not to speak of encouraged. Wadekin feels that if it is not checked, the lack of agricultural labor will increase rapidly and catastrophically. This is so because the outflow of the young affects that part of the farm labor force that must not only compensate for the thinning ranks of the older workers, but offer qualitatively the possibility of achieving a rising agricultural production despite a shrinking labor force.[69] And, if there is an increase in the average skill and cultural level of the farmers, Soviet economists are aware that birth rate would tend to fall off.[70] Thus at such a point the regime would be seemingly irrevocably committed to a "labor productivity" approach and all that implies in the way of investments in machinery and amenities for the rural areas and a loosening of central controls, with the consequent economic autonomy of local farm leaders threatening to spill over into political channels. If the qualitative approach to farm labor were taken and the regime later had second thoughts, nothing less than a "second collectivization" trauma would be necessary to reimpose the old order by forcing ex-farmers back on the farms and holding down those already there.

Wadekin suggests that the regime had better, if it wishes to choose quality over quantity in farm labor policy, train the skilled and semiskilled workers before the bulk of material inputs in the form of new machinery, fertilizers, equipment, and so on, is given out. He feels that all these remain largely ineffective without the necessary trained personnel, and perhaps this does explain how in the last decade and a half the new upsurge in farm equipment production has wrought so little a change in labor productivity. Wadekin's belief is that the more modern the means and methods of agricultural production applied, or to be applied, the greater becomes the need for trained personnel. For example, Wadekin says the application of insecticides and pesticides is severely hampered by the lack of people who know how to handle them properly. The intensification of socialized agricultural production, he concludes, is impossible without a great number of trained specialists and managers.[71]

As Wadekin sees it, many Soviet rural areas are in such a poor state that the success of big investments could bring greater and quicker yields in other sectors of the economy. He feels that only big investments in agriculture can head off the need to import food.[72] Wadekin's conclusion on the Soviet rural manpower crisis is:

> The problem . . . has grown into a social crisis which in our opinion cannot be healed by economic measures alone. The outlow from the land, typical in itself of any industrialization, has been distorted by the effects of Stalin's and Khrushchev's agricultural policy. Socially and demographically, the critical movement has only just arrived. . . . The agricultural measures of Brezhnev and Kosygin are a last attempt to overcome the crisis of Soviet agriculture by conventional means, so to speak.[73]

RECENT SOVIET RESEARCH ON THE CAUSES OF RURAL OUTFLOW

Recent Soviet research on agricultural migration indicates that the number of persons oriented toward city life increases from the older to the younger, from persons without education to the more educated, from natives of the locality to those with a rich experience of geographic mobility. And their instability indicates that, in perspective, the share of the urban-oriented will increase.[74] As for the motivation for this urban orientation, the most fundamental reasons were found to be the desire to improve one's work conditions and the possibility of getting education.[75] When these general motives were further investigated in Novosibirsk Oblast of west Siberia, it was found that among those who migrated there was most likely to be a negative attitude to heavy manual labor.[76] The second most important source of dissatisfaction of those likely to migrate in this study was found to be their low level of pay.[77] A quarter of kokhozniks polled in a study of Kuban kolkhozniks by a Soviet sociologist reported they were dissatisfied with their unskilled manual labor.[78]

A source of discontent among the young workers, but also of general applicability, was found to be apathy toward the results of their work. They did not feel like co-owners of the kolkhoz, as in theory they are, but rather like hired help. Their alienation is expressed not only in their work but also in the withdrawal from any participation in administrative offices of the kolkhoz.[79] A survey conducted by sociologists in Kalinin Oblast in the Tatar Republic indicates that contrary to the notion that the kolkhoz as a cooperative has the advantage of institutionalizing rank-and-file participation to a far greater extent than state enterprises, kolkhozniks felt uninfluential in respect to the making of important decisions to a far more significant extent that did sovkhoz and industrial workers.[80] These revelations seem to confirm the views of the Lairds. The Soviet study making this finding suggests as a method of overcoming this alienation the organization of mechanized brigades and also of smaller links. Workers, especially the young, were found to be more interested in their work and derived more satisfaction from it when in links. Part of this was attributable to their independent decision-making role in these units and a heightened feeling of collectivism and responsibility for the land and equipment under their care.[81]

In yet another in-depth Soviet sociological field study of three kolkhozy, this finding was confirmed. The link system was found to raise the levels of care for the land entrusted to a particular group and as conducive to liquidating impersonality and irresponsibility. And this is believed to be not only economical but positive in moral-psychological terms. It personalizes responsibility for the land. Moreover, this study confirms the general data on the "flight of youth" problem. It indicates that on the three investigated kolkhozy the average age of workers studied was over forty and that the numbers of youth in the age group sixteen to twenty-nine constituted no more than 8 to 10 percent of the adult kolkhozniks.[82]

Another major cause of discontent among rural youth who want to leave or have left is the length of the work day. Few have only a seven-hour day, and youth seem to want a five-day week. The study regards a two-shift work system already introduced in Sverdlovsk Oblast as very successful in livestock farms, especially as to milkmaids. Also, sanitary and hygienic conditions and the physical heaviness of agricultural labor are much complained of, especially from the unskilled and semiskilled.[83] In the study of three kolkhozy, the least satisfied with their work were field crop workers.[84] Field workers said their work was tiresome and unvaried, and they had to

work in poor weather. Especially arduous is sugar beet work.[85]
Soviet investigators have found that young people who have not finished
their school education are generally among the most discontented. Most
of them are aware of the great income differential between themselves
and the managerial personnel of their kolkhoz, or the urban workers.[86]
Wadekin feels that it is a common attitude of the young to regard it
as a disgrace to remain in the village, since agricultural work is
mainly physical and thus below them.[87]

An examination of the mechanizers of both sovkhozy and kolkhozy of Novosibirsk Oblast by Soviet experts showed that two-thirds
of them were fully satisfied by their work, its social prestige, its
creativity, the high qualifications they have, and their pay. The study
concludes that this satisfaction was based on an understanding on
their part of the social significance of their work. But of the un-
satisfied minority the study showed that dissatisfaction increases
with the amount of education.[88] Wadekin feels that although manual
labor is spurned as menial by youth and mechanizers enjoy prestige,
still the young consider agricultural mechanized work less desirable
than other technical work, apparently since so many mechanizers,
many of them young, are leaving the farms.[89]

Wadekin raises two other points of interest—the particularly
intense discontent of livestock workers and the sex imbalance problem
within the farm work force. Livestock workers, he relates, are notorious for having an extremely long work day and too few days off.
Not only is mechanization of their work minimal, but it is also difficult for them to improve their qualifications.[90] They make more than
field workers, but only because they work more and longer man days,
and this has the side effect of taking away much of the time necessary
for house work and for private agricultural activities on their garden
plots. And this indirectly reduces their supplemental income. Especially resented by them is the so-called interrupted work day,
which means that idle hours in a normal daily cycle of work in animal
husbandry are not paid in working time, although people cannot generally make use of these "breaks" or dead time. Wadekin cites the
case of a milkmaid's work day consisting of only 57 percent actual
work time. On the average the trip from home to the stables and back
takes two or more hours.[91] Wadekin feels that this explains why
milkmaids usually have to get up very early—at 3:00, 4:00, 5:00 a.m.
—and return home late at night. The problem has resulted in much
talk of late of introducing two shifts and a five-day week. Wadekin
concludes that all this accounts for the fact that many people are not
inclined to take livestock jobs despite its usually higher pay. It is
mostly girls or single elderly women who take such jobs.[92] A recent
Soviet economics book discusses two-shift work in livestock as growing, but cautions that in doing so the general level of pay for workers

involved in it should not decrease, which means that they must be more productive per work unit than previously. But without mechanization this does not seem likely to happen, and hence the increased productivity of labor precondition to installing two-shift work would seem to forestall any wholesale imminent implementation.[93]

As for the problem of sexual imbalance, of the total kolkhoz population, 57.1 percent is female. Wadekin feels that the rural exodus is mainly a male exodus, especially because "male" kinds of work were most susceptible to mechanization, for example, plowing, sowing, and reaping, while work in animal husbandry was least mechanized and traditionally predominantly "female." Now there is a deficit of males in the agricultural population. The younger and more skilled males tend to leave, leaving behind the older unskilled men. In sovkhozy the situation is similar but less extreme because of the more favorable age and sex structure there and because of the higher degree of mechanization of field work.[94] Wadekin concludes that the lower stratum in kolkhozy society is predominant female.[95]

THE KOSTROMA EXPERIMENT

Alexander Yanov describes the experiment conducted by the Kostroma party organization to retain young kolkhozviks. Administrative measures, such as the passport system, were rejected. Instead privileges were guaranteed to the young, such as a level of pay surpassing anything they could expect in the city. Obviously this was quite expensive and created some anger on the part of older, more experienced hands, who would be earning less than the favored youngsters. But Yanov reports it succeeded. Yanov goes on to identify three separate streams of youth that flow out of the rural areas. First, those school dropouts who fail to complete their eight-year schooling. They take city jobs that urban youth find unattractive. Yanov reports that it is this group that is most easily influenced by means of guaranteed pay and material and housing privileges dangled in front of them by the Kostroma experiment. The second stream is recruited from the fourteen- and fifteen-year-olds who have completed the eight grade but who at this age are still entirely under their parents' thumb, and the parents usually send them to fill the craft and factory schools in the cities, looking down on agricultural work and wishing their children a better future. To undo this requires the erosion of the negative image of the peasant in the minds of the parents. And, finally, the smallest stream is the graduates of secondary schools, the potential transformers of rural life. They almost all leave to become skilled specialists. Ninety percent of middle management personnel on farms have only elementary education. This testifies to the flight of group three. Yanov goes on to advocate contracting the use of the piece-work system for farm work because it overlooks the quality of work. In so doing he attacks the brigade form of organization of labor because it enshrines the piece-work system. What he advocates is the unassigned mechanized link, studied in the Kostroma experiment. This form is oriented toward the independence, initiative, and intelligence of workers, so that they are creators rather than robots. With this form of work teams, he holds, every inch of land acquires a specific, collective master. This form, he claims, revives for the farmer-collective all the integrity of the production cycle. This, he urges, is a contemporary form of labor that the contemporary kolkhoz's gifted and intelligent young people need.[96] Here, then, we find the link advocated as a method of stemming the outflow of the young rather than primarily as a method for increasing productivity.

Another negative aspect of the shortage of skilled machine operators caused by the outflow problem is the necessity of relying on transient machine operators at harvest time. They often arrive late and find equipment in bad shape. Moreover, they feel no obligation to do a good job, since for them it is often a one-shot proposition. Nor do they take good care of the machinery entrusted to them, since they will not be there to answer for its condition.[97]

Thus the rural exodus is continuing, and it is resulting in an increasingly older, predominantly female and unskilled, underemployed, undereducated work force with poor morale and low productivity and relatively low pay, increasingly aware of the disparity between their conditions of life and those of the more fortunate and much admired urban population. The rural youth are alienated and regard farming as menial and unchallenging. It is unrealistic to assume that even with the best intentions, the rural infrastructure necessary to dramatically transform rural life into something comparable to urban life is attainable in the near future, and meanwhile the frustrations of a much more ambitious, better-educated, and better-informed youth, as well as older specialists, build up. Soviet students of the problem tend to denigrate the traditional answer to this problem, administrative controls to hold them down on the farms—internal passports, registration of arrivees in urban areas, the illegality of industry hiring kolkhozniks not properly released by the kolkhoz.[98] There is the weapon of agricultural resettlement, a concept encompassing the relocation of both urban and rural populations to certain areas where new lands are being opened up. Supposedly voluntary, state agencies yearly carry out resettlement and grant new settlers tax, credit, and land use benefits.[99] Is this denigration of such methods because they genuinely feel such techniques are outmoded or simply not fruitful solutions to the underlying problem, or is it simply masking embarrassment over the continued use of such policies, since this amounts to a confession of failure to win over the peasantry voluntarily to the agricultural system after so many decades? Again, the absence of an unequivocal, explicit right to leave the kolkhoz in the new kolkhoz Model Charter is indicative of a possible reluctance to risk all on a positive policy of winning over the great majority of the peasantry to the virtue of staying put. Still, the new realism on the issue is apparent in the guaranteed wage and new pension and social security reforms, all increasing the benefits to kolkhozniks. And it is becoming more common in Soviet literature to see the admonition of agricultural experts to the effect that only after material interests of kolkhozniks are satisfied can the role of moral stimuli grow.[100] Thus the regime is being counseled that concrete material improvements must come before and instead of propagandistic exhortations to work harder and longer and with a communist spirit, although the latter approach costs far less. Yet there is another dimension to the flight of the young, educated, and skilled. How real can "kolkhoz democracy" be when the thin veneer of experts is subservient to the all-powerful kolkhoz chairman, while the best element below escape to the cities? There is left only the passivity of the old, and the very young, the lazy and unambitious, and a high proportion of women, all of which does not add up to a very effective curb on the arbitrariness or unwisdom of the powerful kolkhoz chairman.[101] Such then is the present posture of the discussion of this rather pressing problem as viewed by both Soviet and non-Soviet sources. One is left with the impression that the Soviets are indeed continuing to pay a high price for their continuing marriage to the myth of voluntary collectivization.

NOTES

1. Problemy Izmeneniia Sotial'noi Struktury Sovetskogo Obshchestva (Moscow: Izdat. "Nauka," 1968), p. 163.
2. V. N. Iakimov, Problemy Trudovykh Resursov Kolkhozov (Moscow: Izdat. "Ekonomika," 1969), pp. 11-12.
3. Arthur Adams and Jan Adams, Men Versus Systems (New York: The Free Press, 1971), p. 29.
4. Iakimov, op. cit., p. 15.
5. S. I. Semin, Razvitie Obshchestvenno-Ekonomicheskykh Otnoshenii v Kolkhozakh (Moscow: Izdat Nauka, 1968), p. 197.
6. Migratsiia Sel'skogo Naseleniia (Moscow: Izdat. Myl', 1970), p. 4.
7. Karl-Eugen Wadekin, "Manpower in Soviet Agriculture," Soviet Studies XX, No. 3 (January 1969): 286.

8. V. M. Alekseeva, Razvitie Soiuza Rabochikh i Krest'ian v Period Perekhoda k Kommunizmu (Leningrad: Izdat Leningradskogo Univ., 1967), p. 19.

9. Migratsiia Sel'skogo Naseleniia, p. 8.

10. Ekonomika Sotsialisticheskogo Sel'skogo Khoziaistva v Sovremennykh Usloviiakh (Moscow: Izdat. "Ekonomika," 1971), p. 282. Hereafter cited as Ekonomika.

11. Narodnoe Khoziaistvo SSSR v 1970 (Moscow: Izdat, Statistika, 1971), p. 22.

12. V. Yeropkin, "Analiz Rasshirennogo Vosproizvodstva v Kolkhozakh i Sovkhozakh," Ekonomika Sel'skogo Khoziaistva, no. 8 (1972): 32.

13. Ekonomika, pp. 282-283.

14. Klassy, Sotsial'nye Sloi, i Gruppy v SSSR (Moscow: Izdat. "Nauka," 1968), pp. 85-86.

15. Ibid., p. 122.

16. Narodnoe Khoziaistvo SSSR v 1970, p. 378.

17. Strauss, op. cit., pp. 253-254.

18. Ernest Mandel, Marxist Economic Theory, Vol. II, (New York: Monthly Review Press, 1970), p. 575.

19. Strauss, op. cit., p. 270.

20. Ibid., p. 269.

21. Ibid., p. 270.

22. S. Sdobnov, "Ekonomika Sel'skogo Khoziaistva v Period Razvitogo Sotsializma," Ekonomika Sel'skogo Khoziaistva, no. 7 (1972): 15.

23. Narodnoe Khoziaistvo SSSR v 1970, p. 507.

24. Ekonomicheskie i Sotsial'nye Problemy Industrializatsii Sel'skogo Khoziaistva (Moscow: Izdat. Mock. Univ., 1971), p. 4.

25. Ibid., p. 55.

26. Sherman, op. cit., pp. 169-170.

27. Norton T. Dodge, "Recruitment and the Quality of the Soviet Agricultural Labor Force," in The Soviet Rural Community, edited by James R. Miller (University of Illinois, 1971), p. 182.

28. Ekonomika, p. 31.

29. Ibid., p. 38.

30. Klassy, Sotsial'nye Sloi i Gruppy v SSSR (Moscow: Izdat. "Nauka," 1968), p. 91.

31. Ekonomika, p. 39

32. Ibid., pp. 39-40.

33. N. P. Kopach, Obshchestvennyi Trud v Sel'skom Khoziaistve i Rezervy Ego Ekonomii (Moscow: Izdat. Ekonomika, 1972), pp. 26 and 192.

34. Klassy, Sotsial'nye Sloi i Gruppy v SSSR, pp. 120-121, 126-131.

35. M. I. Sidorova, Obshchestvennye Fondy Potrebleniia i Dokhody Kolkhoznikov (Moscow: Izdat. Kolos, 1969), p. 101.

36. Iakimov, op. cit., p. 39.

37. Karl-Eugen Wadekin, "Manpower in Soviet Agriculture," Soviet Studies XX, no. 3 (January 1969): 289.

38. Klassy, Sotsial'nye Sloi i Gruppy v SSSR, pp. 121-122.

39. T. I. Zaslavskaya, "Ways of Controlling Labor Movement and Employment In The Rural Economy of Siberia," in The Human Factor in Agricultural Management (Warszawa: Panstwowe Wydawnictwo Naukowe, 1970), p. 26.

40. G. P Bulavin, Prevrashchenie Sel'skokhoziaistvennogo Truda v Raznovidnost' Industrial'nogo (Moscow: Izdat. "Ekonomika," 1970), p. 48.

41. Ibid., p. 107.

42. Ibid., p. 111.

43. Migratsiia Sel'skogo Naseleniia, p. 228.

44. Bulavin, op. cit., p. 113.

45. Ibid., p. 117.

46. Ibid., pp. 120-121.

47. Jerzy Karcz, "Some Major Persisting Problems in Soviet Agriculture," Slavic Review, 29, no. 3 (September 1970): 424.

48. Ibid., p. 425.

49. Migratsiia Sel'skogo Naseleniia, p. 112.

50. For a brief discussion of some aspects of the problems of seasonal harvest helpers, see Boris Anashenkov, "For Both Countryside And City," Literaturnaya Gazeta, no. 3 (January 17, 1968): 10, translated in CDSP XX, no. 5 (February 21, 1968): 2-4, 6.

51. Strauss, op. cit., p. 54.

52. Osnovy Ekonomiki Kolkhoznogo Proizvodstva (Kazan': Tatarskoe Knizhnoe Izdat. 1966), pp. 196-197.

53. Bulavin, op. cit., pp. 32-33.

54. Ibid., p. 11.

55. Ibid., p. 12.

56. Kollektiv Kolkhoznikov—Sotsialno-Psikhologicheskoe Issledovanie (Moscow: Izdat. "Mysl'," 1970), p. 106.

57. Problemy Izmeneniia Sotsial'noi Struktury Sovetskogo Obshchestva (Moscow: Izdat. "Nauka," 1968), p. 198.

58. Bulavin, op. cit., p. 13.

59. Ibid.

60. Ibid., pp. 124-125.

61. Ibid., p. 126.

62. Ibid., p. 127.

63. V. N. Iakimov, Problemy Trudovykh Resvrsov Kolkhozov (Moscow: Izdat. "Ekonomika," 1969), pp. 37-38.

64. Ibid., p. 41.

65. Ibid., pp. 45-46.
66. Ibid., p. 49.
67. Ibid., pp. 72-73.
68. Karl-Eugen Wadekin, "Manpower in Soviet Agriculture," op. cit., p. 287.
69. Ibid., p. 293.
70. Iakimov, op. cit., p. 15.
71. Karl-Eugen Wadekin, "Manpower in Soviet Agriculture," op. cit., p. 296.
72. Ibid., pp. 303-304.
73. Ibid., p. 304.
74. Migratsiia Sel'skogo Naseleniia. p. 154.
75. Ibid., p. 165; see also G. Zinchenko, "Agrarnyi Otriad Rabochego Klassa SSSR." Kommunist, no. 14 (September 1972): 67.
76. Ibid., p. 184.
77. Ibid., p. 187.
78. P. Simush, The Soviet Collective Farm (Moscow: Progress Publishers, 1971), p. 66.
79. Migratsii Sel'skogo Naselenii, op. cit., p. 200.
80. Iu. V. Arutiunian, Sotsial'naia Strukura Sel'skogo Naseleniia SSSR (Moscow: Izdat. Mysl', 1971), p. 106.
81. Ibid., p. 201.
82. Kollektiv Kolkhoznikov—Sotsial'no-Psikhologicheskoe Issledovanie, op. cit., p. 59.
83. Migratsiia Sel'skogo Naseleniia, op. cit., pp. 205-206.
84. Kollektiv Kolkhoznikov—Sotsial'no-Psikhologicheskoe, Issledovanie, op. cit., p. 99.
85. Ibid., p. 103.
86. Karl-Eugen Wadekin, "Soviet Rural Society—A Descriptive Stratification Analysis," Soviet Studies XXII, no. 4 (April 1971): 525.
87. Ibid., p. 515.
88. Migratsiia Sel'skogo Naseleniia, op. cit., pp. 214-215.
89. Karl-Eugen Wadekin, "Soviet Rural Society—A Descriptive Stratification Analysis," op. cit., p. 531.
90. See S. Gumadeev, "Zabota o Nuzhdakh Zhivotnovodov," Kommunist, no. 13 (September 1971): 69-71; also A. Emel'ianov, "Technical Progress and Structural Changes in Agriculture," Voprosy Ekonomiki, no. 4 (1971), as translated in Problems of Economics, IASP, XIV, no. 4 (August 1971): 22.
91. Karl-Eugen Wadekin, "Soviet Rural Society . . . ," op. cit., p. 527.
92. Ibid., pp. 527-528.
93. Ekonomicheskie i Sotsial'nye Problemy Industrializatsii Sel'skogo Khoziaistva (Moscow: Izdat. Mosk. Univ.. 1971), p. 116.

94. Karl-Eugen Wadekin, "Soviet Rural Society . . . ," op. cit., pp. 524-525.

95. Ibid., p. 525.

96. Alexander Yanov, "The Kostroma Experiment," Literaturnaya Gazeta, no. 52 (December 27, 1967): 10.

97. D. Moskalenko, "It's Worth Thinking About: Before Setting Off for the Virgin Lands," Pravda, August 5, 1971, p. 3, as translated in CDSP XXIII, no. 31 (August 31, 1971): 28-29.

98. Migratsiia Sel'skogo Naseleniia," op. cit., p. 61.

99. A. Z. Maikov and P. A. Gureev, "Legal Principles Governing the Distribution of Labor Supply," SGIP, no. 3 (1971), as translated in Soviet Law And Government, IASP, X, no. 2 (Fall 1971): 177-179.

100. Kollektiv Kolkhoznikov, op. cit., p. 119.

101. Arthur Adams and Jan Adams, Men Versus Systems (New York: The Free Press, 1971), pp. 29-30.

The "link" (zveno) issue is currently a major problem for the Brezhnev regime within the agricultural sector. The issue emerged explicitly in Stalin's last years only to become an "un-issue" after the late dictator's anti-link position led to the political demise of Politburo agricultural expert Andrei Andreev. It reemerged from its "un-issue" status in the late 1950s in the context of a generally stagnant agricultural situation, and it has most recently played a role in the political demise of the pro-link Politburo agricultural specialist Gennadi Voronov, a rival of fellow Politburo agricultural expert Dmitri Poliansky.[1] The emphasis below will be on the present status of the issue, although ample background on the evolution of the issued will be provided.

DEFINITIONS 1958, 1965, AND 1970: SOME COMPARISONS

According to an official Soviet economic dictionary published in 1958,[2] a link is an internal brigade form of cooperation of labor in kolkhozy used for the cultivation of labor-intensive and some technical crops. It is a constitutent part of the permanent production brigade of the kolkhoz. The organization of this link is said to be conditioned on the necessity of liquidating impersonality during hand work on sown areas of cultivated crops. Such work does not require joint work of a great number of kolkhozniks but is a crucial factor in yield rates. The 1958 definition states that a link includes usually from eight to twelve persons, depending on the number of able-bodied kolkhozniks in the brigade and the area of cultivated crop per man. The link (as of 1958) was widely used in field production and in the crop production brigades raising cultivated crops and vegetables, the cultivation of which was still insufficiently mechanized and which demand great systematic expenditures of hand labor for the whole of a work period. Each link is given a plot containing sown areas with cultivated crops on which it alone applies its hand labor for a whole agricultural year—from preparation for sowing to harvest—under the general control of the brigadier of the permanent production brigade of which it is a constituent part. At the head of the link is a link leader, designated by the kolkhoz board from among the members of the link, and he fulfills the function of guiding the link while jointly and equally working in it. For each link the kolkhoz board establishes a production task for the coming year.

The Soviet Encyclopedia Dictionary Of Legal Knowledge,[3] published in 1965, describes the link as one of the forms of organization of labor in kolkhoz production created for the cultivation of all kinds of crops. It notes that especially widespread use is being made of complex mechanized links. The article states that links can be independent or part of a mechanized brigade, which goes beyond the 1958 definition. The kolkhoz board creates the link and secures for it by an act a definite plot of land and the necessary machinery, if it is to have any. Each link is assigned a production task by the kolkhoz board in which is indicated what kind of crops should be raised, what kind of yields should be achieved, what labor production expenditures per unit of produce and its value should be, as well as what the gross harvest target is. In kolkhozy where internal cost accounting is used, links are given an accounting plan-task and a piece-work premium pay based on final results of production. The link is constituted as a rule by from six to twelve workers, headed by a link leader designated by the kolkhoz board or the brigade meeting. In the new kolkhoz Model Charter enacted in 1969, the practice of designation by the brigade meeting was adopted as the norm, whereas before designation was generally by the board. The link leader distributes work among members of the link, organizes it, and checks on observation of the order of the day, on fulfillment of norms of output, and on the quality of work.

Despite the general coincidence of these two definitions of links, both limit links to kolkhozy. There are some significant differences in these formulations, indicating that a new attitude toward the link has developed between 1958 and 1965. First of all, the 1965 description does not restrict the link to particular kinds of crops, as does the 1958 formulation. Moreover, in the 1965 description the link is not necessarily a subdivision of the brigade. It can be independent of the brigade. Also, the association of the link with hand work in the 1958 description is severed in the 1965 description. In fact, the 1965 definition talks of mechanized links, thus considerably enlarging on both the concept and the form of the link, as well as in general upgrading their significance. The tone of the 1965 formulation is not at all apologetic. The 1958 formulation implicitly looks upon the link as a necessary evil, a device resorted to in default of the appropriate machinery or mechanization. Certainly the tone of the 1965 formulation is more positive, although it hardly betokens recognition of the link as universally applicable to all farms or as a key to the solution of the productivity of labor and work incentive problems.

The link is usually smaller than the brigade, although this is not always the case. Also, although link leaders or heads are not full-time administrators, brigadiers normally are, although, again, there is an exception: the brigadiers of some small brigades are not always full-time administrators. Thus size and the type of administrator are not the crucial distinctions between link and brigade. What is supposedly the crucial difference is that the brigade is an independent collective that works through a complete production cycle, whereas a link normally completes only a part of the production cycle. However, even this distinction is questionable since the advent of so-called mechanized detachments and consolidated complex mechanized links that work a whole production cycle or crop rotation period.[4]

The link is still defined as a subunit of the brigade. Insofar as a consolidated link utilizes its own membership exclusively and its own equipment and plot for the whole cycle of work, it does not transcend the brigade, but rather becomes in essence a brigade.[5] Thus, by definition, a link that comes to resemble a brigade is no longer a link, even if it is still called a link. The dogma that a link is a subunit of the brigade requires some semantic juggling.

THE LINK ISSUE AFTER STALIN

The link has obvious economic implications, but it is the ideological implications that have until recent years eclipsed the purely economic criteria being applied to judge its economic performance and in fact have long retarded its use on a large scale. In fact, the link issue has loomed large in the postwar agricultural-political issues among Soviet leaders.[6] In essence, the link represents an attempt to use the piece-work system as opposed to the collective work system of the much larger brigade. The first serious attempt to get away from the brigade collective work principle was embodied in a Central Committee Plenum decree of February 1974 entitled "On Measures to Improve Agriculture in the Postwar Period."[7] This decree stated, inter alia, that it was necessary to work out and apply a better system of payment of labor so as to encourage those working well. To this end and taking into account the serious problem of the presence of impersonality in the use of kolkhoz land, especially the frequent transfer of land from one brigade to another, which hindered the raising of productivity, it was recognized that kolkhozy should, in the shortest possible time, liquidate this impersonality and secure to field production brigades permanent plots for crop rotation, including cattle and inventory, and not allow fluidity in the composition of these brigades. The kolkhozy were also told to create links within the brigades to cultivate technical, vegetable, and seed crops and, where possible, graincrops. The decree took note of a series of obstacles to the further rise of labor productivity, the growth of yields, and the productivity of livestock. It cited leveling in pay among kolkhozniks, and the fact that the individual and small group piece-work system was not sufficiently utilized. It was stated that links and brigades with higher yields should receive higher pay. But, as Alexander Vucinich notes, with kolkhoz work fluctuating seasonally and requiring several specializations on the part of each member, a complex agricultural operation is not as easily broken down into its measurable components as a complex industrial operation. Also, results of agricultural work hinge on favorable weather, so that results alone are an inadequate criterion for the measurement of the amount and intensity of labor put into work.[8] Moreover, since agricultural work lacks the spatial concentration of work in a factory, it requires proportionately more technicians to appraise and register the results of work. Vucinich reports that for all these reasons the Soviets were apparently unable to devise a comprehensive system for the appraisal of labor productivity on an individual and link basis.[9]

But, in a _Pravda_ editorial of February 19, 1950, the production brigade was declared the only form that opens wide possibilities for the application of large-scale work processes in agriculture. And it further specified that in grain production the link hampers the application of large-scale technological processes, and that therefore the demand for their widespread dissemination would be contrary to the interests of strengthening the kolkhoz.[10] Links, the official line of the 1950s charged, obstructed the use of complex machinery and split the kolkhozy into uneconomically small units, dispersing their resources. The political scapegoat for the abrupt eclipse of the link experiment of the past three years was Politburo member Andrei Andreev, the Minister of Agriculture, who was not blamed for inspiring the links in grain cultivation. In _Pravda_ of February 28, 1950, he confessed that his inaccurate formulations had led to it appearing that he had advocated replacing brigades with links.[11] The superseding policy of merging smaller kolkhozy into larger ones, a policy associated with Andreev's rival Khrushchev, the other Politburo agricultural expert, proceeded at breakneck speed after beginning in 1950.[12] The official reason for these mergers was that they created conditions for a more efficient use of machinery in the fields and improved the utilization of agricultural specialists.[13] About 250,000 small kolkhozy, some so small as to encompass only ten to thirty households, were amalgamated into 93,000 large farms, which had on the average three to four times as much land, labor, and livestock.[14] Relatively large brigades were formed on these large kolkhozy and, as Vucinich relates, although the link was not abolished, its role became a secondary one. It was relegated to carrying out special assignments that required small work groups. In grain production it was fully dismissed, since this does not call for breaking up work into small groups. In general, says Vucinich, links were retained for work where mechanization was minimal. The brigade became the basic unit for calculating supplemental pay.[15]

THE LINK ISSUE REEMERGES

As Alec Nove puts it, the issue was not whether or not there should be links. There always had been. Rather it was and still is whether there "should be a semi-permanent link which was a long-term attachment to a specified area of land and equipment, and which is left to perform broadly agreed upon tasks as it sees fit, with its income depending upon its results?"[16] Yet the links of today are more varied both in structure and in purpose than those of the 1950s. And they are commonly used in sovkhozy as well as kolkhozy. Those who advocate their use claim they are the only way to introduce a responsible owner-like attitude to land and its produce short of reintroducing private property. Today's link is a primary work unit of from three to eight members that has varying degrees of autonomy. The Western student of Soviet agriculture Dimitry Pospielovsky characterizes the contemporary link as follows:

> It is small and informal enough for a relatively "personal" type of farming with more clearly established, recognized and felt responsibilities for the whole production cycle on a particular piece of land, rather than for a single type of operation.[17]

Opposed to the link principle is the more prevalent one based on division of labor into large brigades. Each brigade deals with a particular operation, which may be over in one day to be superseded by another operation. Pay under this system is normally a piece-work basis and thus not dependent on the final product, except insofar as the total income of the parent farm depends on the work of each brigade. Hence, as Pospielovsky concludes, in the brigade system there is no direct correlation between the income criteria of the farm as a whole and of each individual member of the farm, with consequent lack of incentive.[18]

Although in a state of eclipse throughout the early and middle 1950s, a revival of interest in the links materialized after 1958, when Khrushchev allowed link experiments to begin again on a limited scale. Pospielovsky credits the post-1958 agricultural stagnation for this, as well as the very poor agricultural results in 1963.[19] This general stagnation was due to the rising costs of inputs needed by the farms exceeding the rising prices paid out by the state to the farms for produce. Although a decade-long policy of raising prices for agricultural produce had succeeded in stimulating a rise in marketable produce, the rise in inputs exceeded rises in farm incomes and in addition the growth in the volume of marketable grain affected the level of payments in kind to kolkhozniks, thus checking their ability to market grain or to use it for raising livestock on their private plots to sell on kolkhoz markets. Moreover, a repressive policy during Khrushchev's last years toward the private sector further reduced the real incomes of kolkhozniks and thus acted as a disincentive to increase output.[20]

THE PROPONENTS OF THE LINK GAIN

The new links were often mechanized, that is, they were endowed with a full complement of farm machinery and a plot of land. The link was to be paid by the parent farm on the basis of how much it produced or sold to the farm at previously agreed rates. Also, mechanized brigades of fifteen to fifty appeared. These were thus considerably smaller than the regular piece-work field brigades, although much larger than the link. But, as Pospielovsky points out, they both shared the characteristics of being based on internal economic accounting, of being independently responsible for the whole cultivation cycle on a specific piece of land, and of being paid on the basis of their total performance rather than for just performing on one function, say plowing.[21] The link is seen as conducive to creating a spirit of common material incentive for each member and a common responsibility for the return on their work. So, with this system, tractor drivers no longer try to increase their income by plowing as much land as they can regardless of the quality of plowing. A smaller crop affects their income as well as that of the whole team.[22]

V. Zhulin, chief agronomist of a sovkhoz in the Altai District of west Siberia, in an article in Komsomol'skaia Pravda of August 7, 1964, defended the principle of workers doing all the operations on their fields—sowing, plowing, harvesting, and so on—as distinct from performing merely one or two specialized operations. He preached the doctrine of personal responsibility for the whole agricultural cycle on a given land mass. Zhulin urged that legally binding written contracts be concluded between the individual farms on the one hand and the links on the other, assigning definite plots of land and definite machinery and fixing prices for the final product that the farm will buy from the individual link. Zhulin argues that such a legalized and stable system would put an end to the harmful attitude of the land belonging to the "whole people" or the "state," which, he feels, means it is without "real masters." Zhulin anticipates the criticism of the links as kindling petty bourgeois private property tendencies by touting them as true schools of communism, creating true group feelings of cooperation to achieve final results that all are responsible for, as opposed to the "petty individualism" of the piece-work system of the brigade.

A conference on links held in the Kuban was reported in Komso-mol'skaia Pravda of September 29, 1965. Pospielovsky notes that one of its major conclusions was that wherever links are introduced, the need for numerous controllers, supervisors, and auditors, who check on field work, disappears, with obvious savings in administrative expenses to the farm.[23] Apropos of this is a description by the Soviet sociologists O. I. Zotova and V. V. Novikov of a link (team) experiments' results:

> The increase in self-administration has made the primary
> group so mature, strong and united that it has been possible
> to do away with the services of bookkeepers and storemen.
> The accounts are kept by the team leader, who relies on the
> reports sent him by the team members and rarely checks
> them. The keys to the stores are also held by the team
> leader. If anyone wants to get some grain, fodder, etc.,
> . . . he obtains the key from the leader and goes to the
> store on his own. . . . No one in the group wishes to cheat
> anyone because to do so would really be to cheat himself.[24]

The Soviet Doctor of Economics V. Tikhonov, at a round-table discussion of agricultural economists, pointed out that the present-day kolkhoz brigades were too large, which necessitated piece-work pay. This in turn complicated direct ties between pay and the final results of the work of the collective. Tikhonov advocates hourly pay as a guaranteed minimum with supplemental pay for quality, quantity, and cost reduction. Such a system, he emphasized, requires smaller production units.[25] Official approval of the link experiments came by way of a Pravda editorial of December 10, 1966, entitled "Creative Search in the Countryside." It described an experiment by an Omsk Oblast sovkhoz that aimed at liquidating impersonality in land cultivation and raising the responsibility of each worker for yields and the condition of machinery. Experimental mechanized links were created. Tremendous reductions in labor productivity were realized. The tone of the editorial is one of sober optimism. The mechanized link has, in certain cases, proven highly successful. It could be used elsewhere although there is no call for a campaign to universalize it. What the editorial amounts to is a green light to go ahead with hitherto sensitive, limited, and isolated experiments on a modest scale without fear of being accused of ideological heresy.

The economist I. I. Dmitrashko stresses that mechanized links consisting of one tractor and one or two mechanizers assigned to 100-200 hectares of plowed crops operate inefficiently, requiring supplementary workers and poorly utilizing equipment. He claims that experience with corn or sugarbeets indicates that mechanized links with ten to fifteen men and five or six tractors, cultivating a few crops with various sowing periods and cycles, is better.[26] He also indicates that links with permanent personnel achieve higher yields and with lower costs.[27]

The ideas of M. Lemeshev, a pro-link Soviet economist, go well beyond Zhulin's advocacy. Writing in the March 1966 issue of Problem of Economics,[28] Lemeshev opposes any form of centralized production or product-mix planning for farms and also opposes predominantly market-regulated prices. He would only like government interference in the price system when a marked imbalance in the national agricultural product mix develops, so as to induce the farms to increase production of the products needed. Lemeshev argues that efficiency requires a feeling that the peasant is master of the land, a phrase often used by link advocates. Lemeshev advocates that each farmer must be personally interested in the end result. He favors breaking up the huge kolkhozy, if the farmers so desire, and reconstituting the original village-based small work links, with the parent farm acting as the connection with state agencies on behalf of the link. In general the parent farm would handle transportation, storage, repair, and auxiliary enterprises. It would formulate written contracts with the individual links stating the prices and quantities of products it would buy from them, charging them rent for machinery used to produce such or simply deducting it from the prices it pays for them. The link itself would provide its members with social insurance by reserving part of its income for that purpose.

Pospielovsky opines that one of the causes for the long-delayed Congress of Kolkhozniks was ambivalence over the link issue.[29] As Pospielovsky points out, some critics of the link mask their ideologica arguments over the problem that quarrels among members of the link over relative shares of the income may cause or over the problems of dissolving a link torn by internal dissension. But behind these argu ments, he feels, is the aversion felt by those who feel the links promot de facto private farming. They suspect that a link is too much like a large extended family:

In fact, it is possible that the more empirically minded
Soviet experts and even party functionaries foresee this
development (of the viable links toward a modified private
land tenure) of links as a quiet and relatively painless return to a form of functional private farming without the
reconversion of land into a private market commodity.[30]

But not all types of farm work lend themselves to link-type organization, and the use of huge machines on large fields, especially grain
operations, is not ripe for link-type, small-knit groups. So this de
facto decollectivization could not be applied across the board but rather
selectively. Besides this technical problem, Pospielovsky suggests a
practical problem that works against the link. And that is rural underemployment and rural overpopulation, all of which amount to a surplus
of unskilled manual labor.[31] The use of links would economize on the
use of this overabundant commodity, thus causing the regime to provide
other work for it or allow these unskilled workers to drift to the urban
centers in violation of the regime's elaborate internal passport restrictions.

Pospielovsky suggests that in order to get benefits in terms of
long-term care and improvement of the soil, permanency, and certainty
by way of introducing legally binding contracts between the farms and
their links, the links must become legal persons fully protected by law
from either dissolution by the kolkhoz chairman or state agencies, or
from the arbitrary transfer of their members to other work on the
farm.[32] So far there has been no reflection of such a policy in the
press. And the new kolkhoz Model Charter does not reflect any decision on the link question. The draft Model Charter of April 1969, in
Article 14, went beyond the 1935 charter provision for production
brigades by naming links in a list of production subdivisions, and
specified that all of these were to be allocated land and equipment
for a period of several years. As Keith Bush observed, this left the
door open for mechanized links.[33] Article 26 of the final version of
the Model Charter also names links as one of the possible forms of
organizing production and labor, but weakens the link by replacing the
draft provision for securing the production units for years with machinery, land, etc., with a simple statement that these units are secured
with machinery, land, etc., without reference to how long, an omission
Keith Bush finds notable.[34] Sidney Ploss also feels that this omission
was very significant. He believes that Gennadi Voronov, a Politburo
champion of the link, had been beaten on this issue by Brezhnev and
Poliansky, representing a more cautious attitude toward the link.[35]
Pospielovsky sees this as leaving it up to local kolkhoz management
whether to give these units a sense of permanency.[36]

SOME LEGAL RAMIFICATIONS OF
THE LINK ISSUE

In an important article the jurist I. F. Kuz'min combats the notion apparently abroad in certain circles that the production subdivisions of the kolkhoz, operating on a khozraschet basis, are the owners of the assets assigned by the parent kolkhoz to them. He feels that the view of some that these subdivisions are legal persons is both theoretically and practically erroneous. He feels the subdivisions' relations with the kolkhoz are strictly an intrakolkhoz matter, therefore are outside the civil code, and hence cannot concern relations between two legal persons. Moreover, the practical consequences of treating the subdivision as a legal person, he feels, would lead to a weakening of the organizational unity of the kolkhoz and thus deprive it of the advantages connected with the conduct of a huge economy, also thereby promoting localism, which in turn leads to unjustifiable pay differentials among subdivisions of the same kolkhoz. Kuz'min criticizes those like the Latvian jurist Ia. Strautmanis who even deny that a subdivision can be the subject of internal kolkhoz property relations, that is, that it can have any rights as against the parent kolkhoz. Yet, he argues, Strautmanis is inconsistent, since he recognizes the kolkhoz household to be a subject of internal kolkhoz relations without being a legal person. In sum, the Kuz'min view, although not as extreme as that of Strautmanis, is an obstacle to a Lemeshev reform. He concludes that the subdivisions can have property rights as against the kolkhoz without being a legal person and that this is essential, since otherwise it would be difficult for them to function as a khozraschet unit. Kuz'min does not even exclude the use of internal kolkhoz prices being used in subdivision-parent kolkhoz relations.[37] The use of contracts is also approved to implement those relations, but he notes that both the use of contracts and prices now in a few kolkhozy is strictly on an experimental basis. He emphasizes that he opposes the economist Lemeshev' advocacy of full economic independence for the production subdivisions.[38] Yet interestingly, he never once mentions the word "link." This indicates the present sensitivity of the link issue. Also very interesting is Kuz'min's mild treatment of the ideologically heretical breakup of kolkhozy into independent subdivisions as merely legally fallacious and economically unsound.

THE STATUS OF THE LINK TODAY

The tenor of today's presentation of the link is positive but cautious. And the focus in on the less radical version of the link. Love of the particular plot assigned is stressed as a crucial advantage of the link. The temporary master of land does not love it. And a group that does not have to nurse a crop through its whole cycle does not care about the whole cycle. The link overcomes these deficiencies in the highly specialized, impersonal, one-function brigades.[39]

A recent Soviet agricultural economics text describes an experiment with the normless or "order-free" link in Kazakhstan and Dagestan. The essence of this system is that each link consists of ten to fifteen highly qualified mechanizers who are allotted four to five thousand hectares of arable land plus the necessary tractors, agricultural machines, fertilizers, and other supplies. They are given a technological chart in which is indicated: the volume of production; the quantity of sown hectares per crop and all the technology needed to produce it; the gross harvest; expenses based on norms, including the pay funds. These are the only obligatory documents given the link. There are no norms of output or orders within the link. Link members work according to the principle "one for all, all for one", and strictly adhere to the technological chart. Payment of labor is as follows: up to the reception of the harvest workers received advances in a size of up to 100 rubles a month, and after taking account of gross produce a final calculation of earnings is made, based on the quantity and quality of produce raised by the link as compared to the agreed upon evaluation made at the beginning of the year. For 1968, with a grain yield of twelve centners from one hectare, the cost of one centner in links was 1 ruble 60 kopeks, whereas with a neighbor working in the old way costs were 6 rubles 38 kopeks per centner. The average monthly earnings of link members were 360 rubles. This high pay was based on the colossal growth in productivity of labor. On the production of one centner of grain the link expended twenty minutes, whereas its neighbor spent from two to five hours. Moreover, the link's administrative and overhead expenses practically disappeared. But the description of this fabulously positive link experiment ends on a cautious note:

> Of course, the mass inculcation of the given system, when the experiment is still not complete, would be premature, although it is now already evident that it was a tremendous advantage.[40]

In the same vein is another item about link experiments related by A. Duduk, a sovkhoz chief economist, and B. Krugliak, an economics candidate. They report on mechanized links in Zaporozh'e Oblast, where the links were given great economic independence and put on khozraschet. They were also operating on a "without orders" basis of payment of labor. The system operates as follows. At the beginning of each month on the basis of the technological chart, the volume of planned work for each crop and the period for fulfilling it for the month are noted down in the linkbook. The link leader fixes daily the actual volume of the fulfilled work and the expenses of labor in man days and man hours. Members of the links themselves communicate to the link leader data on output, expenditure of gas, and so on. Expenses on repair work and technical servicing of equipment and machines are entered in the link book. At the established time, this book goes to the farm bookkeeping department, where the earnings of each member of the link are calculated.[41] This is far from the Lemeshev idea, or even Zhulin's idea of actual bilateral contracts between parent farm and link. Moreover, the "link without orders" still has its targets set from above, and it certainly is not a legally independent and economically autonomous entity, as Pospielovsky proposes. The orderless link is hailed by V. V. Gusev as the best method of economizing in today's agricultural conditions, and he even claims that in addition to its greater ability to promote incentive, it also promotes a feeling of collectivism, that is, that the link is ideologically preferable.[42] And the economist I. Krasil'nikov hails links as progressive and highly conducive to improving the skills and knowledge of link members.[43]

FUTURE DEVELOPMENTS

So at the present time the regime has passed by the opportunity of dramatically upgrading the link afforded by the writing of a new kolkhoz Model Charter. It has not seen fit to sponsor a dialogue in the scholarly and specialized press on the case for a legally and economically independent link dealing with a parent farm on a basis of legal equality. But it continues to allow selective praise for certain types of link, especially the mechanized ones. The regime focuses on the positive side of the links from their standpoint, their demonstrated greater economic ability. This is explained by their "group spirit" as opposed to the piece-work mentality of the larger brigades, with their built-in impersonality. Still, the regime is not willing to give up the "myth of the superiority of huge brigades," just as it is not willing to give up the myth of the superiority of the sovkhoz over the kolkhoz, although this has been relatively deemphasized in recent years. The myth of the voluntary collectivization of agriculture is still enshrined.

What of the future of the links? Perhaps their fate is tied to studies of the optimal size of farms and internal subunits. The Soviets are more willing to admit that the great size of some kolkhozy, with consequent dispersal of work sites, requires top-level managers to spend too much of their valuable time simply going to and returning from check-up trips and information-gathering expeditions.[44] To the extent that the Soviets learn and acknowledge that "gigantomania" in farms is unscientific and uneconomical, the link offers a means of retreat without decollectivizing. So does the private subsidiary economy. It is in many ways a case similar to that of the links. It too is victimized by myths and irrational ideological prejudices. Perhaps, as Roy Laird put it, nothing short of another revolution or a series of production failures far more serious than those yet experienced can be expected to result in a serious challenge to the basic myth associated with Soviet collectivization.[45] The stagnancy of the post-1958 period, the merely incremental, marginal improvements of the Brezhnev-Kosygin era, and the growing bottleneck aspect of agriculture in the context of the whole economy, all perhaps present bases for a turnabout on the link issue and an end to the present ambivalent, selectively positive approach to limited link experiments. Yet there are counter trends. The newly created branch system of farm organization, whereby farms are broken down into construction, mechanization, livestock, and crop branches and then integrated with each other on an oblast level, could obliterate the orderless link. For as Paige Bryan remarks, as farming becomes more mechanized, it is very difficult on an ideological level to justify the essentially private use by five or six people—usually a family—of large pieces of machinery.[46] Bryan feels that whenever this regime requires high labor productivity, because of poor performance in the socialized sector, it encourages the use of links.[47] Such is the situation today with grain. Thus, the greater the mechanization, the less the use of links. Yet those areas of agricultural production least amenable to mechanization are prime link areas.

NOTES

1. For the political rivalry between Voronov and Polyansky in general and over the link issue in particular, see Werner G. Hahn, The Politics Of Soviet Agriculture, 1960-1970 (Baltimore and London, The Johns Hopkins University Press, 1972). Pravda of April 28, 1973 (p. 1), announced that Voronov had, together with Pyotr Shelest, been dropped from the Politburo.
2. Kratkii Ekonomicheskii Slovar' (Moscow: Gospolitizdat, 1958).
3. Entsiklopedicheskii Slovar' Pravovykh Znanii (Moscow: Izdat. Sovetskaia Entsiklopediia, 1965).
4. Progressivnye Formy Organizatsii Truda v Kolkhozakh i Sovkhozakh (Moscow: Izdat. Kolos, 1970), pp. 18-19.
5. Ibid, p. 54.

6. See Sidney I. Ploss, Conflict and Decision-Making in Soviet Russia: A Case Study of Agricultural Policy, 1953-1963 (Princeton: Princeton University Press, 1965).

7. For text, see Resheniia Partii i Pravitel'stva po Khoziaistvennym Voprosam (1917-1967), Tom III (Moscow: Izdat, Polit. Lit., 1968), pp. 381-427.

8. See Michael E. Bradley and M. Gardner Clark, "Supervision And Efficiency in Socialized Agriculture," Soviet Studies XXIII, no. 3 (January 1972): 466.

9. Alexander Vucinich, Soviet Economic Institutions (Palo Alto: Stanford University Press, 1952), p. 75.

10. "Against Distortions in Kolkhoz Labor Organization," translated in CDSP II, no. 10: 12.

11. Andreev's statement is translated in Soviet Studies II: 79-80.

12. Istoriia Narodnogo Khoziaistva SSSR (Moscow: Izdat. "Vyshaia Shkola," 1964), p. 210.

13. For an examination of the reasons for the amalgamations, see Robert C. Stuart, The Collective Farm in Soviet Agriculture (Lexington, Toronto, and London: D. C. Heath & Co., 1972), pp. 49-50.

14. A. Podkolzin, A Short Economic History of the USSR (Moscow Progress Publishers, 1968), pp. 224-225.

15. Vucinich, op. cit., p. 78.

16. Alec Nove, "Soviet Agriculture Under Brezhnev," Slavic Review 29, no. 3 (September 1970): 392.

17. Dimitry Pospielovsky, "The 'Link System' in Soviet Agriculture," Soviet Studies XXI, no. 4 (April 1970): 411-412.

18. Ibid., p. 412.

19. Ibid., p. 416.

20. Arcadius Kahan, "Agriculture," in Prospects for Soviet Society, edited by Allen Kassof (New York: Praeger Publishers, 1968), p. 288.

21. Pospielovsky, op. cit., pp. 417-418.

22. O. I. Zotova and V. V. Novikov, "The Development of Collectivist Attitudes Among Agricultural Workers," in Town, Country and People, edited by G. V. Osipov (London: Tavistock Publications, 1969), p. 212.

23. Pospielovsky, op. cit., p. 421.

24. O. I. Zotova and V. V. Novikov, op. cit., p. 213.

25. "Problems of Rural Economics," Pravda, April 24, 1966, p. 3.

26. I. I. Dmitrashko, Vnutrokolkhoznye Ekonomicheskie Otnosheniia (Moscow: Izdat. Ekonomika, 1966), pp. 69-70.

27. Ibid., p. 72.

28. See the section "A Discussion on Draft Directives for the Twenty-Third Congress," in Voprosy Ekonomiki, no. 3 (1966).

29. Pospielovsky, op. cit., p. 428.

30. Ibid., p. 429.

31. Ibid., p. 430.

32. Ibid., p. 431.

33. Keith Bush, "The New Draft Kolkhoz Model Charter," Bulletin, Institute for the Study of the USSR, XVII, no. 7 (July 1969): p. 38.

34. Keith Bush, "The Third All-Union Congress of Kolkhozniks," Bulletin, Institute for the Study of the USSR, XVII, no. 1 (January 1970): 22.

35. Sidney I. Ploss, "Soviet Politics on the Eve of the 24th Party Congress," World Politics XXXIII, no. 1 (October 1970): 70-71.

36. Pospielovsky, op. cit., p. 434.

37. I. F. Kuz'min, "Pravovye Sredstva Povysheniia Effektivnosti Proizvodstvennoi Deiatel'nosti Kolkhozov," SGIP, no. 8: 72-73.

38. Ibid., p. 74.

39. Ekonomicheski i Sotsial'nye Problemy Industrializatsii Sel'kogo Khoziaistva (Moscow: Izdat. Mosk. Univ., 1971), pp. 127 and 136.

40. Ekonomika Sotsialisticheskogo Sel'skogo Khoziaistva v Sovremennykh Usloviiakh (Moscow: Izdat. "Ekonomika," 1971), p. 233.

41. "Knizhka Zven'evogo," Ekonomicheskaia gazeta, no. 36 (September 1971): 11.

42. V. V. Gusev, Kolkhoz kak Samoupravliaemaia Sotsial'naia Sistema (Moscow: Izdat. Mysl', 1971), p. 43.

43. I. Krasil'nikov, "Istochnik Rosta Produktov Zhivotnovodstva," Kommunist, no. 12 (August 1971): 61.

44. V. P. Reshetniak, Upravlenie v Kolkhozakh (Moscow: Izdat. "Kolos," 1970), pp. 83 and 98-100.

45. Roy Laird, "Collectivization: New and Old Myths," in The Development of the Soviet Economy, edited by Vladimer Treml (New York: Praeger Publishers, 1968), p. 88.

46. Paige Bryan, "Soviet Agriculture—Where Does It Go From Here?" Radio Liberty Dispatch, September 21, 1972, p. 8.

47. Paige Bryan, "Feed Crops and the Zveno", Radio Liberty Dispatch, July 18, 1972, p. 2.

CHAPTER

9

THE PRESENT AND FUTURE
OF THE PRIVATE
SUBSIDIARY ECONOMY

The "acre and a cow" economy primarily refers to kolkhozniks, although the sovkhoz workers, as well as certain other workers and employees, have in fact similar rights on a smaller scale[1] and, to a lesser extent, indulge in subsidiary farming on their smaller plots.[2] The kolkhoz general meeting may give plots up to one-quarter of a hectare to pensioners, state employees, physicians, and teachers living in farm villages.[3] In fact, the contribution to gross agricultural production of the nonfarm workers and employees, a category that includes town, suburban, and even city dwellers with garden plots, is growing. It has been estimated as contributing some two-fifths of all private production or about 13 percent of gross Soviet agricultural production. This leaves approximately three-fifths of private production as the product of kolkhozniks and sovkhoz workers.[4] Traditionally that is, since 1935, the gardens of kolkhozniks totaled only an insignificant percentage of all kolkhoz land—2.3 percent as of January 1, 1938, and the size of the average kolkhoz household or dvor holding was .49 hectares, or about 1.2 acres, although somewhat larger in the less populated areas.[5] Khrushchev's restrictions on the private plots (to be noted below), especially burdensome after 1958, were based primarily on the notion that time spent on them was at the cost of participation in the kolkhoz public sector. Khrushchev objected to private plots as ideologically subversive because they perpetuated the petty private property, small-scale personalized farming spirit and mentality. His restrictions on them had pronounced negative effects for Soviet agriculture. Khrushchev's successors reversed these policies almost immediately after ousting him,[6] not because they were in any way less ideologically vigilant or "liberal" than Khrushchev, but on pragmatic grounds. In putting forward a more liberal policy, they made no ideological concessions to private property. They simply condemned Khrushchev's un-Marxian penchant for administrative solutions and his subjectivism in arbitrarily restricting the private economies before they had outlived their usefulness. According to Brezhnev and Kosygin, the private plots were destined to disappear as soon as the public sector of the kolkhoz was stronger. Meanwhile the private sector continued to supply the urban population with a variety of products, as well as certain types of produce, and the kolkhozniks themselves with supplemental income. While Brezhnev and Kosygin accused Khrushchev of trying to impose an arbitrary timetable on the abolition of private plots, they argued with increasing emphasis that kolkhozniks would voluntarily give up their private plots once they realized that cheaper and better (or at least equivalent) produce in sufficient quantities could be bought from their own kolkhoz or the state stores.[7] Until that time, kolkhozy were ordered by the regime to facilitate the development of the private sector by making available feed, hay, pastures, better breeds of livestock, etc., to individual kolkhozniks. And the new kolkhoz Model Charter, directives of the Twenty-Third and Twenty-Fourth Party Congresses, and various party and state decrees afforded better protection of the right to indulge in private subsidiary farming.

The new kolkhoz Model Charter certainly did not liberalize the size of the garden plots or the limits on private livestock applicable to kolkhozniks. In comparison to the 1935 charter, these rights were slightly restricted. Nevertheless the regime's subsequent emphasis on helping the private sector and protecting it from arbitrary curtailment and discrimination at the hands of kolkhoz officials added up to a much more positive policy toward the private sector than under Khrushchev, and this shift in policy was based on economic pragmatism, not any sudden enthusiasm for a sector that remained ideologically repugnant.[8] Ideological inflexibility had yielded to economic pragmatism.

The liberal "swing" in the regime's policy toward the private sector was significant for this reason. It did not represent a basic change in long-term policies or goals. But it may have set the stage for further "erosions" should agricultural productivity in the public sector continue to stagnate or perhaps even decline. Such a situation would in fact be practically intolerable to a regime committed to increasing the output of consumer goods and food products, both of which depend on a far more productive and profitable agriculture. Should production continue to stagnate, the agricultural bottleneck may become more severe as popular pressures for more and better food and consumer goods, pressures fanned by the regime's promises to deliver such goods after the Twenty-Fourth Congress, continue to grow. Also, the commitment to defense and defense-related industries puts a tremendous strain on the finite capital investment funds available to agriculture. Yet the inability or unwillingness to satisfy consumer appetites once they have been stimulated will increasingly create political risks for the regime as a whole, or certainly for individual members of the Politburo associated with unfulfilled promises. If the conflict between the seemingly infinite appetite of the industrial-military complex for more capital investments on the one hand and the almost equally infinite need for agricultural capital on the other become too severe, the regime might abandon its liberal policy in favor of yet another round of retrenchment, recentralization, and repression in agriculture. Should there be such a reversal, one of the first indicators would be a change in attitude toward the private plot. Khrushchev's economically irrational attack upon the private plot after 1958 was in part attributable to the need for a scapegoat for the failures of his agricultural policies.

The survival of the private plot is attributable to two seemingly contradictory needs of the regime. The first is this scapegoat function. There are limitations on the sins that can be plausibly attributed to the private sector. It cannot be blamed for undermechanization or the absence of vital infrastructural networks. Yet it can be held up as a subverter of the collective work ethic, as an illicit example for the young, a symbol of the petty bourgeois private property mentality. It can also be argued that the very existence of private plots continues to kindle the hopes of the unredeemed anti-collectivist minority that the regime will decollectivize if only they can shirk work in the public sector and convert others to regard the private plot as primary rather than subsidiary, especially if they can make it more productive than the public sector. In any case the regime may find the private plots a convenient excuse for low morale and low productivity in the public sector in spite of numerous reorganizations and attempts to create incentives.

A second reason for the survivial of the subsidiary private sector is simple economic pragmatism. For various reasons it is not practical for the collective farms to grow certain crops that the population needs. So the private sector, machine poor but labor-intensive, is left to meet these needs without the state being required to divert resources from higher priorities. Also, to the extent farmers satisfy their own needs via their private plots, they preserve the public sector for growing more of the top-priority crops. And, since the typical private plot products—milk, eggs, butter, vegetables—are so labor-intensive and generally unmechanized, these would cost the public sector great amounts of labor. This is avoided by tolerating the private plots. Moreover, the state was able to avoid the problem of a minimum annual guaranteed wage for kolkhozniks by giving them private plots and letting them supplement their income up to a minimum level. The state is relieved of the need to provide capital investments, higher prices, or guaranteed minimum wages, and the burden

is shifted from the state to the kolkhozniks. Now since the advent in
1966 of a minimum guaranteed income—primarily guaranteed by the
individual kolkhoz, with the state's guarantee only secondary—the
rise in most kolkhoz incomes because of fairer prices being paid out
by the state and less discrimination against kolkhozy in many areas,
the individual kolkhozniks realize a far higher percentage of their
annual income from the public sector than they traditionally did.
Still, the percentage of income derived from the private sector is
very significant, and moreover the private plot provides a more secure source of those products that the individual dvor prefers.

In the following pages of this chapter the economic significance
of the private sector and the problems it poses for the regime will
be examined in depth, as will be the institution by which the private
economy is engaged in, the kolkhoz dvor, a remnant of Russian peasant law.

THE PRESENT ECONOMIC ROLE OF THE PRIVATE SECTOR
IN SOVIET AGRICULTURAL PRODUCTION

Major aspects of the private subsidiary economy concern Soviet
economy and, in Soviet agriculture in particular, the role the subsidiary
economy plays in providing kolkhozniks with personal income and sus-
tenance, and the effects of the subsidiary economy on the kolkhoz public
economy. Does the labor time spent on the private economy come at
the expense of the public economy? How do labor costs involved in
the two sectors for production of the same crops compare? In general,
which sector is the more efficient economically? There is the question
of the regime's views on the private sector today, the possibility of
any dramatic change in the present policy, and, if so, the likely direction of such a change.

In 1953 the personal subsidiary economy produced 45.6 percent
of total agricultural goods. By 1968 this percentage had slipped to
29 percent.[9]

Andrei Babich, drawing upon official Soviet statistical handbooks,
sketches the present extent of the private sector. In the USSR today,
there are 14,700,000 kolkhoz dvors occupying 4,800,000 of the 360,100-
000 hectares of kolkhoz land. In 1969, 5,200,000 out of a total of
10,000,000 hectares used for growing potatoes and vegetables were
on private plots (including those belonging to nonkolkhozniks). Private
farmers owned 15,900,000 of the nation's 40,500,000 cows, 13,800,000
of its 56,000,000 pigs, 27,400,000 of its 130,600,000 sheep, and no less
than 4,200,000 of its 5,100,000 goats. In 1967, produce to the value
of 13,600 million rubles was produced on the private plots of kolkhozniks, and to the value of 10,200 million rubles on those of workers.

The total value of the gross production of all categories of farms was 78,100 million rubles. As of January 1, 1968, less than one-third of the total number of cattle in the USSR, and a little over one quarter of the number of pigs and one-fifth of the total sheep were in the private sector. In that year the private sector accounted for 38 percent of the USSR's total meat production and the same percentage of the total milk production.[10]

In a study of three kolkhozy by a team of Soviet social scientists done during the middle and late 1960s in Orlovsk Oblast, it was discovered that the subsidiary private economy was the most important source of dvor income outside of work in the public sector of the kolkhoz, providing from 30 to 75 percent of dvor income in the three investigated kolkhozy. And, of the dvor production in these three kolkhozy, from 20 to 70 percent of it was sold on the market.[11] Even in the face of a long-term trend of increase in the share of kolkhozniks' income from the public sector during the period from 1951 to 1967—it increased by four times over this period[12]—the share from the personal economy is still estimated to be 35 to 42 percent by one source,[13] and 40 percent by another.[14] Approximately one-fifth of the produce of the subsidiary economy as a whole finds its way to the kolkhoz market or to the state.[15] Hence, the overwhelming amount of its production supplies the dvors themselves. Still, it is approvingly noted that the subsidiary economy provides a substantial amount of food for the city population and that in absolute volume of supply this role is growing.[16]

Let us examine the economic role of the subsidiary economy in greater detail and with an eye on recent trends. The subsidiary economy of kolkhozniks, workers, and employees accounted in 1963 for 23.8 percent of all produce grown in the USSR, and in livestock products production the percentage was 45.6 percent.[17] At the beginning of 1963 the heads of cattle in the personal subsidiary economy of kolkhozniks amounted to 38.5 percent of the social herds of kolkhozy The percentage sizes of personal herds in terms of kolkhoz herds for pigs, sheep, and goats were respectively 31.6 percent, 29 percent, and 31.3 percent. At this time the total sown area of garden plot of kolkhozniks constituted approximately 37 percent of the total sown area of kolkhozy.[18] It is apparent from this that the private sector is especially significant nationally in terms of livestock products. But a goodly portion of the fodder for the private sector's livestock comes from collective farm fields[19] either as payments in kind or through nocturnal requisitioning. According to Wadekin, over 70 percent of today's payments in kind are in grain, most of which is used for fodder for private livestock.[20] Thus the prosperity of private livestock production is directly attached to the kolkhoz public sector.

As far as the crop production side is concerned, it is less important in general but very significant in regard to a limited number of types of produce. The economist Shmelev makes the point that most private or subsidiary economy crop production involves those kinds of produce the production of which in the public sector is insufficiently mechanized, for example, potatoes and vegetables, both of which are of insignificant weight in the public sector. In 1962 the share of potatoes, vegetables, and melons in the subsidiary economy of kolkhozniks, workers, and employees was 75.3 percent of all their sown area, whereas the total percentage for these crops in the public sector sown area was only 3.1 percent.[21] As of 1966, for the average RSFSR kolkhoz family, the personal subsidiary economy supplied 7 percent of its grain, 90 percent of its potatoes, 80 percent of its vegetables, and practically all of its meat, butter, and eggs, plus 52 percent of its hay needs.[22] Thus it is evident from this that the private sector more or less makes the dvor self-sufficient in all its basic food needs except bread. As far as the effect of it on the general volume of Soviet agricultural production, its weight as of 1966 was 17 percent overall, or 6 percent of grown produce and 30 percent of all livestock. But for certain products it was a most significant source. It accounted for 60 percent of all potatoes, approximately 40 percent of all vegetables, more than 40 percent of the meat, approximately 39 percent of all milk, and almost 68 percent of all eggs.[23] Such figures are impressive, especially since they involve staple foods.

THE PRIVATE PLOT AND THE INCOME
OF KOLKHOZNIKS

The historian Yu. Arutiunian, using data from certain Ukrainian villages statistically typical of rural areas for the whole of the USSR, confirms that the per capita income of a kolkhoz dvor from the communal or public sector is one-third less than the per capita income of workers and employees. In the country as a whole, payments for the labor of kolkhozniks were 30 percent below the yearly wages of sovkhoz workers in 1958, 42 percent below in 1959, and 39 percent below in 1960. But Arutiunian notes that far more substantial than the differences between the sectors—state and kolkhoz—were the differences in income within the sectors, that is, between the various occupationally qualified groups of the population. Those employed in skilled mental labor in the village were paid twice as much as those performing unskilled physical labor. The wages of the most highly paid skilled personnel were six to seven times higher than the payment for the labor of those at the other extreme. Arutiunian then proceeds to see whether income derived from the private plots brings the lower-paid categories up to the upper-level group. The data showed that personal plots were distributed among all income and skill strata of the rural population. The subsidiary plot, he concludes, is popular among all social groups, including workers and employees of state institutions and enterprises. But their plots differ in size. In 1964 the average family garden of a kolkhoznik was approximately .4 hectares in size, while that of a worker was only .17 hectares. Among kolkhozniks there was one cow for approximately every three plots, whereas among workers there was only one cow for every eleven plots. Arutiunian concluded that plot incomes did not serve to equalize the income gap between skilled and unskilled. The skilled had the same livestock holdings and plantings as the unskilled. The personal plot does raise the income of the kolkhozniks toward the level of that of workers and employees, but it does not bridge the income gap between skilled and unskilled in the rural work force.[24]

The private plots, which in the aggregate constitute only 3 percent of the whole sown area of the USSR, provide a very significant proportion of all vegetables, potatoes, fruits, milk, butter, and livestock products. Yet they provide practically no grain[25] or other technical crops. The relative role of the private sector in total agricultural production and in supplying income to kolkhozniks has been declining since the 1950s, yet the private sector has not lost its significance nor will it soon. In fact, the return per day from the private plot still exceeds that from the public sector of the kolkhoz.[26] In absolute terms total production and personal income from private plots have increased. It is only in a relative sense that it has declined, and that decline has not been precipitous. Moreover, it is the tremendous capital investments and reforms in prices and fiscal policy undertaken by the state toward the farms, in particular the kolkhozy, that have significantly increased output from the public sector. The total income per kolkhoz dvor for 1960-67 in the RSFSR increased from 1,495 to 2,142 rubles, or by 43 percent. During this period personal income from the public economy increased by 75 percent. The share of income from the subsidiary economy in total personal income of the kolkhoz family for this period declined from 42 to 35 percent and the percentage of contribution of the public economy increased from 41 percent to 50 percent.[27]

COMPETITION BETWEEN PRIVATE AND PUBLIC SECTORS

A recurrent debate has centered on how the private plot affects the kolkhozniks' work in the public sector of the kolkhoz. Certain Soviet politicians and economists have attacked any liberality toward the private sector on the basis that such liberality only encourages

kolkhozniks to neglect work in the public sector. The Soviet economists G. Shmelev, M. Makeenko, and V. N. Iakimov have defended
the private sector against such attacks. Much of the debate has been
about incentives to work. Shmelev argued that to allow the private
sector to prosper was to create greater incentives to work productivity
in general by making the kolkhozniks more prosperous. For this
reason he opposed Khrushchev's policy of restricting private plots
after 1958, declaring that artificial curtailment of the personal subsidiary economy undermined personal material incentives and led to
unhealthy raises in kolkhoz market prices. Shmelev backed his arguments by pointing out that the liberal policy prevailing prior to 1958
and reverted to under Brezhnev and Kosygin led to periods of increased
agricultural output.[28]

The Soviet economist G. Kuznetsov, who would seemingly cling
to the traditional dogma of the inherent superiority of collectivization,
also stressed his opposition to any premature curtailment of the private
sector on the basis that personal incentives would be undermined.[29]
M. Makeenko, another Soviet economist, labels the belief that work
in the private subsidiary economy lowers participation in the public
sector a "big myth." Both he and Shmelev maintain that the private
sector does not compete with the public sector. Output from the private sector, he says, is primarily consumed rather than marketed.
Private production tends to concentrate on crops that are the most
labor intensive and the least mechanized, and hence of marginal interest to the public sector. And Makeenko adds that female labor predominates in the private sector; hence the latter utilizes the least
skilled as well as a marginal segment of the labor force.[30] These
data are confirmed by data collected by the Soviet sociologist V. N.
Shubkin.[31]

Kuznetsov, Makeenko, and Shmelev want to "de-ideologize" the
criticism of the dvor, and both Kuznetsov and Makeenko are, although
not admitting it, battling the argument current in the West that more
effort is expended on the private plots because they are privately
owned. The American economist Charles Wilber concludes that there
is no evidence to support this, although there is evidence to support
the importance of price differentials between sales to the state and
in kolkhoz markets as an explanation.[32] Roy and Betty Laird agree
with Wilber that ownership as such does not insure efficiency.[33]
Rather it is the clear nexus between effort and reward.

V. N. Iakimov's study of the private sector concludes that the
kolkhoznik sells not just because he has a surplus but in order to
make money. Up to 1965 the percentage of his income from the subsidiary economy was approximately equal to that from the social
economy. But from 1965 on the percentage of income from the public
economy grew significantly.[34] In the RSFSR it grew from 41 percent

in 1960 to 50 percent in 1967, while the share of the personal subsidiary economy decreased to 34.6 percent. But during this period, the absolute size of income derived by kolkhozniks from the personal subsidiary economy increased by 8 percent.[35] Therefore, says Iakimov, it is not just because the public economy is deficient in satisfying the needs for certain produce, but more importantly because it does not yet provide a sufficiently high income for the kolkhoznik that the latter is attached to his private plots.[36] So Iakimov's point is that, given the inadequacies of the wage incentives of the public sector, the investment of time in the private sector is rational, predictable, and justifiable. Iakimov feels that you can insure that enough time is spent on the public sector without attacking the private sector. He condemns the past administrative curtailment of the private sector because the policy failed to benefit the public sector as it was intended. The curtailment did not in fact create supplementary labor resources for the public sector, nor did it raise the level of labor activism among kolkhozniks in the public sector.[37] Iakimov cites figures indicating significant increases in private livestock holdings between 1954 and 1958 with no loss of labor in the public sector of the kolkhozy. On the contrary, he notes that during this period of intense growth in the private sector, labor activity of kolkhozniks grew significantly.[38] For Iakimov the lesson is clear: prosperity in the private sector is consonant with and even a stimulant of increased labor activism in the public sector, rather than a negative influence on it.

THE MOST RECENT ASSAULT ON THE PRIVATE SECTOR AND ITS RESULTS

Khrushchev's crackdown on the private sector began in March 1956, when legislation allowing kolkhozy to adjust the sizes of subsidiary holdings of household up or down, within certain limits, according to the labor participation of able-bodied members of the household in the communal economy, was enacted.[39] From 1958 to 1960 the total sown area in the private sector was reduced by 9 percent, while private livestock holdings dropped. In 1958 the state discontinued sales of food grains to households. In December 1958 Khrushchev exerted pressure on farmers to sell their livestock "voluntarily" to their kolkhoz and on kolkhozy to cease leaving communal fields fallow as summer pasture for private livestock.[40] The result of these steps was a major decline in the private livestock herds. From 1959 through 1964, significant decreases occurred, except for pigs. As to the extent of these livestock declines, the heads of cattle declined by 14 percent in 1963 and in 1964 by 17 percent, cows by 23 percent and 21 percent respectively in these years, and goats and sheep by 18 percent and 28 percent.[41] Also, the number of kolkhoz dvors decreased during this period by 8 percent,[42] probably indicating that the repressive policy forced some families out of agricultural work. Following the 1964 Central Committee decree of October 27, "On Removal of Unjustified Limitations on the Personal Subsidiary Economy of Kolkhozniks," the number of livestock of all types started to increase. Brezhnev made it clear that a new positive policy toward the private sector was in force. Taxes on private livestock holdings were eliminated, as were certain restrictions on the number of animals to be kept. Restrictions on the size of private plots were reduced.[43] Late in 1964 the state began to sell foodstuffs for private livestock, and Gosbank was authorized to extend credit to private livestock owners to purchase more livestock.[44]

With the increased monetization of remuneration of labor in the kolkhozy in recent years, less feed has been distributed to kolkhozniks as payment in kind.[45] Since the advent of guaranteed minimum pay for kolkhozniks in 1966, the already emergent trend away from in-kind pay has been accelerated.[46] The result of this has been to reduce the feed readily available to kolkhozniks for their private livestock. Moreover, there is evidence that, despite the official "liberal" policy at the highest echelons, at the local level party support for private farming is lacking. This manifests itself in cases of private farmers being deprived of pasturage and fodder.[47] In certain localities the fodder shortage has led recently to reductions inprocurable livestock products.[48] The consequence of this unofficial local repression has been a slowed rate of increase for private plot output and a general reduction in the livestock population, which has been pronounced in the private sector. In 1969 alone, the number of large horned cattle in private plots fell by 2,400,000, of cows by 700,000, and sheep and goats by 2,100,000.[49] Andrei Babich feels that this recent decline in private farming has been due to the party's indifference or even encouragement of infringements of private farmers' rights.[50] "At present," he states, there are many in the party who "see in the existence of private farming a concession to the peasants' private interests."[51] Babich sees the present policy of the party toward the private plots as "ambivalent." One can easily detect an instinctual, resilient ideological prejudice within the party cadres that erodes their economic pragmatism.

Still, certain facts admitted to be such by Soviet economists must be sobering to the most ideologically committed, if not grounds for further irrational attacks on the private sector. For example, one man day worked by a kolkhoznik in the private sector brings in more income than a man day worked in the public sector. And although productivity of labor in the private sector is lower than in the public sector, yet the average kolkhoznik spends one-third of his total work time in the private sector, derives approximately 40 percent of his total income from it, and produces approximately 30 percent of the gross produce of agriculture.[52] Yet as the English economist Knox Lovell notes, the intensive application of labor with practically no equipment has enabled the private sector to outdistance the public sector in terms of productivity per unit of livestock. In 1958 the private sector accounted for 52 percent of total meat production with only 37 percent of all meat-producing livestock.[53] The private sector obtains higher yields per animal or per hectare in the production of meat and typical garden crops—fruit, berries, potatoes, and vegetables. The private sector is also as fully productive as the public sector in regard to milk and raw wool. The garden crops, notes Lovell, require a minimum of land area and a maximum of labor time and very little expertise.[54] Lovell concludes, like Iakimov, that most peasant families need their plots to enable them to maintain an acceptable standard of living. Not only is income derived from the public sector insufficient to support a typical family, but the produce of the public sector is normally of the wrong assortment, especially deficient in vegetables, meat, and fruit.[55]

Consequently, the private sector's impact today is far from insignificant. There has been no significant decline in its role as a mainstay for the kolkhozniks as a source of both supplementary income and otherwise unavailable produce.[56] Also, approximately a fifth of all its production finds its way to market.[57] In 1966 three-fourths of all vegetables and melons, 85 to 88 percent of all meat and milk products, and over 90 percent of all potatoes consumed by kolkhozniks came from the private sector. Sovkhoz worker families are much less dependent on the private sector for these items.[58]

Lovell feels that until such time as a significant portion of the investment in agriculture is allocated to improving the agricultural distribution and storage system, a real need for the private sector will continue to exist irrespective of its level of output.[59] He believes that the private sector's most significant role is to cover up for the gross deficiencies in the state distribution system.[60] He feels that the private sector's continued existence is a measure of the public sector's inability or unwillingness to produce certain produce or allocate investments for the trade infrastructure needed to service rural or even urban food consumers.

G. Kuznetsov holds that in order for the private sector to "die out" the following will have to occur: an increase in kolkhoz production to a level commensurate with the public need for produce; a standardization of pay levels and social funds of consumption per capita in city and country; all-around development of state and cooperative trade and continual provision of the population with all necessary agricultural and industrial goods; a struggle with the surviving private property mentality and psychology and the instilling of a communist outlook.61 Such a formidable set of preconditions will not come to pass soon.

Insofar as Kuznetsov's views are orthodox, the private sector will continue to be a significant factor for the near future—the next decade at least. But it is far from certain that the private sector will not be subjected to repressive campaigns from time to time. Andrei Babich sees a threat to the private sector's autonomy in the new state inspectorates for purchases and quality control of agricultural produce announced as being formed in raions, krais, and oblasts as liason agents between farms and procurement, sales, and processing organizations. This was announced in Brezhnev's Central Committee speech of July 3, 1970. Their task is to track down all marketable surpluses and include them in the contract agreements for delivery to state authorities. Babich sees this as contrary to the March 1965 Central Committee plenary sessions, which established fixed delivery quotas and made special provisions for above-quota sales in a spirit of fostering voluntary sales.62 Babich feels that the inspectorates will sooner or later force private plot owners to sell their surpluses and thus ultimately destroy the kolkhoz markets.63 Of course, this remains to be seen, although no doubt the additional pressure the inspectorates apply to kolkhozy to "voluntarily" sell all their above-quota surpluses may even force them in turn to pressure the kolkhozniks to help them meet the actually illegal demands laid on them by turning over private plot produce. If this occurs and if the above-quota prices are well below kolkhoz market prices, it will lead to a crisis of underproduction in the private sector. This will generate more pressure on the public sector to compensate for the loss of marketable produce, as well as to supply the kolkhozniks with the produce they require but may refuse to produce for themselves, since they fear that it will be commandeered by the state at unsatisfactory prices.

The regime's forays against the private sector seem to represent an irrational response to shortcomings in the public sector. It is quite clear that the private and public sectors are and have been complementary rather than competitive and that the continued existence of the private sector is an economic necessity given the regime's investments and financial-economic policies toward the farms. Yet at times the private sector becomes the "whipping boy" or "devil" behind agricultural crises.

Karl-Eugen Wadekin recognized that the private sector represents a potential source of disruption for a Soviet-type centralized economy, rendering it partially dependent on factors that cannot be centrally controlled. It exposes the defects of the state sector and by contrast makes the scale and causes of these failures more visible to the public. It also exploits these faults via the kolkhoz market.64

Roy Laird believes that the regime is as equally determined to eliminate the city kolkhoz markets on which the surplus from private plots is sold. The reason for this, he states, is not just to eradicate private trade but to destroy the kolkhoz's markets role as a communications medium. Without this information center, the kolkhozniks would be largely cut off from contact with what is going on outside their tightly controlled farm-universe.[65]

The ultimate question is to decollectivize or not and, if so, how to do it without seeming to. The enlargement of the scope and maximum limits of livestock and land plots could be a gradual way. So could a more liberal policy in respect of family or dvor partitions, a legal process whereby certain members of a family legally separate from the family or dvor and found their own separate dvor, thereby becoming entitled to their own garden plot and livestock. Proliferating the number of dvors would, of course, increase the total number and area of plots and private livestock. Gradually dvors could rent kolkhoz lands temporarily unused by their kolkhozy. They might also be allowed more generous use of kolkhoz equipment and personnel, perhaps for a fee, and even be allowed to hire a limited number of seasonal help. Moreover, they might even be allowed to buy certain types of machinery so as to better utilize their land and time. The state could retain controls via price-setting for voluntary sales as well as by a tax structure designed to encourage sales to the state. The credit system as well as the sales of machinery could also be used to control the private sector without directly interfering in its day-to-day operations.

THE FUTURE OF THE DVOR AS A LEGAL ENTITY

Perhaps the legal institution of the kolkhoz dvor would be jettisoned by the regime at this point since it served the purpose, among others, of minimizing the extent of the private sector by substituting an extended family instead of the individual as the subject of use of the plot and livestock. It is the official Soviet legal doctrine that the kolkhoz dvor is not a juridical person, like the kolkhoz itself. Rather it is, according to Soviet law, a single subject of the right of land use. Dvor members as individuals have shares of the dvor garden plot but do not have rights as land users.[66] All this creates practical difficulties within the dvor if relationships among its members are unfriendly, and also burdens both the kolkhoz itself and even the state administrative and judicial organs with intra-dvor disputes as well as disputes between the dvor and kolkhoz. In fact the kolkhoz dvor is a complex legal matrix, perhaps too complex. Conceptually it is an underdeveloped institution. Dvor actions can involve it in administrative law, kolkhoz law, financial law, land law, and personal property law. For instance, the dvor pays an agricultural tax based on the size of its garden plot, whereas members of the dvor having nonagricultural income do pay a regular income tax on it individually, and this does not fall on the dvor as a whole.[67] Its relations with its parent kolkhoz are classified as either kolkhoz-legal or civil-legal.[68] According to one Soviet jurist, norms defining the legal position of the subsidiary economy of the kolkhoz dvor and its property relations constitute kolkhoz-legal relations and should be regulated by norms of kolkhoz law.[69]

The issue of whether or not to transfer legal jurisdiction over users of lands within rural population points hitherto under the kolkhoz or sovkhoz to village Soviets has come up of late. The jusist A. M. Turubiner holds to the traditional view that since the use of personal plots of kolkhozniks is involved, this is inherently an internal kolkhoz matter. The jurist V. P. Balezin believes that in light of the trend toward separating the land under and around the house itself from the garden plot, which more and more should be in an area well removed from the house, the former should be placed under town Soviet jurisdiction, while the "leading role" in regulating the purely agricultural plots should remain with the farms.[70] This emphasis on the preferability of splitting up the hitherto united home and garden plot has implications for the viability of the plots as a significant source of income for the kolkhozniks.

In the juridical literature the dvor is defined as a family-labor union of persons who are members of the kolkhoz and participate with their labor in its public economy, from which they receive their basic income while jointly conducting a small personal subsidiary economy on their garden plot.[71] Yet, strangely, there are dvors consisting of only one person and even dvors without a plot.[72] And there are dvors in which some members are not even kolkhozniks.[73] Still, despite all these seeming inconsistencies between the standard definition and the realities, the problem of the informal and indefinite internal administrative relations within the dvor is enough to justify drastic redefinition and overhauling by legislation. Yet none has so far been attempted, despite the opportunity presented by the adoption of a new kolkhoz Model Charter in 1969. At the heart of this internal administrative problem is the theory of the equality of all dvor members. Yet no legislation exists providing any legal teeth to implement this. The underdeveloped legislation on the dvor allows the traditional Russian peasant custom that governed the old peasant dvor to apply by default to the present dvor except insofar as Soviet legislation provides otherwise, which it generally does not. The head of the dvor, as per Russian peasant law, is the "house owner," its representative in its economic affairs. In theory his rights are no greater than other dvor members, yet he alone acts in the name of the dvor as its legal representative and can bind all its members.[74] Yet the rules of liability are far from satisfactory in distinguishing acts done by the head in the interests of the dvor, in which case dvor property is liable, and acts done by him in his own personal interests, in which case only his personal property is liable. It should be noted that the dvor, although not a legal person, still partakes of the nature of a legal person. Dvor property is not available to satisfy the personal debts owed by individual dvor members. Nor is the personal property of dvor members liable for dvor debts.[75]

The right to use the garden plot resides in the dvor as such, not with its separate members. And the size of the plot does not depend on the number of members.[76] In other words, despite the fact that one family has far more mouths to feed and hands to occupy, it is given no more than a half hectare, the maximum stipulated by the Model Charter. Perhaps kolkhozy adjust plot sizes within the minimum-maximum range on the basis of such considerations, but still the maximum itself is too low to really reflect the needs of large families. Apparently illegal extensions of the plots are still widespread, no doubt in good measure due to this situation.[77] The upward revision of the maximum size is one possible response to the problem of how to increase production of certain products without raising purchase prices for them or allowing dvors to rent temporarily unused kolkhoz lands from the kolkhoz. Only in a negative sense is consideration given to the labor efforts of dvor members in regard to plot size. Dvors, any one of whose members fail to earn the minimum number of labor days set by the particular kolkhoz for work in the kolkhoz public sector, have their plots reduced.[78] This is obviously unfair and incentive-destroying in that it punishes all dvor members and not just the guilty one. But it does illustrate the group responsibility principle[79] institutionalized in the dvor, a principle that extends to taxation, insurance, credit, and general legal and administration liability. At one time it could be argued from the regime's standpoint that such collective liability was a necessity so as to instill respect for the regime's goals and production targets in a naturally hostile peasantry that was bent on circumventing its responsibilities. To hold the dvor collectively responsible for tasks and duties was to prevent the evasive individual from getting away with clever circumventions by putting him and his family on notice that they would pay his debts. For most peasants with strong family ties this liability of his family for his defaults inhibited such attempts. Of course, the disincentives inherent in such a negative stimulus to performance are obvious. It produced attempts to meet only the bare minima and to simulate the achievements required. It also engendered a sullen, embittered attitude toward the regime's goals.

Another issue the regime faces in respect to the dvor is whether or not to reconsider its traditional prohibition of the dvor utilizing hired labor in the subsidiary economy.80 There is no evidence that this issue has been brought up in recent years. It certainly goes against a basic principle of Soviet socialism. Still, as long as the terms of such employment are regulated scrupulously by the state and the number of hired hands strictly limited, such a practice would hardly be a threat to reinstitute the classical capitalist wage slavery referred to as the exploitation of man by man. But it could produce a more subtle, incremental, progressive strengthening of whatever residual private entrepreneurial spirit remains on the farms and even lead to an unhealthy income differentiation among the peasantry that could catalyze petty jealousies and resentments. This could in turn create pressures for more state-provided benefits to the less fortunate peasants. Moreover, perhaps what the regime is more worried about in this regard is not merely the breach in the socialist ethic of not employing labor for private enrichment, but rather that they would be opening a veritable Pandora's box by this very limited and restricted breach in the cannon of socialist principles. With kolkhozniks emboldened by such a concession and by the sweet taste of mini-private farming, their next demand, should production and productivity soar under the new dispensation, might be for more liberal hiring provisions. The subsidiary might soon become the primary economy. Moreover, if the limited experiment did prove very successful economically, it would only strengthen the hand of the ultraliberal economists and jurists who advocate more and more decentralized and nimimal state controls over agricultural production and more use of such economic levers as credits, tax, and prices. The regime is sensitive to invidious comparisons between the private and public sectors unless they confirm the bias of the regime in favor of large-scale farming. Success under such a new scheme would by implication cast doubts on the basic soundness of the Soviet commitment to large-scale farm operations. Of course, all of this need not flow out of a limited reform in which one or two hired hands were allowed per dvor during peak seasons, even if this were coupled with liberalization of the maximum sizes of both plots and livestock holdings. But if a limited experiment were to prove successful, the logic of the situation might suggest more of the same. And this logic is very threatening to the ideology. Herein lies a major obstacle to the idea even being put on the agenda for public discussion.

Another possible direction of reform could be revision of the now traditional Soviet prohibition on the renting out of land.81 If a dvor could rent out its plot to others and thereby realize income, it would be very advantageous to a dvor consisting of only elderly or disabled members or women with children. Rentals could be strictly controlled, as could the amount of land any one person or dvor could rent. Again this is ideologically objectionable in principle, although hardly threatening to socialized agriculture if kept within limits. Again the mere public mention of this idea is apparently anathema.

An especially vexing problem for kolkhozniks and the courts involves distinguishing the personal property of dvor members from dvor property. Although this is hardly an acute problem for the regime from the standpoint of the economic performance of farms, still it is one of those peculiar features of kolkhoz life that makes of the kolkhoz peasantry a caste apart from the rest of Soviet society, evidence of their legal separateness, and thus a contributing factor to the generally negative self-image of the peasant. Article 42 of the new Model Charter of the kolkhoz defines the home, economic structures, livestock, petty agricultural inventory, and bees as dvor property. Moreover, all property transferred to the dvor by its members and all objects of domestic use and personal consumption obtained with common means, per article 27 of the USSR Fundamentals of Civil Legislation, are dvor property. And, per article 126 of the RSFSR Civil Code, the property of the dvor belongs to its members by right of joint property. But all this is far from tidy in reality. The complications arise because individual dvor members have their own personal property, which can easily become confused with dvor property. On top of this there is also another distinct category of personal property, the joint property of spouses. The joint property of the dvor is shareless in nature. No one dvor member has a definite, specific share he can identify while the dvor is in existence. Possession, use, and disposal of dvor property is carried out only by common agreement of all dvor members. Only if a member leaves the dvor for good can he demand his share. In contrast, ordinary personal joint property in Soviet civil law—with the exception of joint property of spouses—is share property, with each share being definite before its liquidation, and this share, unlike the share in dvor property, can be sold, pledged, given or willed away, whereas the share in dvor property cannot be alienated in any manner before it becomes definite through what is called partition or apportionment.[82] Another contrast between the two forms of property exists in respect to their liability for debts. For the personal debts of any dvor member, dvor property is not attachable. For common or joint property of citizens there is joint or "solid" liability, which means that the creditor can demand from any one of the copossessors some or all of the property. And whereas ordinary joint property is inheritable in the normal way, a share in dvor property "opens up" only after the last living dvor member dies.[83]

There are recurring legal problems when the circumstances are unclear as to how and with what means certain objects or property were acquired by dvor members, that is, in exactly what capacity an individual dvor member has acted—as agent for the dvor or for

himself. Moreover, as if this concentricity of various types of property in dvor members was not confusing enough, yet another major
source of confusion is the principle that all dvor members are obliged
to contribute to the dvor common pot from their personal earnings,
a unique feature of the old Russian peasant dvor. And when the earnings of individuals go into the common pot, their legal status is transformed. They become dvor property. A big question is just what
share of a dvor member's personal earnings would he contribute. The
problem is that there is no legislation or legal guidance on this. Usually it is left to informal arrangements, and obviously these breed
disputes.[84] And such disputes go to court as do all disputes over use
and disposal of dvor property.[85] Obviously the informality of these
arrangements, the legally fuzzy definitions of just what the characteristics of each type of joint property are, and the failure to adequately
define exactly what happens when and if one dvor member vetoes a
particular use or disposition of dvor property—since the rule of
unanimity is clearly set forth but without describing the consequences
of a veto by any one member—all confound the situation.

Other collective liabilities of the dvor include payment of the
agricultural tax [86] and mandatory property and livestock insurance
premiums.[87] While the regime no doubt still derives some administrative convenience in treating the dvor as a corporate entity for
these purposes, as well as maintaining the general inhibitory atmosphere that is part and parcel of such a collective liability, the dvor
constitutes a rather substantial method of limiting the number of
garden plots and thus of limiting the private sector. If any adult could
get his own individual plot, the private sector would be many times
greater than it is today. In fact this is the nub of the problem of fraud-
ulent partitions. A partition is officially defined in the context of the
kolkhoz dvor as a distribution of property among dvor members and
the formation as a result of two or more dvors. This is to be distin-
guished from apportionment, which is a distribution of property as
the result of which one or more dvor members receives his share
and permanently leaves the dvor without a new dvor being formed.[88]
Many partitions were engaged in just to get another plot. If this is
the actual motive rather than it being based on necessity of some
sort, then it should not be allowed by the court, per Soviet legal authorities. Yet there are no firm and specific criteria upon which to
base the court's granting of the petition for partition. This area is
a legal swampland. The Latvian jurist Ia. Strautmanis bemoans
this.[89] But so far, even with the advent of a new kolkhoz Model Charter, this is still the situation.

Strautmanis favors an approach to the kolkhoz dvor legislatively
that would not stabilize it as an institution. He points out that in the
Baltic republics the dvor has no historical roots, and hence by

implication he is saying it would be easier to dispose of.[90] Yet he
is aware that its preservation by the regime is not based on reverence
for peasant traditions. So when he urges not stabilizing the dvor by
new legislation because it is in the long run a brake on the further
socio-economic development of the kolkhoz,[91] he may be interpreted
as favoring a transformation of the legal status of the family of kolkhozniks into that of the worker's family. As to whether or not he
envisions this as a gradual process or a sudden and complete conversion is not clear. In any case there seem to be no echoes of this in
the Soviet literature. And, as to whether or not he intends by this
the extinction of the garden plot, and thus the private sector, is an
open question. It need not if the right to a plot vests in individuals.
The sblizhenie (merger) theory explains that the dvor and the subsidiary economy will become progressively less important until ultimately
the dvor will be nothing more than a common family with a legal status
indistinguishable from that of the workers, and the garden plots will
be unnecessary because of the growth of the public sector and will
be voluntarily given up by their users.

The Soviet lawyer N. Sirodoev explains away the significance
of the new kolkhoz Model Charter's unprecedented independent section
on the dvor and its economy as reflecting not its growing role, but
rather the necessity of more fully securing the constitutional rights
of citizens in the conduct of their personal economies.[92] Strautmanis
relates incidents that make this explanation of the motive behind the
new treatment of the dvor in the charter appear credible. He reports
cases in Latvia of illegal curtailments of garden plots on the unfounded
basis that they hinder development of the public economy. He notes
that in some kolkhozy inducements in the form of an extra 10- to 20-
ruble addition to basic monthly earnings were offered if kolkhozniks
gave up their garden plots and personal livestock. He states that this
practice was officially condemned and ceased in Latvia in 1966.[93]
So Sirodoev plays down any attempt to attribute to the new section on
the dvor an upgrading of it in the eyes of the regime or even an af-
firmation of its vitality. In any case there are two problems inter-
twined by the dvor. First, whether or not this anachronistic peasant
law institution that stamps the farm family with a badge of inferiority
and that spawns many intricate and complex legal questions is serving
any useful administrative, legal, or economic functions today. Second,
and more important, whether to expand, contract, or freeze the present
scope, size, and function of the private sector and, if so, how will this
affect the dvor? Can the dvor still perform a useful purpose for the
regime if it decides to either abolish or expand the private sector?
Perhaps the regime will open these questions up for public discussion.
So far it has been assumed that the private sector and the dvor, although far from having outlived their usefulness, are progressively

166

declining in importance. Hence any opening up of the public agenda to the question might indicate a shift in thinking, perhaps reflective of a fundamental policy shift in favor of a greater role for the private sector.

NOTES

1. Yu. V. Arutyunyan, "Rural Social Structure," in Town, Country and People, edited by G. V. Osipov (London: Tavistock Publications, 1969), p. 240.
2. As of 1965, 60 percent of all personal subsidiary economy production came from kolkhozniks. V. A. Belianov, Lichnoe Podsobnoe Khoziaistvo pri Sotsializme (Moscow: Izdat. Ekonomika, 1970), p. 55.
3. "Nashi Konsul'tatsii," Chelovek i Zakon, December 12, 1971, p. 85.
4. Karl-Eugen Wadekin, The Private Sector in Soviet Agriculture (Berkeley: University of California Press, 1973), p. 1.
5. Naum Jasny, The Socialized Agriculture of the USSR (Palo Alto: Stanford University Press, 1949), pp. 340-341.
6. N. D. Kazantsev, Utopicheskii i Nauchnyi Sotsializm o Pereustroistve Sel'sko Khoziaistva (Moscow: Izdat. Mosk. Univ., 1969), p. 207.
7. A. I. Kuropatkin, Ekonomicheskie Osnovy Preodoleniia Sushchestvennykh Razlichii Mezhdu Gorodom i Derevnei (Moscow: Izdat. Mosk. Univ., 1971), p. 60.
8. Karl-Eugen Wadekin, The Private Sector in Soviet Agriculture, op. cit., p. 2.
9. G. Kuznetsov, Tovarnye Otnosheniia i Ekonomicheskie Stimuly v kolkhoznom Proizvodstve (Moscow: Izdat. "Mysl'," 1971), p. 290.
10. Andrei Babich, "The Private Plot: A Vital Element in Collective Farmers' Income," Analysis of Current Developments in the Soviet Union, Institute for the Study of the USSR, no. 659 (July 13, 1971): 2.
11. Kollektiv Kolkhoznikov—Sotsial'no—Psikhologicheskoe Issledovanie, op. cit., p. 75.
12. V. A. Tikhonov, "Problemy Truda v Sel'skom Khoziaistve SSSR," in Sel'skoe Khoziaistvo Sovetskogo Soiuza (Moscow: Izdat. Kolos, 1970), pp. 159-160.
13. G. Kuznetsov, Tovarnye Otnosheniia i Ekonomicheskie Stimuly v Kolkhoznom Proizvodstve, op. cit., pp. 290-291.
14. Andrei Babich, "The Private Plot . . .," op. cit., p. 4.
15. Kuznetsov, op. cit., p. 291.

16. A. F. Tarasov, Razvitie Kolkhoznoi Sobstvennosti v Obsh-chenarodnuiu (Rostov: Izdat. Rostovskogo, Universiteta, 1967), p. 317.

17. G. Shmelev, "Ekonomicheskaia Rol' Lichnogo Podsobnogo Khoziaistva," Voprosy Ekonomiki, no. 4 (1965): 27.

18. Ibid., p. 35.

19. I. Lukinov, "Problems in Agricultural Forecasting," Voprosy Ekonomiki, no. 7 (1971), translated in Problems of Economics, IASP, XIV, no. 10 (February 1971): 12.

20. Karl-Eugen Wadekin, "Payments in Kind in Soviet Agriculture—Part II," Bulletin, Institute for the Study of the USSR, XVIII, no. 11 (November 1971: p. 8.

21. Ibid.

22. M. Makeenko, "Ekonomicheeskaia Rol' Lichnogo Podsobnogo Khoziaistva," Voprosy Ekonomiki, no. 10 (1966): 60.

23. Ibid., p. 61.

24. Yu. Arutiunian, "The Social Structure of the Rural Population," Voprosy Filosofii, no. 5 (May, 1966), translated in CDSP XVIII, no. 25 (July 13, 1966): 22.

25. M. Makeenko, op. cit., p. 61.

26. David W. Bronson and Constance B. Krueger, "The Revolution in Soviet Farm Household Income, 1953-1967," in The Soviet Rural Community, edited by James R. Millar (Urbana: University of Illinois, 1971), p. 237.

27. Kuznetsov, op. cit., pp. 290-291.

28. Shmelev, op. cit., pp. 31-33.

29. Kuznetsov, op. cit., p. 292. Kuznetsov strongly condemned a proposal to sell small tractors to the private sector that appeared in Voprosy Ekonomiki, no. 11 (1968): 63. The American economist Keith Bush claims the "minitractors for the private plot issue" has been dormant for the last four years. Keith Bush, "Soviet Agriculture in the 1970's," Studies on the Soviet Union (New Series) XI, no. 3 (1971): 29.

30. Makeenko, op. cit., pp. 58-65.

31. V. N. Shubkin, "A Comparative Sociological Survey of a Moldavian Village," in Town, Country and People, edited by G. V. Osipov, (London: Tavistock Publications, 1969), p. 166.

32. Charles K. Wilber, The Soviet Model and Underdeveloped Countries (Chapel Hill: The University of North Carolina Press, 1969), p. 50.

33. Roy and Betty Laird, Soviet Communism and Agarian Revolution, op. cit., p. 119.

34. Iakimov, op. cit., pp. 83-84.

35. Ibid., p. 84.

36. Ibid., p. 85.

37. Ibid., p. 86.

38. Ibid., p. 87.

39. For a detailed history of the assault on the private sector, see Karl-Eugen Wadekin, The Private Sector in Soviet Agriculture, op. cit., chapters 8 and 9.

40. C. A. Knox Lovell, "The Role of Private Subsidiary Farming During the Soviet Seven-Year Plan, 1959-65," Soviet Studies XX, no. 1 (July 1968): 50.

41. Iakimov, op. cit., pp. 87-88.

42. Ibid., p. 87.

43. Pravda, November 6 and 7, 1964.

44. Izvestia, April 2, 1964.

45. Babich, "The Private Plot: A Vital Element in Collective Farmers' Income," op. cit., p. 3.

46. Karl-Eugen Wadekin, "Payment in Kind in Soviet Agriculture," Bulletin, Institute for the Study of the USSR, XVIII, no. 9 (September 1971): p. 5.

47. Izvestia, March 11, 1971.

48. Pravda, December 27, 1969.

49. Ibid., January 25, 1970.

50. Babich, "The Private Plot . . .," op. cit., p. 4.

51. Ibid., p. 4, based on Izvestia, March 11, 1971.

52. Iakimov, op. cit., pp. 91-92.

53. Lovell, op. cit., p. 58.

54. Ibid., p. 59.

55. Ibid., p. 60.

56. In fact the land area of the private sector increased by 6 percent from 1964 to 1966. C. A Knox Lovell, op. cit., p. 66.

57. Klassy, Sotsialnye Sloi i Gruppy v SSSR, op. cit., p. 94.

58. Z. N. Lekhova, Potrebitel'skaia Kooperatsiia i Sblizhenie Urovnei Zhizni Sel'skogo i Gorodskogo Naseleniia (Moscow: Izdat. Ekonomika, 1969), p. 13.

59. Ibid., p. 64.

60. Ibid., p. 65.

61. Kuznetsov, op. cit., p. 293.

62. Andrei Babich, Soviet Agricultural Procurements System Reshaped, Analysis of Current Developments In The Soviet Union, Institute for the Study of the USSR 3, no. 624 (1970): 4.

63. Ibid., pp. 5-6.

64. Karl-Eugen Wadekin, The Private Sector in Soviet Agriculture, op. cit., p. 368.

65. Roy D. Laird, The Soviet Paradigm (New York: The Free Press, 1970), p. 168.

66. Iu. Zharikov, Pravo Sel'skokhoziaistvennogo Zemlepol'zovaniia (Moscow: Iurid. Lit., 1969), pp. 83-84.

67. D. V. Burmistov, Nalogi i Sbory s Naseleniia v SSSR (Moscow: Izdat. "Finansy," 1968), pp. 53-54.

68. V. Z. Ianchuk, Problemy Teorii Kolkhoznogo Prava (Moscow: Izdat. Iurid. Lit., 1969), pp. 160-161.

69. Ibid., p. 161.

70. V. P. Balezin, "Nekotorye Tendentsii Razvitiia Prava Pol'zovaniia Kolkhozov, Sovkhozov i Drugikh Sel'skokhoziaistvennykh Predpriiatii Zemliami Perspektivnykh Sel'skikh Naselennykh Punktov," Vestnik Moskovskogo Universiteta, Pravo I, seria 12 (1973): 19-21.

71. Kolkhoznoe Pravo, edited by Grigor'ev (Moscow: Iurid Lit., 1970), p. 406.

72. Ibid., pp. 406-407.

73. Ibid., p. 407.

74. Ibid., p. 410.

75. Ibid., pp. 410-411.

76. Ibid., p. 412.

77. M. Maliarov, "Strozhe Sobliudat' Zemel'nyi Zakon," Sots. Zak, no. 4 (1972): 6.

78. Kolkhoznoe Pravo, op. cit., p. 413.

79. For a brief discussion of this, see Stephen Dunn, "Structure and Functions of the Soviet Rural Family," in The Soviet Rural Family, edited by James R. Millar (Urbana: University of Illinois Press, 1971), pp. 328-329.

80. Kolkhoznoe Pravo, op. cit., p. 414.

81. Ibid.

82. Ibid., p. 419.

83. Ibid., p. 420.

84. Ibid., pp. 422-423.

85. Ibid., pp. 423-424.

86. N. P. Voloshin, Pravo Lichnoi Sobstvennosti Kolkhoznogo Dvora (Moscow: Gosiurizdat, 1961), p. 113.

87. Kolkhoznoe Pravo, op. cit., p. 428.

88. See "Razdely i Videly v Kolkhoznom Dvore," in Kratkii Iuridicheskii Slovar' Spravochnik dlia Naseleniia (Moscow: Gosiurizdat, 1960), p. 363.

89. Ia. Strautmanis, Pravovoe Regulirovanie Imushchestvennykh Otnoshenii Kolkhozov (Riga: Izdat. "Zinatne," 1970), pp. 110-111.

90. Ibid., p. 237.

91. Ibid., p. 238.

92. N. Sirodoev, "Pravo Zemlepol'zovaniia Kolkhoznogo Dvora," Sov. Iust., no. 13 (1970): 6.

93. Ia. Strautmanis, op. cit., p. 89.

10

THE PROBLEM OF
THE OPTIMAL SIZE
OF FARMS

According to the economist John Mellor, the principal source of economy in large-scale farm operation lies with the spreading of overhead capital and management over a larger set of other resources and output, while its principal diseconomy lies with special problems of management of large labor forces.[1] The most common source of failure of large-scale units, Mellor claims, arises from rigid application of practices irrespective of the highly variable physical conditions on which they are to be applied. The problem with a large-scale labor force is that it may lack this incentive to notice need for adaptation once the need is recognized. Closely related to the problem of adaptation of knowledge are those aspects of good husbandry that arise from drive in getting jobs done and from particularly hard labor at critical periods. These features are at once more important in agriculture than in most other production systems and at the same time more difficult to achieve through supervision rather than incentive.[2]

Roy and Betty Laird, after studying the growth in the average size of American corporate farms that the Soviets cite to buttress their ideological bias that the bigger the farm the better, conclude that there are important limits on farm size, varying with the type of farm, if peak efficiency in management and production is to be maintained.[3] As the Lairds recount, under Khrushchev between 1950 and 1964, the size of the average kolkhoz, which has always been smaller than the sovkhoz, increased by more than four times. Yet, conclude the Lairds, published Soviet studies on the optimal size of the farms reiterate faith in the present large units despite a new emphasis on intensive, rather than extensive farming techniques.[4] Perhaps this is generally true but there is evidence of a willingness to rethink the proposition that bigger farms are more efficient and the bigger the more efficient. The evidence of a new critical attitude toward farm size will be examined below. It should be kept in mind that the size of the farm is not only an economic, but also an administrative problem as well. It is a factor in assessing the best forms of internal organization of labor on farms, which in turn raises the questions of forms of payment of labor and incentives for labor. As the late Jarzy Karcz noted, the necessity to maintain a large enforcement and control apparatus to regulate procurement and planning deprived the farms of scarce administrative talent.[5] In other words, farm size is not a problem independent of other major problems already discussed. These interrelations will be spelled out below. It is certainly recognized by both Soviet and non-Soviet economists that among the factors influencing production, one of the greatest significance is the size of the enterprise. As N. A. Aitov puts it, there is a certain optimum size of the kolkhoz for each stage in the development of technology and means of communication and transportation, which cannot be exceeded without bad effects on its management and economic activity.[6] The authors of a Soviet work on optimal size of kolkhozy assert that the correct size allows, under various equal conditions, the more effective combination of basic elements of production so as to minimize production expenses and maximize production. The authors believe in fact that one of the reasons for the insufficient tempo of development of kolkhoz production for the last decades is the irregularity in kolkhoz size. In some regions there are still some very small kolkhozy with only up to two hundred hectares of communal sown area. On these it is supposedly difficult to organize rational production by branches as well as for the farm as a whole.[7] The authors also acknowledge that some large kolkhozy are very difficult to administer and production effectiveness is thereby lowered. A widespread problem is that of the all-too-frequent huge farm branches on the one hand and very small ones on the other, both extremes rendering it difficult to organize rational agricultural production and to secure qualified management.[8] The Soviet authors ask by what criteria to judge the optimality of farm size. Their answer is necessarily framed in general terms. First, they offer us technical armament, equipment, agro-technical measures, kinds of crops and breeds of cattle and livestock, and expenses of labor. All these are factors of agricultural production that they feel in some way relate to and bear on optimal farm size. A second factor they offer is the specialization of a given farm. Third, and last, is zonal peculiarities of the farm's location. In other words, optimal size depends in part on the degree of farm specialization and on the soil-climatic zone.[9]

The Soviet economists I. Zemetin and P. O. Pertsev list four arguments in favor of bigger farms. First, on the larger farm the relative size of capital and exploration expenses connected with fulfillment of the function of administration material security and services decreases. In terms of cost defined per hundred hectares of

arable land and per hundred man days of basic expense, the higher
the degree of general concentration of production, the greater the size
of economies achieved. Second, internal transportation expenses of
larger farms are lower relatively than are those on the average size
farms. Third, larger farms receive supplementary economic advantages
in comparison with the average sized from the higher technological
concentration of production. Fourth, the larger farms, unlike the
average size, possess the objective bases for complete, rational administration of production.[10] On closer scrutiny it all boils down to
the assertion that the bigger the farm the bigger the economics of
scale and the better the use of transportation, machinery, and administrative personnel. There is nothing at all compelling in all this. In
the abstract this may be true for some particular types of farm in
relation to others, but it need not be true of all bigger farms in relation to all smaller ones. In any case the economic logic embedded
in these blind assertions, unfettered by facts and data in support, at
best simply says that all things being equal a larger farm with more
equipment can achieve economies of scale that the smaller farm cannot. In no way is the fact that a larger farm is given or allowed to
buy more equipment than a smaller one and thereby better armed
technologically proof of its economic superiority. Their superiority
may simply be attributable to the extra machinery alone, not to size
as such.

The same authors state that experience shows that extremely
large kolkhozy and sovkhozy, like very small ones, do not give the
proper economic results. By comparison with the economically optimal sized farms, their per-hectare production is lower and their
costs higher.[11] As to just what is meant by optimal sized farms, the
authors investigated all farms in certain regions and correlated their
size with their production costs, productivity of labor, and output
volume. Actually their methodological techniques are not well defined.
In any case, their investigations indicated that for grain-livestock
kolkhozy of Rostov Oblast the optimal size is from ten thousand to
sixteen thousand hectares of plow farm and from fourteen thousand
to twenty thousand hectares of arable. The optimal size of kolkhozy
of the northern grain-livestock economies for production plots is
approximately three thousand to five thousand hectares for the north
Caucasus.[12] In terms of the regions investigated the authors conclude
that the size of the village in which it is economically practical to
build schools, clubs, electrical factories, and so on, is five to six
hundred inhabitants, which amounts to 150 to 200 able-bodied kolkhozniks.[13] Their findings as to optimal size for production plots indicate
that in the steppe zone in grain-livestock kolkhozy the most effective
farms are those with four to five thousand hectares of plowland and
as for complex mechanized links, those with one thousand to fourteen

hundred hectares of plowland. Dairy farms operate optimally in these areas with six to eight hundred cows and pig-fattening farms with seventy-five hundred to ten thousand head. As for sheep farms, the figure for the area is twenty-five hundred to six thousand head.[14] There is no point in giving more figures for particular types of farms. The point is that this methodology, imperfect as it is since it does not take into account inequalities in machinery and other qualitative production inputs, is leading to a scientific approach to optimality in farm size. Since this is only the first generation of books on optimal size of farms, one can expect more sophistication later. The very publication of such books and the commissioning of further investigations marks the legitimization of the subject of optimal size, which in itself, regardless of the fuzziness of the methodology now employed, represents a significant inroad of economic pragmatism into the hitherto impervious dogma of the larger the farm the better, along with its extreme manifestation, gigantomania in farm size. There is another aspect to the new awareness of the limits on size. The economist V. Tikhonov condemns brigades on kolkhozy that are so large that piece-work pay for members is complicated or frustrated in implementation because direct ties between pay and final results of the work of the collective are obscured, thus killing incentives.[15]

Now "gigantomania" is a bad word. But this was not always so, as a brief sketch of the history of collective farm size growth will indicate. At the beginning of 1921 many kolkhozy had socialized fields that did not exceed seventeen hectares. And there were practically no kolkhozy with more than 220 hectares of fields. On the average as of October 1927, in the kolkhozy of the RSFSR there were 261 hectares of land per kolkhoz.[16] Of course this was before collectivization. From 1928 to 1940 the size of the public or communal sown area per kolkhoz rose from 42 hectares in 1928 to 72 in 1929, to 443 in 1930, to 476 in 1937, and to 492 in 1940.[17] The majority of these kolkhozy had small mixed livestock farms, but only a few had specialized farms within them.[18] Then after the Second World War came the period of kolkhoz mergers. Out of approximately 236,000 existing in 1940-1945, most were considered too small, including some with only ten dvors. In some oblasts in the central area kolkhozy with only up to thirty dvors constituted half the total of kolkhozy for the oblast. And, says an official economic history, these kolkhozy were too small to fully utilize the power of contemporary technology. So the process of consolidation of kolkhozy began in 1950. In the Ukraine 338,000 kolkhozy were consolidated into 19,300.[19] According to a team of Soviet philosophers and historians, the postwar mergers were dictated by the need to capitalize on the bigger technical facilities and accumulated experience of the larger farms. By 1953 the total number of kolkhozy decreased to 93,300, and then to 69,100 by the end of 1958. In 1966 figure 37,100 was given.[20] As of January 1, 1966, there were 13,400 sovkhozy and 35,600 kolkhozy.[21]

Over the period from 1940 through 1966, on the average, one large kolkhoz was formed from six. Per 1963 data, 1.4 percent of all kolkhozy encompassed from 61 to 100 dvors, 19.6 percent from 101 to 200 dvors, 18.8 percent from 201 to 300, 27 percent from 301 to 500, and 28.9 percent over 500.[22] As of 1969, the average per kolkhoz was 420 dvors, 6,000 hectares of sown area, and more than a thousand head of big horned cattle, about fifteen hundred sheep, and approximately six hundred pigs. In contrast, the average sovkhoz had 21,900 hectares of arable land, 6,700 hectares of sown area, 200 head of big horned cattle, approximately 900 pigs and 400 sheep and goats.[23] Looking at the average size per kolkhoz according to republics, there is a tremendous difference in size. It ranges from 2,100 hectares per kolkhoz in Lithuania to a high of 63,700 per kolkhoz in Turkmenistan.[24] In general the Baltic, Transcaucasian, and European farms are much smaller than the central Asian, which is explainable in terms of the semi-arid terrain of central Asia. In comparing averages of kolkhozy and sovkhozy, the fact that the average sovkhoz is over three times larger than the average kolkhoz, which by non-Soviet standards is extremely large, is striking. This is no new development. The sovkhozy have been generally larger throughout the regime's rule. What is rather interesting is that the economists are not using this stark contrast in size between sovkhozy and kolkhozy as a starting point for their analysis of optimum size of farms. Instead they have generally compared and investigated kolkhozy. The sovkhozy, the ideologically superior farm because they are state property, are also supposedly economically superior because they are, on the average, significantly larger and moreover have been better supplied by the regime with equipment and supplies. According to the dogma that the bigger the size the better, the sovkhozy should be economically outperforming the kolkhozy on the whole. Yet this is not the case, and it is most interesting that optimal size studies so far concentrate on kolkhozy without reflexively applying sovkhoz size standards to them. Moreover, it is also notable that there is practically no in-depth comparative economic performance analysis of kolkhozy and sovkhozy. One might surmise from this that the regime fears that the results might be damaging to their dogma of the natural superiority of the sovkhozy.

So the dramatic kolkhoz consolidation drive of the 1950s resulted in very much less kolkhozy with, on the average, far greater size and work forces. The official catalog of reasons given for the consolidations throws light directly on the Soviet view of the importance of farm size. First, the productive use of time, machinery, and fuel. Of course, this seems to be a purely technical-practical argument. But it is not linked to any empirical data. That is, it may well have been true as far as the very small kolkhozy were concerned, but what about the medium-sized ones? Another reason given for consolidation was that the further development of livestock herds of kolkhozy could be accelerated only if a cheap and abundant feed base and an appropriate infrastructure of livestock shelters and buildings were developed. Since most kolkhozy did not themselves have the resources to attempt this, the answer seemed to be to pool them together to create the necessary resource base. Again, the criticism of this as a justification of the necessity of kolkhozy consolidation or of larger-sized kolkhozy being inherently more economical is that it simply ignores the whole run of possible explanations of why the resource base of the average or smaller kolkhozy were inadequate to self-finance expanded production. Obvious alternatives to consolidation would have been more state capital investments in agriculture, more state loans to individual farms, or more rational price systems for kolkhoz products being set by the state. A third reason for the consolidation was that the large-scale public sector farms required skilled cadres and qualified management that the small kolkhozy could not maintain financially, nor could they subsidize the educating of such. This may or may not be true, but in any case, as presented, it does not command assent, since again it fails to go into the reasons for the apparent financial inability of the smaller farms. Is it due to the nature of their small-scale operation and volume or their human errors or the unfavorable terms—prices, taxes, credits, and supplies—foisted upon them by the regime's policies generated by the ideologically inspired antipathy of the latter toward them, in part because of their small size? Last, it is asserted in favor of consolidation that it resulted in a definite economizing and freed a certain number of administrative workers for use in production.[25]

To sum up the consolidation drive, at the end of 1953 the average kolkhoz exceeded the size of the 1950 kolkhoz by 34 to 47 percent, depending on which indicators are compared—sown area, arable, number of dvors. At the end of 1960 the average kolkhoz exceeded the 1953 average per area of arable land by 1.5 times, per number of dvors by 17 times, per public sown area by 1.5 times, per heads of cattle by 2.7 times. From 1961 through 1967 the average size per dvors, arable, and sown area did not change significantly.[26] So stability in size has set in. Why? Apparently notions of optimality are a factor. One group of Soviet optimality experts admits that the law of the technical-economic advantage of huge production units over the petty is not absolute. Not all huge kolkhozy are more advantageous This source notes that huge kolkhozy encompassing more than ten population points are too hard to manage.[27] So the dogma that bigness is inherently a virtue has been eroded. This new sobriety is reflected in another Soviet work:

Structural changes in property relations will continue in the small collective farms which, in view of their limited material and labour resources, cannot widely apply modern machinery, are unable to buy and maintain them. This process evidently will also affect the larger collective farms, inasmuch as the development of technology and the need for its best use will require the pooling of effort by a number of collective farms. At the same time the process of enlarging the collective farms must keep within the bounds of economic efficiency. Purely administrative decisions are impermissible. Any economically unjustified merger of collective farms may result in adverse consequences. The point is that the enlargement of collective farms has its territorial bounds, is determined by the structure and size of the farm making it possible efficiently to utilize the productive forces, the material and labor resources and to organize production. Some collective farms, as was pointed out at the Plenary Meeting of the Central Committee of the CPSU in March 1965, were so enlarged as to prove to be unmanageable.[28]

Here there is evident some thought that the highly touted inter-kolkhoz movement is, in effect, a substitute for further kolkhoz consolidation or even the conversion of kolkhozy into sovkhozy, so-called "sovkhozization." And, as noted by the American political scientist and student of Soviet agricultural policy Robert F. Miller, Brezhnev has indicated that for the foreseeable future sovkhozization of kolkhozy is strictly a non-issue. The important thing, as Miller reads Brezhnev, is to increase the capacities and attractions of both types of farms, even if it means reducing the size of some kolkhozy.[29] Let the ideologists adjust the dogma to suit the economic imperatives.

What follows is one Soviet attempt to actually define in terms of fundamental principles a science of optimal size for farms, that is to grope toward a framing of objective criteria to be employed in analyzing whether particular farms should be larger or smaller, although optimality is a goal not just as to sheer size but also as to the right mix of types of livestock and crops, and so on. The following enumerated considerations are laid down as affecting the definition of optimal size: specialization; level of intensity; technical equipment level and level of mechanization of labor; peculiarities of the technology of production of basic types of produce; the character of transportation and technical means of communication; the condition of a road network; the configuration, relief, and composition of arable land; its contours and melioration possibilities; the water supply; the distribution of population points; and the ease of administration. Some are factors for increasing size, others for reducing size. Factors for increase include: raising the levels of mechanization (big machines demand large land masses); construction of dense networks of roads (all-weather); getting more transport equipment and also perfecting technical means of communication; creating big, well-built villages of a city type; raising educational and cultural levels and the level of professional specialization of all workers as well as the skill level of officials and specialists. Factors for decrease are: transformation of land, plowing up bad hay lands and pasture and in general using land more productive by watering; increasing the fertility of livestock and fowl.[30] The idea seems to be that intensive care and treatment of land can better be done where smaller total areas are under an administrator's jurisdiction and scrutiny. In any case, my point in exposing this list is not to go into its technical merits or general economic validity but rather to cite it as evidence of a new approach to the "size of farms" problem.

The same Soviet source goes on to generalize that kolkhozy specialized in the production of technical crops, potatoes, and vegetables demand or need less land than grain farms. And farms raising and feeding big horned cattle and sheep require more land than dairy and food-raising farms. The questions to be asked are: Is the land area of the particular kolkhoz sufficient for intensive productive use of contemporary technology and organization of livestock production on a large scale? Or is it too big to administer effectively, or to administer democratically, in line with the duty to observe kolkhoz democracy? Are brigades and farms within a kolkhoz of a rational size?[31] The authors link violations of kolkhoz democracy to the factor of excessive farm size. It is in these huge kolkhozy, they claim, where it is objectively so difficult to call regular general meetings of the rank-and-file kolkhozniks, that the temptation is so great to forego general meetings.[32] Yet these reports of the abuse in practice of kolkhoz democracy on the basis that the great size of some farms thwarts participation have been registered for years. One report in 1966 stated that only those farm workers who lived close to the board offices were invited to the report and election meetings.[33] Hence the new kolkhoz Model Charter recommendation for convening brigade meetings, as well as other democratic institutions that can help reconcile the theory and practice of kolkhoz democracy, is an important one with important implications. The tremendous growth in average size of kolkhozy after consolidations created a situation wherein even with the requisite willingness of the kolkhoz board and president to honor the kolkhoz charter, and the kolkhoz Model Charter, by periodically convening the general meeting of all kolkhozniks to decide the most important business of the kolkhoz, a willingness not to be assumed in any case, it was technically impossible to transact any deliberation over policy in such a huge gathering. So the alternative institution, a meeting of representatives of kolkhozniks,[34] developed first on the larger kolkhozy. Yet in many cases, as Soviet materials indicate, even these have lost their meaning as the highest organs of control over kolkhoz administrators.[35] Will economic efficiency be sacrificed to accommodate the less than honored-in-practice theory of kolkhoz democracy? Perhaps, if their size makes them "unadministrable" from the standpoint of the kolkhoz officials and party and state control organs. In fact it is reported that many unadministrable kolkhozy in recent years were disbanded and reorganized on a more modest scale,[36] although there is no evidence of any significant trend in this. Moreover, this was done apparently not to make grass roots control by rank and file kolkhozniks over their supposedly elected and responsible officials possible or more effective, but rather to rationalize the administrative problems as viewed from above. So the impulse to simplify kolkhozy that are administratively too complex, and thus to cut down their size or stabilize it, hardly betokens any regime sensitivity to the ideal of making actual kolkhoz democracy, although the regime is eager to advertise such actions as serving this cause since it continues to honor the theory, if not the substance, of kolkhoz democracy.

NOTES

1. John W. Mellor, The Economics of Agricultural Development (Ithaca, New York: Cornell University Press, 1966), pp. 364-365.
2. Ibid., pp. 368-369.
3. Roy and Betty Laird, Soviet Communism and Agrarian Revolution, op. cit., pp. 17-18.
4. Ibid., p. 58.
5. Jerzy F. Karcz, "Comparative Study of Transformation of Agriculture in Centrally Planned Economies: The Soviet Union, Eastern Europe and Mainland China," in Erik Thorbecke, editor, The Role of Agriculture in Economic Development (New York: National Bureau of Economic Research, 1969), p. 246.
6. N. A. Aitov, "An Analysis of the Objective Prerequisites for Eliminating the Distinctions Between the Working Class and the Peasantry," in Town, Country and People, edited by G. V. Osipov (London: Tavistock Publications, 1969), p. 129.
7. G. Kotov and I. A. Borodin, eds., Optimal'nye Razmery Kolkhozov (Moscow: Izdat. "Kolos," 1970), p. 3.
8. Ibid., pp. 3-4.
9. Ibid.
10. I. Zametin and P. P. Pertsev, K Voprosu o Spetsializatsii Sel'skogo Khoziaistva (Moscow: Izdat. "Mysl'," 1970), pp. 213-214.

11. Ibid., pp. 235-236.
12. Ibid., pp. 240-241.
13. Ibid., pp. 241-242.
14. Ibid., pp. 248-249.
15. See CDSP XVIII, no. 17 (May 19, 1966): 32.
16. Kotov and Borodin, eds., op. cit., p. 13.
17. Ibid., p. 19.
18. Ibid., p. 23.
19. Istoriia Narodnogo Khoziaistva SSSR (Moscow: Izdat. "Vyshaia Shkola," 1964), p. 210.
20. Society and Economic Relations (Moscow: Progress Publishers, 1969), p. 125.
21. V. V. Matskevich, "Sotsial'no-Ekonomicheskie Preobrazovaniia i Sotsialisticheskaia Sistema Sel'skogo Khozaistva v SSSR," in Sel'skoe Khoziaistvo Sovetskogo Soiuza (Moscow: Izdat. "Kolos," 1970), p. 16.
22. Society and Economic Relations, op. cit., p. 125.
23. Matskevich, op. cit., p. 16.
24. S. A. Udachin, "Zemel'nyi Fond i Zemlepol'zovanie v SSSR," in Sel'skoe Khoziaistvo Sovetskogo Soiuza, op. cit., p. 69.
25. Kotov and Borodin, eds., op. cit., pp. 24-25.
26. Ibid., p. 26.
27. Ibid., p. 28.
28. Society and Economic Relations, op. cit., pp. 125-126.
29. Robert F. Miller, One Hundred Thousand Tractors (Cambridge: Harvard University Press, 1970), p. 363.
30. G. Kotov and I. Borodin, eds., op. cit., pp. 33-34.
31. Ibid., pp. 35-36.
32. Ibid., p. 39.
33. CDSP XVIII, no. 4 (February 16, 1966): 6-7.
34. V. P. Reshetniak, Upravelenie v Kolkhozakh, (Moscow: Izdat. "Kolos," 1970), p. 44.
35. Kotov and Borodin, eds., op. cit., pp. 64-65.
36. Ibid., p. 82.

11

THE LAND RENT
AND KOLKHOZ
COST-PRICE PROBLEM

SECTION 1: THE FREE LAND USE ISSUE

The fact that no rent is charged by the state for the use of its agricultural lands by either kolkhozy or sovkhozy has been held to have two adverse effects by the American economist Howard Sherman. First, those farms with better land in terms of soil, climate, or location tend to have higher incomes than others, although this may be divorced from any greater skill or effort put forth by them in their work. Second, without a rent charge acting as a rationing device so as to better use the finite supply of state land and as an input into cost of agricultural production analysis, it is more difficult to know how to arrive at rational prices policies that both insure reasonable returns to farms as well as encourage or discourage certain crops from being raised on certain lands. The economist Robert Stuart notes that looked at from the land manager's perspective, the absence of a charge for the use of the land he manages creates only a minimal possibility that he will view the land as a scarce resource.[1] As Howard Sherman notes, to a very slight extent there is some element of rent in the differential zonal purchase price system, but as will become clear below, this scheme is very crude. Sherman feels the Soviets are now beginning to edge toward the introduction of a more precise form of rent because this would improve both the allocation of resources and the equity of farm income distribution.[2] Another problem the Soviets face in this respect is that before an accurate system of differential rents can be applied, a cadastral survey or catalogue of land quality for the whole country is needed. As the British economist Michael Kaser notes, cadastral registers or surveys were held to be unnecessary in the absence of private landholding. Now, however, pressure from Soviet economists as well as jurists has mounted, and in December 1968 a law was enacted as a basis for undertaking a cadastre.[3] So far none has been completed. It is the economic policy aspects of the land use and land rent problems that will be explored in this chapter rather than the technical problem of how to make land more productive through amelioration, drainage, irrigation, and application of fertilizers. In other words, the focus here is on the economic problems of dogma and incentive that affect Soviet farm efficiency and productivity.[4]

In the USSR the state is the sole owner of all land. As the exclusive owner it gives out land to users only on the basis of a right of use, a use that is restricted to a designated purpose—in the case of kolkhozy, for agricultural use. Like all land users, the kolkhoz has the right of use without charge. In the USSR land users are forbidden to alienate, rent, pledge, or sell land. The land given to the kolkhoz for use is given on the basis of unlimited use, that is, without charge and without a time limitation,[5] and this takes the legal form of the state assigning specific lands to a kolkhoz by a deed of perpetual use. In theory such assigned lands cannot be taken away once given out to the kolkhoz without the agreement of the kolkhozniks of that kolkhoz.[6]

The negative attitude of the Soviets toward land rent is conditioned by their view of land rent under capitalism. According to official definition, land rent under capitalism is part of the surplus value created in agriculture by hired workers and appropriated by land owners. This involves the exploitation of hired help either by the owner or the lessee of the owner-lessor. The rent charge is part and parcel of private property in certain land and is the difference between the value and the social price of production of the agricultural produce. Absolute rent differs from differential rent in that it is received from all land independent of differences in fertility and location of different plots and of the productivity of added investments of capital in one or the same land plot. Nationalization of land destroys the monopoly private property in land and the absolute rent inextricably tied to it. Differential rent under capitalism is the excess of added value above average profit that is created thanks to the higher productivity of labor of agricultural workers on relatively better land plots and is appropriated by the owner of the land. Differential rent under socialism is supplementary net income in money or in kind created on enterprises located on superior or average land in terms of fertility or on land convenient to markets and also on enterprises conducting a more intensive economy. There are two forms of it. Differential rent I is supplementary net income created on naturally more fertile and better-located land. Differential rent II is supplementary net income received as a result of the growth in the productivity of labor.[7] According to the cannons of orthodox Soviet political economy, in industry the value of a commodity and the price of production are determined by the average conditions of production. In agriculture the price of production of agricultural products is not determined by the average conditions of production, but by the conditions of production on the poorest lands. This is because agricultural land is limited and hence even the worst land in terms of fertility must be utilized, so costs on the worst land determine the socially necessary expenses of agricultural production.[8]

Differential rent is the excess profit over and above the average profit, obtained by those farms that operate under more favorable conditions of production. The three factors that make it possible to obtain differential rent are the difference in soil fertility of lands, the difference in the location of lands in relation to markets, and the difference in productivity derived from the additional capital invested in the land. According to Marx, differential rent connected with variations in fertility and land location was differential rent I. The application of artificial fertilizers, improved machinery, and so on, creates differential rent II. The rent that is paid to the owner of land for its use is called absolute.[9]

Marx recognized that differences in fertility and in closeness to markets of some lands, given similar outlays on them as on the less fertile and less conveniently located farms, would yield more and, in the case of the better located, have lower transportation costs and hence higher profits. Those with higher fertility and superior location were the better lands. Since the output of the best and medium quality lands is insufficient to meet the demands of society, the worst lands must be utilized. And this means that not only the capitalists who farm the best and medium plots, but also farm the worst must receive the average profit. Therefore, the price of production of agricultural commodities equals the costs of production (including rent) on the worst lands plus the average profit. Medium and best lands yield an excess profit—that is, one over and above the average profit. Differential rent I is the excess profit obtained on lands of better quality or those closer to markets as compared with lands of lesser quality or poorer location. It comes about as a result of differences between the individual and market price of production due to the disparity in the quality of land. Excess profit obtainable from any plot as a result of additional capital investment, that is as a result of more intensive farming, is called differential rent II.[10]

Some Soviet economists believe that with the destruction of the capitalist means of production, any kind of land rent is destroyed. Therefore they considered the existence of differential rent under socialism a myth. I. Markov declares that the question of rent in socialist conditions should not be considered in Soviet economic literature because no such economic category exists under Soviet socialism.[11] But the Soviet economist A. V. Bolgov reads Marx differently, and his view is the orthodox one. According to Bolgov, Marx does not state that the destruction of the capitalist method of production excludes any possibility of forming noncapitalist differential rent if the commodity character of production and the identity of market prices of similar goods are pre served.[12] Bolgov states that some Soviet economists, including T. L. Basiuk, consider the following conditions as creating differential rent under socialism: (1) the limitedness of land, (2) different fertility and locational advantages of land, (3) commodity character of production and the operation of the law of value. The direct cause of the formation of differential rent under socialism is the presence of the two forms of socialist property.[13] The factors of differing climates, different soil fertility, nearness to markets, and variants in productivity of different collectives of labor all remain after capitalism disappears. And good-money relations in the transitional period between the end of capitalism and the establishment of socialism were the basic form of relation between city and country, and in the period of socialism and the unfolding of the construction of communism, they develop even more. Consequently, says Bolgov, with the socialist means of production you have all the necessary conditions to produce differentials I and II. But, he emphasizes, differential rent under socialism is essentially different from differential rent under capitalism. And differential rent under socialism was not and cannot take the form of a rent payment for land because the landowner-monopolist has been replaced by the collective of kolkhozniks or the state.[14]

According to Bolgov, socialist practical experience fully confirms Marx's position that raising the fertility of all agricultural land does not destroy the inequality in fertility of separate plots. It either strengthens, decreases, or leaves this unchanged. This point can and should serve as a starting point for an economic evaluation of the land so as to define the size of differential rent I as to fertility.[15] Differential rent in conditions of socialism represents supplementary net income that is created in kolkhozy cultivating better land in terms of fertility or location or utilizing land more productively than other kolkhozy. According to size, differential rent is equal to the difference between the social and individual cost of production of agricultural products or, in other words, between socially necessary and individual expenses of production.[16] All this leads, says Bolgov, to the all-important question of defining social cost of agricultural products in conditions of socialism. And this question suggests the unifying thread running between the problems of agricultural prices, costs, incomes of farms, differential rent, and maximization of agricultural production by specialization and concentration of production. When you talk of differential rent I and II, you are really talking about comparative costs of production and not just different capacities to produce. Some Soviet economists consider that prices for agricultural products, like those for all others should be built upon the law of value, based on the average for all economies of conditions of labor and production. These economists consider that the average norm of profit and price of production and also of differential land rent in socialist agriculture are absent, and therefore to define prices of agricultural products by the costs of production in the worst conditions now where all land belongs to one owner is absurd. Certain other Soviet economists hold that under conditions of socialism there are not and cannot be poor lands, only poor managers, and that therefore the cost of agricultural products should be defined as the cost of their production on the average or even on the best (per fertility or location) lands. But as Bolgov interjects, this would be possible only if all cultivated land or even the overwhelming majority of it were of equal fertility. Bolgov reminds his fellow economists that although all the land belongs to one owner, it has different users.[17] Denying the existence of differential rent in kolkhoz production and considering that, per the law of value, agricultural products' prices should be defined by the average conditions of production of farms on the scale of the whole country, academician S. Strumilin criticizes these economists who recognize the presence of differential rent in kolkhozy but deny its presence in sovkhoz production. Strumilin holds that the cost of sovkhoz production should be defined by the average social expenses of production, and in kolkhozy by the level of those in the worst conditions of production. Bolgov sees in the existence of zonally differentiated purchase prices for both kolkhozy and sovkhozy— although the number of zones for each of the two types of farm differs— proof of the Soviet commitment to the theory of a single differential rent concept equally applicable to both farm sectors.[18]

Those who would define prices for agricultural products on the basis of averages for costs of production for the country as a whole may be forced to propose the establishment of purchase prices separately for each kolkhoz, taking account of its individual expenses and its need to accumulate reserves. Bolgov believes this would introduce arbitrariness into the practice of price formation and undermine the material interest of many kolkhozy in improving their economy and more fully utilizing their land. And, if you make production costs on the average of best lands the norm, then those kolkhozy with the worst natural-climatic and locational situations would have to subsidized directly by the state budget.[19] Yet, reminds Bolgov, the worst land must be used, since land is limited. So the worst conditions of production, meaning the highest objective costs of production of needed produce, must be taken into account in pricing policy, and this means that the social costs of agricultural products can be defined and is defined, as most Soviet economists recognize, by the conditions of production on the worst lands, but under the average or objective costs of production for the majority of kolkhozy working similar lands, that is, under the average level of technological equipment, the average level of use of labor and means of production, and the average level of productivity.[20]

Bolgov discusses zonal cost of agricultural products as the basis of zonal prices. This involves definition of the labor-consuming character of production of various products under differing conditions of production. Just like the cost in general, the zonal cost of agricultural products is defined as the socially necessary expenses of labor and material means on the worst land in a given zone per fertility and location, achieved under average conditions of production, energy use, utilization of technology, agro- and zoo-technical equipment, labor resources, and productivity of labor. Therefore, based on zonal cost, zonal prices should be established not in relation to the expenses of lagging kolkhozy, which produce very little, or of advanced kolkhozy, but rather in relation to the expenses of the average kolkhozy, in economic terms, of the zone, that is, the majority of the kolkhozy of the zone. And most Soviet economists, adds Bolgov, accept zonal cost as the basis of zonal prices.[21] Bolgov is aware that the existing price zones are too big, and in consequence of this the differential purchase prices do not correspond to actual differential conditions of production.[22] Hence some kolkhozy within a zone have different climatic or fertility conditions than others in the same zone and thus objectively higher or lower costs of production than others in the same zone. This is obviously a shortcoming of the existing system. Bolgov, recognizing this, urges the further perfecting of differentiation of purchase prices among zones and within zones in order to place kolkhozy in different natural-economic conditions of production in more or less equal conditions of profitability.[23]

Bolgov, although admitting that sovkhozy in different climatic-natural zones are affected income-wise by these differing cost factors as are kolkhozy, denies that differential rent exists in the sovkhoz sector. What exists among sovkhozy and appears to be differential rent I and II is actually differential income. What is critical is that differential rent is a product of the private property monopoly in land, and the sovkhozy do not have such a monopoly as do the kolkhozy. Their means of production are all state-owned. All the income they generate belongs to the state. All differential rent will disappear when cooperative-kolkhoz property in the means of production disappears.[24] Marx taught that land rent presupposes land property in land, that is, the ownership of definite land by an individual or group of individuals.[25]

Is the receipt by the state of part or all of differential rent I under socialism actually a rent fee in disguised form for land use? This question involves the ultimate question of whether or not there should be a rent charge paid by the land user to the state. Bolgov believes that the receipt by the Soviet state of differential rent I is a transfer from the kolkhozy to society of the surplus income that is formed as a result of different fertility of land, and also as a result of the conditions of production (for example, growth of cities and development of transportation) created by society rather than by the individual kolkhoz.[26] Yet Bolgov does not differentiate this from the simple charge for land use or rent fee. Presumably he feels the rent fee, in contradistinction to the state under socialism taking differential rent I, would be a charge on top of or in addition to differential rent and unjustified since, apparently, he sees socialism as requiring free land use. This, however, is a major question. Is a fee for land use pure and simple incompatible with the principles of socialism and, if not, is it economically or politically desirable? Is Bolgov's position due to ideological prejudice, a mere legacy of a too literal and dogmatic regard for Marx's writings, a prejudice that might explain his unwillingness to consider differential rent I and II as existing as such in the sovkhoz sector and his and most other Soviet economists need to represent what is essentially differential rent I and II in the sovkhoz sector as "differential income"? As the British economist Michael Kaser notes, Soviet economic practice continues to deny the applicability of absolute rent to socialist conditions. Land is national property and no fee for its use is to be made by simple virtue of owner-ship by the state.[27] And the imperfect mechanism of the zonally differentiated purchase prices to recapture differential rent I and II is held not to be incompatible with the principle of usufruct in perpetuity to kolkhozy. Bolgov justifies letting a good part of differential rent I remain with the kolkhozy so as to raise their material interest in production. Yet this should not be allowed to result in unjustified income disparities among kolkhozy, with those operating under more favorable soil-climatic and locational areas enriching themselves through no greater skill or harder work on their part. Socialism demands equal pay for equal work. Bolgov thus justifies the state's taking part of differential rent I as not violating the material interests of kolkhozy but rather as a means of placing all kolkhozy in an equal position in relation to the land and thus realizing to some extent a party program ideal of securing equal economic conditions for raising the incomes of kolkhozy in unequal natural-economic conditions of production.[28] But as to the state taking away differential rent II, Bolgov voices the orthodox Soviet position that this would violate the socialist principle of distribution—for more work and better results, more pay. And, in the end, to do so would result in undermining the material incentive of kolkhozy in intensifying their economies.[29] Yet part of it is levied, he notes, via the income tax on kolkhozy.[30] And this is justified, since society makes capital investments in agriculture and trains agricultural specialists for the farms.[31]

Bolgov is aware of the necessity of some type of comprehensive agriculture land evaluation or cadastral survey in order to more economically use and tax land. He chastises "some economists" who dogmatically interpret Marx's "labor theory of value" to mean that land does not have value in order to oppose any cadastral survey or economic evaluation of land as unscientific. Bolgov interprets Marx's position on land not having value as referring only to uncultivated land. This quoting of Marx by rival groups of Soviet economists is again illustrative of the need to find ideological legitimacy for their positions, especially if it is either directly contrary to past Soviet practices or was attacked as ideologically offensive. The burden of sustaining the ideological purity of a proposed economic innovation seems to be on the innovating forces. There seems to be a presumption of ideological illicitness attaching to unprecedented proposals. Normally the attempt must be made to cite Marx against Marx or to explain away the status quo defender's damaging citation as either taken out of context or as not meaning what the other party claims it means, or, as a last resort, claiming the duty of all good Marxists to creatively adapt Marxian tenets to the changed times, needs, and circumstances, that is the idea of Marxism not as a dogma but rather as a method of analyzing changing reality. Such was the problem facing economists who advocated the sale of the MTS machinery to the kolkhozy. The problem was less acute for those who advocated the link but nonetheless ideologically embarrassing.

The economist I. T. Beliaev feels that in the absence of a land cadastre and the establishment of a rent payment for better land, zonal purchase prices must be used to recapture differential rent I.[32] But once the quality of land is established, a fixed payment from the user should be levied. The economic evaluation would be made periodically, since improvements in land occur, and as do improvements in technique that increase the value of the land.[33] The economist A. Kalnyn'sh also considers a fixed rent payment an alternative.[34]

I. Kebin, an Estonian party official, proposed in 1966 the introduction of a per hectare tax on agricultural land based on its quality.[35] Writing in Pravda on August 31, I. Leontyev advocated land rent as a cost factor. Leontyev notes that until quite recently the idea of the plan as a gigantic, all-embracing summary statement of production and consumption of the whole infinite multitude of highly diverse types of products made and used throughout the country was accepted. This conception of the plan, he notes, is linked with the conception of socialism as a system that excludes every manifestation of creative initiative and independence in the lower cells of the national economy. Yet the new economic reform in general[36] and the Twenty-Third Congress in particular put forward the idea of a sharp reduction in the number of plan indices of enterprises' work that are set from above and advised that centralized planned management should be concentrated primarily on the chief and decisive aspects of the country's economic development. This presupposes the existence of commodity production. Although traditionally commodity production arises and develops on the basis of private property and is connected with a spontaneous kind of economic life, the present form of commodity production is socialist, with its own socialist value relationships inextricably linked with planned management of the economy. Leontyev emphasizes, however, that commodity-money relations will fade away and disappear only with the transition to the highest phase of communism, when a single communist type of property and a communist system of distribution will prevail. The ties between enterprises and even within them today are built on the principles of compensation and equivalence. Without these there can be no genuine economic accountability and the effective economic stimulation of production. Yet, complains Leontyev, there is often found in the literature the opinion that of the economic ties in the socialist national economy, the chief and determining one is the direct and nonequivalent form of tie, while the commodity equivalent form plays only a supplementary role. But this view is a legacy of the time when the purely formal nature of economic accountability was considered the norm, and value categories were regarded as merely accounting tools and not at all as the basis for compensating every normally operating enterprise for the socially necessary expenditures. Leontyev then proceeds to the conclusion that public ownership of the means of production predetermines that these cannot become private property but does not mean that they drop out of the sphere of equivalence ties in the national economy. He considers the assertion that means of production in a socialist economy are not commodities as overturned, and consequently their values serve as much more than a convenience for calculation. The introduction of payment for production assets paid to the state by enterprises, he notes, definitely fixes the commodity nature of production assets. And, says Leontyev, it is no accident that in connection with the transition to genuine economic accountability and the development of economic methods of managing the national economy, the question of introducing into economic usage such a category as the price of land has arisen. Leontyev states that the free assignment of land to farms means that absolute rent is eliminated with nationalization of lands, an orthodox position. As for differential rent, it is created by differences in land equality. And since land is limited, the question of how much particular land is worth is very important.

Leontyev sides with those managers and economists who propose the introduction of land valuation and the establishment of payment for land in accordance with it. This is, Leontyev points out, not at all unprecedented. After all, he notes, the fact is that in a number of cases, payment for land actually exists—in the form of rent payments and zonal purchase and accounting prices. He urges the introduction of the concept of land price and payment for land so as to eliminate a serious source of uneconomical utilization of the country's natural resources. This would fit as well with the overall system of value categories of commodity production under socialism, he urges, and, just like the principle of paying for production assets, it is not the least incompatible with socialist production relations. After all, the payment for land use would constitute part of the surplus value entering the state budget. And this fee, based on a precise stocktaking of the relative renumerativeness of plots of land, would contribute to the creation of more equitable economic conditions for farms and enterprises, which constitutes an important prerequisite for the effectiveness of economic incentive methods.[37]

So Leontyev, in advocating what amounts to, at least in form, absolute rent, does so in the guise of simply extending the same principle reflected in the charge for use on production assets now exacted from industrial enterprises and today considered one of the most important elements in the economic reform program.[38] And he skirts the ideologically anathema absolute rent by arguing that the fee would go to the whole of society through its collection by the state. Moreover it would, like differential rent, act as an equalizer of farm incomes and a force for better analyzing economic performances of farms. So, in effect, absolute rent is not absolute rent if it goes to society rather than private property owners. Yet such is the rigidity of the Marxist liberalists that such terminology must be avoided or shunned. Form worship inhibits substantive analysis. And Leontyev is implicitly arguing that just because it is land rather than capital for which a charge for use is being levied, this provides no basis for ideological distinctions. V. M. Alekseeva agrees that a fee for land based on the quality and quantity of land given to the user is not inconsistent with state ownership of all land and would simply represent an extension to agriculture of the fee for industrial production funds charged by the state and embodied in the 1965 reform.[39]

The economist G. R. Romanchenko disputes the analogy between a land fee and the fee for industrial funds. A fee for land use is absolute rent and absolute rent is incongruous where land has been nationalized. The nationalization of land in the USSR is based on the principle of free use and is enshrined in the USSR Constitution as a basic principle of socialism. It is of international significance. Having based his opposition to it on ideological grounds, he then attacks it on practical grounds. It is difficult to distinguish between that part of differential rent produced by higher productivity of labor and that part produced by the greater fertility of the land. He endorses both zonal prices and a graduated income tax as more flexible than a fixed per hectare fee, which could only be based on possible income rather than actual income. Income estimates are especially difficult in agriculture, he notes.[40]

The economist V. P. Shkredov in a book published in 1967 goes far beyond Leontyev's mere general advocacy of some type of rent charge for land use. In fact Shkredov's reform proposals go beyond anything previously or, to date, subsequently said. They add up to the most radical package of proposals for reform of the present kolkhoz order put forth in decades. Shkredov discusses methods of equalizing the incomes of farms in different climatic-soil and locational positions. He compares a land tax based on land quality and quantity to a charge for land use, preferring the latter after analyzing the implications of both. Moreover, the charge for land use, since it varies with the quantity and quality of the land, is quite like the now orthodox charge for the use of industrial productive assets paid by state enterprises to the state budget in order to encourage fuller utilization of an enterprise's fixed and circulating assets, with the charge being proportional to the value of land and circulating assets. This charge was instituted in 1945.[41]

Unlike the price mechanism, the payment for land use, he feels, is directly related to the individual farm's area and quality of land. The zonally differentiated price device cannot be so individualized or tailored to each farm. The fee for land use directly correlates farm income with the farm's land quality and quantity. And without this, he feels, it is impossible to create for all kolkhozy and sovkhozy economically equal conditions. The rent fee can be sensitive to the actual quality of each individual plot of land.[42] Shkredov is struck by the inflexibility and wastefulness of the traditional free land use principle. The noncorrespondence between the size of land area given to each farm, from the one side, with the quality and quantity or the means of production and work force necessary for its cultivation in conformity with the socially normal level, from the other side, unavoidably lowers the effectiveness of the use of land as well as the means of production. The general area and structure of usable land in the possession of a farm should correspond to its material possibilities, to the present mass of its means of production, and to its labor resources. And this leads Shkredov to the conclusion that it is necessary for farms to either increase or decrease their land areas as their labor and capital and equipment base dictates. Thus the securing of a fixed amount of land for perpetual use is a hindrance to this shifting to more or less land from time to time and should be done away with. But Shkredov is cautious. He advocates not a sudden changeover but rather a gradual shift to the regulated organization of land use on a contractual basis between the state and the farms, a form of rental contracts. These would be true voluntary, bilateral contracts and not arbitrary, unilateral administrative decisions foisted on the farms. The kolkhoz would on its own decide how much land it needed to fulfill its plan. The new principle would be: whoever can best utilize land should get more land.[43]

Shkredov feels that the right to free and unlimited land use led to the economic immobility of land as a means of agricultural production that hinders the economic effectiveness of land use. The new proposed rental contract system would overcome this. Under this sytem the land user will be materially interested in renting the minimally necessary land. If a farm's actual production needs change, it might want to decrease or increase its land. Shkredov proposes that there be two land funds set up, one for long-term rentals and another for short-term. He advocates that farms be allowed to rent out some of their rented land to other farms if they cannot utilize the already rented land themselves. The new lessee should then pay the rent fee directly to the state.[44] Shkredov, anticipating not only ideological objections but also some practical ones, argues that the rental contract can spell out in detail the duties of the lessee for insuring that he will care for the land, leaving it in a good agrobiological condition.[45] Thus he anticipates the argument that short-term users will milk the land without care for the long run and thus will not make the kind of investments in it that insure long-term fertility because they want only to realize short-term pay-offs from any investments they make.

The orthodox answer to this is that the farm that finds itself unable to utilize part of its land would temporarily give it over to another user, with the permission of the local Soviet. What the practical effects of this have been are not to be found in the literature, nor is it clear as to whether the land lender is compensated for the land.

A faint echo of Shkredov's article idea appears in an article in Novy Mir of March 6, 1967, by the economist G. Lisichkin. Taking note of a newly created Czechoslovak tax on land with the rate on the best land being nearly ten times that on relatively poor land and with some kinds of soil not being taxed at all, Lisichkin records that for a long time voices in the Soviet Union have been calling for a restoration of the per hectare tax, differentiated according to the land's natural value.[46] He fails, however, to elaborate on this or describe how the quality of land would be ascertained and just what degree of progressivity in rates is desirable. Nor does he indicate whether the tax would be applied to fallow land or otherwise unused land. Nor does he tackle the problem of how to precisely define the natural-climatic tax zones, the same problem that arises in relation to the present zonal differential price system. In any case, Lisichkin is far less bold than Shkredov and does not directly challenge the orthodox principle of free and perpetual land use for farms. In 1969 Iu. Zharikov broached the idea of using a direct rent for land. He did not commit himself to the idea but rather tossed it out for discussion.[47]

A description of what appears to be the most intricate differential purchase price scheme was presented by the Lithuanian economist B. Poshkus at a scientific conference in Lithuania in August 1971 on the subject of differential purchase prices in agriculture. It was sponsored by the USSR Academy of Science.[48] In another article Poshkus describes in detail how between 1967 and 1970 the Lithuanian Republic created a model for grouping the kolkhozy of the Republic for differential price purposes. The four factors used were: the quality of land; the average yearly basic funds; the average yearly circulating funds; and the labor fund per hectare.[49] The results were equal rates of profit for all the kolkhozy and without leveling of incentives. The best farms (Group I) paid out on the average per man day 26 percent more than the worst (Group II).[50]

SECTION 2: THE FREE SALES ISSUE

The Soviet economist G. Lisichkin is a champion of the application of the industrial economic reforms approach to the farms, that is maximal use of the so-called economic levers—price, credits, taxes—instead of imposing specific production targets from above. Lisichkin is a proponent of what he describes as the "incontestable advantage" of stimulating production participation by the price paid for output in comparison with salaries according to job or with renumeration merely on the basis of scales and rates for a norm of work performed. Based on Lisichkin's study of the effect of the implementation of reforms over the period from 1955 to 1957, he concludes that the kolkhozniks more tangibly related their well-being and their personal earnings to the growth of production and to increasing the sale of output. He also claims the reforms led to more accumulation of funds. For Lisichkin the success of the reforms was in great measure due to the farm's obtaining the possibility to resolve production questions more independently and being able to perfect the structure of their crop areas at their own discretion. All this in response to price signals. As Lisichkin puts it, no farm acted to its own detriment, and in conditions where price correctly informs the producer about the state's economic requirements, the maximalization of the farm's self-interest works in the state's self-interest.[51]

Lisichkin is one of the few economists willing to tout the superiority of the kolkhoz over the sovkhoz, at least in some respects. In doing so he is indulging in a minor heresy. He contrasts the earnings of the sovkhoz worker, which continued to depend basically not on the output he produces but on established scales, rates, and work norms, with those of the kolkhoznik, for whom more and more the reward is based on increased productivity and production. Insofar as the sovkhozy work is evaluated according to "gross volume" of work performed and not according to the final product and income, it remains a fetter on the initiative of the work force. What he neglects to consider, however, is whether the kolkhoznik, with the newly instituted guaranteed pay system, is not now moving into a status more like that of the sovkhoz worker.

Lisichkin feels that income on the whole is meaningless to the sovkhozy since the pay of their labor force is not based on the farm's income, and the farm's funds are also of a magnitude that is almost independent of this. In other words, the sovkhozy can get funds directly from the state and thus independently of earnings. This fact, Lisichkin feels, accounts for the greater level of intensification found by comparison on kolkhozy. The kolkhoz is on a true economic accountability basis, and what feeds it is its own ingenuity.[52]

Lisichkin criticizes the traditional concept of an agricultural policy of planning "from the achieved levels," which he says was engendered by the subjective method of guiding the national economy, and which still regards the development of the sovkhozy. As he sees it, it channels the initiative of sovkhoz executives not into aiming for the maximum profit, but rather into pretending to the planning agencies to be poorer than they are and thus obtaining a plan that is a little lower and easier to achieve. He cites cases where fast-spoiling crops could not be marketed locally after a natural disaster in order to salvage some of their value because the sovkhoz had to undergo a long correspondence with their remote administrative superiors regarding what to do because of these unplanned circumstances. And, he concludes, both the lack of a stake in the amount of income and of the product and the excessive regulation of economic activity prevent the sovkhozy from yielding the quantity of output they could under other conditions. On the kolkhozy, he holds, such problems are not so acute, and that is precisely why they are attaining a faster pace in the development of production, although their material base is not as strong as the sovkhozy and the latter receive more resources. At this point Lisichkin becomes ideologically sensitive. He feels it necessary to justify his need to contrast kolkhozy and sovkhozy, a contrast that transitionally is made only to show the superiority of the latter. He urges that it is not the forms of ownership that should be contrasted, but rather the extent to which the principles of economic accountability are used on both types of farms. On the kolkhozy, he feels, the elements of true economic accountability are functioning, whereas on the sovkhozy economic accountability is formal and fetters the initiative and material interest of the workers.[53]

Lisichkin, anticipating the criticism that he is advocating the abolition of planning in agriculture, claims he is in reality advocating methods of strengthening it. The gist of the matter lies in scientific pricing by the state. The planned price of a commodity should inform the producer what outlays for producing it are socially necessary. The very level of the price determines the economic habitat of the production of the commodity, he stresses, and by raising or lowering the price it is possible to contract or expand the area of the production of the commodity. Every farm will check the established price against its own conditions of production and its consequent production costs and then decide whether it can successfully carry on production in these conditions.[54]

A rejoinder to Lisichkin appeared in the agricultural daily Sel'skaia Zhizn' of September 13, 1967, authored by a Stravropol party first secretary, an economist, and several other local party functionaries, plus some agricultural statisticians and a kolkhoz chairman. They ignore the fee-for-land-use issue. They brand as unrealistic Lisichkin's proposals for the free sale of kolkhoz and sovkhoz produce, and the elimination of the planning of state purchases of products in kind, coupling this with an accusation that he is guilty of making a fetish of commodity-money relations and the law of value as the alleged regulator of socialist production. They assert the orthodox position that the kolkhozy are an inalienable part of the planned economy and that to permit trade in kolkhoz products to be conducted exclusively outside the state plan would upset the entire system of the planned organization and administration of the national economy. They declare that it is a most important advantage for the farms that the state guarantees them the planned purchase of their entire marketable output at prices known in advance.[55] The authors reject Lisichkin's proposal for planning of prices only by the state. This, they hold, would cause disproportions.[56] Yet they fail to give a reasoned explanation of why this is inevitable if Lisichkin's proposal is adopted. Moreover, they fail to make clear why guaranteed state purchase is such an advantage or how it is conducive to maximal production. In substance their rebuttal is simply an ideologically motivated broadside devoid of practical, demonstrable criticisms. And although they accuse Lisichkin of making a fetish of commodity-money relations, they do stop short of accusing him of outright heresy and they cloak their fundamentally ideological objection in the garb of a practical economic critique. This is significant in itself in that it demonstrates that open dialogue involving challenges to long-established "sacred cow" tenets is possible, even if within carefully prescribed limits. As will be evident from what follows, the dialogue over this issue of the maximal use of the price mechanism as a substitute for the traditional clumsy sets of gross output indices dictated from above is far from dormant. Clearly the issue is recognized as an open one. However, the fee-for-land-use issue has become an "un-issue." With the passage of a new Fundamentals of Land Legislation in December 1969, which expressly reaffirmed the principle of free land use by farms, a basic decision to silence proponents of a fee for land use like Shkredov was taken. And when the new kolkhoz Model Charter came out in November 1969, yet another opportunity to reconsider this was presented. But the Model Charter reaffirmed the traditional position reflected in the new Fundamentals of Land Legislation.

Evidence of the present "un-issue" status of the fee-for-land-use issue can be seen in the avoidance of even its mention in two recent articles on land use in the kolkhozy. The jurist L. Fomina does not even indirectly hint at any challenge to the principle of fee land use. It is assumed to be unquestionable.[57] The veteran Soviet land law specialist G. A. Aksenenok discusses the rational use of lands of farms strictly in terms of the new duties spelled out by the new Model Charter and other legislation without ever even alluding to the question of whether or not free use of land itself is economically rational. There is no echo at all of any of Shkredov's proposals, not even a derisive allusion.[58] It would appear then that at least for now and the foreseeable future this is an "un-issue."

However, the issue of the function of price in the planning of agricultural production is far from being an un-issue. Lemeshev and other proponents of maximizing the use of the price mechanism as a replacement for central planning of outputs of various crops and commodities have triggered a rigorous debate not only over the function and scope of the price mechanism but also over the basis for price policy. A group of agricultural economists consisting of S. Kolesnev, an academician of the All-Union Lenin Academy of Agricultural Sciences and head of the Timiryazev Agricultural Academy's Department of the Organization of Socialist Agricultural Enterprises; Doctor of Economics M. Sokolov, professor and head of the Agricultural Economics Department of Moscow State University; and Candidate of Economics I. Suslov, docent in the Economics Department of the CPSU Central Committee's Academy of Social Sciences, produced an article frontally attacking the core of Lemeshev's proposal. While they make it clear they were not proponents of the all-encompassing rigid Stalinist central plan, a complete plan from above that outlaws all spontaneity below, they emphasized that some central planning was and is absolutely required by a socialist system. So far their position is the orthodox one, and Lemeshev and those of his ilk are the unorthodox, radical, but still loyal opposition. It is notable that Lemeshev's earnestness and motives are not questioned. Although they attack his ideas, they do not question his right to advocate them. And apparently the unorthodox economists like Lemeshev, Venzher,

G. Lisichkin, and L. N. Kassirov do have access to the scholarly periodicals and, on occasion, to the popular press. So, unlike the free land use issue, this one in almost all its aspects is, if not wide open, at least not an un-issue. It is discussable even though the regime has made it quite clear which viewpoint it adheres to. This leads one to believe that the regime is willing to keep its future options open by not absolutely anathematizing the unorthodox views of Lemeshev and the others. Moreover, the unorthodox economist camp includes some rather renowned men, who have at one time made major contributions to the modernizing of the Soviet economy and the dismantling of some of its archaic, overcentralized, cumbersome, initiative-stifling, incentive-smothering features. So they have built up some value in the regime's eyes to protect them from the more irresponsible, opportunistic, and highly dogmatic critics.

Kolesnev, Sokolov, and Suslov are alarmed by Lemeshev's proposals that the exchange of agricultural and industrial products be conducted on the basis of free supply and demand. They attack Lemeshev's presumption that centralized planning hampers and restricts the development of commodity-money relations. They criticize individual economists who are drawing incorrect conclusions from the criticism of the mistakes and miscalculations in the planning and management of agriculture exposed by the March 1965 Central Committee Plenum. These economists derive from the mistaken notion that planning from above in principle is incompatible with the democratic forms of managing kolkhozy. They would restrict the state management and planning agencies to the role of regulating prices, credit, and taxes, which are regarded by the reformers as the sole levers of state influence over the farms. All other economic functions of the state agencies they regard as administrative interference incompatible with economic methods of management and planning of the national economy and incompatible also with the co-operative nature of the kolkhozy. They quote V. G. Venzher, the economist who incurred the wrath of Stalin by first advocating the sale of the MTS machinery to the kolkhozy (a step later taken by Khrushchev in 1958), as urging the exclusive use of the value levers of price, profit, credit, privileges, and other stimuli to influence the development of kolkhozy in the direction desirable for the national economy. Venzher would reduce the role of the centralized state regulation of the farms to merely the collection and distribution of economic information and indirect influence via price, credit, and tax regulation. G. S. Lisichkin urges the replacing of orders for production of whole lists of crops by the use of voluntary bilateral contracts. L. N. Kassirov calls the setting of assignments by the state for the farms in terms of the amount and structure of their output to be sold to the state nothing but administrative dictation. M. Lemeshev advises granting kolkhozy the complete right to plan the sale of their products to the state. All of these schemes call for development of free market relations and a rejection of centralized planning of procurements of agricultural products, that is, a rejection of one of the major achievements of the Soviet social system, say the authors.[59]

The authors insist that the objective basis in the sense of a compulsion for planning is socialist public ownership as the means of production. The guideline for prosperity is the correct combination of centralized planning with the development of the economic initiative of the farms. Both the farms and the state have an interest in the planned procurement of agricultural products. The state requires such a plan in order to guarantee the country's needs for foodstuffs and agricultural inputs into industry will be met, and for the farms it is a guarantee of marketing their commodity output at economically advantageous prices. As output rises, the importance of its guaranteed sale will increase for the farms. So the mutual interests of both society and the farms are served by planned procurements. Yet the authors recognize that agricultural planning should make fuller use of the mechanism of commodity-money relations and value categories, should take more operative account of the farms' initiative and deepen their specialization.

They hold that if the state, as the exponent of national interests, creates conditions for the sale of commodity outputs that are economically sound and profitable for the kolkhozy, then they have a material interest in producing such commodities. Moreover, it is a vital necessity and prime duty of the kolkhozy to do so. So the authors insist that the point is not the special nature of kolkhozy, but simply the soundess of the plan. Central planning being an objective necessity, it must continue to exist. Moreover, it influences, the direction of farm development.[60]

V. Venzher, G. Lisichkin, and M. Lemeshev advance the idea of selling farm output mainly through the free market. This would force the kolkhozy to somehow adapt their production to market requirements. They would have to study the level of market prices in different areas or wait till local market prices rose to the desired level as a result of an increase in demand.[61] Venzher feels the state procurement organizations would be confronted with the necessity of purchasing a given product precisely where its production is cheaper and where prices consequently are lower. He feels that peaceful competition between competing farms would lower the price.[62]

The authors, however, feel there are grounds to suppose that, on the contrary, as long as the demand for agricultural output exceeds supply, it would lead to higher rather than lower market prices for agricultural products. And, they hold, this would mean that the main efforts of the managers and specialists of kolkhozy would inevitably be bent not so much toward an increase in the production of output as toward skill in marketing it profitably. And this would lead to mounting individual farm expenses being incurred to create their own storage and marketing facilities rather than going into the production process. Moreover, the planning of agricultural production without coordinating it with national economic needs would lead to the emergence of major disporportions between industry and agriculture. They also claim that turning loose free market forces would cause a considerable increase in purchase and retail prices for agricultural products, speculation, a lack of control in the work of the procurement organizations, and, in the final analysis, a breakdown in the fulfillment of the purchase plan. The kolkhozy needed free sales on the kolkhoz market or to state purchase agencies where the purchase price did not insure them a normal income, but now, when the level of purchase prices is satisfactory, central, planned marketing of their output becomes economically profitable for them. So free sales are not the most in keeping with the nature of kolkhoz production. Rather, mass marketing to a wholesale purchaser is. So the task is to work extensively to perfect the planning and procurement system, not to dismantle it, say the authors. Lisichkin's view that the lag in agriculture before the March 1965 Central Committee Plenum was caused merely by a violation of the law of value is a gross oversimplification. The crux of the matter is the correct use of the whole complex of economic factors, and first of all the economic laws of planned and proportional development of expanded socialist production, the law of value, and also the principles of combining public and personal interests and material incentives. It is wrong to simply counterpose such categories as the plan and the market. It is not the market, they argue, but uncontrolled market conditions that counteract development according to a plan. Under socialism the very mechanism of commodity-money relations has a planned nature, not only because the basic, key positions of the economy are determined by the plan centrally, but also because prices, interest, credit, production costs, profits, and profitability are formed in planned and other economic services of the socialist enterprises. So, conclude the authors, under the conditions of socialism the market is planned and its development is systematic.[63]

What these three orthodox economists say boils down to a dogmatic assertion that even with the state controlling the tax, price, and credit levers, and even with the leverage of the state agricultural inputs monopoly, they will not allow or trust the kolkhozy to produce spontaneously whatever they feel will best serve their own interests. They are stung to their ideological quick by the notion of spontaneous production even within a controlled macro-economic environment within which a large part of the agricultural production sector, the sovkhozy, would remain inside the plan and hence could be relied on to supply a significant share of the absolutely essential commodities and, by their competitive marketings, to affect the prices kolkhozy could get for identical produce. They are not impressed by the argument implicit in the Lemeshev proposal of the state's control power resting not only in its manipulation of the economic levers but also in its role as the inevitable, even monopolist buyer. Rather Kolesnev, Sokolov, and Suslov fasten on the seemingly minor problems implicit in the obviously limited free market proposal, such as some speculation, undue expenditures on nonproductive marketing facilities, and the unhealthy potential for exploiting regional commodity deficiencies. They use the "big scare" argument that the implementation of the proposal would inevitably lead to gross disproportions in the economy, whereas in reality—and they admit this—up to the present the disproportions already are there, are substantial, and are working against the agricultural sector. Moreover, they were planned. It is ironic to hear the proponents of the plan plead its case on the basis that it alone guards against disproportions. Perhaps the reaction betokens an instinctive distaste on the part of the orthodox for anything that is unplanned and spontaneous. The anarchy of the free market is a Marxist bogey. Certainly to compare the limited free market proposed by the reform economists to the classic free market of Adam Smith, Ricardo, or even its much tamer and less spontaneous contemporary mixed economy progeny is a gross distortion.

Perhaps they are simply afraid that, in the short run, the abrupt transition to the proposed system would cause major dislocations temporarily disruptive both economically and, perhaps, politically in that they would challenge the vested interests of the adversely affected economic potentates and their conservative-minded, bonus-conscious, and plan-fulfillment-oriented colleagues. These interests would sabotage its operation from within to discredit it. Certainly the planning bureaucracy would fight this reform, since it would imperil their function at least as to the agricultural sector. The local state and party control apparatus would also lose its powers over the farms, and hence it would also oppose the free sales system, believes the American economist Morris Bornstein.[64] Moreover, perhaps some of the orthodox economists sense in this proposal a Pandora's box of economic heresy, which might spread to the industrial sphere if it works in agriculture. The idea of opposing it may be perhaps then attributed to not so much a fear of the immediate economic disruption it might cause—which in fact might be welcomed by the ideological zealots as proof of its basic unsoundness and thus would discredit the reformers—but rather to a fear that it might succeed and hence result in further concessions to the economic independence of the kolkhozy. This might then spread to the sovkhozy and from there to industrial enterprises. So these economists hope to nip it in the bud. Perhaps what other antireform economists are reacting to is the incipient political autonomy on the part of the kolkhozy. They fear that this economic autonomy, limited as it would be, would lay the foundation for the kolkhozy to become a major economic interest, especially if they continued their trend toward more and more regional and ultimately national association. Perhaps even the politically feeble— from the standpoint of grass-roots kolkhoz control—fledgling system of regional and All-Union Kolkhoz Councils, carefully controlled as it now is by the party, seems an ominous development as far as the more nervous antireformers are concerned. And yet another possible source of opposition may simply be those true conservatives who fear the necessity of rethinking the orthodox fundamentals and finding them wanting. The reform constitutes an intellectual challenge to those of mediocre mind. They find the prospect of a painful reevaluation that would require them to approach economic problems on an ad hoc, experimental basis simply too frightening. The Marxian economic orthodoxy furnishes a core of beliefs and principles that both simplifies and orders reality, subsuming the idiosyncratic, exceptional, and even spontaneous within its ordered and omniscient perspective, thereby, at least theoretically, suspending the need to investigate, account for, or experiment with these disharmonious intrusions in a supposed economic universe of regularity, order, and law-governed socioeconomic progress.

The economist G. Kuznetsov is also critical of the reformers Venzher, Lemeshev, and Kassirov. Venzher is criticized for demanding absolute observance of the principle of equivalence in relations between the state and the kolkhozy. Kassirov is wrong in believing mere use of the economic levers can correct produce shortages that arise in consequence of going over to a voluntary contract system of procurement. All three of the reformers, according to Kuznetsov, err in six respects. First, they underestimate state planning as the most important advantage of socialism over capitalism. Second, they do not take into account the contradiction between value and consumer value of goods. Free purchase replacing planned centralized purchase would create market spontaneity and obviate the advantages of the central plan. Third, free purchase would lead to a goods exchange basis for agriculture, meaning expansion of the market sphere at the expense of the production sphere. Fourth, the liquidation of planned tasks contradicts the correct combination of the interests of the state, of all society, and the interests of the individual collective and personal interests. Fifth, absolute observance of the principle of equivalence in relations between the state and the agricultural enterprises is scarcely possible. It is only realistic to talk about exchange that allows kolkhozy to cover expenses and have enough left over to provide for accumulation funds. The state must exact rent via price, taxes, and so on. Sixth, economists like Lisichkin contrast the planned directive with goods-money relations. Yet under socialism, goods-money relations are one of the forms of planned economic ties, although hardly exhausting the totality of them.[65]

This criticism of the liberals by Kuznetsov adds nothing to what was said by Kolesnev, Suslov, and Sokolov. It is, however, of some interest that Kuznetsov is far from being a rigid adherent of the status quo. As will be seen below, he puts forward many significant reform proposals in the realm of price, credit, and tax policy that indicate a receptivity to experimentation and tampering with the established modus vivendi. So his opposition to the free market idea would seem to be an indicator that such opposition is far from limited to only the less imaginative, rigid neo-Stalinist elements among the economists. In other words, the opposition to the free market idea is not a monolithic one. In fact it runs the gamut from arch conservative to very liberal. The economist V. P. Boev calls Lisichkin's claim that the main cause for the lagging of livestock production is low purchase prices for milk and meat too simplistic, ignoring technological problems. To allow kolkhozy to respond to demand spontaneously would lead to deployment of sums needed for investment into transportation needs and practical shipment problems. In fact, perfecting rational specialization requires stable planned procurements.[66] Here is another example of at least criticism on grounds other than ideological.

SECTION 3: AGRICULTURAL PRICE POLICY

It seems that today Soviet economics has come a long way in terms of emancipating itself from the degrading role of rationalizer of Stalin's theories. According to a study of Soviet economists by the American economist Richard W. Judy, analytical economics had been denied a role in the political economy of socialism and competent economists had been liquidated or driven underground during Stalin's days. Judy quotes the Soviet academician A. A. Arzumanyan as saying that Stalin's fear of autonomous economic research doomed it to being only an abstract, closed, and scholastic study of socialist property ownership, with the result that theoretical economics became significantly isolated from life and from the study of economic problems. He also quotes academician L. F. Ilyichev as describing the effect of Stalinism on Soviet economics as encouraging economists who could not analyze concrete factual material but who instead could adroitly manipulate citations.[67] Judy detects little change in things till July 1955. Political economists continued to occupy themselves with irrelevancies and ideological considerations retained their dominance, with ideologues continuing to control the important editorial and directoral posts. But after the July 1955 Central Committee Plenum, economists were criticized and demands were thereafter made on them to solve problems. They were accused by Khrushchev of divorcing themselves from practical work.[68]

The thrust of the criticism was to make Soviet economics relevant to the problems facing policy-makers. The analytical poverty, as Judy calls it, of Soviet political economy in the face of the painful and ubiquitous economic malfunctions of the day dictated cogent analysis, not anecdotal descriptions of the ills coupled with appropriate citations from the Marxist classics. Economists were censured, inter alia, by the political leadership for their inability to formulate the theoretical basis of price formation or to develop ways of stimulating higher productivity.[69] According to N. O. Karotamm, a Soviet Doctor of Economics, the aim today of Soviet agricultural economists is to determine the most rational means of developing the material and technical basis of socialist agriculture and, in doing this, to establish criteria for the rational specialization and distribution of agricultural production in the various zones and regions as well as making economic assessments of the techniques used in agriculture, working out with greater precision the criteria for measuring the effectiveness of capital investments and new techniques in a socialist agricultural system. The economists are concerned with the problem of raising the level of labor productivity and are working on methods of assessing and comparing productivity. A great deal of work has been done on the question of introducing cost accounting in agricultural enterprises and making them more profitable. A great deal has also been written on ways of applying on kolkhozy the principle of material incentives to make workers more productive. This involves the formulation of a rational wage system. Yet another major concern is the question of differential rent under socialism, its social character, its process of formation and distribution. And yet another major area of concern is the way the two forms of socialist property can be brought closer together and ultimately merged into a single form, the property of the whole people. This involves the question of the gradual elimination of existing differences between town and country.[70] All these are of course practical preoccupations, excepting perhaps the last topic.

Today Soviet economists are freely discussing the importance of money and prices. And it is generally admitted by all in the post-Stalin period that the law of value does apply to a socialist economy. After this was admitted, Howard J. Sherman discerns three different views of the value of manufactured means of production as current among Soviet economists. The economist K. B. Ostrovitianov, assumes, like Stalin, that the law of value operates under socialism only where there is market exchange. Since, however, means of production are owned and exchanged only between state enterprises and kolkhozy, "value" exists only in the market exchange between state enterprises and kolkhozy alone. This is, says Sherman, a very limited view of the role of value, and does not allow the rational circulation of values or prices of the manufactured means of production exchanged between state enterprises. The second view of value is that of I. A. Kronrod, who assumes that "value" operates wherever there is "exchange." He argues, however, that state enterprises do exchange goods, are autonomous units and may not be treated as one big firm, and must exchange equivalent value products in order to provide material incentives for their workers. So he concludes that the law of value does operate in the state sector of the economy, not just in the state-kolkhoz exchange sector and in the kolkhoz market sector.[71] The third and most radical view, that of I. S. Malyshev, argues that value does not arise from exchange in socialism at all, nor from any automatic market process. Rather in socialism value as a need or category arises from the necessity in the planning process of measuring the amount of labor expended on each product and in the aggregate. This view sees the need then for a rational calculation of value on all products coming within the plan.[72]

Sherman explains the recent concentration of both Stalinist and liberal economists on the question of the need for rational evaluation and calculation within the economy as growing out of the increased complexity of the Soviet economy. And with this there are more technological possibilities and variants open to the planners in each industry.[73] To obtain the optimum balance in agriculture, as well as in industry, the most outputs from the least inputs, you have to do things in the way that produces the most value output with the least costs. As Sherman notes, either to calculate costs or to evaluate output, one must have prices that rationally reflect social costs and social needs. This can be done by either minimizing costs or by maximizing the value of output.[74] Yet some Soviet economists, whose views are labeled "voluntarist," simply feel the planners should set prices as they desire, since they hold that the law of value has no application to the socialist economy and that prices need have no effect on planning. This view has few supporters anymore, although, as Sherman notes, the present Soviet price structure still does not reflect any particular value theory. The price system does reflect a Marxist notion that price must equal the value in labor terms, which must represent the total of the wage cost plus the cost of materials and capital depreciation plus a profit margin.[75] In the agricultural context, up to the advent of a guaranteed wage of kolkhozy, in theory it was not possible to use wage and other cost data to arrive at prices, since the wage cost, being uncertain since it was a residual, could not be known beforehand. Even today

the wage bill for the new year cannot be predicted. So price calculations are complicated. Moreover, the question arises as to calculating
the profit margin or surplus value. Here, notes Sherman, there is
considerable disagreement among Soviet economists as to exactly
how the calculations should be made.[76]

The concept of the costs of production is crucial to the rational
price system. The Soviets are increasingly recognizing not just
direct labor production costs, that is of living labor, but moreover
the labor costs embodied in the used-up plants, equipment, and materials. This is how such costs are rationalized in terms of Marx's
labor theory of value. Far more ideologically troublesome, however,
are the more indirect labor costs of using natural resources and
capital in one project rather than another, that is, the opportunity
costs of using scarce resources. Since capital and natural resources
are limited, they must be used on the more desirable project. Consequently, a rationing system must be developed. One possibility is
charging a rate of interest on loans or a rent charge for land use so
as to discourage frivolous use or tying up scarce capital for too long.
Ideologically, however, interest charges and rent charges are suspect.
These necessarily imply the productivity of capital, and this conflicts
with the labor theory of value. Yet, as Sherman notes, the planners
must take into account the necessary rate of profit or uniform return
on capital and natural resources in order to determine whether it is
worthwhile for the society to use it for X rather than Y, and in order
to bring an equality between the aggregate supply and demand for
capital and natural resources. In both capitalist and socialist societies,
the rates of profits, interest, and rent function as devices to allocate
scarce resources, but in a socialist society they cannot act, as they
do in a capitalist context, to affect the distribution of income among
individuals. So, notes Sherman, "The objections of Soviet dogmatist
to such words as 'profit' and 'productivity of capital' in this context
are formal and purely semantic, and have no foundation either in
Marxist value theory or in real issues."[77] As Sherman points out,
Marx himself said nothing against the technical economic concept of
profit, rent, or interest as an allocational device. Only dogmatic
Soviet economists find the use of profitability or rent to judge economic
performance "un-Marxist." Yet in 1965 as an integral part of the so-
called Kosygin reforms, interest charges in the form of a tax were
levied on fixed and working capital put at an industrial enterprise's
disposal by the state. Why not charge the farms a rent fee for the
hitherto freely given in use land?

The agricultural price policy debate today centers on the criteria
to be used to base prices on rather than the function of agricultural
prices, although one must qualify this by referring back to the now
somewhat subsided debate over the maximization of the use of price

as one of the only methods of controlling or planning agricultural production. It is now orthodox wisdom to grant to the price mechanism a major role in agricultural planning along with tax, credit, and investment policies. The ongoing dialogue today concerns more precisely the relative role of price as a planning mechanism, it being assumed by the orthodox economists that agricultural prices are an integral part of a planned agricultural procurement system. And questions of tax reform and the concept of costing agricultural production, as well as land rent I and II, all enter the picture through the discussion of price.

Agricultural procurement prices are those set by the state for sales by both kolkhozy and sovkhozy to state procurement agencies. The Soviet government has, says Morris Bornstein, pursued two conflicting objectives in setting them: first, to fix the terms of trade so as to make the kolkhozniks bear a large share of the burden of industrialization and, second, to provide incentives to produce. Bornstein concludes that the former objective clearly dominated during the Stalin era, while after 1953 the latter has been more characteristic of Soviet kolkhoz price policy.[78] Procurement prices for various products have been raised many times since 1953, most recently for milk and certain other livestock products in 1970.[79] Even the new prices instituted in 1958 were not, however, related to costs of production because of a lack of appropriate cost data. As Bornstein puts it, for decades, as long as average procurement prices were extremely low, reference to costs was politically inexpedient, and kolkhozy did not calculate their production costs. The notion that the concept of cost was inapplicable to kolkhozy was widely accepted. Bornstein states that only in 1955 did the state begin to investigate the level and structure of kolkhoz costs and only in 1958 did farms begin to calculate their costs.[80] Bornstein concludes that successive increases in agricultural procurement prices, together with adjustments in prices of industrial inputs and of consumer goods, have markedly improved the kolkhozniks' terms of trade since 1953 and, in conjunction with other measures, helped to bring about a large increase in agricultural output between 1953 and 1958. Subsequent price increases have been more selective, focusing on lagging commodities, especially livestock products.[81] This is especially true of the 1965[82] and 1970 price increases. As to the sovkhozy, the prices paid to them were generally lower than those paid to kolkhozy, since state subventions made good their losses. Now the emphasis as to their prices is also on insuring profitable operation by sensitivity to costs.[83]

Certain issues emerge out of the more technical aspects of the present price structure debate. These are ultimately connected with the questions of rational farm specialization, farm autonomy, land rent, and equalization of farm incomes for farms working with different levels of technology and labor or in different climate, soil, and locational environments, where equal efforts and use of available assets results in different income.

Among the proposals put forward to remedy the shortcomings in the level, structure, and regional differentiation of agricultural procurement prices, Bornstein notes the following: (1) basing prices on marginal rather than average costs; (2) revising the boundaries of regional price zones; (3) using instruments other than price differences to take differential rent; (4) varying prices in accordance with harvest fluctuations.[84] Each of these will be taken separately.

Today the zonal price is supposed to be based on the average cost of production in that zone. Those kolkhozy in a zone with higher than average costs may not cover their expenses of production. Assuming that the labor component in such a farm's cost is within the zonally socially necessary expenses of labor limits, then is it fair, as Alex Nove asks, to punish a kolkhoz condemned by the plan to grow and sell a certain crop at a certain price that fails to insure it a profit by judging its performance as wanting economically?[85] According to Soviet doctrine, socially necessary expenses of labor in agriculture are determined not by the worst conditions of production, but rather by socially normal conditions of production activity on the least fertile land needed to produce the quantity of a given product necessary for society. Thus, not the expenses of the worst operating farm in the zone but the expenses of a farm that is in the relatively worst natural-climatic conditions and operating its production activities in socially normal conditions and incurring the socially norm expenses under such conditions defines the cost base of the price zone.[86]

As Bornstein notes, although a few members of the marginal cost school favor basing price on the national marginal cost of the product, most accept the principle of zonal price differentiation and urge instead that price be based on the marginal cost of the zone, not the national average. They advocate basing the price on production costs of farms on the worst lands in the zone in terms of fertility and location but with average conditions of production as to mechanization, labor productivity, and managerial efficiency. Bornstein notes that prices based on marginal costs would mean higher procurement costs for the state, although these might be at least in part recouped by raising wholesale and retail prices, or the state could hold down retail prices and recapture some of this by taxes on the differential income of the low-cost farms. The counter argument is made that it is undesirable to set retail prices below procurement prices, as this would encourage farms to keep agricultural products at retail prices in order to resell them to the state at procurement prices.[87] The answer to this is to outlaw this practice and severely punish it. Another problem not mentioned by Bornstein is that of farms with

marginal lands having less than average conditions of production as
to mechanization and hence lower labor productivity, although working
at maximal efficiency given their technological level and skill level.
Is the price that fails to give them a profit fair to them since they are
working just as hard and as skillfully as is objectively possible to
fulfill a socially necessary task?

G. Kuznetsov tackles the problem of the marginal versus the
average expense school. His starting point is that if public demand
for good cannot be covered by use of the best and average lands, then
relatively poorer lands must be brought into production. So the resulting higher costs of production that result are socially necessary
costs if they arise from work done under normal economic conditions.[88]
Kuznetsov criticizes proponents of the "average expense" school because they ignore the implications of the above and would punish, in
effect, the high-cost producer.[89] Kuznetsov favors breaking larger
price zones down into more meaningful smaller ones so costs can
be more sensitive to local cost conditions. He feels the present zones
encompass too many climatic and soil differences. Expenses that
in larger zones were considered high would then become average in
smaller zones. Kuznetsov feels that local state executive organs in
oblast, krais, or autonomous republics within which natural conditions
differ greatly should be given the right, within limits, to differentiate
prices for groups of raions within their republic, oblast, or krai.[90]
Although he opposes the "dogmatists" who insist on average costs as
the basis of zonal prices, he attacks the other extreme, personified
in the views of V. D. Shkredov, who refuses to recognize the validity
of any zonal prices. Shkredov disparages zonally differentiated prices
as manifestations of naked administrative arbitrariness. Kuznetsov
defends zonal prices as an unavoidable means of determining the level
of development of production forces and of planning rational specialization and concentration of production as a form of insuring the social
division of labor.[91] Some of the economists denying zonal value propose to introduce identical purchase prices for the same produce on
the scale of the whole country. They hold that rent income differentials
thereby created could be levied away by the state's tax on farm incomes. Kuznetsov feels this would, even though the prices utilized
the worst lands' cost on a national scale, be disincentive-creating
as to the more profitable farms because it would take away their incentive to keep their costs down so as to increase their profits.[92]

The economist E. S. Gorodetskii also opposes a uniform profit
rate for all agricultural products on the scale of the whole country.
Due to the size and variety of climatic zones, he feels it is not practical
to have a corrective mechanism in a uniform price per product for
the whole country. He feels it would be best to allow Union Republics
and their administrative subdivisions to decide independently on

corrective prices but under defined rules.[93] Gorodetskii, like Kuznetsov, attacks the proponents of a single price for a product on the scale of the whole country. To these economists differential purchase prices contradict the law of value and do not stimulate production. They advocate use of a payment for the use of land. Gorodetskii feels it is wrong to condemn zonal prices, even though Marxism regards value as an economic category reflecting general rather than singular or special relations and in spite of the Marxist belief that the character of value relations presupposes the universality of price, that is of the money expression of value. Yet, says Gorodetskii, zonal value is real and in definite conditions exists and is an unavoidable, intermediary link in the process of reducing individual value to social value. Zonally differentiated prices reflect the necessity of recognizing cost differentials based on objectively different conditions of production.[94] Gorodetskii feels that the system of individual prices for each separate farm is not practical because price would then cease to perform as a specific value category and could not fulfill the function of accounting for expenses of social labor and distribution and redistribution of the surplus value. Very small price zones, not to speak of individual prices, are a brake on specialization and concentration of production.[95] The economist L. M. Kravchuk agrees with Gorodetskii that individualizing purchase prices for each farm would be wrong. His reasons are the complexity of the task and the loss of the stimulus function of prices and profit.[96]

The economist M. F. Kovaleva feels that prices used in trade between industry and agriculture should be such as to insure each sector ability to extend its productive capacity, insure equal pay for equal work, and, finally, result in each sector putting an equal share into the society's social funds of consumption and in return receiving back equal benefits therefrom.[97] She also recommends breaking down larger zones into the smaller, more naturally homogeneous area, thus creating more meaningful cost zones. Kovaleva raises the question of the level of profitability to be insured by the price mechanism. The economist L. Braginskii notes that while most Soviet economists consider zonal enterprise cost of production to be the basis for the differentiation of purchase prices, there is no unity on the question of the proportion of accumulations in price. According to Braginskii, some economists believe that price should incorporate a standard accumulation norm even though such a norm cannot stimulate reduced agricultural production costs, while others focus attention on the stimulating function of price for the development of products that are of primary importance, noting that there are sharp differences in the profitability of production of individual agricultural products. The question arises as to the justification for these variations. Braginskii perceives the theoretical prerequisite for determining the level of profitability in pruchase prices for regions to be the formation of social value of agricultural output on the basis of objectively marginal production conditions. Yet the average level of kolkhoz profitability for a zone does not take into account, says Braginskii, the actual need for accumulation resources and does not serve to lower production costs. And the purchase price also fails to perform its stimulatory role because the volume of net income received from production on the worst land is lower than that on the better land. Braginskii's view is that the best criterion for determining the profitability norm in price is the necessary rate of expanded reproduction required for strengthening the production base and for increasing consumption. This means that there can be no single accumulation norm in price for all types of products.[98]

G. Kuznetsov notes that for the country as a whole during the period from 1958 to 1962, livestock prices were too low to insure profitability. With the rise in purchase prices in 1965, by 1967 the general level of purchase prices was 145 percent above the 1958 level.[99] In 1966 the norm of profitability of crops was 70 percent nationally, whereas for livestock products it was 8 percent. The norm of profitability for grain crops in 1967 was 142 percent, for sunflower 371 percent, for pork 23 percent, for fowl 6 percent, and -4 percent for milk. Up to 1970 purchase prices for livestock products were still too low to create material incentives, despite price increases in 1962 and 1965. In 1970 purchase prices for milk, cream, and meat were significantly raised.[100] These increases, concludes Kuznetsov, significantly closed the gap between the profitability of livestock and crop production.[101] Yet Kuznetsov leaves us no criterion by which to set prices other than that of simply insuring profitability.

Kuznetsov advocates the introduction of seasonal prices. He argues that in the north and central raions of the USSR the period of yearly applying higher prices should be longer than in the south. This would not only compensate in part for different natural conditions of production but also overcome existing seasonal inequality in supply of milk to urban centers. This would interest farms in meeting year-round milk needs, which they are loathe to do now because the cost of milk is higher in the stall period than in the pasture period in many oblasts. With year-round prices the same, farms strive to deliver more in the summer and cut down sharply on deliveries in the winter.[102]

Seasonal milk prices have existed but often were not sufficiently differentiated. Today seasonal differentiated prices exist for meat, vegetables, and potatoes as well, although they are far more crucial for milk, which is the fastest spoiling product.

Kuznetsov thus is attacking the rigidity of the Soviet agricultural price system, which holds prices stable despite yearly variations in

harvests. Perhaps the state should raise procurement prices and
retail prices temporarily when harvests are especially poor. Kuznetsov's aforementioned proposal is for prices to reflect seasonal supply-
demand relationships. As Bornstein notes, the present premium
prices for above-plan deliveries of grain and a few other crops, like
the dual price system in effect until 1958, cause the effective price
to vary directly with the size of the harvest. In good years, average
realized prices are higher because more of the commodity is put into
the above-quota sales at higher prices. Conversely, in bad years
both the quantities and the average procurement prices are lower.
Bornstein concludes that, as a result, farm incomes tend to fluctuate
more than if prices varied inversely with the size of the harvest.
Also, since procurement prices of perishable commodities are uniform throughout the year, there is no incentive to produce or store
them for the colder months.[103] What Bornstein fails to mention is
that this system rewards the farms that have better natural-economic
production conditions, unless taxes take away most of their advantage.

I. Lukinov favors raising prices to compensate for poor harvests
due to bad weather so that society as a whole rather than the individual
farm shoulders the burden. Lukinov argues that in terms of the
Marxian value theory that in poor years the average cost per unit of
output, and therefore the product's value, is greater, and so the price
should be higher. Opponents argue that prices should be fixed on the
basis of average costs over a number of years and be revised periodically. During poor harvest years, farms in trouble could get state
credits.[104] Lukinov is far from alone in advocating prices geared to
the size of harvests, so-called sliding prices. E. S. Gorodetskii notes
that shifts in farm profitability reflecting changes in weather are
inequitable since the farms are not responsible for the weather conditions.[105] Kuznetsov also advocates sliding prices, as they protect
the stability of farm accumulation in bad years. He feels that they
should only move up, never down.[106] Yet if the burden of nature's
fickleness is not to be blamed on the farm, then why should a farm
be allowed to gain added income because of very good weather since
this too is "unearned." Gorodetskii, to be consistent, would have
to oppose Kuznetsov on the "only move up" condition. P. D. Polovinkin
defends the stability of price principle embodied in Brezhnev's fixed
five-year planned prices. He argues that stability of price stimulates
the economy to achieve definite goals is sets on the basis of these
prices and thus allows price to fulfill its function as an instrument
of planning. He holds that with sliding prices there is subjectivism
in establishing prices.[107] This amounts to putting a rather high
premium on price as a planning mechanism in disregard of the obvious
inequity of the farm being a hostage of the weather.

As to the level of profitability, there seems to be no theory behind the variations of profitability among crops caused by the procurement prices paid out for these. In industry a profit markup above branch average cost assures sufficient profitability to every normally operating enterprise. To transfer this idea to agriculture is not as simple as it might seem. First of all there is the evaluation of land problem, since land is a prime means of production in agriculture. Moreover, the labor cost has traditionally been undefinable because, on the kolkhozy, it was a residual. And, since the labor day pay unit was worth more on the more successful farms, its use in comparisons of farms would mean that the more successful farms, that is the more efficient, had higher labor costs since they paid out higher amounts for labor. Some Soviet economists urged the use of sovkhoz pay rates in monetizing labor costs in kolkhozy. The problem was that generally sovkhoz workers' pay was well above that of the average kolkhoznik. Even today with the advent of guaranteed pay, supposedly at approximately the sovkhoz level, there still is uncertainty during the course of the year as to the exact labor costs because of premia, bonuses, and the often conditional and merely minimal level aspect of the guaranteed pay. Another aspect of the cost calculation controversy is whether the profit markup should be applied to the cost of materials plus labor costs and plus depreciation or rather to only fixed and working capital. Since the adoption in industry of a profitability markup on capital, many advocate this approach in agriculture. There is a serious problem with regard to the calculation of amortization. The norms of amortization for machinery are often arbitrary. They were earlier based on the work done by the machine rather than its actual condition. To revert to the old system just because present norms are arbitrary, says R. G. Askerov, would ignore the fact of a machine's obsolescence, which occurs independent of its use and which is a commonplace in agriculture.[108] Bornstein poses some important questions as to the use of the industrial profit calculation method. Will it be possible to determine the amount of capital involved in the production of individual commodities?[109] Moreover, not just cost but also desired accumulation levels must be taken into account in setting levels of profit. So must the prices of industrial inputs like machinery and chemical fertilizers be taken into account. All this creates tremendous complications.

Kuznetsov feels that it is wrong to have norms of profitability of different agricultural products vary by as much as one hundred times. Cutting down on the variation would, he feels, be more stimulating overall in production terms. Yet he emphasizes that he is not advocating absolutely equal profitability norms for all products, as this would frustrate specialization. Kuznetsov urges that besides correlating profit with expenses of production, it is necessary to take into account the mass yield of each crop per hectare or sown area, per man day, and per weight of the unit of produce. In 1966-67, he notes, the greatest mass of profit per 1,000 rubles of expenses of a farm, per one expended man day, and per weight of the unit of produce was generated by sunflower seeds. But going only by the highest profit per sown hectare, cotton was best. By comparison with sugar beets, grain crops often get larger profits for equal expenditures, but per unit of sown area they generate less profit. In light of this, if a single identical norm of profitability were established, then it would sharply weaken a farm's interest in production of grain, barley, and sunflower seeds, since these crops give a very small mass of profits per hectare. Kuznetsov holds that those crops that secure less income per hectare, even though they do not demand large labor expenses per unit of land, and grow quicker, do need a higher profitability norm than those crops the raising of which gives greater gross income per hectare and involves higher intensity of land use.[110]

Noting that on the whole industry's norm of profit is higher than agriculture's, he holds that agriculture requires a higher norm of profitability than industry. First, because of agriculture's much lower material production base. The value of basic production funds per worker in agriculture is 2.8 times lower than in industry. Also, inherently land as a means of production requires more energy resources because of the distance and dispersal of labor sites in comparison to industry. He argues that agriculture involves nature's influence, a factor that is maximal in this sphere and minimal in industry. Industry needs practically no insurance against nature. Finally, changes to higher wholesale prices in connection with recent industrial economic reforms have led to more expensive industrial inputs for agriculture.

The ninth five-year plan (1971-75) has committed the regime to a far greater capital investment in building the agricultural technical base in an attempt to increase productivity and profitability. The combined state-kolkhoz investment will be 1.6 times greater than during the eighth five-year plan.[111] Of this, roughly two-thirds is state supplied.[112] Roy Laird sees the current investment commitment in light of that of the previous plans as indicative of the regime's awareness that gains in agriculture are becoming increasingly more expensive.[113]

E. S. Gordotskii raises some thorny problems in respect to calculating the profitability of kolkhozy. Since there is a difference between the mass of produce a kolkhoz produces in a year and that part of this mass that takes the form of goods, goods production cannot be used as the sole criterion of kolkhoz production.[114] In other words, some produce goes back into production. Is this part a legitimate production cost and, if so, how is it costed, that is by reference to what price? Gorodetskii holds that it is very important to measure

213

profitability by correlating the mass of profit with applied production funds so as to determine thereby the norm of profitability. Production expenses, he feels, do not exactly reflect the costs or degree of use of production funds. A significant part of the circulating funds of kolkhozy are seed and fodder reserves. So are natural insurance funds. The kolkhoz with more insurance funds, under equal conditions, is less profitable than another with less. And, in analyzing the profitability of sectors of production, it is very difficult to define exactly the amount of production funds applied in production of a given product or crop. He feels that profitability should be defined by comparing profit with the money expression of applied production funds. Yet, as he notes, today land is not included as a constituent element in the money expression of production funds. Gorodetskii also feels that it is necessary to correlate profit with the amount of land of the farm.[115] By implication he might be interpreted as being in favor of a land use fee or some type of land tax.

Yet the problem of evaluating land as a constituent part of farm production costs has not been solved, since no land cadastre has been completed despite the voices of many economists being raised on behalf of just this. The land evaluation problem affects both scientific costing and pricing as well as the resource allocation problem. It also affects the specialization of agricultural production. The economist B. A. Baimukhambetov feels strongly that the economic calculation of land and the establishment of a scale of normative sizes of profit per unit of arable of a certain quality land would introduce an essential correction into the process of determining the sizes of planned and actual profit per unit of arable land.[116]

Braginskii believes that after the introduction of the land cadastre, income tax should be supplemented with a differential tax system that takes into account the qualitative assessment of the productivity of farmland. As a result he feels society will be able to redistribute income for the good of the entire economy in proportion to the actual effectiveness of labor inputs. Braginskii feels that the distribution of a kolkhoz's net income must provide enough for adequate accumulation and be sufficient to stimulate production.[117] He bemoans the absence of a criterion for distributing the net income between accumulation funds and public consumption funds, or for establishing the proportions for deductions to be used for the replenishment of fixed and working capital. He proposes that the state use its credit system as a key means for augmenting the intrakolkhoz distribution. The economic limits to credit must, he urges, be determined by the optimal sum of the farm's own resources that the farm can draw on the basis of accumulation norms. These norms, he notes, do not exist today, and hence credit would seem to fill the existing resource gap. Credits should be used to promote specialization. Braginskii favors the introduction of long-term loans to replenish working capital in order to increase the intensification of production on kolkhozy experiencing financial difficulty. Also, on economically weaker farms, credit can make it possible to secure more rational proportions between consumption and accumulation. The same goal, he notes, can be served by extending loans to kolkhozy to pay wages to their members, a practice officially sanctioned in 1966 in order to institute a guaranteed minimum wage for kolkhozniks. But he conditions such credits on the need for additional funds for wages arising from higher labor productivity.[118]

Braginskii feels that the stimulatory impact of credit and trade on all processes in production and distribution can be realized only if the main indices of kolkhoz development are defined. These are the norm of expanded reproduction and the normative level of wages. The expanded reproduction norm is calculated on the basis of average data over a period of many years. These data include the level of net income and the amount of net channeled into fixed and working capital. The kolkhoz's own accumulations and the long-term credit it obtains must be sufficient to insure a given growth rate of fixed and working capital and to attain an optimal capital-output ratio in agriculture.[119] Braginskii feels that in determining the consumption growth rate, it is advisable to proceed from the norms of wages on sovkhozy and from the assigned growth of labor productivity of kolkhozy, taking the volume of production into account. And, in order to form such a plan, he urges that an "ideal" mathematical model of the con- solidated economic plan of kolkhozy be created, so as to find the specific numerical dependencies and relationships of all the afore- mentioned instruments of commodity and monetary relations between city and village. This might, he believes, become a component part of the national economic plan.[120]

Braginskii fails to propose any specific mandatory norm of yearly accumulation for kolkhozy out of their net income. Article 36 of the new Model Charter, which deals with the distribution of the kolkhoz's gross income, states that income shall be so distributed as to insure the proper combination of accumulation and consumption and that allocations for increasing the fixed and circulating assets are obligatory. With the annual allotment's size fixed annually taking into account the need to insure further continuous expansion of pro- duction, the question arises as to whether there should be a mandated minimum accumulation expressed as a percentage of either kolkhoz net income or gross income. It is an open question. As matters now stand, the direct participation of kolkhoz profits in the purchase or renewal of farm machinery is insignificant, its share in this not exceeding 22 percent. State long-term credits provide more than half of all means for this, and the single most important reason for this seems to have been the advent of guaranteed pay for kolkhozniks in 1966, which made the kolkhozy without the available special credit dip into capital investment funds to make good the guaranteed pay. This was and is especially true for the weaker kolkhozy.[121] So it seems the guaranteed pay, which comes primarily from the kolkhozy, has impaired their ability to self-generate the accumulation funds necessary to some kind of optimal production and expansion. It has helped ameliorate the problem of poor material incentives by presumably leveling-up the lower wages but at the cost of the accumulation side. So, if the state desires to promote expanded production among kolkhozy at some particular level, it must reform the credit system. One of the traditional differences between kolkhozy and sovkhozy was that the former were self-financing while the latter were subsidized by state funds. If the state refuses to solve the accumulation problem by increasing procurement prices, then it must get more capital to the kolkhozy by the credit mechanism. And even with the orthodox cannon that wage increases cannot exceed rises in the productivity of labor except in the cases of the weaker kolkhozy,[122] still this has happened in 1966 and can happen whenever there is bad weather, especially with the new guaranteed pay system. So perhaps the credit system must be reexamined.

R. G. Askerov finds great arbitrariness in the rules governing the dates when various credits for certain agricultural equipment must begin to be repaid, as well as in the number of years over which repayment is to be completed. Askerov submits that perhaps the East German technique of raising the material interest in quicker repayments of credits by lowering the interest rate if the principal sum is paid off before the deadline should be used. He also opposes Braginskii's proposal that repayment start simultaneously with the beginning of the use of the equipment. Normally repayment begins after the third year or beyond. Askerov feels that in extreme cases perhaps one year after receipt of the machinery is fine but, in general, Braginskii's proposal would place kolkhozy in a very difficult financial position and would force them to decline the use of credits, thus hindering production.[123]

G. Kuznetsov approaches the credit problem from the perspective of helping the weaker kolkhozy, now burdened with providing guaranteed pay, obtain enough funds for proper accumulation. He proposes noninterest bearing credits to them, as is already done in Bulgaria. For the economically strong and average kolkhozy, he proposes introducing a differentiated interest rate that would increase with the length of the period within which it can be paid off, as is done in East Germany.[124] Kuznetsov goes beyond Askerov in posing the ultimate solution to the accumulation problem caused to kolkhozy by the burden of guaranteed pay: creation of a single centralized state-kolkhoz fund of guaranteed pay for kolkhozniks, intended to supplement the pay of kolkhozy unable to self-generate the requisite guaranteed pay. This would be similar to the present centralized kolkhoznik pension fund. In 1962-63 Bulgaria, he notes, set up a guaranteed pay fund from yearly contributions from the state and from 2 percent yearly deductions from the income of kolkhozy.[125]

The territorial specialization of agricultural production has been mentioned as a goal of the regime. It is a means of maximizing production and minimizing costs of production by matching crop production to the soil-climatic area or areas where they are best suited. The idea is to take the USSR average productivity per hectare of each crop as the criterion and then compare the local yield per crop to this average. If each crop is located in the area where its yields are highest and its costs of production lowest, this will maximize productivity. The key is to reduce production costs. In the first stage of this general scheme, the attempt would be made to minimize costs of production rather than to maximize productivity of land, using a comparative index of costs of produce in various locations. Often the lowest cost and highest productivity areas for crops coincide, but not always.[126] Probably the priority of the "lowest cost" variant is because it involves much less in the way of capital outlays and inputs, as specialization is intimately connected to the procurement price, profitability, and land cadastre problems. Present procurement prices are notoriously poorly related to natural conditions. But within present territorial price zones and between zones major differences in production costs are ignored by the application of a single procurement price. It has been concluded by the territorial specialization experts that given the basis of contemporary procurement prices, it is practically impossible to realize rational specialization of production. According to these experts, procurement prices should secure equality of profitability for all farms working in equal production conditions and encourage production of those crops best suited to particular locations in those areas. The prices should not punish those whose production costs are higher because of objectively poorer work conditions that they cannot overcome but should stimulate production of certain crops in areas best suited to them by insuring higher profits to such lower-cost, higher-productivity producer farms.

As it now stands, many farms specialize in products that have relatively high purchase prices and not those that are best suited to their natural and economic conditions. The result is that the social costs of production are higher for such products than if rational specialization were implemented by the price system.

It has been suggested that every five years prices be reviewed and corrected to take into account technical and cost reduction developments.[127] In this connection a thorough land cadastre is needed in order to lay a foundation for specialization. It would classify soils and land quality, and ultimately yield an economic evaluation expressing the value of gross production of crops per price zone and the costs of production per zone per crop. On this basis procurement prices could stimulate the most advantageous use of land[128] and help determine the correct amount of differential rent to be taken by rental payments.[129]

Yet some Soviet economists feel that all this can be better achieved by tax reform rather than through the mechanism of state procurement prices. The question involves how best to recapture for the state the differential rent generated by different climatic, soil, and technological endowments of farms. The tax on kolkhozy was, until 1965, based on a flat rate of 12.5 percent on all gross revenues, except those devoted to productive expenditures and other minor exceptions.[130] On April 10, 1965, a ukaz of the USSR Supreme Soviet Presidium reformed the tax so that it fell on net income exclusive of the first 15 percent of it and exempted also the income of kolkhozniks below 60 rubles a month.[131] Those who advocate the use of the tax mechanism as a more flexible medium for recapturing unearned farm income and for inculcating a rational material incentive to production feel it can better be differentiated to each farm's objective production conditions than can prices. Also it can be directly related to the quantity and quality of land, thus promoting more efficient land use and more production. Moreover, using the price mechanism ties recapturing differential rent to sales to the state, whereas the tax falls independent of this and thus contains no built-in disincentive to marketing.[132] Proponents of the tax mechanism urge that it be reformed in order to perform these functions. E. S. Gorodetskii voices what appears to be a growing sentiment in favor of a progressive tax rate instead of the flat 12 percent rate. As he sees the problem with the present tax, its flat rate is neither directly connected with the level of profitability nor with the quality of land. He proposes it be differentiated according to the natural-economic zones and within these zones. It should take into account the level of profitability and output in terms of net income per unit of land of a certain quality.[133] V. R. Boev also favors a tax based on the level of profitability.[134] G. Kuznetsov advocates a progressive tax rate as a tool for aiding the decrease in economic differentiation among farms and cutting down on the great fluctuation of pay levels among kolkhozy. He proposes increasing the tax immunity to the first 30 percent of net income and then imposing a progressive income tax rate. He would free from taxation the labor fund of the kolkhoz up to the level of 60 rubles per month per worker. Thereafter the state could use the income tax rate to punish kolkhozy paying out too much in wages at the expense of accumulation by applying a steeply progressive rate to higher

level pay.[135] In other words, Kuznetsov wants to discourage excessive
wage bills and encourage more investments in increased production
by the tax system. The problem is that to go too far in this direction
will undermine material incentives of the workers. Moreover, while
this may encourage the stronger kolkhozy to cut consumption in favor
of accumulation, it will not necessarily help the weaker kolkhozy
directly, beyond the benefit that the firm 30 percent of their profit
is tax free, admittedly a substantial benefit in itself but hardly a direct
and scientifically based proportionate response to their objectively
higher costs of production, which limit their ability to generate the
level of profitability necessary to assure the proper level of accumulation as well as to provide their workers the necessary salaries to
insure material incentives. In other words, Kuznetsov's 30 percent,
while obviously better for the weaker kolkhozy than the present 15
percent immunity, is still not justified in terms of economic data.
It is pulled out of the air. In any case, regardless of the particulars
not being justified, some reform in this direction seems to be in the
offing. At the October 1968 Central Committee Plenum, Brezhnev
stated that an income tax differentiated per the farm's level of profit
would be better than the present flat fee income tax.[136]

SECTION 4: WAGE POLICY

The price problem is obviously a function of the costs of production. It is the wage bill that comprises a major cost of any farm's
production. To keep it down toward subsistence or even below—as
was the case traditionally with the kolkhozy, allowing the private plots
to provide for subsistence—proved a bottleneck to increased production and generally undermined material incentives. Hence the commitment to some uncertain level of minimum wages for kolkhozniks in
1966 not only made cost production and hence rational price planning
more feasible but also promoted material incentives. The idea was
that a kolkhoznik's basic wage was to approximate that of the sovkhoz
workers and ultimately that of the industrial workers. It was, however,
not to increase any faster than the increase in his labor productivity,
which, of course, was only in part a function of his own efforts and
rather more a function of the equipment, education, and other macro-
economic factors beyond his control to improve. And obviously with
the rise in wages envisaged for most kolkhozy by the guaranteed pay
principle—and it should be kept in mind that no definite amount as
such is guaranteed, only a definite amount for work done—[137] there
is a real danger that consumption will come at the expense of accumulation and that the guarantee of a certain minimum pay per month, as
was always the case with the sovkhoz workers, could, instead of

increasing material incentives to work harder, as it was intended to do, prove a disincentive since, regardless of results of work, a certain minimum pay would be guaranteed. Unless work norms for the minimum necessary work are well grounded and unless an attractive bonus or premium system for above-norm work is used rather than a straight time work unit that disregards results both quantitatively and qualitatively, the costs of low-level security in wages for kolkhozniks will be very high for the state and have no great stimulatory value as such on kolkhozniks to increase their productivity. Moreover the new guaranteed wage scheme will not doubt increase labor costs and hence production costs. If it is not accompanied by increased capital and machinery inputs from the state to the farm so as to technologically arm kolkhozniks objectively to increase their productivity instead of simply relying on the effect of the guaranteed wage principle as a sufficient impetus in itself to increased productivity, it will not be conducive to improving the quality or the quantity of output. The kolkhoz itself is largely indifferent to the quality of its output, since state prices fail to distinguish between different varieties of the same crop.[138] So this would constitute the starting point for reform.

It is quite clear from Soviet economic literature that increasing purchase prices cannot be considered the route to increasing the productivity of kolkhozy or their profitability. Rather the strengthening of their material-technical base and the concomitant industrialization of agricultural labor is seen as the key to this.[139] This is not put forward as a rationale for holding back purchase prices today for certain products when these prices do not guarantee a fair return on legitimate production costs but rather as a warning that farms had better subsidize their own increased labor productivity by a self-accumulation level that restricts consumption, especially consumption in the form of excessively high wage payments. In 1967 expenses for payment of labor constituted 62 percent of all agricultural production costs in kolkhozy. Yet this was down by 8 percent by comparison with 1962,[140] despite guaranteed pay. This does not necessarily indicate any increase in the productivity of labor in general or any particular benefit derived from the guaranteed pay scheme. The avowed purpose of the guaranteed pay reform was to raise kolkhozniks wages to the level of sovkhoz workers and industrial workers, not necessarily as an economic stimulus but rather as a long-overdue removal of an inequitable burden shouldered by the kolkhoz peasantry. In fact, figures for 1962-67 indicate that the major cause of cost increases for all agricultural products that occurred in this period was increased expenses of labor.[141] So the regime, in righting a wrong, cannot expect to recoup the added costs of its righteousness in the short run, as it seems to be saying when it demands that pay increases via the guaranteed wage not outstrip rises in the productivity of labor.[142]

What in fact has happened to kolkhozniks' wage levels in relation to those of sovkhoz and industrial workers since 1966? Taking the pay per work day in industry in 1964 as 100 percent, the same work day in the sovkhoz was approximately 65 percent of this. In 1966 it went up to 75 percent, and in 1967 to 77 percent. By 1968 it was 85 percent. In 1968 the average monthly pay in sovkhozy was 76 percent and in kolkhozy 55 percent of that of industry. In 1968 the pay per man day in kolkhozy was 87 percent of that in the sovkhoz and the average monthly pay in the kolkhozy was 72 percent of the sovkhoz level.[143] But yet another Soviet source put the kolkhoz per man-day rate at only 87 percent. It should be emphasized that the per worked day figure is significantly higher than the yearly earnings percentage. For instance, in 1954-55, while the percentage of the average kolkhoznik's man-day earnings to those of the sovkhoz worker was 61 percent, the yearly earnings percentage was only 49 percent. In 1968-69 the figures were respectively 87 percent and 73 percent.[144] Alec Nove reports that despite the general upward surge in kolkhoz pay, Estonian kolkhozy, which had paid 46 percent above the USSR average kolkhoz pay as of 1963—whereas Belourussian kolkhozy then paid 38 percent below the average—as of 1968 still paid 2.5 times the Belourussian amount, although both rates had gone up absolutely. Nove concludes that many kolkhozy could not afford to pay the sovkhoz rates recommended by the 1966 guaranteed pay decree. And Nove cites Soviet statistics that indicate that post-1958 pay increases for kolkhozniks have greatly exceed the increases in productivity, thereby adding significantly to labor cost. From 1958 to 1965 labor productivity rose by 35 percent and total kolkhoz pay by 81 percent, while the seven-year plan had envisaged 100 percent and at least 40 percent respectively.[145]

The differences between the top and the bottom salaries within the kolkhoz, although reportedly somewhat reduced during the period 1965-67,[146] are still quite large. In the period 1960-64 the differential had risen significantly.[147] Many Soviet economists hold that kolkhoz chairmen's salaries should be approximately equal to those of nearby sovkhoz chairmen's and that, as a rule, the pay of managerial personnel should not exceed two or three times that of the average kolkhoznik.[148]

Karl-Eugen Wadekin reports that official rebukes directed at kolkhozy have been frequent in recent years, because their wage level over the period 1966-70 rose faster than their gain in labor productivity. Article 27 of the new kolkhoz Model Charter incorporates the position that wages are not to rise faster than labor productivity. It has even been said that earnings of kolkhozniks in very strong kolkhozy should rise less than gross income and should not be allowed to rise markedly above the sovkhoz level.[149] Wadekin notes that there is no analagous problem in the sovkhozy since their wage rates are fixed by the state, excepting, within limits, their premia. Wadekin also confirms that labor productivity of kolkhozniks has, in recent years, not risen as fast as kolkhozniks' wages. Wadekin notes that the 1965 state procurement price increases directly benefited kolkhoz wages, especially the wages of livestock personnel. The eighth five-year plan directives called for an increase in average monthly kolkhoz wages by 35 to 40 percent to be accompanied by a rise in agricultural productivity of 40 to 45 percent. In 1966 came the guaranteed kolkhoz wage, meant to benefit the lowest wage groups.[150] Wadekin concludes that for the period 1966-70 kolkhoz wages did rise faster than labor productivity, raising production costs over 1964-68 by 25 percent. By 1968 the percentage of labor costs in kolkhoz production costs was over 50 percent, but this was not much different from sovkhozy.[151] Wadekin concludes that there was no special failure in the kolkhozy, as official criticism imputes, but rather it was the overall context of the Soviet system and the aftermath of past neglect of agriculture that made the labor productivity rise less than was hoped for.[152] What this amounts to is a deflating of the Soviet claim that the income redistribution in favor of agriculture, especially the kolkhozy, necessitated by the accumulated discriminations against this sector by the state until less than a decade ago, can now be self-financed largely by increased kolkhoz productivity of labor. So, despite Soviet claims, hopes, or plans, it would seem unrealistic in the near future to expect to hold the line on state procurement prices unless there occurs some combination of a very significant increase in the technological base of the average kolkhoz plus a more rational price system that encourages maximal crop specialization in low-cost production conditions. The dogma that the rise in kolkhoz wages cannot be allowed to exceed the rise in kolkhoz labor productivity is simply unrealistic if the regime really intends to bring the kolkhoznik's wage level up to that of the industrial worker. Those who wish to condition the realization of this goal on the observance of this dogma are in reality only paying lip service to the attainment of the goal.

NOTES

1. Robert C. Stuart, The Collective Farm in Soviet Agriculture (Lexington: Heath & Co., 1972), p. 139.

2. Sherman, op. cit., p. 172.

3. Michael Kaser, Soviet Economics (New York and Toronto: McGraw-Hill, 1970), p. 170.

4. W. A. Douglas Jackson, "Wanted: An Effective Land Use Policy and Improved Reclamation," Slavic Review 29, no. 3 (September 1970): 411.

5. Kolkhoznoe Pravo, (Moscow: Gosiurizdat, 1970), pp. 118-120.

6. Ibid., p. 121.

7. For various definitions, see Politekonomicheskii Slovar' (Moscow: Izdat. Polit. Lit., 1964) and Kratkii Ekonomicheskii Slovar' (Moscow: Gospolitizdat, 1958).

8. R. Iu. Kuvatov, Sebestoimost' Sel'skokhoziaistvennoi Produktsii (Alma Ata: Izdat. Kainar, 1969), p. 43.

9. P. Nikitin, Fundamentals of Political Economy (Moscow: Progress Publishers, 1966), pp. 123-125.

10. S. Vygodsky, Capitalist Economy (Moscow: Progress Publishers, 1966), pp. 64-65.

11. A. V. Bolgov, Differentsial'naia Zemel'naia Renta v Usloviiakh Sotsializma (Moscow: Izdat. Akad. Nauk, SSSR, 1963), p. 35.

12. Ibid., p. 38.

13. Bolgov, op. cit., p. 39.

14. Ibid., p. 50.

15. Ibid., pp. 75-76.

16. Ibid., p. 113.

17. Ibid., p. 114.

18. Ibid., p. 115.

19. Ibid., p. 119.

20. Ibid., p. 122.

21. Ibid., p. 128.

22. Ibid., p. 138.

23. Ibid., pp. 140-141.

24. Ibid., pp. 158-159.

25. Ibid., p. 166.

26. Ibid., p. 167.

27. Kaser, op. cit., pp. 167-168.

28. Bolgov, op. cit., p. 170.

29. Ibid., p. 172.

30. Ibid., p. 187.

31. Ibid., p. 176-177.

32. I. T. Beliaev, Differentsial'naia Renta v SSSR (Moscow: Izdat. Mysl', 1967), p. 52.

33. Ibid., p. 119.

34. A. Kalnyn'sh, "Opyt Material'nogo Stimulirovaniia Rukovoditel'ei i Spetsialistov Kolkhozov," Ekonomika Sel'skogo Khoziaistva, no. 10 (1971): 75.

35. B. V. Erofeev, Osnovy Zemel'nogo Pravo (Moscow Izdat. Iurid. Lit., 1971), p. 211.

36. For a statement of the essence of the economic reform as it is now understood, see Ekonomicheskaia Reforma: Yeye Osuschestvlenie i Problemy, red. A. M. Rumiantsev i P. S. Bunin (Moscow: Izdat. Polit Lit., 1969), p. 22.

37. For the English translation, see L. Leontyev, "Questions of Theory: On Commodity Production Under Socialism," Pravda, August 31, 1966, pp. 2-3, translated in CDSP XVIII, no. 35 (September 21, 1966):

38. Ekonomicheskaia Reforma: Yeye Osushchestvlenie i Problemy, op. cit., p. 230.

39. V. M. Alekseeva, Razvitie Soiuza Rabochikh i Krest'ian v Period Perekhoda k Kommunizmu (Leningrad: Izdat. Leningradskogo Univ., 1967), p. 40.

40. G. P. Romanchenko, Rentabel'nost Kolkhoznogo Proizvodstva (Moscow: Izdat. Kolos, 1969), pp. 257-259.

41. V. Pereslegin, Finance and Credit in the USSR (Moscow: Progress Publishers, 1971), p. 103.

42. V. P. Shkredov, Sotsialisticheskaia Zemel'naia Sobstvennost' (Moscow: Izdat. Mosk Univ., 1967), pp. 130-131.

43. Ibid., p. 140.

44. Ibid., pp. 141-142.

45. Ibid., p. 145.

46. For the translation, see CDSP XIX, no. 42 (November 7, 1967): 29-37.

47. Iu. Zharikov, Pravo Sel'skokhoziaistvennogo Zemlepol'zovaniia (Moscow: Iurid. Lit., 1969), pp. 131-134.

48. For the report of the proceedings, see "Differentsiatsiia Zakupochnykh Tsen," Ekonomika Sel'skogo Khoziaistva, no. 11 (1971): 121-126.

49. B. Poshkus, "Vnutrizonal'naia Differentsiatsiia Zakupochnykh Tsen," Ekonomika Sel'skogo Khoziaistva, no. 12 (1971): 16.

50. Ibid., p. 21.

51. CDSP XIX, no. 42 (November 7, 1967):

52. Ibid., p. 31.

53. Ibid.

54. Ibid., p. 33.

55. Ibid., p. 38.

56. Ibid., p. 39.

57. L. Fomina, "Zemlepol'zovanie Kolkhozov," Sov. Iust., no. 13 (1971): 5-6.

58. G. A. Aksenenok, "Pravo Sel'skokhoziaistvennogo Zemlepol'zovaniia v Usloviiakh Nauchno-Tekhnicheskogo Progressa," SGIP, no. 7 (1971): 25-32.

59. S. Kolesnev, M. Sokolov, and I. Suslov, "On the Question of the Plan and the Market," Sel'skaia Zhizn', September 22, 1966, as translated in CDSP XVIII, no. 37 (October 5, 1966): 7-8.

60. Ibid., p. 8.

61. Ibid.

62. Ibid., pp. 8-9.

63. Ibid., p. 9.

64. Morris Bornstein, "The Soviet Debate on Agricultural Price and Procurement Reforms," Soviet Studies XXI no. 1 (July 1969): 20.

65. G. Ia. Kuznetsov, Tovaryne Otnosheniia i Ekonomicheskie Stimuly v Kolkhoznom Proizvodstve (Moscow: Izdat. "Mysl'," 1971), pp. 4-7.

66. V. R. Boev, Zakupochnye Tseny i Chistnyi Dokhod Kolkhozov (Moscow: Izdat. "Kolos," 1969), p. 10 and 24.

67. Richard W. Judy, "The Economists," in Interest Groups in Soviet Politics, edited by H. G. Skilling and Franklyn Griffiths (Princeton: Princeton University Press, 1971), p. 223.

68. Ibid., p. 225.

69. Ibid., p. 228.

70. N. G. Karotamm, "The Economics of Agriculture," in Social Sciences in the USSR (New York: Basic Books, Inc.; Paris and The Hague: Mouton and Company, 1965), pp. 183-185.

71. Howard J. Sherman, "The 'Revolution' in Soviet Economics," in Economics in Social Thought in the Soviet Union, edited by Alex Simirenko (Chicago: Quadrangle Books, 1969), p. 233.

72. Ibid., pp. 233-234.

73. Ibid., p. 234.

74. Ibid., p. 238.

75. Ibid., p. 239.

76. Ibid.

77. Ibid., p. 242.

78. Morris Bornstein, "Soviet Price Theory and Policy," in George Feiwel, editor, New Currents in Soviet - Type Economics: A Reader (Scranton: International Textbook Company, 1968), pp. 237-238.

79. Ekonomicheskie i Sotsial'nye Problemy Industrializatsii Sel'skogo Khoziaistva (Moscow: Izdat. Mosk. Univ., 1971), p. 58.

80. Bornstein, "Soviet Price Theory and Policy," op. cit., p. 239.

81. Ibid., p. 241.

82. Roger Clarke, "Soviet Agricultural Reforms Since Khrushchev," Soviet Studies XX no. 2 (October 1968): 160.

83. Bornstein, "Soviet Price Theory and Policy," op. cit., pp. 241-243.

84. Ibid., p. 245.

85. Alec Nove, "Soviet Agriculture Under Brezhnev," Slavic Review 28, no. 3 (September 1970): 396.

86. E. S. Gorodetskii, Obshchestvenno Neobkhodimye Zatraty Truda, Soitmost' i Tsena v Kolkhoznom Proizvodstve (Moscow: Izdat. "Ekonomika," 1970), p. 41.

87. Bornstein, "Soviet Price Theory and Policy," op. cit., p. 245.

88. G. Ia. Kuznetsov, Tovarnye Otnosheniia i Ekonomicheskye Stimuly v Kolkhoznom Proizvodstve, op. cit., p. 51.

89. Ibid., pp. 60 and 65.

90. Ibid., pp. 65-66.

91. Ibid., pp. 85 and 90.

92. Ibid., p. 94.

93. Gorodetskii, op. cit., pp. 160-161.

94. Ibid., p. 164.

95. Ibid., p. 180.

96. L. V. Kravchuk, "Nekotorye Voprosy Vyravnivaniia Ekonomicheskikh Uslovii Vosproizvodstva v Kolkhozakh," in Ekonomicheskie Otnosheniia Mezhdu Gosudarstvom i Sel'sko Khoziaistvennyi Predpriiatiiami, edited by M. F. Kovaleva and S. V. Rogachev, (Moscow: Izdat. Mysl', 1969), p. 127.

97. M. F. Koveleva, "Ekonomicheskie Osnovy Tsenoobrazovaniia pri Sotsializme i Problemy Sovershenstvovaniia Tsen na Sel'skokhoziaistvennuiu Preduktsiiu," in Ekonomicheskie Otnosheniia Mezhdu Gosudarstvom i Sel'sko Khoziaistvennymi Predpriiatiiami, op. cit., p. 92.

98. L. Braginskii, "On the Interaction of Economic Levers in Collective-Farm Management," Voprosy Ekonomiki, no. 3, (1971), translated in Problems of Economics, IASP, XIV, no. 5 (September 1971): 63-64.

99. Kuznetsov, Tovarnye Otnosheniia i Ekonomicheskye Stimuly v Kolkhoznom Proizvodstve, op. cit., pp. 140-141.

100. Ibid., pp. 145-146.

101. Ibid., p. 148.

102. Ibid., p. 149.

103. Morris Bornstein, "The Soviet Debate on Agricultural Price and Procurement Reforms," Soviet Studies XXI no. 1 (July 1969): 7.

104. Ibid., p. 9.

105. Gorodetskii, op. cit., p. 159.

106. Kuznetsov, op. cit., p. 151.

107. P. O. Polovinkin, Rezervnye Fondy: Vosproizvodstvo v Kolkhozakh (Moscow: Izdat. "Ekonomika," 1970), pp. 108-109.

108. R. G. Askerov, "Tekhnicheskii Progress i Sovershenstvovania Istochnikov Obnovleniia Sel'skokhoziaistvennoi Tekhuniki na Rasshirennoi Osnove," in Ekonomicheskie Otnosheniia Mezhdu Gosudarstvom i Sel'sko Khoziaistvennymi Predpriiatiiami, op. cit., pp. 166-167.

109. Bornstein, "The Soviet Debate on Agricultural Price and Procurement Reforms," op. cit., p. 11.

110. Kuznetsov, op. cit., pp. 154-155.

111. N. Gusev, "Sel'skoe Khoziaistvo v Deviatoi Piatiletke," Ekonomika Sel'skogo Khoziaistva, no. 2 (1972): 8.

112. Keith Bush, "More Light on Soviet Investment in 1966-70 and 1971-75," Radio Liberty Dispatch, May 4, 1971, p. 1.

113. Roy D. Laird, "Prospects for Soviet Agriculture," Problems of Communism XX (September-October 1971): 34.

114. Gorodetskii, op. cit., p. 102.

115. Ibid., pp. 103-105.

116. B. A. Baimukhambetov, "Ekonomicheskaia Otsenka Zemli kak Faktor Sovershenstvovaniia Khozraschetnogo Planirovaniia," in Ekonomisheskie Otnosheniia Mezhdu Gosudarstvom i Sel'sko Khozia-istvennymi Predpriiatiiami, op. cit., p. 50.

117. Braginskii, op. cit., p. 66.

118. Ibid., pp. 69-71.

119. Ibid., pp. 72-73.

120. Ibid.

121. Askerov, op. cit., p. 159.

122. A. N. Blanovskii, "Nakoplenie i Potreblenie v Kolkhozakh," in Ekonomicheskie Otnosheniia Mezhdu Gosudarstvom i Sel'sko Khoziaistvennymi Predpriiatiiami, op. cit., p. 185.

123. Askerov, op. cit., p. 173.

124. Kuznetsov, op. cit., pp. 177-178.

125. Ibid., pp. 180-182.

126. Zametin and Pertsev, op. cit., pp. 44-46.

127. Ibid., pp. 76-79.

128. Ibid., pp. 80-81.

129. Bornstein, "The Soviet Debate on Agricultural Price and Procurement Reforms," op. cit., p. 13.

130. Alec Nove, The Soviet Economy, 2nd rev. ed. (New York: Praeger Publishers, 1969), p. 55.

131. Kolkhoznoe Pravo (Moscow: Iurid. Lit., 1970), p. 325.

132. Bornstein, "The Soviet Debate on Agricultural Pirce and Procurement Reforms," op. cit., p. 12.

133. Gorodetskii, op. cit., pp. 182-183.

134. Boev, op. cit., p. 106.

135. Kuznetsov, op. cit., pp. 167-168.

136. Kravchuk, op. cit., p. 129.

137. Clarke, op. cit., p. 162.

138. N. I. Kuprii, "Vzaimootnosheniia Gosodarstva i Kolkhozov v Protsesse Realizatsii Produktov Sel'skogo Khoziaistva," in Ekono-micheskie Otnosheniia Mezhdu Gosodarstvom i Sel'sko Khoziaist-vennymi Predpriiatiiami, op. cit., pp. 76-77.

139. Ekonomicheskie i Sotsial'nye Problemy Industrializatsii Sel'skogo Khoziaistva, op. cit., p. 9.

140. Ibid., p. 37.

141. Boev, op. cit., pp. 51-52.

142. Ekonomicheskie i Sotsial'nye Problemy Industrializatsii Sel'skogo Khoziaistva, op. cit., pp. 120-121.

143. Problemy Ekonomiki Truda v Sel'skom Khoziaistve (Moscow: Izdat. Ekonomika, 1971), p. 219.

144. Ekonomika Sotsialisticheskogo Sel'skogo Khoziaistva v Sovremennykh Usloviiakh, op. cit., p. 221.

145. Nove, "Soviet Agriculture Under Brezhnev," op. cit., pp. 398-399.

146. Ibid., p. 398.

147. Robert C. Stuart, "Managerial Incentives in Soviet Collective Agriculture During the Khrushchev Era," Soviet Studies XVII, no. 4 (April 1971): 550.

148. Ibid., p. 546.

149. Karl-Eugen Wadekin, "Have Kolkhoz Wages Risen Too Much?" Radio Liberty Dispatch, December 10, 1970, p. 1.

150. Ibid., pp. 2-3.

151. Ibid., p. 5.

152. Ibid., p. 6.

CHAPTER

12
CONCLUSIONS

The post-Khrushchev leadership's agricultural policies have been characterized by their conservatism, impersonality, and incrementalism. Brezhnev has spared himself the personal identification with highly innovative policies. The more innovative the policy the less apparent have been its Politburo sponsor or sponsors. The Brezhnev-Kosygin regime has eschewed any penchant toward the Krushchevian "campaigning" approach. All this is not to deny that significant innovations have occured under this regime, but rather that the style, atmosphere, and expectations of the leadership have markedly suffered in the face of the realization that agriculture's problems are profound, deep-rooted, and fraught with consequences for the whole economy. Hence, perhaps the most "positive" element to date in their policy has been to undo the frantic, "half-baked," and often superficial approach that they inherited. This is to say that constant churning out of bogus remedies and hasty reorganizations has been replaced by a more sober, cautious, objective, and pragmatic approach. But at the same time there is, as with Khrushchev, a distinct reluctance to reconsider the fundamentals of the kolkhoz-sovkhoz system. And this is in good measure due to a strong residual Soviet Marxist dogmatism mixed with a belief that radically reorganizing the agricultural production units would undermine the claims of the Soviet system to have found the key to rural industrialization.

The search for scapegoats to cover up systemic failure and malfunctions, together with the pseudo-therapy of administrative reshuffling often characterized by oscillating waves of centralization-decentralization-recentralization, has not entirely gone out of style. However, failure to address the faulty economic problem in economic terms is increasingly becoming costly to the regime's overall priorities and to the economy as a whole. This the regime is increasingly aware of. To the extent that agricultural problems can be insulated from the "infighting" within the Politburo and hence depoliticized in this narrow sense, economic pragmatism will increasingly erode the traditional dogmatism. A stable leadership group, or even the emergence of a single powerful leader such as Brezhnev, would allow the attack upon the problems of the agricultural sectors to proceed insulated from the ebbs and flows of political demagoguery and unprincipled critiques of rivals in the power struggle. It would be more realistic to expect a de-ideologized approach in substance in a political context in which the leaders sponsoring it are not fearful of being branded ideological deviants by powerful rivals. Concessions in substance if not in form are readily made if there exists little likelihood of any opposition calling them into question.

The particular dogmas besetting the regime in the area of agriculture are the misguided beliefs that industrial techniques are always applicable and progressive in the context of agriculture, and that the private sector is ultimately a threat to the public sector; belief in the inherent virtue of very large production units and an all-encompassing plan; and a distrust of decentralized decision-making and of spontaneity in solving local problems. Add to this the vested interest in perpetuating the myths that collectivization was a voluntary movement and that collective farms are true cooperatives, and the Marxian bias against the peasantry. All this is set within the context of a seemingly inherently decentralized agricultural process that evades standardization. The fruit of these myths and biases is the tradition of discrimination practiced against the kolkhozy and the private sector and the existence of huge, difficult-to-administer farms.

The rural population outflow continues despite administrative controls over population movements and legal prohibitions on state-subsidized agricultural trainees leaving their assigned jobs. The result is a serious and unabating loss in both the quality and quantity of younger agricultural personnel. In good measure this is due to the poor quality of rural life, as reflected in reduced educational facilities and opportunities and a lower level of cultural and domestic services than exists in urban areas. Poor roads, lack of entertainment facilities, and the long and severe winters in semi-isolated communities are not appealing to the rural youth and certainly not to their urban counterparts. Add to this the poor working conditions characterized by longer hours, more physically burdensome work due to undermechanization, and the low social esteem in which the rest of Soviet society holds agricultural labor. The result of all this is a pronounced negative attitude toward farm life—very conspicuously reflected in the few Soviet opinion polls of rural youths. The rural farm workers in general reflect at best a minimal satisfaction with their work. Some express dissatisfaction with the long hours involved and others with the monotonous and unchallenging nature of their work. No doubt part of this is due to the realization that their urban cousins have far more domestic and cultural amenities available to them and receive more material incentives and fringe benefits. As a result of the lower pay, poorer benefits, and generally lower standard of living on the farms, the agricultural work force is, despite significant improvements in pay and social benefits under Brezhnev and Kosygin, still largely a demoralized, sullen, and relatively unproductive mass of workers whose labor productivity has not improved significantly. The rural work force is increasingly made up of older women and middle-age males, and the present regime seems resigned to perpertuating the chronic rural underemployment that is the necessary price paid for tolerating a low level of mechanization and a primitive rural transportation, communication, and domestic cultural infrastructure.

The inability of agricultural leadership and the constant turnover of agricultural specialists to some extent negatively affect farm morale and are indicative of the enduring nature of the underlying problems of the underfinancing of farm capital stock and the failure to institutionalize an adequate incentive system. It is also indicative of the hollowness of the claim that the kolkhozy are genuine cooperatives that their supposedly elective leaders tend to be outside experts thrust upon the collective for a relatively short time to fulfill the externally imposed output targets. They are rotated out even if successful, since the regime favors a device whereby local roots will not be laid down. Moreover, sustained overfulfillment of output targets will only earn higher future planned output targets, so consistent success does not necessarily pay off.

The Soviets under Khrushchev and especially under his successors have made progress in attempts to solve the seasonality of labor on the farms by broadening the scope of handicrafts and subsidiary farm enterprises. Much publicity has been given to farm-operated canneries, mills, brick factories, and food processing enterprises. There has been much made of the ever-increasing number of agraro-industrial complexes and kolkhoz-sovkhoz enterprises and the recently vitalized kolkhoz councils are to further promote these forms of interfarm cooperation aimed at promoting rational specialization and concentration of production on the basis of greater mechanization. These are the prototypes of the ultimate wholly industrialized agricultural enterprises, the farm factories. But to date these much vaunted showpiece enterprises have not appreciably affected the plight of dairymaids, field workers, and livestock workers, that is the least skilled stratum, and to proliferate these enterprises requires a major reallocation of scarce capital.

In part the low social prestige that attaches to farm work is a result of the Soviets' continued glorification of the urban worker as epitomizing the spirit of the revolution. No doubt there has been a negative image of the farmer in Soviet literature and in the public mind. But this has merely exacerbated the situation of an objectively deprived and underpriviledged class that has been, in effect, enserfed by the internal passport system and the poor rural educational opportunities.

One of the most hopeful developments under the Brezhnev regime has been the apparent willingness to experiment in a quiet, even at times secretive way with a wide variety of sub-brigade production units, the so-called "links." While extravagant claims have sometimes been made on their behalf by certain farm officials and agricultural experts, on the whole the Politburo leaders have been very cautious and qualified in their praise of various link experiments and have cautioned against universalizing the use of them. The links have the virtue of disaggregating the performance of the huge brigades, which have grown to resemble the old pre-amalgamation kolkhozy in size. But the ten- to fifteen-man links, with their stability of personnel and land tenure through the whole crop cycle, are ideologically suspect as being a retrograde revived version of the old family farm. They are praised for pinpointing individual responsibility more clearly and inculcating greater love for the particular land they are alloted. Perhaps the mechanized link is the best hope for a more rational approach to creating a decentralized production unit that is more responsive to material incentives and capable of maximizing production and doing so without indulging in such typical Soviet work force responses as simulating performance, and applying husbandry techniques that in the long run undermine the soil for the sake of short-run plan fulfillment. The link could become the typical kolkhoz or sovkhoz production unit for most labor-intensive field and livestock operations without decollectivizing or even compromising the principles of large-scale socialized agriculture. The more responsibility the links assume, either by individual contract or by a new comprehensive law on link-parent farm relations, the greater the chance to tap the reservoir of personal incentive among the more ambitious kolkhoz-sovkhoz workers. Moreover, this would be a flexible vehicle for reducing the army of control personnel and the multilayered agricultural bureaucracy. It would allow for a flexible and localized pricing mechanism to operate within certain limits between individual links and the parent farm and extend the khozraschet principle to the grass-roots level.

Another "escape valve" from the pressures of gigantic farms mired in unproductive layers of district administrators far removed from the operative farming operations would be to localize the "acre and a cow" private plot economies by allowing them to expand their operations within well-defined limits. This would ease the burden on the state sector in respect to providing the peasants themselves with vegetables, fruit, meat, milk, and other dairy products that the public sector is hard-pressed to provide. Of course, this too is ideologically retrograde in the eyes of the orthodox and far more so than any expanded use of the link. But to revise upward the limits on livestock holdings and the number of hectares per plot would alleviate the public sector's problem in providing the rural population with those types of produce that are very labor-intensive. Even more daring and ideologically reprehensible would be a reform that would legalize the buying of certain types of machinery by peasants for use on their private plots. So would the liberation of the limitations on hired labor by possessors of private plots. Perhaps private plots of adjoining homeowners could be jointly worked by their families to create a limited but genuine mini-cooperative.

In any case, the conclusions I have reached in examining Soviet perceptions of the private sector and its role are that it is no longer perceived as a direct threat to the public sector and that it has been able to provide the urban population with what the public sector is least able or willing to provide, as well as to relieve the regime of the burdens of providing its own farmers with their food needs. In the future there need develop no essential rivalry between the two sectors. Why not a broadening and a deepening of the allocation of crop and livestock specialization between the two sectors? Surely there is no real possibility of the private sector substantially infringing upon the public sector or weaning the farm work force away from the public sector. The machinery supplying, credit, tax, price, and labor legislation levers are all available to hedge in an expanded and dynamic private sector. All the commanding heights would still be in the hands of the state. In the rational division of labor the private sector could continue to play a vital complementary role if emancipated from irrational, ideologically inspired constraints. What little balm the regime obtains by periodic repression in the private sector triggered by failures in the public sector could be more than compensated for by a more contented, less constrained, and prosperous collective farmer. The regime's continued emphasis on the gradual voluntary curtailment of the private sector as the state sector increases in efficiency and scope need not preclude such a development.

The problem of devising an economically rational set of criteria for determining the optimal size of farms is critically linked to the problem of establishing a scientific approach to the costing of agricultural production to base rational agriculture prices on. Ideological constraints play a negative role in this sphere too. So far much of the Brezhnev reforms has employed merely efficiency in carrying out the plan. This market mechanism and, as part of it, a pricing system that is a means to stimulate the maximal efficiency in production have not been utilized. Rather, cost accounting is narrowly seen as a means to the end of judging the efficiency of plan fulfillment. The market mechanism and market prices are seen as essentially capitalistic devices, and the anarchy of the market place is contrasted to the planned, proportional development characteristic of socialism. While "gigantomania" has become a bad word, brigades today are gigantic and are as large as pre-amalgamation collective farms. Yet the difficulty of controlling performance on these huge farms, the time wasted circumnavigating them, and an awareness of the law of diminishing returns on economies of scale have all sobered the regime and are evidence of a firm commitment to reexamine farm size in terms of optimality. The Khrushchevian penchant for uncritically embracing bigness in farm size seems definitely a thing of the past. There seems to be an awareness that very large farms are not administrable. But as of the moment, Soviet studies of optimal size are in their infancy.

The problem of devising a rational price system for agricultural commodities, on the basis of which farms could produce just those commodities and products best suited to their climate, soil, locational, technical and labor factors, is one that the regime is tackling in a rather half-hearted way. There is growing awareness that the ideological imperative of apportioning land to farms without exacting a direct rental fee is at war with rational land use and a scientific analysis of production costs. The Marxian notion of absolute rent as a capitalist category hobbles the regime in this respect. Their concept of differential rent I and II, although helpful in mitigating the consequences of the aversion to absolute rent, is in practice a very difficult concept to translate into a workable system of complex differentiated price zones, given the diversity of soils, climates, locations, and especially the varying levels of mechanization and technical skills prevalent among the farms' work forces. Some wieldy systems of exacting a fee related to the quantity and quality of land, together with an allowance for different technological, mechanical, and human skill levels of farms, must be implemented in order to reward farms equally for equal efforts and to overcome the persistent lag between the better-off and the poorer farms. Perhaps the tax mechanism can be used in conjunction with a scientifically based land cadastre.

A decompressing of the centrally devised and imposed output targets and an increase in the use of the central levers—credit, tax, purchase prices—together with more emphasis in determining the purchase price policy on the quality of produce as well as premiums for off-season production, could free the farms of the fetters on their ingenuity and minimize unnecessary and counterproductive petty tutelage from distant, out-of-touch bureaucrats. This decompression would take a load off the central planners, allowing them to concentrate on the minimal number of output targets. It would decongest the channels of communication swollen by upward, downward, and horizontal flows of petty details and unrealistic and out-of-date orders and appraisals. Again it would be a step toward a real measure of autonomy for the kolkhozy, more in keeping with their supposedly cooperative nature. And again the state could use its financial, insurance, credit, supply, tax, and purchase price controls to insure that the farms produced at least the minimum amounts of critical products necessary to insure the population's needs to the extent that this is a realistic proposition. Naturally the new-found autonomy of the farms would represent a limited power on their part to minimize their production of various products. This would give them some bargaining power for the first time since NEP. The regime would have to make it worthwhile for them to maximize production. This would require higher procurement prices, more and better equipment supplies, and greater wage, pension, consumer goods, and welfare benefits for collective farmers. The regime might also allow for the freer flow of manpower out of the rural area by easing up on administrative constraints on the rural population. In effect, all this would amount to a monumental redistribution of national income in favor of the agricultural sector, particularly the kolkhozy. It would require a revision of the Soviet dogma that industrial workers must always be preferred over rural workers both in salary levels and social security benefits. It would result in a rolling back of the regime's traditional favoritism toward the urban community. In the agricultural sector itself it would imply an even-handed policy toward both kolkhozy and sovkhozy. The ideologically preferable sovkhozy would have to lose their privileges. The guaranteed wages instituted under Brezhnev for collective farmers would have to be given a far greater subsidy by the state than has been the case, at least for a transitional period until the new decompressed system allowed the free play of price incentives to raise the technological and mechanical level of the average farm to such a point that labor productivity could rise dramatically as a result of both the new objective and subjective factors. To insist, as the regime now does, that kolkhoz wages should not exceed rises in labor productivity is clearly inappropriate and irrational in the context of this transitional period following decades of general party and state neglect of agriculture coupled with the traditional discrimination against the kolkhozy in particular.

In sum, the ideological constraints on the undertaking of meaningful reforms are formidable but the relative inefficiency of Soviet agriculture and its growing bottleneck effect on the regime's economic and political priorities is so great that the pressures for radical innovation are also growing. An atmosphere of creeping pragmatism is eroding the ideological constraints. But incrementalism in the face of the need to rethink the fundamentals can prove to be confusing and counterproductive. Lenin's "one step forward and two steps back" is a poor strategy to follow at this critical juncture, following the decades of stagnancy under Stalin and the crazy quilt flittings and oscillations of Khrushchev. The Brezhnev regime has had some nine years to muddle through. The grain crisis in 1972 was a major crisis for them policitically. It was indicative that patches do not make a new garment. Unfortunately the reasonably good 1973 harvest will relieve some of the pressure and make the role of the reformers all the more difficult. But it only takes some poor weather to cause a large-scale agricultural crisis in the USSR given the chronic under capacity production the system has institutionalized, set against rising population levels, higher protein expectancies, and commitments to supply grain to the bloc and other allies. So one can confidently predict that unless fundamental price, wage, administrative, and organizational reforms or some significant combination of these are attempted soon, the periodic crisis will continue to embarrass the regime, necessitating significant periodic grain and soybean imports and generating the need for political scapegoats, since the Soviets would have it that the system never fails, only men do.

13

POSTCRIPT:
THE 1972 GRAIN DEALS,
THE SECOND FALL
OF MATSKEVICH,
AND THE 1973 HARVEST

A series of events has occurred since July 1972 that crystallizes in dramatic fashion some of the present dimensions of the perpetual crisis in Soviet agriculture. On July 8, 1972, a three-year $750 million grain purchase by the Soviet Union from U.S. sources was announced.[1] The U.S. Department of Agriculture one month later announced that the Soviets would purchase a billion dollars worth of farm products from the U.S. over the next year.[2] Practically simultaneous with this, the Soviets reportedly purchased U.S. soybeans valued at about $125 million, the first Soviet purchase of soybeans from the U.S.[3] The U.S. Department of Agriculture estimated that Soviet agricultural purchases for fiscal year 1973 would total $1.2 billion, compared with about $150 million in 1972. Of this, wheat purchases figured to be around $660 million, feed grains $400 million, and soybeans $135 million.[4] Department of Agriculture experts interpreted the soybean deal as indicating that the USSR was in the midst of a dilemma over vegetable oil supplies, apparently caused by declining sunflower seed output since 1968.[5]

Personnel changes in January and February 1973 among top-level agricultural administrators have brought home the seriousness with which the Politburo regarded the grain shortfalls of 1972 and the generally poor agricultural performance of recent years. On January 31, 1973, Pravda carried a brief announcement that S. Shevchenko was relieved of his position as President of the All-Russian Association for the Sale of Agricultural Equipment and Supplies "for violation of state discipline."[6] Three days later Pravda's back page announced that Vladimir Matskevich had been relieved of his position as USSR Minister of Agriculture, while its front page carried the news that Dmitri Poliansky, a Politburo member, had succeeded Matskevich as USSR Minister of Agriculture and had been relieved of his post as a First Deputy Chairman of the USSR Council of Ministers.[7] Shevchenko had been this agency's head since its establishment in March 1961.[8] The seeming demotion of Politburo member and agricultural expert Poliansky may be an attempt by the Politburo to bring greater authority and prestige to the Ministry of Agriculture in order to head off another poor agricultural performance in 1973. It is unprecedented to have a Politburo member simultaneously head a ministry, and the office does thrust Poliansky into a most exposed position, for his fate is now squarely tied to future agricultural results, especially the grain harvest. Fortunately, the summer and fall of 1973 proved good and the Soviet grain harvest appeared to be a near record one, with bunker weight computed to reach 195 million metric tons.[9] Matskevich had been ousted by Khrushchev as Minister of Agriculture in 1960 after serving in that post since 1955. In 1960 the crop was again bad. But after Khrushchev's fall, Matskevich was reappointed USSR Minister of Agriculture in 1965 and held that post till now.[10]

Before describing the agricultural failure of 1972-73 that prompted these personnel changes, it is worthwhile to characterize the careers of Matskevich and Poliansky as agricultural policy specialists. Matskevich has consistently championed strict state control over kolkhozy, opposing Khrushchev's plans in 1960 to create some sort of kolkhoz union and thereby undercutting the Ministry of Agriculture. This, along with his opposition to Khrushchev's corn campaigns and the poor harvest of 1960, contributed to his initial ouster as USSR Minister of Agriculture. Poliansky and N. Podgorny at this time supported the idea of kolkhoz unions.[11] Poliansky's rivalry with G. Voronov for the role of prime Politburo agricultural expert dates from 1961. Poliansky's enthusiasm for the charlatan Trofirm Lysenko injured him. In the immediate aftermath of Khrushchev's fall, his weakening of the Ministry of Agriculture's role was reversed and Matskevich was restored as its head. Poliansky's opposition to this coupled with Voronov's support for it further boosted Voronov. It also dealt a blow to those desiring a kolkhoz union, among whom were Poliansky and Brezhnev.[12] The kolkhoz union issue was raised again in 1966, and the pro-union forces were advocating by means of the union idea the reduction of the role of the Ministry of Agriculture. Poliansky became spokesman for the union and found strong support in Brezhnev and Ivan Bodyul, the Moldavian Party First Secretary and a protégé of Brezhnev. In connection with the move to draft a new kolkhoz Model Charter, which emerged from the March 1965 Central Committee Plenum, the issue of kolkhoz unions gained currency. At the Twenty-Third Party Congress in 1966 Brezhnev raised the question of kolkhoz unions. According to Werner Hahn, the Politburo was badly divided on the issue, with Brezhnev, Shelest, Podgorny, Pel'she,

Poliansky, and Kirilenko in favor and Suslov, Voronov, Mazurov, Kosygin, and Shelepin against. Matskevich was thus able to resist the pro-union forces within the commission to draft a new kolkhoz charter, which was created in 1966.[13]

Poliansky still continued to play the role of chief lobbyist for agriculture within the Politburo, and it was he who publicly warned against the shifting of resources away from agriculture in 1966-67, following the record harvest of 1966. As Hahn puts it, the bumper 1966 harvest weakened the argument for continued aid to agriculture, and over Poliansky's public objections, resources were shifted to other sectors, especially light industry.[14] Brezhnev revealed at the October 1968 Central Committee Plenum that the current five-year plan's call for 21.2 billion rubles of central state investments in agricultural construction and equipment in the first three years of the plan had in fact fallen short by almost four billion. This resulted in reduced fertilizer and agricultural equipment production and deliveries.

The "climax" of the kolkhoz union issue came at the November 1969 Congress of Kolkhozniks with its adoption of a new kolkhoz Model Charter that included recognition of the right of kolkhozy to join "councils" rather than "unions," a term now used by Poliansky and Brezhnev. The powerless elective "councils" created by the Congress represented a victory for Matskevich, Voronov, and other anti-unionists. Ironically, Matskevich himself became the head of the All-Union Kolkhoz Council, which included many government agricultural officials.[15]

Voronov had been a champion of the mechanized link. But like Poliansky, he suffered a defeat when the new kolkhoz Model Charter's final draft dropped a clause on long-term assignment of land and machinery to farm production subdivisions.[16] On other issues Voronov was succeeding. He pushed for specialized meat cattle herds in the late 1950s and early 1960s, a policy Khrushchev had thwarted. In view of the manifest meat shortages of 1968 and 1969, Voronov's approach seemed worth pushing. Yet in 1969-70 Voronov's Politburo ranking dropped to the bottom. This in the face of stagnant meat production in 1968 and 1969. Brezhnev's technique for dealing with the meat shortage was to raise meat prices, especially for pigs and poultry. Voronov called for specialized meat cattle farms based on meat and cattle breeds. Brezhnev in late 1970 advocated increases in purchase prices for livestock products as a proper technique for solving the problem.[17] Voronov had opposed Brezhnev's and Poliansky's emphasis on building hundreds of huge livestock raising complexes as a solution to the meat shortage. In late July 1971 Voronov was removed from his post as Russian Republic Premier. Although continuing on as a Politburo member, his new post as chairman of the

USSR's People's Control Commission did not justify his status as Politburo member.[18] Clearly his direct conflict with Brezhnev on the meat shortage strategy rather than with Poliansky led to his eclipse. On this issue Brezhnev emerged as the personal champion of a particular approach. While he had hitherto carefully avoided becoming personally associated with particular initiatives in agricultural policy, where the risks of failure were great, he had "blown his cover" on this issue. Hitherto he had been able to use Poliansky as his stalwart or to allow sensitive and unpredictable policy initiatives generated by acute immediate problems to be sponsored by very top-level agricultural specialists like Voronov or Poliansky or by second-rank figures like Matskevich. The duels on the very sensitive issues like the unions were fought out with only guarded secondary support from Brezhnev. He certainly hedged on the link issue.

While the fall of Voronov was not occasioned by the failure of a policy linked directly to him or by the need for a scapegoat for a fiasco, Matskevich's second ouster seems to be a classic example of the scapegoat approach. True, Matskevich has long been a prime enemy of Poliansky and a sometimes ally of Voronov, but that alone would probably not have caused his fall at this time. It was the grain failure of 1972 that did him in, requiring as it did an offering on the altar of public humiliation. Matskevich became a scapegoat for the accumulated institutionalized failings of the whole agricultural system. Brezhnev is now using Poliansky as a shield. If the upswing of 1973 proves ephemeral and the failures of 1972 are soon repeated, requiring grain imports on the scale of 1972, then Poliansky figures to be cast down in disgrace so as to deflect criticism away from Brezhnev. Poliansky is in a most unenviable position. Having faithfully served both Khrushchev and Brezhnev as chief agricultural trouble shooter, he may have passed the point of his usefulness now that he has been given the almost "Kamakaze-like" role of pulling the USSR out of its grain and meat shortage crises.

Just what are the dimensions of this most recent failure? The economist Paige Bryan correctly predicted that the 1972 gross agricultural output would likely have fallen about 4 percent below that of 1971 due to large shortfalls in grain and forage crops. This would mean that the 21.7 percent planned growth in gross agricultural output for 1971-75 over 1966-70 has become impossible of attainment.[19] The ninth five-year plan has gotten off to a disastrous start with two bad crop years in a row: 1971 and 1972. The planned output targets for grain and meat are practically impossible of attainment and state grain reserves have been reduced to a minimum.[20] The 1972 gross grain harvest was approximately 168 million tons, only some 10 percent below the all-time high of 186.8 million tons in 1970. Yet 28.5 million tons were to be imported within 1973. The 1966-70 average gross output was 167.6 million tons and the yield was 13.7 centners per hectare.[21] It was planned to average 195 million tons over 1971-75 and with a yield of 17.8 centners per hectare.[22]

The 1972 report on plan fulfillment indicated that 1972's agricultural output was 95.4 percent of 1971's. The agricultural statistics section is preceded by the defensive introduction stating that agriculture operated under extremely poor weather conditions in 1972. Keith Bush's above approximation was quite accurate as to the 1972 grain harvest, which was officially 168 million tons. State grain purchases totaled 60 million tons in 1972. Sugar beet production was slightly up over 1971 but well below the average per year during 1966-70, while sunflower seed output was below that of 1971 and well below the average for 1966-70. Potato production was well below the 1971 level—77.8 million tons to 85.2 million in 1971—and well below the yearly average over 1966-70 (94.8 million tons). Vegetable production went down from 20 million tons in 1971 to 19.1 million in 1972.[23] The fallout from this? Soviet grain imports during 1972-72 will probably exceed 30 million tons as compared to a mere 10.4 million tons imported by Khrushchev during 1963 and 1964. As for livestock results for 1972, the number of cattle increased from 102.4 million to 104 million, while the hog total slipped from 71.4 to 66.5 million, and the sheep and goat population went down slightly.[24]

Keith Bush concludes that the 1972 setback has merely stiffened the Soviets' resolve to attain self-sufficiency in staple foodstuffs as soon as possible. Great hopes for grain increases have been posited on extensive use of irrigated acreage in Central Asia and Kazakhstan. Bush feels strongly that these feed grain imports are only a medium-term expedient until the domestic base becomes adequate. That this grain autarchy goal is pursued seemingly regardless of cost is evidenced by the continued commitment to growing wheat on irrigated land, an extremely costly business.[25]

A few days after Matskevich's fall, Ivan Bodyul, the Moldavian First Secretary, came out with a proposal that would seem to vitalize the kolkhoz councils. He proposed that they be entrusted with the functions of economic management of kolkhozes and interkolkhoz associations. Thus these primarily advisory organs would become actual administrators of the kolkhozes. This is what Matskevich opposed. However it would be naive to believe that the Soviet leaders mean by supporting this proposal to create a powerful, independent, nationwide kolkhoz movement. Rather it would seem more likely that Christian Duevel is closer to the truth in observing that the new kolkhoz councils would be a better manipulative device than the traditional one of utilizing directly party or state organs.[26] In fact, Bodyul's star has been rising. He has increasingly come to the fore as a pro-council man and leading proponent of agraro-industrial association.

In fact, his republic is a leader in the development of such associations, especially in processing of grapes, vegetables, fruits, and sunflower seeds.[27] His stock has been further boosted by the publication of a book he authored entitled Social Changes in the Countryside, which was positively reviewed in the leading Soviet economic weekly.[28]

On March 9, 1973, Bodyul delivered a report to the Second Congress of Moldavian Republic Collective Farmers that gave in detail the new powers he had in mind for the Moldavian farm council. In effect, Moldavia, Bodyul's bailiwick, with Kremlin approval, was running a pilot project for the nation. Bodyul prefaced his revelations about the actual powers to be given the council with the assertion that it was necessary to have a management agency whose leadership would fully encompass all the economic elements of the cooperative sector and would be able to regulate the development of economic conditions and maneuver material and technical resources on the scale of the entire system. Bodyul related that the assembled collective farmers, having considered this, decided to transfer the management of the economic activity of the kolkhozes and interkolkhoz enterprises to the jurisdiction of the council, which they had elected democratically. The councils were to be vested with the right to manage all the affairs of kolkhozes and interkolkhoz enterprises, directly to plan and manage production, to receive procurement assignments from the state, distribute them, and insure their fulfillment. They are to plan production and directly manage it, introduce scientific-technical innovations, distribute material and technical resources, and insure their rational utilization. They are to insure the correct proportions between accumulation and consumption, as well as the growth of fixed production assets. They are to concentrate and distribute capital investments to develop interkolkhoz cooperatives and to resolve questions of output norms, the pay system, and the training of cadres. Having full administrative powers over interkolkhoz enterprises and associations and creating centralized capital investments and seed, fodder, and foodstuff stocks, they will be able to exert a direct influence on the redistribution of differential rent.[29]

It had been announced on March 6th that Poliansky had been elected chairman of the USSR All-Union Kolkhoz Council, replacing Matskevich.[30] The Moldavian councils are now in farm unions along the lines envisioned by the original union proponents. Of course, it remains to be seen whether the Moldavian experiment will be allowed to spread. In any case, this represents a daring new initiative and one that Brezhnev cannot avoid identification with. Moreover, Bodyul's political fate is clearly tied to it, and if he is successful and Poliansky is not in his role as the overall "Tsar" of agriculture, Bodyul would loom large as a most logical replacement for him in the Politburo, or in any case as his counterweight.

Talk of extensive agricultural consolidation reflected in a Pravda editorial of December 16, 1973, which was supposedly based on an unpublished Brezhnev speech to a plenary session of the Central Committee, triggered rumors that the impending Soviet agricultural reforms could eliminate the collective farms. This rumor circulated at the same time the Party revised the report of the 1973 record grain harvest upward from the 215 million metric ton total reported by Brezhnev in October 1973 to 222.5 million tons.[31] In late July of 1973, Brezhnev's tone had been one of qualified optimism on the 1973 grain harvest. It had been planned to be 197.4 metric tons. Brezhnev's remarks betrayed an expectation of a grain harvest slightly below this at the 186.8 ton level.[32] The 1973 grain crop proved to be the best in Soviet history and some 37 million more tons than that of 1972. While generally favorable weather during the 1973 growing season, especially generous spring rainfall in the principal grain areas, was probably not the major factor in the grain turnabout,[33] the rumor seemed to indicate that the regime might be crediting its revamped agricultural leadership with some contribution to the dramatic reversal of 1972. This pilot project in Moldavia, which might provide the model for wholesale transformation of the collective farms, was apparently meeting some resistance on the part of farm managers who did not relish ceding their functions of production planning, resource allocation, and other important investment functions to raion kolkhoz councils.[34] However, despite this, the purported Brezhnev speech of December, coupled with the ongoing pilot projects in the Baltic and Moldavia, and the record grain harvest of 1973, fueled speculation of a dramatic administrative solution to the "kolkhoz problem." However, Deputy Minister of Agriculture Leonid Khitron's news conference of December 24, 1973, while not denying that transformation of the collective farms remained a long-term goal, unequivocally denied that the experimental interfarm cooperation programs were about to be generalized.[35]

Ironically, the Soviets purportedly offered to help tide over the U.S. until its 1974 grain harvest came in, since it developed in late 1973 that U.S. grain stocks had been drawn down to low levels after heavy exports, especially to the USSR in 1972-73. (The Soviets, in dire need after their 1972 grain fiasco, had bought American wheat at bargain prices of about $1.65 a bushel. As of January 1974, the price had risen to $5.80 a bushel.)[36] The Soviet trade official concerned, however, soon claimed the alleged offer was due to a "complete misunderstanding" but that the USSR had agreed to delay taking delivery of the remaining 18.4 million bushels of the 125 million bushels of wheat it had purchased from the U.S. until after July 1, 1974.[37]

The 1973 sunflower seed crop, while apparently lower than expected, is definitely an improvement over that of 1972. The poor sunflower and soybean harvests of 1972-73 prompted Soviet imports of U.S. soybeans. These imports were utilized to enrich Soviet livestock feeds with protein.[38] Feed crop failures in 1972 caused the lowering of 1973 production goals for meat and milk. Apparently 1973 production goals were lowered to ensure growth of livestock herds so as to attain planned meat and milk output for 1974-75. Figures for the first half of 1973 indicate marginal increases in both meat and milk marketing relative to the corresponding period of 1972.[39]

Criticism of the minister in charge of fertilizer supply followed a March 1973 Central Committee special decree on the fertilizer problem. The gist of the degree was an accusation that the Ministry of the Chemical Industry has made poor use of its production capacity and that, in addition, it was turning out too much poor quality fertilizer.[40] Less than a month later, it was announced that the Occidental Petroleum Corporation had signed a twenty-year multibillion dollar chemical-fertilizer barter arrangement with the USSR that provides for the export of American technology and equipment for a new Soviet fertilizer complex, special piping to link it to seaports, and shipments of American superphosphoric acid, to be paid for by Soviet shipments of ammonia, urea, and potash. Tass put the overall value of the deal at $8 billion. Present at the signing was not only Minister of Foreign Trade Patolichev, but the recently criticized Minister of the Chemical Industry, Leonid Kostandov.[41]

In January 1974, Leonid Kostandov announced that in 1973 the USSR had become the world's leading producer of chemical fertilizer, surpassing the U.S. for the first time. When their crash development program was launched in the late 1950s, Soviet production represented about one-third of that of the U.S.[42] Still, the Soviets are going ahead full steam with the Occidental Petroleum deal and seem quite interested in accelerating their acquisition of American agricultural technology and techniques. Strong evidence of this is the June 19, 1973 U.S.-USSR agreement on cooperation in the field of agriculture. In part this agreement provides for cooperation in research and technology, including possible joint research programs on crops, livestock, machinery, and equipment. To implement the agreement, a U.S.-Soviet Joint Committee on Agricultural Cooperation will be established to meet annually. The Soviets are especially interested in improving the mechanization of their agriculture generally with U.S. technology. There is a special concern with regard to harvesting and management of large enterprises. From the U.S. standpoint, this represents a potentially great market for U.S. companies selling machinery and equipment.[43]

What then is the significance of the 1972 grain crisis and what are its costs? Obviously the quality of chemical fertilizer has been low, hence the Occidental Petroleum deal. But above and beyond this, the grain shortfall is evidence of agricultural stagnation under Brezhnev of late. Brezhnev has consistently advocated and secured large appropriations for the agricultural sector, but after seven years, two poor crop years in a row have depleted grain reserves and forced unprecedented purchases of grain from abroad. This will most likely adversely affect meat production, as has the falling off of sunflower seed output with its high-protein oil content so important to the production of high-quality mixed feeds. The use of potatoes as livestock feed, an increasingly widespread phenomenon of late, is a terribly costly alternative.[44]

Paige Bryan emphasizes and documents the fact that the yearly percentage growth of agricultural output since 1965 has not been in proportion to the yearly growth in productive agricultural investment. The disproportions of 1967, 1969, and 1971 were especially strong. In 1967 6.9 percent more was invested in agriculture, which yielded only a 1.4 percent percentage growth in agricultural output. In 1969 the figures were respectively 4.1 percent and 3 percent, and in 1971 10.6 percent and 0 percent.[45]

Not only are the ninth five-year plan's output targets for grain and meat out of reach, but the mobilization of millions of workers from outside the agricultural sector and the deployment of tremendous amounts of transportation equipment to get in the harvest, with the consequent disruption to the affected sectors, are also costs. And there has not been any official acknowledgment by the Soviet government to the public that they have been forced to purchase grain abroad. Since at least some of the Soviet public has learned this via Western radio broadcasts, the credibility of the regime has to that extent been compromised,[46] and moreover, this news is bound to bring into question the adequacy of a collective agricultural system that is unable to feed the growing population. All of this suggests that we are witnessing in the present grain crisis a "re-run" of the previous ones. The present crisis, although in part a result of bad weather, is primarily due to the inherent weakness of the system: an overly centralized and remote central administration, farms too large to administer rationally, an incentive-smothering wage and price system, an inflexible planning system, and a massive coordination apparatus overloaded with problems and contingencies foreseeable and unforeseeable. The link system could be an invaluable tool for inculcating the crucial linkage between effort and reward, and the encouragement of the private sector by means of new and more liberal tax, land use, credit, price, and livestock limitation policies could go far toward making agriculture more efficient. But the regime's actions in handling the present crisis are bereft of any indications of an inclination to reconsider the fundamentals of the system. The grain, soybean, and chemical deals are merely patches fashioned to tide the country over till good weather returns, and even the potentially radical innovation involving the Moldavian kolkhoz councils is merely another example of the attempt to use administrative restructuring as a buffer against a more agonizing reappraisal of the root causes of these periodic crises. The Soviet leaders simply refuse to face the bedrock issues involved, and the price they will continue to pay for this is periodic grain and meat crises and a politically embarrasing dependence upon imports. Brezhnev has stumbled, just as Khrushchev did, on the seemingly intractable problem of agriculture. That he has been able able to deflect criticism from himself so far on to Voronov, Matskevich, Shevchenko, Kostandov, and, perhaps, Poliansky is certainly no defense against an ultimate reckoning. For Brezhnev, as the chief, is ultimately responsible for agriculture and he will find it increasingly difficult to utilize scapegoats. Perhaps more than any other single domestic issue, agricultural performance will be a decisive one for Brezhnev's political future. For the time being, "action" has been taken and Bodyul has become Brezhnev's new prophet on agricultural questions. But the scapegoat-finding and administrative-juggling scenario is the standard Soviet medicine tried time after time to no great effect. Perhaps it will buy a few years more of "muddling through," although another 1971-72 could be Brezhnev's last act unless his much vaunted détente initiative provides substantial enough gain to more than compensate for agricultural stagnancy. Still, the risk Brezhnev is running in possibly implementing a drastic centralization of the kolkhoz administration at a time of serious lag in performance of the current five-year plan, which has already necessitated unprecedentedly large grain imports, is very great indeed. This holds despite the 1973 recovery. For the crucial farm performance indicators in Soviet agriculture still contrast poorly with those of the U.S., despite the Soviet lead in fertilizer production. Output per farm worker in the USSR is only one-ninth of American productivity, and the Soviet Union uses about 30 percent of its labor force in agriculture, compared with 4 percent in the U.S.[47] Also, while the size of U.S. and Soviet farms continues to grow, American labor productivity continues to rise while Soviet productivity lags. The biggest American farms are the most productive, but on the average the American farm as of 1974 is some 385 acres,[48] while, as of 1970, the Soviet kolkhoz was over 6,000 hectares and the sovkhoz almost 21,000 hectares.[49] The "big" U.S. farms are midgets compared to Soviet farms.

NOTES

1. The Wall Street Journal, July 10, 1972, p. 4.

2. "Soviet Purchasing Grain from U.S. May Total Billion," New York Times, August 10, 1972, p. 1.

3. "Reports Say Russia Buying U.S. Soybeans," New York Times, August 9, 1972, p. 45.

4. Foreign Agriculture 10, no. 46 (November 13, 1972), Foreign Agricultural Service, U.S. Department of Agriculture, p. 3.

5. George E. Wanamaker and Roger S. Euler, "USSR Import of U.S. Soybeans May Indicate Difficulties in Meeting Oil Needs," Foreign Agriculture 4, no. 46 (November 13, 1972): 4.

6. Pravda, January 31, 1973, "Khronika," p. 6.

7. Pravda, February 13, 1973, pp. 1 and 6.

8. Werner G. Hahn, The Politics of Soviet Agriculture, 1960-1970 (Baltimore: The Johns Hopkins University Press, 1972), p. 49.

9. Paige Bryan Toprak, "The Soviet Grain Harvest, 1973-74," Radio Liberty Dispatch, September 7, 1973, p. 1.

10. For a sketch of Matskevich's career, see Prominent Personalities in the USSR (Metuchen, N.J.: The Scarecrow Press, 1968).

11. Hahn, op. cit., p. 29.

12. Ibid., p. 154.

13. Ibid., pp. 185-186.

14. Ibid., p. 189.

15. For analysis of the pre-Congress and post-Congress anti-union forces, see Sidney Ploss, "Soviet Politics on the Eve of the 24th Congress," World Politics XXXIII (October 1970): 71-72.

16. Ibid., pp. 70-71.

17. Hahn, op. cit., p. 235.

18. Ibid., p. 268.

19. Paige Bryan, "An Evaluation of the Soviet Agricultural Product in 1972," Radio Liberty Dispatch, November 16, 1972, p. 1.

20. Keith Bush, "The Weather and Mr. Brezhnev," Radio Liberty Dispatch, Quarterly Review of Soviet Affairs, July-September 1972, p. 2.

21. Keith Bush, "Soviet Grain Output, Deliveries and Imports," Radio Liberty Dispatch, October 16, 1972, p. 2.

22. N. Gusev, "Sel'skoe Khoziaistvo v Deviatoi Piatiletke," Ekonomika Sel'skogo Khoziaistva, no. 2 (1972): 2.

23. Pravda, January 30, 1972, pp. 1-2.

24. Ibid., p. 2.

25. Keith Bush, "Soviet Grain Output, Deliveries and Imports," op. cit., pp. 8-9.

26. Christian Duevel, "After Matskevich: Real Power to the Kolkhoz Councils," Radio Liberty Dispatch, February 14, 1973, p. 3.

27. M. Bazin, Soiuz Zemledeliia i Promyshlennosti (Kishinev: Izdat Kartia Moldoveniaske, 1969), p. 9.

28. See Ekonomicheskaia Gazeta, no. 10,(March 1973): 22.

29. See the report by Bodyul in Sovietskaia Moldavia, March 10, 1973, pp. 1-3, translated in CDSP XXV, no. 10 (April 4, 1973): 1-7.

30. Sel'skaia Zhizn, March 6, 1973, p. 2.

31. Christopher S. Wreo, "Soviet Farm Reform Could Eliminate Collectives," New York Times, December 17, 1973 p. 2.

32. Hedrick Smith, "Brezhnev Optimistic on Crops, But Record Yield Isn't Forecast," New York Times, July 27, 1973, p. 39.

33. Fletcher Pope, "Brezhnev Reveals Record Soviet Grain Harvest of 215 Million Tons," Foreign Agriculture 11, no. 47 (November 19, 1973): 4.

34. Paige Bryan Toprak, "Progress of Reform in the Kolkhoz Councils," Radio Liberty Dispatch October 23, 1973, p. 1.

35. "Soviet Aide Denies Any Plan to End Collectives," New York Times December 25, 1973, p. 2.

36. Theodore Shabad, "Soviet Offers to Sell Grain to U.S. to Replenish Depleted Supplies," New York Times January 29, 1974, p. 1.

37. "Soviet Aide Denies Any Intention to Sell Wheat Back to U.S.," New York Times February 3, 1974, p. 2.

38. George Wanamaker, "USSR Sunflower Crop Continues Under the Weather," Foreign Agriculture 11, no. 43 (October, 22, 1973): 2.

39. Davie M. Schoonover, "Soviet Livestock and Dairy Marketings Gain Despite 1972 Feed Crop Losses," Foreign Agriculture no. 40 (October 1, 1973): 16.

40. Theodore Shabad, "Soviet Minister Answers Critics," New York Times, March 21, 1973.

41. Hedrick Smith, "Soviet and Occidental Oil In Multibillion-Dollar Deal," New York Times, April 13, 1973, pp. 1 and 57.

42. Theodore Shabad, "Soviet Claims Lead Over U.S. in Output," New York Times, January 21, 1974, p. 37.

43. "U.S.-USSR Agreement Calls For New Agricultural Cooperation," Foreign Agriculture, 11, no. 28 (July 9, 1973), pp. 5 and 16.

44. Paige Bryan, "Another Soviet Livestock Setback and Response," Radio Liberty Dispatch, December 22, 1972.

45. Paige Bryan, "Soviet Agriculture—Where Does It Go From Here?" Radio Liberty Dispatch, September 21, 1972, p. 2.

46. Keith Bush, "Soviet Grain Output, Deliveries and Imports," op. cit., p. 9.

47. Theodore Shabad, "Soviets Claim Lead Over U.S. in Output," op. cit., p. 44.

48. "Study Reports Fewer Farms and Less Land in Agriculture," New York Times, January 9, 1974, p. 19.

49. Sel'skoe Khoziaistuo SSSR, Izdat Kolos: Moscow, 1972, pp. 19 and 21.

APPENDIXES

A SKETCH OF THE EVOLUTION OF THE
COLLECTIVE FARMS AND
THEIR PRESENT WEIGHT IN THE ECONOMY

In 1913 75 percent of the population of Russia was involved in agriculture.[1] Lenin's strategy of a "smychka," or alliance, of proletariat and peasant was therefore a necessity in 1917. In the Bolshevik "land, bread, and peace" slogan during 1917, the promise of land distribution was calculated to cement the "smychka." The land was "nationalized" in two stages. By the first decree of October 26, 1917 (old style), landlord properties were transferred to local communities for redistribution.[2] By a second decree of February 19, 1918, all land was nationalized although left in the use of the peasants. All land became in principle state property. Peasants, subject to prohibition on the sale or hiring out of land and labor, were allowed to remain independent of the few state and collective farms formed during the period of "war communism" (1918-20). At the end of 1918, there were 1,579 collective economies and 3,101 state farms in a sea of 16 million individual farms, with the number of the latter increasing to 25 million in 1927.[3]

The word "kolkhoz" literally means "collective economy." Actually it is a contraction of the Russian words for collective economy—"Kollektivnoe khoziaistvo." This term has become synonomous with the specific type of agricultural producer's cooperative known as the "artel." The artel competed with two other types of producer's cooperatives, the TOZ and the commune, eventually absorbing these two by the end of collectivization. The commune differed from the artel and TOZ forms in that within it all the means of production and the personal economies of family members were socialized.[4] From the regime's standpoint, it was ideologically the purest form of producer's cooperative, but due to lack of skills—only the poorest of the rural population were attracted to it[5]—and the incentive-killing form of equal distribution it was based on, it failed to generate surpluses needed by the state. The communes were ultimately converted into artels.[6] The TOZ, or association for joint working on the land, was the simplest form of kolkhoz. Labor was socialized, but the livestock and agricultural tools of its members remained their private property, as did some of the land.[7] The artel differed from the TOZ in that not only were land and labor socialized, but basic tools and implements and the means of production of its members were as well. Graden plots, however, were individually cultivated, and distribution in general was based on the amount of work done rather than on the equalitarian basis as in the commune.[8] Theoretically all three types were voluntarily constituted and self-governing producer's cooperatives.

The state farm or sovkhoz was totally a state enterprise, and at first these were organized on former specialized farms that the Soviets were loath to see broken up. From the beginning they were on the average larger in size individually than all the types of collective farms but far fewer in number. Their number only began to increase significantly after 1928.[9]

The following table indicates the relative percentages of the three types of kolkhozy among the total number of kolkhozy per year.[10]

	1918	1919	1920	1927	1928	1929	1930	1931
Commune	61.7	31.7	18	9	5.4	6.2	8.8	3.6
Artel	38.3	58.3	73.6	48.1	34.8	33.6	73.9	91.7
TOZ	—	10	8.4	42.9	58.8	60.2	17.3	4.7

The following table[11] indicates distribution of groupings of the noncollectivized peasant economies in terms of the size of their land holdings among all peasant economies for twenty-two gubernias of the RSFSR.*

Year	Landless	Up to 4 Desiatinas	4 to 10 Desiatinas	Above 10 Desiatinas
1917	10.6%	60.5%	25.2%	3.7%
1919	4.7%	79.5%	15.3%	00.5%

In 1923 Lenin's article "On Cooperation" established the official theory justifying gradualness in dealing with the multimillions of small peasant farms. Marx and Engels left no blueprints for industrializing agriculture other than to talk of it as ultimately involving large-scale cultivation by armies of workers. Lenin emphasized that cooperatives of all sorts—credit, consumer, sales, and so on—would gradually educate the peasantry to the advantages of cooperation. Socialism in the countryside would come by degrees. At first the simplest cooperative associations and then the simpler form of producer cooperatives would be taken up by the peasantry on a strictly

---

*One desiatina = 2.7 acres (approx.); gubernia = tsarist administrative unit.

voluntary basis.[12] And the voluntary aspect of Lenin's cooperative plan is still stressed today.[13]

Under the New Economic Policy (NEP),* which began in 1921, the number of cooperating peasants grew so that by 1925, 6.5 million belonged to various types, 3.2 million alone to credit cooperatives. The so-called seredniaks, or middle peasants, in 1924-25 constituted some 67.5 percent of all cooperatives' members and the poor peasants about 24.5 percent. Eight percent of the cooperatives' total membership was made up of the "better-off" (Zazhitochnykh) peasants.[14] The cooperative movement by 1929 still embraced only a third of the agricultural population and benefited mainly the middle peasants rather than the poor ones, or bedniaks.[15] It should be noted that the cooperative movement was distinct from the collective farm movement.

As of 1926-27, the richer peasants, or kulaks, provided 20 percent of the bread for the nation and the seredniaks and bedniaks 74 percent, although as of the period just before collectivization only 5 percent of all peasants were considered kulaks.[16] Obviously right up to the eve of collectivization, the collective and state farms were a minor factor in production. The average size of the kolkhozy from 1918 up to collectivization remained virtually unchanged. From 12 to 13 families per kolkhoz in 1918, they reached only 13.4 in 1928.[17] And while the number of sovkhozy remained roughly the same in numbers from 1925 through 1929, their average hectarage per farm more than tripled, from 220 to 747 hectares, by 1929.[18]

In 1928 the shortage of procurable grain reached crisis proportions and a policy of compulsory grain procurement ensued, which, in 1929, led to the first massive collectivization drive in the name of eradicating the kulaks. Alec Nove attributes the crisis of 1928 to the party's faulty agricultural machinery and grain procurement price policies of 1926.[19] According to Moshe Lewin, Stalin some time in 1929 had given up on the future of small-scale agriculture. In the light of the grain crisis, which the regime had created and which Stalin had exacerbated by his forced procurement campaign of 1928, and given Stalin's overly ambitious industrialization goal embodied in the first five-year plan of 1929, Stalin chose to collectivize en masse in order to secure a mechanism by which to control the hitherto independent peasantry. This was seen as a solution to both

---

*NEP represented a period of liberalization during which the regime encouraged petty commodity producers to increase their production by allowing, within limits, the hiring of labor and machines and a general expansion of freedom of enterprise, albeit small-scale enterprise.

the grain problem and the problem of obtaining extra capital to subsidize rapid industrialization. Stalin saw lagging agricultural production as a threat to industrialization.[20] The pace of mass collectivization from 1929 to 1932 was tremendous although spasmodic. As late as June 1, 1929, only 3.9 percent of all peasant economies were collectivized.[21] In 1932 there were over 200,000 kolkhozy (mainly artels) encompassing over 60 percent of all peasant economies.[22] And while the total sown area of the sovkhozy increased by 6.5 times between 1929 and 1932, 77 percent of the total sown area in 1932 belonged to the kolkhozy.[23] By the end of 1934 agriculture was substantially collectivized. The private sector was reduced essentially to the aggregate of private plots held by kolkhoz and sovkhoz members plus plots allocated to various other rural inhabitants, together with an insignificant number of nonfarmers usually located in isolated mountainous terrain. As of 1937, 93 percent of all peasant households were within the kolkhozy.[24]

The machine tractor stations (MTS) were created in the late 1920s to provide expert mechanical service to the kolkhozy and to maintain control over the very small stock of scarce agricultural machinery. With their concentration of the few rural party members, they became the party's control mechanism at the farm level and watched over individual farm agriculture operations as well until their abolition in 1958. They were state agencies.[25]

In 1950 there were 254,000 kolkhozy, many only containing between 10 and 30 households. As a result of the kolkhoz amalgamation campaign of 1950-53, the number of kolkhozy was reduced to 93,000. The size grew by 2.5 times to an average hectarage per farm of 1,407 hectares.[26] As of 1938 there were 3,961 sovkhozy, which averaged per farm 12,411 hectares of sown area alone. The number jumped from 4,988 to 9,176 in 1963.[27]

Data indicate that in 1970 there were 33,200 kolkhozy, with each kolkhoz averaging 433 households, or dvors, and 6,100 hectares of land. At the same time there were 14,958 sovkhozy, averaging per sovkhoz 21,000 hectares.[28] In terms of total state purchases of major agricultural produce, the relative shares of the kolkhozy and sovkhozy as suppliers for the following three years are shown in the table on the following page.[29]

The figure for kolkhozy is derived from the official data given for sovkhozy and other state enterprises.

As for total agricultural production, kolkhozy as of 1966 provided approximately two-thirds, which consisted of 41 percent from the communal or public sector and 20 percent from the private plots of kolkhozniks.[30] The total land mass at the disposal of sovkhozy in 1968 was over 655 million hectares, as opposed to a total of 388 million for the kolkhozy and some 8.6 million in the private plot sector.[31]

As of 1970 the share of the sovkhozy in total production of the following

	Kolkhozy			Sovkhozy and Other State Enterprises		
	1940	1965	1970	1940	1965	1970
Grain	90	63	50	10	37	50
Cotton	94	80	77	6	20	23
Sugarbeet	96	91	91	4	9	9
Sunflower	98	86	82	2	14	18
Potatoes	98	67	61	2	33	39
Vegetables	94	43	43	6	57	57
Cattle and Fowl	78	55	57	22	45	43
Milk	84	59	58	16	41	42
Eggs	97	55	35	3	45	65
Wool	82	58	56	18	42	44

commodities was: grain, 46 percent; cotton, 23 percent; sugarbeet,
9 percent; sunflower, 20 percent; potatoes, 14 percent; vegetables,
35 percent; meat, 32 percent; milk, 28 percent; eggs, 33 percent;
wool, 41 percent.[32] By subtracting these figures from 100 percent
and allowing for a deduction from the remaining percentage for
that part of total production from the private sector, we arrive at the
figure for the kolkhoz sector. The official 1970 statistical handbook
USSR in Figures gives the combined percentage of kolkhozy and sovkhozy in total production of the main agricultural produce. Taking the
remainder as the share of the private sector, we arrive at the following figures: grain, 1 percent; cotton, 0 percent; sugarbeet, 0 per-
cent; sunflower, 1 percent; potatoes, 65 percent; vegetables, 40 per-
cent; meat, 34 percent; milk, 36 percent; eggs, 54 percent; wool, 19
percent.[33] As for the overall share of the private sector in total
agricultural production today, one American economist estimates
it to be approximately 25 percent.[34]

NOTES

1. Jean Chombart De Lauwe, Les Paysans Sovietiques (Paris:
Editions Du Seuil, 1961), p. 263.
2. For the text, see Istoriia Kolkhoznogo Prava, Tom I (Moscow: Gosiurizdat, 1959), pp. 17-18.
3. A. Goncharov and L. P. Luniakov, V. I. Lenin i Krest'ianstvo
(Moscow: Izdat, Polit. Lit., 1967), pp. 98 and 178.
4. For the definitive work on the communes, see Robert G.
Wesson, Soviet Communes (New Brunswick: Rutgers Univ. Press,
1963).

5. S. A. Ignatov, Leninskie Printsipy Organizatsii Sotsialisti-cheskogo Sel'skokhoziaistvennogo Proizvodstva (Moscow: Izdat "Mysl", 1970), p. 13.

6. See the article "Kommuna" in Kratkii Ekonomicheskii Slovar' (Moscow: Gospolitizdat, 1958).

7. M. Lewin, Russian Peasants and Soviet Power (Evanston: Northwestern Univ. Press, 1968), p. 111.

8. M. Lewin, Ibid., p. 110.

9. See the article "Sovkhozy" in Politicheskii Slovar' (Moscow: Gospolitizdat, 1958).

10. V. F. Stanis, Sotsialisticheskie Preobrazovaniia Sel'skogo Khoziaistva (Moscow: Izdat. Mysl', 1971), pp. 136-137.

11. V. N. Iakovtsevkii, Agrarnye Otnosheniia v SSSR v Period Stroitel'stva Sotsializma (Moscow: Izdat Nauka, 1964), p. 102.

12. V. Lenin, Selected works, Vol. 3 (Moscow: Foreign Languages Publishing House, 1961), pp. 814 and 819.

13. G. V. Ivanov, "Voploshchenie i Dal'neishee Razvitie Idei Leninskogo Kooperativnogo Plana v Novom Primernom Ustave Kokhoza," Vestnik Mock. Univ., Pravo. No. 2 (1969): 73-74.

14. Iakovtsevskii, op. cit., p. 281.

15. Lenin, op. cit., p. 401.

16. V. F. Stanis. op. cit., pp. 176-177.

17. Ibid., p. 193.

18. Iakovtsevskii, op. cit., p. 316.

19. Alec Nove, "The Decision to Collectivize," in W. E. D. Jackson, editor, Agrarian Policies and Problems in Communist and Non-Communist Countries (Seattle and London: Univ. of Washington Press, 1971), p. 70.

20. Lewis, op. cit., pp. 372 and 401.

21. Iv. S. Kukushkin, Sel'skie Sovety i Klassovaia Bor'ba v Derevne (Moscow: Izdat, Mock. Univ., 1968), p. 198.

22. Ekonomicheskaia Istoriia SSSR (Moscow: Sotsekgiz, 1963), p. 373.

23. Istoriia Narodnogo Khoziaistva SSSR (Moscow: Izdat. Sotsialno-Ekonomicheskaia Lit., 1960), p. 538.

24. Ibid., p. 553.

25. Roy D. Laird and Kenneth E. Beasley, "Soviet Tractor Stations—Policy Control by Auxiliary Services," Public Administration Review, XX, no. 4 (Autumn 1960): 214. For a definitive study of the origin and evolution of the MTS, see Robert Miller, One Hundred Thousand Tractors (Cambridge: Harvard University Press, 1970).

26. Ekonomicheskaia Istoriia SSSR, p. 449.

27. Ignatov, op. cit., pp. 45 and 48.

28. SSSR v Tsifrakh v 1970 Godu (Moscow: Izdat. Statistika, 1971), pp. 134, 136, 138, 139.

29. Ibid., p. 130.

30. M. I. Terentev, Kolkhozy Tovarnodenezhnie Otnosheniia (Moscow: Izdat. Ekonomika, 1966), p. 3.

31. Ekonomika i Organizatsiia Sel'skokhoziaistvennogo Prois-vodstva (Moscow: Izdat. Mysl', 1970), p. 185.

32. SSSR v Tsifrakh v 1970 Godu, p. 106.

33. Ibid., p. 106.

34. Keith Bush, "A New Agricultural Statistical Compendium," Radio Liberty Dispatch, April 17, 1972.

THE NEW KOLKHOZ COUNCIL STATUTES

It was reported in the Soviet press on March 12, 1971, that a
session of the Union Council of Kolkhozy had approved draft statutes
on kolkhoz councils at the Union, Republic, Autonomous Republic,
krai, oblast, and raion levels.[1] It was later reported that a Presidium
of the Union Council was chosen whose president was USSR Minister
of Agriculture Matskevich.[2] Then in August 1971 it was announced
that the USSR Council of Ministers had confirmed the Statute on the
Union Council of Kolkhozy of Union Republics, Autonomous Republics,
krais, oblasts, and raions presented to it by the Union Council of
Kolkhozy.

The Statute on the Union Council of Kolkhozy, with adaptation
taking into account the subordinate role of each lower level, seems
to be the model for all lower-level councils.[3] According to article
1, the Union Council ia a "centralized elective social organ" of kolkhozy,
not kolkhozniks, formed so as to further develop kolkhoz democracy,
to collectively service the more important problem areas of kolkhoz
life, to generalize their experiences, and work out recommendations
for fuller use of kolkhoz reserves. It also aims at carrying out the
party's agricultural development plans. What is conspicuously absent
in article 1 is any reference to defending the rights of kolkhozy as
such or of unifying the efforts of kolkhozy or kolkhozniks on a national
scale to effect changes in their behalf. Article 2 makes clear that
the Union Council is guided by the party and state, as well as by the
All-Union Congress of Kolkhozniks and the All-Union Meeting of
Representatives of Kolkhoz Councils of Union Republics. What is
not at all clear, as will be seen below, is the relationship between
the All-Union Congress of Kolkhozniks, whose structure and jurisdiction
remain sketchy, and the Union Council of Kolkhozy.

Article 3 describes the membership in the Union Council. It
is composed of elected experienced kolkhoz presidents, kolkhoz shock
workers, agricultural specialists, representatives of interkolkhoz
unions, agricultural organs, social organizations, scholars, ministry
and department heads of the All-Union government connected with
kolkhoz activities. In what proportions these motley representatives
of various interest are to be elected and how is not discussed, thus
strengthening the suspicion that the composition of the Union Council
will be strictly dictated from above and thereby by insulated from

grass-roots pressures and sympathies. Article 4 explores the jurisdiction at greater length and in more detail than article 2. According
to it, the Union Council examines questions connected with observance
of the Model Charter, gives jointly with the USSR Ministry of Agriculture explanations of the application of the Model Charter, and prepares propositions to supplement or change it. It introduces recommendations on land use, resource use, reclamation, chemicalization,
and electrification. It discusses results of the production-economic
activities of interkolkhoz and state-kolkhoz enterprises and makes
recommendations to improve their work. It generalizes valuable
experiences and works out recommendations for perfecting the administration of production, planning and internal economic accounting,
organization, and pay and protection of the labor force of interkolkhoz
enterprises and organizations; it works out recommendations for the
correct distribution of income, the effective use of basic and circulating funds, the improvement of control-audit work; it works out
proposals for widening interkolkhoz and state-kolkhoz ties, improving
the sale and processing of agricultural products, and the developing
of subsidiary enterprises; works out proposals for improving preparation and raising the qualifications of kolkhozniks, guiding cadres
and specialists, for fuller use of labor resources, for raising the
material and cultural level, for perfecting the social security of
kolkhozniks; makes recommendations on social insurance of kolkhozniks; examines preliminarily the petitions of Union Republic Councils
of Ministers on transforming kolkhozy into sovkhozy and into other
state agricultural enterprises; directs and coordinates activities of
councils of kolkhozy of republics, krai, oblast, and raion, examining
their proposals and aiding them; examines other important questions
and works out recommendations and proposals and presents these to
the USSR Ministry of Agriculture as well as to other organizations.
What emerges from this is that its decisions are ultimately recommendatory. It has no power to legislate on or dispose of any matter.
It is clearly conceived of as an adjunct to the USSR Ministry of Agriculture and its section on kolkhoz affairs.

Article 5 simply states that it establishes and exchanges experience with foreign cooperative organs. Apparently the regime hopes
to use the Union Council as a public-relations and propaganda organization in part for foreign consumption, no doubt heavily in the "Third
World," especially in Africa and parts of Asia where agricultural
cooperatives are much discussed and even employed in various forms.
Perhaps the use of kolkhoz representatives abroad as ambassadors
of Soviet agriculture will give some psychological balm to this traditionally very deprived sector of the Soviet economy, boosting its
stock at home as a sort of "feedback" effect of its missionary work
abroad. Moreover, one cannot discount the possible motive of drumming

up publicity for the kolkhoz in the third world as a means of undercutting the Chinese critique of the Soviets as ideologically soft and
having no "models" appropriate to the underdeveloped world.

Article 6 states that the Union Council convenes an All-Union
Meeting of Representatives of Councils of Kolkhozy of Union Republics
once every five years and an All-Union Congress of Kolkhozniks as
needed. The Union Council of Kolkhozy can convene extraordinary
sessions of the All-Union Meeting of Representatives of Councils of
Kolkhozy of Union Republics or it can be convened by demand of one-
third of the Councils of Kolkhozy of Union Republics themselves. The
Union Council of Kolkhoz establishes the norms of representation at
All-Union Congress of Kolkhozniks and All-Union Meeting of Representatives of Councils of Union Republics. Just what the desideratum
for convening the Congress as opposed to the Meeting of Representatives
of Union Republic Councils is is not mentioned. Nor is it spelled out
which organ decides whether the one-third of all Union Republic Councils needed to convene an extraordinary meeting or representatives
has been achieved in proper form and according to proper procedures.
In fact, no procedures are mentioned.

Article 7 states that the Union Council of Kolkhozy is elected
by open ballot at the All-Union Meeting of Representatives of Union
Republic Councils of Kolkhozy, or, at the All-Union Congress of Kolkhozniks, for a five-year term. It would seem that providing two ways to
elect the Union Council without specifying any precondition to the use
of either, or any explanation of why the luxury of an alternative method
is provided, is bound not only to focus attention on the motives for
this but also to stimulate speculation on the different interests and
constituencies that might coalesce around the two, as well as the
theoretical and actual powers each is to have or may acquire. It is
surely very rare to provide institutional alternatives in the Soviet
Union, and even though one may be subordinate in fact to the other,
yet the granting of theoretical equality to potentially rival institutions
is a most interesting phenomenon. Only time will tell whether the
two institutions develop and if so whether on the basis of different
constituencies. Will the leadership use the one as a counterpose to
the other or simply as an alter ego? Perhaps the use of the Congress
is a democratic "front."

In periods between All-Union Congresses of Kolkhozniks and
All-Union Meetings of Representatives of Union Republic Councils
of Kolkhozy, the Union Council can, as an exception, per Article 7,
take in new members, with consequent confirmation of them at the
All-Union Meeting of Representatives of Union Republic Councils.
The obvious "packing" potential of this provision could serve the
regime well in future if, in fact, the Congress of Kolkhozniks jells
as an institution reflective of grass-roots kolkhozniks' interests.

Article 8 states that the Union Council chooses from its membership a Presidium, a President, a Deputy President, and also confirms a Council Secretary. The Union President is simultaneously President of the Presidium. Article 9 enjoins the Union Council to form "sections" to study questions and to prepare for Council sessions. Obviously these sections have a role analogous to the Party Secretariat and will be able to predigest the issues to appear on the Council's agenda and thereby, in effect, to manipulate the Congress.

Article 10 states that the Union Council is to hold sessions at least two times a year. Extraordinary sessions can be convened by the Council Presidium or on demand of one-third of the Council membership. Both Council and Presidium sessions require a two-thirds quorum. Their decisions are adopted by simple majority vote. The internal procedures of the Presidium other than the quorum and decision by simple majority are not described. Nor are there any details on how the Presidium members are chosen by the Union Council. It would seem to be reasonable to believe that this Presidium will become the all-important power center of the Union Council. It is intended to be the Council executive. According to Article 11, it realizes organizational work in periods between Council sessions, composes draft work plans for the Council, and gives its conclusions to the Council. It hears reports from the Union Republic, krai, oblast, and raion councils. As for the President, he convenes Presidium sessions when needed but at a minimum of at least once a quarter. Obviously the power to convene is a major power, and the role of the President seems analogous to that of the kolkhoz president or that of the chairman of the Presidium of the Supreme Soviet. According to article 12, the President, and in his absence the Deputy President, organizes the work of the Council as well as that of the Presidium and carries out the decrees of both. Thus the President may dominate the Presidium and thereby the whole Council, aided by the "responsible secretary," who, according to article 13, organizes the work of Council sections and prepares materials for Council and Presidium sessions, giving answers in writing to requests.

According to article 14, the Council is to observe the rights of kolkhozy, interkolkhoz, and state-kolkhoz enterprises, preserving their economic independence and initiative. It is stressed that decrees of the Union Council for kolkhozy and interkolkhoz organizations are recommendatory. Yet "recommendations" in the Soviet context are tantamount to binding official orders in fact though not in theory. According to article 15, the USSR Ministry of Agirculture prepares materials for Union Council and Presidium sessions on technical and economic questions.

The Model Statute on Union Republic Councils of kolkhozy is substantially similar to the Union Council Statute, as are the other model statutes. According to article 5, the Union Republic Council convenes once every five years a Republican Meeting of Representatives of Councils of Kolkhozy of Autonomous Republics, krais, oblasts—and in Union Republics without oblasts, Raion Councils of Kolkhozy—and, as needed, a Congress of Kolkhozniks of the Union Republic. The Model Statute on the Council of Kolkhozy of the Autonomous Republic, Krais, and Oblasts, in Article 5, provides for the convening once every two to three years of a Meeting of Representatives of Councils of Kolkhozy of Raions and, when needed, of Republican, Krai, and Oblast Conferences of Kolkhozniks.

According to article 6, the Council of Kolkhozy of Autonomous Republics, Krais, and Oblasts are elected by open ballot at Meetings of Representatives of Councils of Kolkhozy of Raions or at Republican, Krai, or Oblast conferences of Kolkhozniks at two- or three-year intervals. Like the Union Republic Councils, those of the Autonomous Republics, Krais, and Oblasts meet at least three times a year (article 9). The Model Statute of Councils of Kolkhozy of Raions provides that these councils are to be convened at least once a year (article 5) and elected via open ballot at a Meeting of Representatives of Kolkhozy for a two- to three-year period. In terms of structure all the below All-Union level councils substantially follow the Union Council Statute.

Although little in the way of practice has accumulated to date, the jurist Z. S. Beliaeva claims that the councils will issue normative-legal acts as well as recommendations, although the former must be approved by state organs to be legally effective. Beliaeva notes that the Union Council on March 4, 1970, recommended a Model Rules of Internal Order of the Kolkhoz, and she urges that in the future the councils take over the issuance of recommendatory acts for kolkhozy hitherto issued by the government organs.[4]

The new series of statutes on kolkhoz councils formalize something less than a tight-knit, cohesive centralized national kolkhoz organization. No kolkhoz parliament has been set up. However, at least in theory, a kolkhoz system of sorts has been launched. But the system is more confederative than unitary in theory. It is multilayered, with no direct line between the individual kolkhoz and the center, except insofar as the still sketchy All-Union Congress of Kolkhozniks may provide this. The multirepublic nature of the national organization insulates the various component suborganizations from one another. It makes it more difficult for a spontaneous national kolkhoz consensus to emerge. It allows for regionalism, localism, income stratification, crop specialization, and other divisive factors to more easily assert themselves. This is all built into the organizational structure. It will be interesting to see just which occupational groups come to the fore in the councils and whether the local level councils develop different emphases than the Republican and All-Union levels. Only time will tell whether these councils will merely be classic Soviet transmission belts or develop into genuine kolkhoz interest groups. Certainly the regime did not create them for the latter purpose. It is probable that for the regime the council's usefulness is its mere existence. That is, the regime has created a national kolkhoz organization, thus granting a certain recognition to kolkhozy as a major sector of the economy. Recognition is certainly cheaper than more capital investments. This recognition, although devoid of any practical consequences as of the moment, is widely advertised as ushering in a new stage in the development of the kolkhozy. It is hailed as a significant action and cited by the regime as proof positive of its sensitivity to the need for action on the kolkhoz front. Moreover, although a centralized national kolkhoz interest group would be a threat to the regime, a puppet central kolkhoz organization, supposedly elected by the kolkhozy themselves, would be the perfect instrument for enforcing comprehensive prescriptions from above for the kolkhozy without doing damage to the theory of kolkhoz democracy, and also for insulating the regime somewhat from the blame for innovative policies that fail. Also, it could be the instrument that most legitimately could, in effect, convert the kolkhozy into a highly disciplined, closely coordinated branch of the national economy, overcoming the semi-anarchic economic disassociation characteristic of the relationship among kolkhozy traditionally. In other words, the councils could be accelerators of administrative centralization within the kolkhoz sector through administrative coordination of production planning, specialization, material supply, credit, capital investment, and labor resources training and allocation policies. What this would amount to would be "nationalization" of the kolkhozy seemingly by self-action rather than by decision of the state and party. Moreover, it would be gradual rather than sudden, and thus appear to be a natural process rather than the product of arbitrary administrative fiat. Such then are some of the possible uses of the new kolkhoz councils.

It is beginning to appear that the regime, and particularly Brezhnev, has decided to experiment with the kolkhoz council as an agency for centralizing the economic management of the kolkhozy. A mere few days following the dismissal of Minister of Agriculture V. Matskevich, Brezhnev's ally, Moldavian First Secretary I. Bodyul, unveiled a major proposal to grant Moldavian councils real managerial power over their kolkhoz members. It has also become known that Estonia and Belorussia are presently experimenting by assigning varying degress of power over resource allocation, investment priorities, and production planning to their councils. Although the Estonian pilot project apparently involves the granting of far fewer powers to the councils than those granted to Moldavia, it is nonetheless a dramatic escalation in their power in relation to 1969. And as Christian

Duevel warns, although the council or union in their now vitalized form are in part going to attempt to equalize economic levels of kolkhozy within their jurisdiction, giving some of the profits of the stronger kolkhozy to the weaker, this will act as a disincentive for the stronger.[5] Duevel concludes that the three variants or pilot projects are the first step in the probable implementation of next higher phase of development of Soviet agriculture, regional integration of farm management. After a trial period, some variant will probably be applied throughout the USSR. Duevel is surprised that at a time of crisis in the development of Soviet agriculture the regime is willing to experiment with so fundamental a reorganization of agricultural management. This, taken in conjunction with an article by the economist Ia. Kronrod in Voprosy Ekonomiki, no. 2, February 1973, which puts forward the idea that kolkhozy will disappear at a relatively early stage of the present phase of socialism, indicates to Duevel that the present majority of the Politburo would seem to have supported Kronrod's thesis.[6]

The economist D. Vanin, writing in Ekonomicheskaia Gazeta, no. 9 of February 1973, proposes a single kolkhoz investment fund be created out of kolkhoz profits and that it be used to subsidize the allocation of machinery and other material inputs to weak kolkhozy to thus aid in kolkhoz income equalization. Paige Bryan sees this as an even more far-reaching proposal than the three other pilot projects, since it calls for a nationwide reorganization of the economic management of kolkhozy.[7] In essence, funds to subsidize the weaker would come from the more profitable farms through the mechanism of payments based on their normal profit levels in the raion, oblast, or republic. All the funds would eventually flow into a central all-union fund administered by an all-union council. Vanin dismisses another method that involves deductions from prices for products having relatively high profitability and using this money as a supplement to the price paid for low-profit products, a method used in Georgia.[8]

Paige Bryan condemns the plan because it simply redistributes profits instead of attacking the problem, which involves faulty price, financial, and socio-economic structures. Bryan feels, moreover, that this essentially new "collectivization" could have adverse effects on the morale of the more prosperous kolkhoz and would violate the guarantees of the 1969 Kolkhozy Model Charter.[9]

Bryan's criticism seems well grounded. What this amounts to is a scheme that, if adopted, could betoken a reluctance by the regime to invest its own funds in the weaker farms. So it is forcing the stronger farms to subsidize the weaker. This could be done by some form of income tax as well. While I cannot agree with Bryan that this scheme represents a far more fundamental reorganization of farm management than the three kolkhoz council pilot projects, it certainly represents in a real sense a nationalization of individual kolkhoz assets.

I would think that the regime will go far along the road of generalizing, developing, and embellishing the pilot projects before it resorts to a Vanin-type proposal. My reasoning is that this would be more consonant with the traditional penchant of Soviet regimes for administrative reorganization and with their belief in the magical qualities of applying new managerial layers and forms. Moreover it would be a more gradual approach than the more shocking overnight quasi-nationalization of individual kolkhoz assets.

NOTES

1. Sel'skaia Zhizn', March 12, 1971, p. 2.
2. Ibid., March 13, 1971, p. 3.
3. For the texts of all the statutes, see Ekonomicheskaia Gazeta, no. 32 (August 1971): 12-13.
4. Z. S. Beliaeva, "Normativno-Pravovye Akty Kolkhozov," SGIP, no. 1: 48-49.
5. Christian Duevel, "Kolkhoz Union Projects in Estonia and Belorussia," Radio Liberty Dispatch, March 13, 1973, p. 4.
6. Ibid., pp. 10-11.
7. Paige Bryan, "Centralized Economic Management of Kolkhozy Appears Imminent," Radio Liberty Dispatch, April 12, 1973, p. 2.
8. D. Vanin, "Vazhnyi Ekonomicheskii Faktor," Ekonomicheskaia Gazeta, no. 9 (February 9, 1973): p. 19.
9. Paige Bryan, "Centralized Economic Management of Kolkhozy Appears Imminent," op. cit., pp. 5-6.

BOOKS

Soviet

Aksenenok, G. A. Pravovoe Polozhenie Sovkhozov v SSSR. Moscow: Izdat. Akad. Nauk SSSR, 1960.

Alekseeva, V. M. Razvitie Soiuza Rabochikh i Krest'ian v Period Perekhoda k Kommunizmu. Leningrad: Leningradskogo Univ., 1967.

Arutiunian, Iu. V. Sotsial'naia Struktura Sel'skogo Naseleniia SSSR. Moscow: Izdat. Mysl', 1971.

Bazin, M. Souiz Zemledeliia i Promyshlennosti. Kishinev: Izdat. Kartia Moldoveniaske, 1969.

Beliaev, I. T. Differentsial'naia Renta v SSSR. Moscow: Izdat. Mysl', 1967.

Belovsenko, G. Oborotnye Sredstva Kolkhozov i Kredit. Moscow: Izdat. Finansy, 1968.

Belianov, V. A. Lichnoe Podsobnoe Khoziaistvo pri Sotsializme. Moscow: Izdat. Ekonomika, 1970.

Boev, V. R. Zakupochyne Tseny i Chistnyi Dokhod Kolkhozov. Moscow: Kolos, 1969.

Bolgov, A. V. Differentsial'naia Zemel'naia Renta v Usloviiakh Sotsializma. Moscow: Akad. Mauk SSSR, 1963.

Brezhnev, L. I. Leninskim Kursom. Tom I. Moscow: Izdat. Polit. Lit., 1970.

_____. O. Neotlozhnykh Merakh po Dal'neishemu Razvitiiu SSSR. Doklad na Plenume Ts.K. KPSS, March 24, 1965. Moscow: Politizdat, 1965.

_____ . Ocherednye Zadachi Partii v Oblasti Sel'skogo Khoziaistva. Doklad na Plenume Ts.K. KPSS, July 2, 1970. Moscow: Politizdat, 1970.

Bulavin, G. P. Prevrashchenie Sel'skokhoziaistvennogo Truda v Raznovidnost' Industrial'nogo. Moscow: Izdat. Ekonomika, 1970.

Burmistrov, D. V. Nalogi i Sbory s Naseleniia v SSSR. Moscow: Izdat. Finansy, 1968.

Direktivy i Stimuly v Mekhanizme Opravleniia Ekonomikoi. Moscow: Izdat. Mysl', 1969.

Dmitrashko, I. I. Vnutrokolkhoznye Ekonomicheskie Otnosheniia. Moscow: Izdat. Ekonomika, 1966.

Ekonomicheskaia Istoriia SSSR. Moscow: Sotsekgiz, 1963.

Ekonomicheskie i Sotsial'nye Problemy Industrializatsii Sel'skogo Khoziaistva. Moscow: Izdat. Mosk. Univ., 1971.

Ekonomika i Organizatsii Sel'skokhoziaistvennogo Proizvodstva. Moscow: Izdat. Mysl', 1970.

Ekonomika Sotsialisticheskogo Sel'skogo Khoziaistva v Sovremennykh Usloviiakh. Moscow: Izdat. Ekonomika, 1971.

Entsiklopedicheskii Slovar' Pravovykh Znanii. Moscow: Izdat. Sovetskaia Entsiklopediia, 1965.

Erofeev, B. V. Osnovy Zemel'nogo Pravo. Moscow: Izdat. Iurid. Lit., 1971.

Erzina, Z. Kh., and N. P. Shcherbukov. Oplata Truda v Kolkhozakh RSFRS. Moscow: Rossel'khozizaat, 1968.

Galnika, E. I. Spetsializatsiia Kolkhoznogo Proizvodstva. Moscow: Izdat. Nauka, 1970.

Grigorev, ed. Kolkhoznoe Pravo. Moscow: Izdat. Iurid. Lit., 1970.

Gusev, V. V. Kolkhoz kak Samoupravliaemaia Sotsial'naia Sistema. Moscow: Izdat. Mysl', 1971.

272

Iakovtsevskii, V. N. Agrarnye Otnosheniia v SSSR v Period Stroitel'
stva Sotsializma. Moscow: Izdat. Nauka, 1964.

Iakimov, V. N. Problemy Trudovykh Resursov Kolkhozov. Moscow:
Izdat. Ekonomika, 1969.

Ianchuk, V. Z. Problemy Teorii Kolkhoznogo Prava. Moscow: Izdat.
Iurid. Lit., 1969.

Ignatov, S. A. Leninskie Printsipy Organizatsii Sotsialisticheskogo
Sel'skokhoziaistvennogo Proizvodstva. Moscow: Izdat. Mysl', 1970.

Istoriia Kolkhoznogo Prava. Tom I. Moscow: Gosiurizdat, 1959.

Istoriia Narodnogo Khoziaistva SSSR. Moscow: Izdat. Sotsialno-
Ekonomicheskaia Lit., 1960.

Istoriia Narodnogo Khoziaistva SSSR. Moscow: Izdat. Vyshaia
Shkola, 1964.

Kazantsev, N. A. Zakonodatel'nye Osnovy Zemel'nogo Stroiia v SSSR.
Moscow: Iurid. Lit., 1971.

Kazantsev, N. D. Utopicheskii i Nauchnyi Sotsializm o Pereustroistve
Sel'skogo Khoziaistva. Moscow: Izdat. Mosk. Univ., 1969.

Klassy, Sotsial'nye Sloi i Gruppy v SSSR. Moscow: Izdat. Nauka,
1968.

Kolkhoz: Shkola Kommunizma dlia Krest'ianstva. Moscow: Izdat.
Pravda, 1969.

Kollektiv-Kolkhoznikov: Sotsial'no-Psykhologicheskoe Issledovanie.
Moscow: Izdat. Mysl', 1970.

Kolychev, L. I. Kredit i Effektivnost' Kolkhoznogo Proizvodstva.
Moscow: Izdat. Finansy, 1972.

Komachenko, Iu. Prevrashchenie Sotsialisticheskoi Sobstvennosti.
Moscow: Izdat. Mosk. Univ., 1970.

Kopach, N. L. Obshchestvennyi Trud v Sel'skom Khoziaistve i
Rezervy Ego Ekonomii. Moscow: Izdat. Ekonomika, 1972.

Kotov, G., and I. Borodin, eds. Optimal'nye Razmery Kolkhozov.
Moscow: Izdat. Kolos, 1970.

Kotsiuba, T. Ia. Garantirovannaia Oplata i Zakon Raspredeleniia po Trudu v Kolkhozakh. Moscow: Izdat. Ekonomika, 1969.

Kovaleva, M. F., and S. V. Rogachev, eds. Ekonomicheskie Otnosheniia Mezhdu Gosudarstvom i Sel'skokhoziaistvennymi Predpriiatiiami. Moscow: Izdat. Mysl', 1969.

Kratkii Ekonomicheskii Slovar'. Moscow: Gospolitizdat, 1958.

Kratkii Iuridicheskii Slovar': Spravochnik dlia Naseleniia. Moscow: Gosiurizdat, 1960.

Kukushkin, Iu. S. Sel'skie Sovety i Klassovaia Bor'ba v Derevne. Moscow: Izdat. Mosk. Univ., 1968.

Kuropatkin, A. I. Ekonomicheskie Osnovy Preodoleniia Sushchestvennykh Razlichii Mezhdu Gorodom i Derevnei. Moscow: Izdat. Mosk. Unit., 1971.

Kuvatov, R. Iu. Sebestoimost' Sel'skokhoziaistvennoi Produktsii. Alma Ata: Izdat. Kainar, 1969.

Kuznetsov, G. Tovarnye Otnosheniia i Ekonomicheskye Stimuly v Kolkhoznom Proizvodstve. Moscow: Izdat. Mysl', 1971.

Lekhova, Z. N. Potrebitel'skaia Kooperatsiia i Sblizhenie Urovnei Zhizni Sel'skogo i Gorodskogo Naseleniia. Moscow: Izdat. Ekonomika, 1969.

Lenin, V. Selected Works, 3 volumes. Moscow: Foreign Languages Publishing House, 1961.

Migratsiia Sel'skogo Naseleniia. Moscow: Izdat Mysl', 1970.

Nakoplenie i Potreblenie v Kolkhozakh. Moscow: Izdat. Nauka, 1967.

Narodnoe Khoziaistvo SSSR v 1970. Moscow: Izdat. Statistika, 1971.

Nitikin, P. Fundamentals of Political Economy. Moscow: Progress Publishers, 1966.

Osnovy Ekonomiki Kolkhoznogo Proizvodstva. Kazan': Tatarskoe Knozhnoe. Izdat., 1966.

Pankratov, I. F. Gosudarstvennoe Rukovodstvo Sel'skim Khoziaistvom SSSR. Moscow: Izdat, Iurid. Lit., 1969.

Pereslegin, V. Finance and Credit in the USSR. Moscow: Progress
    Publishers, 1971.

Peshekhonov, V. A. Rol' Tovarno-Denezhnykh Otnoshenii v Planovom
    Rukovodstve Kolkhoznym Proisvodstvom. Leningrad: Izdat.
    Lenin Univ., 1967.

Petrov, VI. V. Primernyi Ustav i Problemy Sotsialisticheskoi Zakon-
    nosti v Kolkhozakh. Kazan: Izdat. Kazanskogo Univ., 1971.

Podkolzin, A. A Short Economic History of the USSR. Moscow:
    Progress Publishers, 1968.

Politicheskii Slovar'. Moscow: Gospolitizdat, 1958.

Polovinkin, P. D. Rezervnye Fondy i Vosproizvodstvo v Kolkhozakh.
    Moscow: Izdat. Ekonomika, 1970.

Problemy Ekonomiki Truda v Sel'skom Khoziaistve. Moscow: Izdat.
    Ekonomika, 1971.

Problemy Izmeneniia Sotsial'noi Struktury Sovetskogo Obshchestva.
    Moscow: Izdat. Nauka, 1968.

Progresivnye Formy Organizatsii Truda v Kolkhozakh i Sovkhozakh.
    Moscow: Izdat, Kolos, 1970.

Resheniia Partii i Pravitel'stva Khoziaistvennym Voprosam, Tom 5.
    Moscow: Izdat. Polit. Lit., 1968.

Reshetniak, V. P. Upravlenie v Kolkhozakh. Moscow: Izdat. Kolos,
    1970.

Romanchenko, G. R. Rentabel'nost Kolkhoznogo Proisvodstva. Moscow:
    Izdat. Kolos, 1969.

Rumiantsev, A. M., and P. S. Bunin, eds. Ekonomicheskaia Reforma:
    Yeye Osushchestvlenie i Problemy. Moscow: Izdat. polit.
    Lit., 1969.

Sbornik Reshenii po Sel'skomu Khoziaistvu. Moscow: Izdat. Sel'
    skokhoziaistvennoi Lit., 1963.

Sel'skaia Partiinaia Organizatsiia. Moscow: Izdat. Polit. Lit., 1970.

Sel'skoe Khoziaistvo Sovetskogo Soiuza. Moscow: Izdat. Kolos, 1970.

Semin, S. I. Razvitie Obshchestvenno-Ekonomicheskikh Otnoshenii v Kolkhozakh. Moscow: Izdat. Nauka, 1968.

Shredov, V. P. Sotsialisticheskaia Zemel'naia Sobstvennost. Moscow: Izdat. Mosk. Univ., 1967.

A Short History of the Communist Party of the Soviet Union. Moscow: Progress Publishers, 1970.

Sidorova, M. I. Obshchestvennye Fondy Potrebleniia i Dokhody Kolkhoznikov. Moscow: Izdat. Kolos, 1969.

Simush, P. The Soviet Collective Farm. Moscow: Progress Publishers, 1971.

Society and Economic Relations. Moscow: Progress Publishers, 1969.

SSSR v Tsifrakh. Moscow: Izdat. Statistika, 1971.

Spravochnik Partiinogo Rabotnika, Vypusk Desiatyi. Moscow: Izdat. Polit. Lit., 1970.

Stanis, V. F. Sotsialisticheskie Preobrazovaniia Sel'skogo Khoziaistva. Moscow: Izdat. Mysl', 1971.

Strautmanis, Ia. Pravovoe Regulirovanie Imushchestvennykh Otnoshenii Kolkhozov. Riga: Izdat. Zinatne, 1970.

Suslov, I. F. Ekonomicheskie Problemy Razvitiia Kolkhozov. Moscow: Izdat. Ekonomika, 1967.

Terentev, M. L. Kolkoznye Tovarnodenezhnie Otnosheniia. Moscow: Izdat. Ekonomika, 1966.

Tarashchanskii, A. S. Pravo Sotsial'nogo Obespecheniia Chlenov Kolkhozov. Kishinev: Izdat. Shtiintsa, 1972.

Tarasov, A. F. Razvitie Kolkhoznoi Sobstvennosti v Obshchenarodnuiu. Rostov: Izdat. Rostovskogo Universiteta, 1967.

Twenty-Fourth Congress of the CPSU, 1971, Documents. Moscow: Novosti Press Agency Publishing House, 1971.

Voloshin, N. P. Pravo Lichnoi Sobstvennosti Kolkhoznogo Dvora. Moscow: Gosiurizdat, 1961.

Vygodsky, S. Capitalist Economy. Moscow: Progress Publishers, 1966.

Zametin, I., and P. P. Pertsev. K Voprosu o Spetsializatsii Sel'skogo Khoziaistva. Moscow: Izdat. Mysl', 1970.

Zaslavskaia, T. I. Raspredelenie po Trudu v Kolkhozakh. Moscow: Izdat. Ekonomika, 1966.

Zelenin, I. Ye. Kolkhozy v Pervoe Desiatiletie Sovetskoi Vlasti, 1917-1927. Moscow: Izdat. Nauka, 1972.

Zemlianskii, F. T. Ekonomika Podsobnykh Predpriiatii i Promyslov v Kolkhozakh. Moscow: Izdat. Kolos, 1971.

Zharikov, Iu. Pravo Sel'skokhoziaistvennogo Zemlepol'zovaniia. Moscow: Izdat. Iurid. Lit., 1969.

Non-Soviet

Adams, Arthur E., and Jan S. Adams. Man Versus Systems. New York: The Free Press, 1971.

Amalrik, Andrei. Involuntary Journey to Siberia. New York: Harcourt Brace Jovanovich, Inc., 1970.

Conklin, David W. An Evaluation of the Soviet Profit Reforms. New York: Praeger Publishers, 1970.

Conquest, Robert, ed. Agricultural Workers in the USSR. New York: Praeger Publishers, 1969.

DeLauwe, Jean Chombert. Les Paysans Sovietiques. Paris: Editions Du Seuil, 1961.

Dirscherl, Denis, ed. The New Russia. Dayton: Pflaum Press, 1968.

Feiwel, George, ed. New Currents in Soviet-Type Economies: A Reader. Scranton: International Textbook Company, 1968.

277

Hahn, Werner G. The Politics of Soviet Agriculture, 1960-1970. Baltimore and London: The Johns Hopkins University Press, 1972.

The Human Factor in Agricultural Management, International Association of Agricultural Economists, The First International Seminar, Warszawa, May 27-June 1, 1968. Warszawa: Panstwowe Wydawnietwo Naukowe, 1970.

Jackson, W. A. D., ed. Agrarian Policies and Problems in Communist and Non-Communist Countries. Seattle and London: University of Washington Press, 1971.

Jasny, Naum. Khrushchev's Crop Policy. Glasgow, Scotland: George Outram and Co., Ltd., 1966.

_____. The Socialized Agriculture of the USSR. Palo Alto: Stanford University Press, 1949.

Joravsky, David. The Lysenko Affair. Cambridge: Harvard University Press, 1970.

Kaser, Michael. Soviet Economics. New York and Toronto: McGraw-Hill, 1970.

Kassof, Allen, ed. Prospects for Soviet Society. New York: Praeger Publishers, 1968.

Laird, Roy D. The Soviet Paradigm. New York: The Free Press, 1970.

_____, and Betty Laird. Soviet Communism and Agrarian Revolution. Baltimore: Penguin Books, 1970.

Lewin, M. Russian Peasants and Soviet Power. Evanston: Northwestern University Press, 1968.

Mandel, Ernest. Marxist Economic Theory. Volume II. New York: Monthly Review Press, 1970.

Mellor, John W. The Economics of Agricultural Development. Ithaca: Cornell University Press, 1966.

Medvedev, Z. The Rise and Fall of T. D. Lysenko. New York: Columbia University Press, 1969.

Millar, James R., ed. The Soviet Rural Community. Urbana, Chicago, London: University of Chicago Press, 1971.

Miller, Robert. One Hundred Thousand Tractors. Cambridge: Harvard University Press, 1970.

Nove, Alec. The Soviet Economy, 2nd rev. ed. New York: Praeger, Publishers, 1969.

Ploss, Sidney. Conflict and Decision-Making in Soviet Russia. Princeton: Princeton University Press, 1965.

Prominent Personalities in the USSR. Metuchen, N.J.: The Scarecrow Press, 1968.

Rigby, T. H. Communist Party Membership in the USSR, 1917-1967. Princeton: Princeton University Press, 1968.

Sherman, Howard J. The Soviet Economy. Boston: Little, Brown and Co., 1969.

Simirenki, Alex, ed. Social Thought in the Soviet Union. Chicago: Quadrangle Books, 1969.

Skilling, H. G., and F. Griffiths, eds. Interest Groups in Soviet Politics. Princeton: Princeton University Press, 1971.

Social Sciences in the USSR. New York, Paris and The Hague: Basic Books, Inc., and Mooton and Co., 1965.

Strauss, Erich. Soviet Agriculture in Perspective. New York: Praeger Publishers, 1969.

Stuart, Robert C. The Collective Farm in Soviet Agriculture. Lexington: D.C. Heath and Co., 1972.

Thorbecke, Erik, ed. The Role of Agriculture in Economic Development. New York: National Bureau of Economic Research, 1969.

Treml, Vladimir, ed. The Development of the Soviet Economy. New York: Praeger Publishers, 1968.

Vucinich, Alexander. Soviet Economic Institutions. Palo Alto: Stanford University Press, 1952.

Wadekin, Karl-Eugen. The Private Sector in Soviet Agriculture. Berkeley: University of California Press, 1973.

Walston, Lord. Agriculture Under Communism. New York: Capricorn Books, 1968.

Wesson, Robert E. Soviet Communes. New Brunswick: Rutgers University Press, 1963.

Wilber, Charles K. The Soviet Model and Underdeveloped Countries. Chapel Hill: The University of North Carolina Press, 1969.

ARTICLES

Articles, items, and stories from the following newspapers and weeklies are footnoted but not always included in the Bibliography.

Ekonomicheskaia Gazeta

Izvestia

Komsomol'skaia Pravda

Literaturnaia Gazeta

Pravda

Sel'skaia Zhizn'

Sovetskaia Rossia

New York Times

Wall Street Journal

Soviet

Adikhanov, F. "Otvetstvennost' za Samovol'noe Zaniatie Zemel' Sel'skokhoziaistvennykh Predpriiatii," Sov. Iust., no. 5, (1971): 30.

"Against Distortions in Kolkhoz Labor Organization," translated in CDSP II, no. 10: 12.

Aksenenok, G. A. "Pravo Sel'skokhoziaistvennogo Zemlepol'zovaniia v Usloviiakh Nauchno-Tekhnicheskogo Progressa," SGIP, no. 7 (1971): 25-32.

Anashenkov, V. "For Both Countryside and City," Literaturnaia Gazeta, no. 3 (January 17, 1968): 10, as translated in CDSP XX, no. 5 (February 21, 1968): 2-4, 6.

Arutunian, Yu. "The Social Structure of the Rural Population," Voprosy Filosofii, no. 5 (May 1966), translated in CDSP XVIII, no. 25 (July 13, 1966): 22.

Bakai, P. "Above Plan Scale of Grain," Ekonomicheskaia Gazeta, no. 12 (March 1971): 14.

Bakhovkina, L. N. "Zakupki Kolkhoznoi Sel'skokhoziaistvennoi Produktsii," SGIP, no. 3 (1971): 56-63.

Balezin, V. P. "Nekotorye Tendentsii Razvitiia Prava Pol'zovanie Kolkhozov, Sovkhozov, i Drugikh Sel'skokhoziastvennykh Predpriiatii Zemliami Perspektivnykh Sel'skikh Naselennykh Punktov," Vestnik Moskovskogo Universiteta, Seriz XII, Pravo I (1973): 13-21.

Balezin, V. P. "K Voprose o Normirovanii Razmerov Pridomovykh Zemel'nykh v Sel'skykh Naselennykh Puntakh," Vestnik Mosk. Univ., no. 1 (1972): 11-18.

Batov, Ivan. "Development of Subsidiary Production in a Kolkhoz in Rovensk Oblast," Ekonomicheskaia Gazeta, no. 18: 18.

Beliavea, Z. S. "Normativno-Pravovye Akty Kolkhozov," SGIP, no. 1 (1971): 46-53.

Bezina, A., and M. Mavliatshin. "Uvol'nenie iz Predpriatii i Uchrezhdenii Nepravil'no Priniatykh Chlenov Kolkhozov," no. 23 (1970): 9-10.

Botvinnik, S. "Shchapovskii Kompleks—2,000 Korov pod Odnoi Kryshei," Sel'skaia Zhizn', July 7, 1971, p. 2.

Braginskii, L. "On the Interaction of Economic Levers in Collective Farm Management," Voprosy Ekonomiki, no. 5 (1971), translated in Problems of Economics, IASP, XIV, no. 5 (September 1971): 60-73.

Buslov, D. "Partiinaia Zhizn," Pravda, May 11, 1971, p. 2.

Chikanchi, I. "Po Akkordnomi Nariadu—Dogovoru !" Ekonomicheskaia Gazeta, no. 29 (July 1971): 19.

Dementsev, V. "V Interesakh Dal'neishego Ukrepleniia Kolkhoznogo Proizvodstva," Finansy SSSR, no. 11 (1969): 6-14.

Dem'ianenko, V. N. "Sovershenstvovat' Kolkhoznoe Proizvodstvo," SGIP, no. 6 (1971): 11-18.

Denisenkov, I. Sel'skaia Zhizn', June 23, 1971, p. 2.

Denisov, A. "Iuridicheskoe Obsluzhivanie Kolkhozov i Sovkhozov," Sov. Iust., no. 12 (1971): 3-4.

"Differentsiatsiia Zakupochnykh Tsen," Ekonomika Sel'skogo Khoziaistva, no. 11 (1971): 121-126.

Dimin, A. "Slovo Truchenikov Sela," Partiinaia Zhizn', no. 6 (1971): pp. 71-73.

"A Discussion of Draft Directives for the Twenty-Third Congress," Voprosy Ekonomiki, no. 3 (1966).

Dobrovol'skii, G. "Material'naia Otvetstvennost' Kolkhoznikov po Novomu Primernomu Ustavu Kolkhoza," Sov. Iust., no. 14 (1970): 5-6.

_____. "Material'naia Otvetstvennost' Kolkhoznikov za Ushcherb, Prichinennyi Kolkhozom," Sov. Iust, no. 18 (September 1971): 20-21.

Dobrovol'skii G. F. "Spory O Material'noi Otvetstvennosit Chlenov Kolkhoza," SGIP, No. 3 (1972), pp. 49-55.

Dontsov, S. "Material'naia Otvetstvennost Dolzhnosthykh Lits Kolkhoza i Inykh Lits za Vred, Prichinennyi Kolkhozom," Sov. Iuts., no. 5 (March 1971): 13-14.

_____. "Sudebnaia Praktika Razresheniia Sporov, Odnoi iz Storon v Kotorykh Iavliaetsia Kolkhoz," Sov. Iust., no. 16 (1971): 15-16.

Egorev, V. "Sudebnaia Praktika po Delam o Vozmeshchenii Vreda Prichinennogo Nepravomernym Ispol'zovaniem Zemel'," Sov. Iust., no. 2 (January 1971): pp. 29-30.

Emel'ianov, A. "Technical Progress and Structural Changes in Agriculture," Voprosy Ekonomiki, no. 4 (1971), translated in Problems of Economics IASP, XIV, No. 4 (August 1971): 3-24.

Erofeev, B. "Pravovoi Rezhim Zemel' Perspektivnykh Sel'skikh Naselennykh Puntov," Sov. Iust., no. 9 (May 1970): 22.

Esin, A. "Internal Accounting in Kolkhozy," Ekonomicheskaia Gazeta, no. 27 (July 1971): 18.

Fomina, L. "Zemlepol'zovanie Kolkhozov," Sov. Iust., no. 13 (1971): 5-6.

Georgiev, A. "Sel'skii Trud i Molodezh'," Kommunist, no. 1 (1971): 25-36.

Goriachev, F. "Ukrepliat' Soiuz Nauka i Sel'skokhoziaistvennogo Proizvodstva," Kommunist, No. 1 (1971): 80-89.

Glinka, M. "Dva Podkhoxka k Odnoi Probleme," Sel'skaia Zhizn', July 8, 1971, p. 2.

Granberg, A. "Agriculture in the System of Interbranch Balances," as translated in Problems of Economics, IASP, 10, no. 6 (October 1976): 33-44.

Gumadeev, S. "Zabota o Nuzhdakh Zhivotnovodov," Kommunist, no. 13 (1971): 69-71.

Ekonomicheskaia Gazeta, no. 32 (August 1971).

Ermin, L. "Nash Kurs—Spetsializatsiia," Pravda, July 19, 1971.

Foteev, S. "Sotsialisticheskie Zemel'nye Otnosheniia i Ratsional'noe Ispol'zovanie Zemli," Kommunist, no. 16 (1969): 66-77.

Golikov, V. A. "O Nekotorykh Voprosakh Politiki KPSS v Oblasti Sel'skogo Khoziastva na Sovremennom Etape," Voprosy Istorii KPSS, no. 7 (1972): 16-30.

Gusev, N. "Sel'skoe Khoziaistvo v Deviatoi Piatiletke," Ekonomika Sel'skogo Khoziaistva, no. 2 (February 1972): 1-12.

Iakovlev, V. "Strakhovanie Imushchestva Kolkhoza," Sov. Iust., no. 22 (1971): 3-4.

Ianov, A. "Kostromskoi Eksperiment," Literaturnaia Gazeta, no. 52 (December 27, 1967): 10.

Iuldashev, Ia. "Ekonomicheskie Rezul'taty Perestroiki Gosudarstvennogo Strakhovaniia Imushchestva Kolkhozov," Finansy SSSR, no.
10 (1969): 77-79.

Ivanov, G. V. "Voploshchenie i Dalneishee Razvitie Idei Leninskogo
Koopertivnogo Plana v Novom Primernom Ustave Kolkhoza,"
Vestnik Mosk. Univ., Pravo No. 2 (1970): 72-84.

Ivanovich, N. A. "Nekotorye Voprosy Oplaty Truda v Kolkhozakh,"
Vestnik Mosk. Univ., Pravo. No. 2 (1969): pp. 61-70.

Izvestiia, August 15, 1970.

Kalambet, A. "Ispol'zovanie Osnovnykh Fondov v Agrarno-Promyshlennykh Ob'edieniiakh," Ekonomika Sel'skogo Khoziaistva, no. 1
(1972): 80-86.

Kalandadze, A. M. "Printsip Dispozitivnosti v Deiatel'nosti Kolkhoza,"
Pravovedenie, No. 1 (1971): 73-81.

Karavaev, V. "Priamye Sviazi i Puti Ikh Dal'neishego Razvitiia,"
Ekonomika Sel'skogo Khoziaistva, no. 12 (1971): 73-80.

Kolotinskaia, Ye. N. "Otsenkha Zemel' po Sovetskomu Zemel'nomu
Kadastru," Vestnik Moskovskogo Univ., Pravo No. 3, (1972):
26-35.

Kosholev, V. "Polnyi Vnutri Khoziastvenni Raschet—Vazhnyi Proizvodstvennyi Rezerv," Kommunist, no. 9 (1971): 51-52.

Kharatshvili, G. G. "Chlenskie Pravootnosheniia po Primernomu
Ustavu Kolkhoza," SGIP, no. 2 (1972): 46-53.

"Knizhka Zven'evogo," Ekonomicheskaia Gazeta, no. 36 (September
1971): 11.

"Kolkhoznoe Krest'ianstvo," Pravda, July 22, 1971, p. 1.

Komissarov, V. "Kadry Srednego Zvena v Kolkhozakh i Sovkhozakh,"
Partiinaia Zhizn', no. 16 (August 1971): 24-27.

Komsomol'skaia Pravda, April 14, 1970 and April 24, 1970.

Kolesnev, S., M. Sokolov, and I. Suslov. "On the Question of the Plan
and the Market," Sel'skaia Zhizn', September 22, 1966, as
translated in CDSP XVIII, no. 37 (October 5, 1966): 7-8.

Kornoukhov, V. "Rabota Narodnykh Sudov po Preduprezhdeniiu Khishchenii Kolkhoznogo Imushchestva," Sov. Iust., no. 5 (1970): 26-27.

Kovalenko, M. "Nov' Kolkhoznogo Sela," Kommunist, no. 4 (1971): 33-35.

Kozhevnikov, A. "Nikto Ne Stoit v Storone," Sel'skaia Zhizn', August 5, 1971, p. 2.

Kozyr', M. "Pravo i Sel'skoe Khoziaistvo," SGIP, no. 6 (1972): 10-18.

_____. "Primernyi Ustav Kolkhoza i Problemy Zakonodatel'stva," Sots Zak., no. 2 (1971): 6-9.

_____. "Zakon Kolkhoznoi Zhizni," Chelovek i Zakon, no. 8 (1971): 11-18.

Kozyr', P. "Sochetanie Obshchestvennykh i Lichnykh Interesov v Kolkhozakh," Kommunist, no. 16 (1969): 44-53.

Krasil'nikov, I. "Istochnik Rosta Produktov Zhivotnovodstva," Kommunist, no. 12 (1971): 55-62.

Kuz'min, I. F. "Pravovye Sredstva Povisheniia Effektivnosti Pro- izvodstvennoi Deiatel'nosti Kolkhozov," SIGP, no. 8 (1971): 67-74.

Lemeshev, M. "On the Elaboration of a Program for the Development of the Agraro-Industrial Complex in the USSR," Izvestiia Sibir- skogo Otdeleniia, Akad. Nauk. SSSR, No. 11, Issue 3, translated in Problems of Economics, IASP, XIV, no. 4 (August 1971): 25-44.

Leontyev, L. "Questions of Theory: On Commodity Production Under Socialism," Pravda, August 31, 1966, pp. 2-3, as translated in CDSP XVIII, no. 35 September 21, 1966 : 8-10.

Lobanov, P. "Ekonomicheskaia Politika Partii v Oblasti Sel'skogo Khoziaistva," Ekonomika Sel'skogo Khoziaistva," no. 9, (1972): pp. 31-42.

Loza, G. "Razvitie Agrarno-Promyshlennykh Kompleksov i Ob' edinenii," Ekomomika Sel'skogo Khoziaistva, no. 11 (1971): 98-107.

Luk'ianenko, S. "Pensionnoe Obespechenie Chlenov Kolkhozov," Sots. Zak., no. 12 (1971): 39-42.

Lukinov, I. "Problems in Agricultural Forecasting," Voprosy Ekonomiki, no. 7 (1971), translated in Problems of Economics, IASP, XIV, no. 10 (February 1972): 3-18.

Lur'e, S. "Pravovoe Regulirovanie Kontraktsii Sel'skokhoziaistvennoi Produktsii," Sov. Iust., no. 23 (1971): 20-21.

Maikov, A. Z., and P. A. Gureev. "Legal Principles Governing the Distribution of Labor Supply," SGIP, no. 3 (1971), as translated in Soviet Law and Government, IASP, X, no. 2 (Fall 1971): 177-179.

Makeenko, M. "Ekonomicheskaia Rol' Lichnogo Podsobnogo Khoziaaistva," Voprosy Ekonomiki, no. 10 (1966): 57-67.

Maliarov, M. "Strozhe Sobliudat' Zemel'nyi Zakon," Sots. Zak., no. 3 (1972): 3-8.

Markovaskaia, K., and A. Voronov. "Balance of Money Incomes and Expenditures of the Urban and Rural Population," Den'gi i Kredit, no. 5 (1971), as translated in Problems of Economics, IASP, XIV, no. 10 (February 1972): 37-50.

Masaulov, I. "Primer Mekhanizatorov," Sel'skaia Zhizn', June, 30, 1971, p. 2.

Matveev, A. "Income Tax on Kolkhozy," Ekonomicheskaia Gazeta, no. 25 (July 1971): 18.

Mikulich, V. "Obkom i Sel'skie Partiinye Organizatsii," Partiinaia Zhizn', no. 12 (1971): 39-45.

Mikulovich, I. "Sovershenstvuem Organizatsiiu Truda i Upravleniia v Sel'skom Khoziaistve," Partiinaia Zhizn', no. 5 (1971): 27-32.

Moskalenko, D. "Its Worth Thinking About Before Setting off for the Virgin Lands," Pravda, August 5, 1971, as translated in CDSP, XXIII, No. 31, (Aug. 31, 1971) pp. 28-29.

"Nadzor za Ispolneniem Zakonov v Sel'skom Khoziaistve," Sots. Zak., no. 8 (1970): 18-22.

"Nashi Konsul'tatsie," Chelovek i Zakon (December 12, 1971): 84-86.

Nikolenko, A. "Strogii Spros i Pomoshch," Sel'skaia Zhizn', August, 1971, p. 2.

Nikonov, M. "Kommunisty v Brigade," Pravda, July 20, 1971, p. 2.

Novikov, A. "Akkordnaia Oplata," Ekonomicheskaia Gazeta, no. 25 (June 1971): 11.

"Novyi Otriad Sel'skikh Spetsialistov," Sel'skaia Zhizn' July 30, 1971, p. 1.

Paniugin, V. "Materialnaia Otvetstvennost Chlenov Kolkhoza," Sots. Zak., no. 4 (1971): 9-13.

Pavlov, I. V. "Pravovoe Polozhenie Agrarno-Promyshlennykh Kompleksov," SIGP, no. 9 (1971): 29-37.

Pervushin, A. "Ispolnenie Dogovora Kontraktatsii Sel'skokhoziaist-vennoi Produktsii," Sov. Iust., no. 14 (1971): 6-7.

_____. "Zashchita Sub'ektivnykh Prav Chlenov Kolkhoza," Sov. Iust., no. 19 (October 1971): 11-13.

Polataev, P. "Capital Investment in Agriculture," Voprosy Ekonomiki, no. 7 (1971), translated in Problems of Economics, IASP, XIV, no. 10 (February 1972): 19-36.

Poshkub, B. "Vnutrizonali'naia Differentsiatsiia Zakupochnykh Tsen," Ekonomika Sel'skogo Khoziaistva, no. 12 (1971): 14-21.

"Problems of Rural Economics," Pravda, April 24, 1966, p. 3.

Pshenichnyi, V. "Vyogoda Priamykh Sviazei," Sel'skaia Zhizn', July 13, 1971, p. 2.

Razumovskii, I., and V. Siviakov. "Za 280 Tsentnerov Klubnei s Gektara," Sel'skaia Zhizn', July 23, 1971, p. 2.

Rimachenko, V., and G. Vasilenko. "Agrarno-Promyshlennye Ob'edineniia—Progressivnaia Forma Organizatsii Proizvodstva," Ekonomika Sel'skogo Khoziaistva, no. 12 (1971): 69-73.

Romanov, V. "Spornye Voprosy Primeneniia Kolkhoznogo Zokono-datel'stva," Sov. Iust., no. 3 (February 1972): 14-15.

Rusanov, E. "To Develop Agraro-Industrial Complexes," Ekonomicheskaia Gazeta, no. 32 (March 1971): 14.

Sakhipov, M. S. "Otvestvennost' po Kolkhoznomu Pravu," SGIP, no. 4 (1971): 29-36.

Savielev, M. "From the Experience of Local Soviets: The New Generation of Peasants," Izvestia, August 11, 1971.

Sdobnov, S. "Ekonomika Sel'skogo Khoziaistva v Period Razvitogo Sotsialisma," Ekonomika Sel'skogo Khoziaistva, no. 7 (1972): 12-28.

Sel'skaia Zhizn', April 22, 1971 and March 5, 1971.

Seslavin, M., and A. Trubnikov. "Liuboe Delo Distsiplinoi Krepitsia," Sel'skaia Zhizn', August 17, 1971, p. 2.

Shershukov, A. "Na Mezhe Kontrastov," Ekonomicheskaia Gazeta, no. 28 (July 1971): 19.

_____. "V Interesakh Razvitiia Obshchestvennogo Khoziaistva," Ekonomicheskaia Gazeta, no. 32 (August 1971): 18-19.

Shmelev, G. "Ekonomicheskaia Rol' Lichnogo Podsobnogo Khoziaistva," Voprosy Ekonomiki, no. 4 (1965): 27-37.

Shvets, G. "Nekotorye Voprosy Sviazennye s Primeneniem Primernogo Ustava Kolkhoza," Sov. Iust., no. 24 (December 1971): 14-15.

Sirovatko, A., and A. Khamlak. "Novye Rubezhi Kolkhoznogo Sela," Partiinaia Zhizn', no. 9 (1971): 37-40.

Sovetskaia Rossia, April 24, 1969.

Sirodoev, N. "Pravo Zemlepol'zovaniia Kolkhoznogo Dvora," Sov. Iust., no. 13 (1970): 6-7.

Stepanov, N. "Kliuchevaia Problema Razvitiia Sel'skogo Khoziaistva," Partiinai Zhizn', no. 8 (1971): 27-33.

Storozhev, N. V. "Material'naia Otvetstvennost' Kolkhoznikov," SGIP, no. 11 (1971): 34-41.

Sviatetskaia, T. "Pravovoe Regulirovanie Distsiplinarnoi Otvestven-
nosti Chlenov Kolkhoza," Sov. Iust., no. 17 (1970): 8-10.

V. Taratuta in Sel'skaia Zhizn', July 27, 1971, p. 2.

Tarchokov, K. "Dukhovnyi Rost Kolkhoznogo Krest'ianstva," Kommunist, no. 16 (1969): 78-79.

Trunov, M. "Za Uglublenie Spetsializatsii v Sel'skokhoziaistvennom
Proizvodstve," Partiinaia Zhizn', no. 13 (1971): 16-23.

Vanin, D. "Vazhnyi Ekonomicheskii Faktor," Ekonomicheskaia Gazeta,
no. 9 February 1973): 19.

Vasilenko, M. "Effektivnost' Sochetaniia Sel'skokhoziaistvennogo i
Podsobnogo Promyshlennogo Proizvodstva," Ekonomika Sel'
skogo Khoziaistva, no. 2 (1972): 84-90.

Vavilin, E. "Rabochii Den' Doiarki," Sel'skaia Zhizn', July 20, 1971,
p. 2.

Yeropkin, V. "Analiz Rasshirennogo Vosproizvodstva v Kolkhozakh
i Sovkhozakh," Ekonomika Sel'skogo Khoziaistva, no. 8 (1972):
28-36.

Zharikov, Iu. "Okhrana Imushchestvennykh Prav Zemlepol'zovatelei,"
Sov. Iust., no. 7 (1971): 12-13.

_____. "Okhrana Prava Zemlepol'zovaniia, " SGIP, no. 12 (1971):
46-52.

Zhumagaliev, B. "Politicheskaia Rabota Sredi Zhivotnovodov,"
Partiinaia Zhizn', no. 3 (1971): 25-30.

Zinchenko, G. "Agrarnyi Otriad Rabochego Klassa SSSR," Kommunist,
no. 14 (1972): 60-69.

Zolotukhin, G. "Pod'em Sel'skogo Khoziaistva Trebovanie Vremeni,"
Kommunist, no. 3 (1971): 28-39.

Non-Soviet

Abouchar, Alan. "The Private Plot and the Prototype Collective
Farm Charter," Slavic Review XXX, no. 2 (June 1971): 355-360.

Babich, Andrei. "The Private Plot: A Vital Element in Collective Farmers' Income," Analysis of Current Developments in the Soviet Union, Institute for the Study of the Soviet Union, No. 659 (July 13, 1971).

_____. "The Party Issues Draft Directives for the Ninth Five-Year "Prosperity" Plan," Analysis of Current Developments in the Soviet Union, Institute for the Study of the Soviet Union, No. 644 (March 30, 1971).

_____. "Soviet Animal Husbandry Attempts a 'Great Leap Forward,'" Analysis of Current Developments in the Soviet Union, Institute for the Study of the USSR, No. 671 (October 5, 1971).

_____. "Soviet Agriculture: Present State and Prospects," Analysis of Current Developments in the Soviet Union, Institute for the Study of the USSR, No. 635 (January 26, 1971).

_____. "Soviet Agricultural Procurements System Reshaped," Analysis of Current Developments in the Soviet Union, Institute for the Study of the USSR, III, No. 624 (November 3, 1970).

Bornstein, Morris. "The Soviet Debate on Agricultural Price and Procurement Reforms," Soviet Studies XXI, no. 1 (July 1969): 1-20.

Bradley, Michael. "Prospects for Soviet Agriculture," Current History (October 1970): 226-231 and 244.

_____, and M. Gardner Clark. "Supervision and Efficiency in Socialized Agriculture," Soviet Studies XXIII, no. 3 (January 1971): 465-473.

Bryan, Paige. "An Evaluation of the Soviet Agricultural Product in 1972," Radio Liberty Dispatch, November 16, 1972.

_____. "Another Soviet Livestock Setback and Response," Radio Liberty Dispatch, April 4, 1972.

_____. "Bacon Prices Causing Production Problems," Radio Liberty Dispatch, April 4, 1972.

_____. "Centralized Economic Management of Kolkhozes Appears Imminent," Radio Liberty Dispatch, April 12, 1973.

_____. "Feed Crops and the Zveno," Radio Liberty Dispatch, July 18, 1972.

_____. "Investment and Planning: Soviet Agriculture's Performance and Outlook—1971-72," Radio Liberty Dispatch, February 1972.

_____. "Soviet Agriculture—Where Does It Go From Here?" Radio Liberty Dispatch, September 21, 1972.

_____. "The Soviet Feed Grain Crisis," Radio Liberty Dispatch, December 16, 1971.

_____. "Soviet Grain Trade Policy and the Grain Situation," Radio Liberty Dispatch, March 21, 1972.

Bush, Keith. "More Light on Soviet Investment in 1966-70 and 1971-1975," Radio Liberty Dispatch, May 4, 1971.

_____. "A New Agricultural Statistical Compendium," Radio Liberty Dispatch, April 17, 1972.

_____. "The New Draft Kolkhoz Model Charter," Bulletin, Institute for the Study of the USSR, XVI, no. 7 (July 1969): 36-41.

_____. "Soviet Agriculture in the 1970's," Studies on the Soviet Union (New Series), XI, no. 3 (1971): 1-45.

_____. "Soviet Grain Output, Deliveries and Imports," Radio Liberty Dispatch, October 16, 1972.

_____. "The Third All-Union Congress of Kolkhozniks," Bulletin, Institute for the Study of the USSR, XVIII, no. 1 (January 1970): 16-23.

_____. "The Weather and Mr. Brezhnev," Radio Liberty Dispatch, Quarterly Review of Soviet Affairs (July-September, 1972).

Clarke, Roger, "Soviet Agricultural Reforms Since Krushchev," Soviet Studies XX, no. 2 (October 1968): 159-178.

De Pauw, John W. "The Private Sector in Soviet Agriculture," Slavic Review XXVIII, no. 1 (March 1969): 63-71.

Domar, Evsey. "The Soviet Collective Farm as a Producer Cooperative," The American Economic Review LVIII, no. 11 (September
1966): 734-757.

Duevel, Christian. "After Matskevich: Real Power to the Kolkhoz
Councils?" Radio Liberty Dispatch, February 14, 1973.

Hammer, Darrell. "The Dilimma of Party Growth," Problems of
Communism XX, no. 4 (July-August 1970): 16-21.

Jackson, W. A. D. "Wanted: An Effective Land Use Policy and Improved Reclamation," Slavic Review XXIX, no. 3 (September
1970): 415-416.

Kabysh, S. "New Policy on the Private Plots," Studies on the Soviet
Union VI, no. 1 (1966): 26-34.

Karcz, Jerzy. "Some Major Persisting Problems in Soviet Agriculture," Slavic Review XXIX, no. 3 (September 1970): pp. 417-426.

Laird, Roy D. "Prospects for Soviet Agriculture," Problems of Communism XX, no. 5 (September-October 1971): 31-40.

_____, and Kenneth E. Beasley. "Soviet Tractor Stations—Policy
Control by Auxiliary Services," Public Administration Review
XX, no. 4 (Autumn 1960): 213-218.

Lovell, C. A. Knox. "The Role of Private Subsidiary Farming During
the Soviet Seven-Year Plan, 1959-1965," Soviet Studies XX, no.
1 (July 1968): 46-66.

Millar, James R. "Financial Innovation in Contemporary Soviet Agricultural Policy," Slavic Review XXXII, no. 1 (March 1973):
91-114.

Nove, Alec. "Soviet Agriculture Under Brezhnev," Slavic Review
XXIX, no. 3 (September 1970): 379-410.

Oi, Walter Y., and Elizabeth M. Clayton. "A Peasant's View of a
Soviet Collective Farm," The American Economic Review
LVIII, no. 11 (March 1968): 37-59.

Olgin, C. "The Ninth Five-Year Plan: Economics and Party Politics,"
Bulletin, Institute for the Study of the USSR, XVIII, no. 4 (April
1971): 34-40.

Ploss, Sidney, "Politics in the Kremlin," Problems of Communism XIX, no. 3 (May-June 1970): 1-14.

————. "Soviet Politics on the Eve of the 24th Congress," World Politics XXXIII, no. 1 (October 1970): 61-82.

Pospielvosky, Dimitry, "The Link System in Soviet Agriculture," Soviet Studies XXI, no. 4 (April 1970): 411-435.

"Soviet Purchase of Grain From U.S. May Total Billion," New York Times, August 10, 1972.

"Soviet to Buy Grain From U.S. for $750 Million," The Wall Street Journal, July 10, 1972.

Stuart, Robert C. "Managerial Incentives in Soviet Collective Agriculture During the Khrushchev Era," Soviet Studies XXII, no. 4 (April 1971): 539-555.

Toprak, Paige Bryan. "The Soviet Grain Harvest, 1973-74," Radio Liberty Dispatch, September 7, 1973.

Wadekin, Karl-Eugen, "Have Kolkhoz Wages Risen Too Much?" Radio Liberty Dispatch, December 10, 1970.

————. "Manpower in Soviet Agriculture," Soviet Studies XX, no. 3 (January 1966): 281-305.

————. "Payment in Kind in Soviet Agriculture," Parts I and II, Bulletin, Institute for the Study of the USSR, XVIII, no. 9 (September 1971): 5-18, and no. 11 (November 1971): 5-24.

————. "Private Production in Soviet Agriculture," Problems of Communism XVII, no. 1 (January-February 1968): 22-30.

————. "Soviet Rural Society: A Descriptive Analysis," Soviet Studies XXII, no. 4 (April 1971): 512-537.

Walker, Frederick A. "Industrialization of Soviet Agriculture," Studies on the Soviet Union (New Series) , XI, no. 3 (1971): 46-66.

Wanamaker, George E., and Grover S. Euler, "USSR Import of U.S. Soybeans May Indicate Difficulties in Meeting Oil Needs," Foreign Agriculture 10, no. 46 (November 13, 1972).

Monetization, 157
MTS: dissolution of, 4; role of, 16, 255

Natural pay or payment in kind, 4

Pension Funds, 5, 18, 20-21
Pricing of agricultural produce, 11, 14-15, 109, 210-212
Private livestock, 42, 156-158; fodder for, 11, 19; holdings, 33-34, 42; new legislation on maximum, 26
Private sector: aid to, 11, 13-14, 42-43; economic significance of, 11-12, 54, 148, 157-160; periodic repression of, 6, 30, 56, 156-157
Procurement organs: criticism of, 68; new relation with kolkhozy, 84-85
Procurement policy, 6, 13, 14-15, 21, 41-42, 59, 61
Profitability: level of in agriculture, 65, 212; level of in industry, 212, 213; norms for, 212-214

Regional differentiation of farm income, 206-209

Seasonality of labor, 20, 71-72 118-123
Seredniaks, 254
Smychka, 252
Social security, 15
Soiuzsel'khoztekhnika, 43; criticism of, 15-16, 39; material liability of, 16
Sovkhozization, 4, 14, 177
Sovkhozy: favoritism toward, 107-109, 175-176
Specialists: problems with, 64;

shortage of, 17, 116
Specialization, 8, 62-63, 214, 217
Standard of living, 52-53
State purchase prices: above-plan, 13, 20; basic, 206; firm, 13; seasonal, 210-212; sliding, 13
Subjectivism, 13; Khrushchev guilty of, 3, 10
Subsidiary enterprises, 6, 18, 20, 61, 71-72, 119
Success indicators: distortion factor with, 66-67, 68, 69; problem of measuring quality, 67, 74

Taxes: agricultural, 165; on kolkhozy, 15, 82-83, 218; progressive income tax proposal 15, 191, 218
TOZ, 252
Two-shift work system: on live-stock farms, 63-64, 125-126

Urban-rural differences: method of overcoming, 127, 203

Vil'yams grassland system, 8, 13
Virgin Lands, 4

Women: burdensome aspects of farmwork for, 124, 125-126; disproportionate share in work of private sector, 12

Youth: problem of outflow from farms, 116-117; psychological alienation from farm work, 123-125

Zazhitochnykh, 254

ABOUT THE AUTHOR

STEPHEN OSOFSKY is Assistant Professor of Political Science at the University of Tennessee. He earned his Ph.D in political science, and a Certificate, from the Russian Institute of Columbia University. Mr. Osofsky is also a member of the District of Columbia Bar.

THE POLITICS OF ECONOMIC REFORM IN THE
SOVIET UNION
Abraham Katz

INPUT-OUTPUT ANALYSIS OF THE SOVIET
ECONOMY: An Annotated Bibliography
Vladimir G. Treml

AN EVALUATION OF THE SOVIET PROFIT
REFORMS: With Special Reference to Agriculture
David W. Conklin

THE SOVIET QUEST FOR ECONOMIC EFFICIENCY—
EXPANDED AND UPDATED EDITION: Issues,
Controversies, and Reforms
George R. Feiwel

M